POLITICAL ANIMAL

POLITICAL ANIMAL

THE LIFE AND TIMES OF
STEWART BUTLER

FRANK PEREZ

FOREWORD BY ROBERT W. FIESELER

University Press of Mississippi / Jackson

Willie Morris Books in Memoir and Biography

The University Press of Mississippi is the scholarly publishing agency of the Mississippi Institutions of Higher Learning: Alcorn State University, Delta State University, Jackson State University, Mississippi State University, Mississippi University for Women, Mississippi Valley State University, University of Mississippi, and University of Southern Mississippi.

www.upress.state.ms.us

The University Press of Mississippi is a member of the Association of University Presses.

Any discriminatory or derogatory language or hate speech regarding race, ethnicity, religion, sex, gender, class, national origin, age, or disability that has been retained or appears in elided form is in no way an endorsement of the use of such language outside a scholarly context.

All quotations of intertitles or dialogue from films are the author's direct transcriptions from film prints or video copies.

First printing 2022
∞

Library of Congress Cataloging-in-Publication Data

Names: Perez, Frank, 1968– author. | Fieseler, Robert W., writer of foreword.
Title: Political animal : the life and times of Stewart Butler / Frank Perez ; foreword by Robert W. Fieseler.
Other titles: Willie Morris books in memoir and biography.
Description: Jackson : University Press of Mississippi, [2022] | Series: Willie Morris books in memoir and biography | Includes bibliographical references and index.
Identifiers: LCCN 2022008042 (print) | LCCN 2022008043 (ebook) | ISBN 9781496841292 (hardback) | ISBN 9781496841308 (epub) | ISBN 9781496841315 (epub) | ISBN 9781496841322 (pdf) | ISBN 9781496841339 (pdf)
Subjects: LCSH: Butler, Stewart, 1930–2020. | Gay men—United States—Biography. | Gay rights—United States. | Gay liberation movement—United States. | Transgender people—Civil rights—United States.
Classification: LCC HQ75.8.B88 P47 2022 (print) | LCC HQ75.8.B88 (ebook) | DDC 306.76/62092 [B]—dc23/eng/20220404
LC record available at https://lccn.loc.gov/2022008042
LC ebook record available at https://lccn.loc.gov/2022008043

British Library Cataloging-in-Publication Data available

FOR BILL HAGLER

Long before I knew I was gay I was a political animal.
—STEWART BUTLER, 2008

CONTENTS

FOREWORD

ROBERT W. FIESELER

THE MOST IMPORTANT PERSON IN THE HISTORY OF QUEER LOUISIANA politics never held elected office. He was an old, bald, gay, white hippie who wore dashiki hats and was once arrested at Louis Armstrong New Orleans International Airport for the possession of twenty-two joints. He did not hold rallies or give rousing speeches, nor did he present himself as a moral example. Rather, he was a gay Gandalf character who enjoyed the company of wayward young men, some of barely legal age. In style and in substance, Stewart P. Butler was not a member of the American "political class." No, they who honed debate skills at Princeton and spent their lives plotting the perfect resumes never found their way to the dining-room table of Stewart's home at 1308 Esplanade Avenue in New Orleans. At that den, dubbed the "Faerie Playhouse" by its sundry tenants, Stewart toiled for decades. He proclaimed himself a "political animal," a relentless organizer engaged in the daily trench work of social change.

I first met Stewart in 2014 while researching my debut book *Tinderbox: The Untold Story of the Up Stairs Lounge Fire and the Rise of Gay Liberation* (Liveright, 2018). The book would go on to win several awards, but before it did, I was a queer history novice failing in my efforts and needing help. *Tinderbox* is a nonfiction account of a notoriously unsolved arson at a gay bar that Stewart had lived through in the early 1970s. My book-in-progress demanded that I speak to the few remaining survivors and witnesses of said calamity. I was so nervous when I first called Stewart, feeling so much of the weight of history, that I spoke unintelligibly fast into his answering machine. He couldn't make out my phone number, though he tried and tried by replaying the message, so he personally called around town to track me down. When I first heard his puckish voice over the line, it was the sound of Stewart chiding me for talking too fast while simultaneously agreeing to help me as much as I needed.

Stewart had a generous spirit. We spoke more than twenty times at the
Faerie Playhouse, that unmistakable pink residence dotted with red hearts
on a tree-lined boulevard, and our talks lasted about an hour each. Though
Stewart's health was fading in his mid-eighties, though he shuffled with
oxygen tubes in his nostrils, his mind had bursts of energy and clarity. These
were some of the most illuminating conversations of my life. They were also
hilarious and wayward encounters. "How old are you, honey?" he'd sometimes
ask, making a jolly pass at me in the middle of a serious inquiry about queer
Louisiana politics. I'm convinced that he did this not because he was attracted
to me but because I was a younger man in his space, and he needed to
remind himself that he was alive and vigorous. So I'd tell him my age, which
varied somewhere in my late thirties. "Oh, I thought you was a sweet young
thanggg," he'd say, letting the *g* drag. Taking a beat, he'd follow with, "Well,
you were"—conveying in gay speak that though he found me ancient by his
standards, he might, with some convincing, consider me a special case. I'd
laugh. He'd laugh. How could you not laugh? It was the same three lines every
time. How could you not admire such an obvious pass from a man hooked
to an oxygen tank? That was Stewart, still intact as a gay octogenarian, still
helping the next generation with all due irreverence but also an earnestness
that transcended virtue signaling.

The origins of Stewart's queer activism moved me deeply. He began the
Sunday night of June 24, 1973, believing that keeping "body and soul together,"
as he put it, was enough to constitute a well-lived life as a gay American. He
approached his favorite New Orleans watering hole, a gay bar called the Up
Stairs Lounge, possessing much. At forty-two years of age, he had several
joints in his pocket, a lover of enviable looks and wealth, a steady job, a beautiful rental home, and a bounty of friends. Sure, he was legally second-class.
Closeted at work, he knew an employer could fire him without recourse if his
sexuality became known. State laws could have him and his lover arrested in
their bedroom for "crimes against nature," with mandatory prison sentences
if convicted. Local ordinances could have them locked up for drinking a
beer in a bar while gay or occupying space on a sidewalk while homosexual
or evicted for creating a "house of ill repute" by virtue of living together in
a rental. Living as a sex criminal, as defined by law, Stewart accepted that he
could never viably run for public office or be seriously courted by a major
party. Yet, he was proud to be honestly and truly himself in the life of his
choosing. Besides, a homosexual of his era could build an enviable private
world so long as he played it cool with flagrant behaviors that would brand
him a criminal and an outsider.

So Stewart thought until that Sunday. He and his lover, Alfred Doo-little, ducked down Iberville, a side street bordering the French Quarter, and trudged up thirteen wooden steps of a twisting staircase, which led to a working-class gay haven. They opened a nondescript metal door and entered an oasis chamber teeming with beefcake posters on red-flocked wallpaper and the frolicsome laughter of gay friends. Gossip and singing and piano music flowed through the Up Stairs Lounge like warm currents. Alfred imbibed his fill of the Beer Bust, the bar's Sunday night drink special of one dollar for two hours of unlimited draft beer, while Stewart stuck to vodka and dished with his gay barber Louis "Horace" Broussard. The night's revelry was only briefly disturbed when a drunken hustler picked a fight in the bar and had to be forcibly removed. The dejected man bizarrely screamed "I'm going to burn you all out" as bar staff dragged him toward and then down the front staircase, which served as the bar's sole entrance and exit.

But the music and fun recommenced, and only Alfred seemed to take the hustler's threat seriously. It was at Alfred's insistence that Stewart felt compelled to leave the Up Stairs Lounge for another bar around 7:40 p.m. The couple fought about Alfred's paranoia on the staircase landing to the bar, then at ground level, then all the way down Iberville Street to a rougher dive called Wanda's, where they ordered another round. The booze had barely touched their lips when sirens blared and a fire engine blurred past. The engine plowed aside a taxi as it headed straight in the direction of the Up Stairs Lounge. Something horrific clicked in Stewart's head, and he retraced the path that he and Alfred had just walked.

Stewart traced the plumes of smoke down the street to their source. "I kind of approached it slowly," Stewart recalled. "And all this [throwing up his hands], gradually." He would remember this walk, 145 steps from the door of Wanda's to the blazing bar, for the rest of his life. As I wrote in *Tinderbox*, "The street reflected the blowout of an explosion: fire leaped from windows and smoke wafted off bodies, with friends pointing and officials yelling. Everything seemed to shout for Stewart's attention; few details connected or made sense." Friends were dead in that second-story bar. How many, he could not tell, although he could not find his barber Louis "Horace" Broussard among the survivors, some who lay screaming with scorched or flayed skin on the sidewalk. Men he stood beside as equals minutes before, compatriots in a secret lifestyle, had burned upstairs in a horrific mass. They were now reduced to memories, little more than ashes, their voices silenced.

On the street, Stewart heard a police officer explaining to a newspaper reporter, "Some thieves hung out there, and you know this was a queer bar."

He personally witnessed the Up Stairs Lounge bartender spot and grab the soot-covered hustler, who'd only so recently been ejected from the Up Stairs Lounge threatening to "burn" the place down. Dragging the hustler toward a police officer holding back the gathering crowds, drawn to the spectacle of flames, the bartender demanded that the hustler be arrested and questioned as a suspect. Stewart stood aghast as the police officer feigned distraction and then told the Up Stairs Lounge bartender to "move along," demanding the release of the restrained man.

Stewart watched that hustler, the primary suspect for an arson that would claim thirty-two lives, the deadliest fire on record in New Orleans history, melt into the crowds of the French Quarter and disappear, dead by suicide nearly a year later. Police would never question that hustler even though, at one point in their investigation, they held him in their custody. The fire, it became understood, was not a crime that Greater New Orleans demanded to be solved, as the victims were of a criminal class. This was a sordid example of deviants killing deviants, some justified, part of a broader community warning to install sprinkler systems in old buildings but not an occasion to prosecute an arsonist through the courts.

Up to that moment, Stewart had bought the line fed to New Orleans's large, yet cowed queer population: stay hidden, stay discreet, and you can revel alongside all the other vice-takers in our live-and-let-live community. But where was "live and let live" in that panorama of death? Where was the reward for lifelong discretion? Where was the law's protection when a likely killer stood before a police officer who could only see two criminal fairies having a scrape? What do you do when an entire society, and its people, will not hear you? Stewart asked himself these questions for nearly a decade, during which he ruled the Up Stairs Lounge fire as a catastrophe "no good came from." Stewart eventually processed his grief with a personal answer. What do you do when people refuse to hear you? "Make them hear you, honey," as he liked to say. Where? In the arena of politics, standing openly among the first-class citizens of New Orleans, though he was never accepted as one of them.

So was the "political animal" born from the scorched seeds of trauma and tragedy. So did he finally engage his stubborn political campaigns that would endow civil rights to queer folk, starting in 1980. Stewart's efforts would result in the effective decriminalization of queer life in New Orleans years before *Lawrence v. Texas* (2003), when the US Supreme Court would make it so on every grain of American soil. Throughout his early campaigns, as this book demonstrates, Stewart maintained his zeal in the face of mounting losses and a devastating plague. He possessed the foresight to believe in a country that did not yet believe in people like him. He held true to the American promise that if you engage wholeheartedly in civic life, and don't care who gets credit, you will see meaningful change in your lifetime. Stewart also recognized that this promise was a tough shake for aggrieved citizens, seeking immediate redress, but a better shake than most societies offered their underclasses. He spoke his name publicly when his identity was illegal, imagining the day when he would cease to be a criminal. A gay senior citizen throughout most of his crusades in the late twentieth century, Stewart won congressmen and city council members and ministers as allies to his side. He also recruited and mentored countless protégés, who continued the work when he eventually fatigued. Every morning, Stewart's kitchen landline would ring incessantly with these voices. All sought counsel from Stewart in his humble seat, that den on Esplanade Avenue, even when the "Faerie" sodomy that so brazenly occurred within there was a crime against the state.

As Stewart aged venerably, he became a man of great political victories who needed very little recognition. Perhaps that's why he kept so many of his genuine political friendships: he cared so little for the victory lap. When the ACLU of Louisiana attempted to honor Stewart with the Ben Smith lifetime achievement award in 2014, he arrived at the gala in shorts and gave an acceptance speech of less than fifty words in which he reminded the crowd that he couldn't have accomplished anything without his lover Alfred's fortune. Unlike other queer contemporaries who sought legitimization through respectability politics, Stewart did not follow the model blazed by Harvey Milk, that legendary gay hippie who ran a Castro Street camera store but put on a suit when it was time to be a real contender in San Francisco. Indeed, rather than project success, Stewart always preferred to be himself. A meandering speaker who much preferred to listen, there was no trickery to his game. Cantankerous and flirty, he occasionally smelled musty from the cannabis smoke that hung about him in veritable wisps. To the chagrin of Democratic politicos, he refused to anesthetize his own sexuality while fighting for gay rights ("What would the point be in that? Aren't we saying these freedoms are good and decent?"). And even when he was a major financial donor, liberal candidates hesitated to seat him in any front row, which suited him just fine.

Clearly, some things mattered in the moral universe of Stewart P. Butler and some did not. Stewart believed in the causes of equal rights and equal dignity, and social activism to achieve those ends, but he didn't care for applause and could easily be embarrassed by attempts to lionize his muckraking. And he was a rare man for whom enough was truly enough, materially speaking. In the end, Stewart's civic accomplishments far exceeded his dreams, and he was happiest when doing big things without having to be a big person. Stewart stood as a constant figure in the background of virtually every campaign or event expanding LGBTQ+ rights in Louisiana. New Orleans, for example, was the first major city the Deep South to pass a nondiscrimination ordinance protecting sexual orientation and gender identity in the twentieth century, and it was Stewart who lobbied as a prime mover in that multi-decade effort beside his protégés Courtney Sharp and Rich Magill. As another example, Louisiana was the first and only state in the Deep South to pass a hate crimes law protecting sexual orientation in the twentieth century. A coalition helmed by the Louisiana Lesbian and Gay Political Action Caucus (LAGPAC), an organization of which Stewart Butler was a founding member in 1980, shepherded this law through Baton Rouge in 1997. Such direct and dotted lines, tracing back to the "political animal," are commonplace. There is simply no way of understanding queer Louisiana in the late twentieth century and the queer American South in the same period, more broadly, without understanding the legacy of this one gay hippie.

Political Animal represents the first and only work of scholarship to address this gap in public knowledge by revealing the groundwork of how a major human rights movement unfolded regionally, through coalitions assembled by an unlikely citizen powerbroker who would then cry, "Who, me?" Neither James Sears's venerable Southern queer history book *Rebels, Rubyfruit, and Rhinestones: Queering Space in the Stonewall South*; nor Jim Downs's paean to 1970s queer religious and community activism *Stand by Me: The Forgotten History of Gay Liberation*; nor Frank Perez's own love letter to gay New Orleans *In Exile: The History and Lore Surrounding New Orleans Gay Culture and Its Oldest Gay Bar* has ever provided an insider's account that draws the threads of queer advancement back to Stewart, a modest but determined puppeteer.

Lastly, Stewart engaged these campaigns of meaningful change without ever having to change or contort himself. He began his work as a sexually liberated, gay hippie, and he died as a sexually liberated, gay hippie. For all of these reasons, Stewart's life stands as a model of fulfillment in civic engagement, although he never sought to be an exemplar. Were he still alive, and were you a nineteen-year-old male, he would hit on you in a shameless attempt to shirk such sanctimony. Yet his was a life to be admired and emulated, body and soul.

When it came time for Stewart to pass at the age of eighty-nine, in March 2020, he'd helped the world evolve into a world he much preferred. He'd participated in the willful act of shaping the future. He pulled his daydreams and his wet dreams into reality and went for a swim, so to speak. So when it came time for him to bid his adieu, with his mind drifting and his body failing, Stewart P. Butler embraced death as a darkroom companion. He pursued capital-D Death in a way loved ones could hardly fathom—they did not wish to let him go—and in a way I have never before seen. A lifetime of political engagement in America had annihilated his fear. The political animal died smiling.

POLITICAL ANIMAL

Chapter 1

WANDERLUST

I didn't think I was gay, but I didn't have any problem with the fact that this guy whom I was already friends with came into my room one night when my roommate was gone. He's crying because he just broke up with his boyfriend and he told me. In other words, he came out to me. And I had no problem with accepting him. He used to try to tell me I was gay, and I would say, "ah you're kidding me."

—STEWART BUTLER

SPRING, 2013. STEWART BUTLER IS RIDING SHOTGUN AS HIS FRIEND BILL Hagler drives north along the fabled Old River Road. On the left, the Mississippi River winds its way in graceful curves as it flows south to New Orleans and the Gulf beyond. On the right, green pastures and sugarcane fields are dotted with petrochemical plants and the decayed ruins of old plantation homes haunted by ghosts of the past.

Stewart Butler, aged eighty-three, is riding through his childhood.

I tried to retrace the route we used in the old days when once you left the old Airline Highway at Gonzales it was all gravel the rest of the way to Carville and on until you hit Highland Road about 4 or 5 miles from Baton Rouge. Of course it's paved all the way now with all sorts of business along much of the way. Once you hit the River Road most of what used to be peaceful woods and farming and pastures had been replaced with obnoxious petrochemical plants that obliterated the once serene atmosphere. About two miles before we got to the reservation we almost missed the old Carville Store and Post Office from which political advisor and commentator James Carville hails. The reservation is now a National Guard base that permits limited access for self-guided auto tours. There were about eight information voice boxes along a designated road route from which I could see every building that was there when we lived there was still standing, including our home.[1]

With every mile, he travels back in time, cutting through eight decades, cutting through all the lovers and drugs and jobs and travels and campaigns. He arrives at his beginning—a colony for people with leprosy.

In early 1942, shortly after the beginning of World War II, my father, mother, younger sister (by three years) and I (age eleven) moved to what was then known as the U.S. Public Health Service's National Leprosarium at Carville when my father was transferred there to serve as its Maintenance and Supply Officer. We lived there until the summer of 1949.

So we had our Victory Gardens to grow our own vegetables and there was a huge scrap pile for metal and rubber near the front gate. But also, on the levee, was an elevated airplane watch tower which was staffed from dusk to dawn by volunteers, including teenagers, who called in all aircraft sightings as to speed, direction and type. Also there were practice air raid warnings and blackouts along with Civil Defense patrolpersons who checked to make sure no lights could be seen. In hindsight I think these two things were unnecessary but were really designed for propaganda purposes to make us feel the war was closer to us than it was, thereby making us feel more personally involved.

Looking back on that period, especially after the war, I can best describe it as being like "Country Club" living. We had our own tennis court, swimming pool, nine-hole golf course, ping-pong room, a free movie every week and we explored the adjoining woods and the batture behind the Mississippi River levee in front of the hospital grounds and our house.

The personnel were allowed on the patient side for medical treatment and specified occasions such as softball games and church. Both the Roman Catholic and Unified Protestant churches had personnel sections. The only rules were we weren't supposed to touch anything and to wash our hands upon our return to the personnel side.

We socialized with the medical staff, who lived in the front row of houses; the trade persons, who lived in the second and third rows of houses, and a few people living in the surrounding community.

Since my father was a commissioned officer in the U.S. Public Health Service, we lived in one of the four or so duplexes in the first row of houses. There were also two single houses, one of which the commanding officer Dr. Faget lived in and the other in which the second in command Dr. Johannsen lived. A wide parkway separated the first and second rows with a street between the second and third rows.

All the staff socialized with each other and members of the "outside" community. I remember the families of Drs. Prejean, Johannsen, Faget, and Fite. Dr. Fite was a fellow stamp collector who played chess with me on the side while playing poker with the grown-ups and Mrs. Fite became a very close friend of my mothers. Other staff families I remember were the Turners, Huevels, Nicolosis, Barbays, Rev. and Mrs. Rash and especially the Dubreuils whose son became my closest friend. My father paid for the traps and bait Mr. Dubreuil used crawfishing in the batture behind the levee in exchange for some of Mrs. Dubreuil's delicious crawfish bisque.

And then there was the Sunshine Lady, so called because she lived in the wide place in the River Road on the way to Baton Rouge named Sunshine, La., or was it the other way around? In any case, once when her son was visiting, my mother asked him if he knew how to play poker, to which he drawled, "Why Mz. Butler, I was borned under a poka table."[2]

It is difficult to appreciate fully how experiences in a person's formative years affect the development of his or her personality and belief system. It is reasonable, however, to assume that Stewart's adolescence in the leprosarium instilled in him certain characteristics that would shape his adult life, chief among them compassion, empathy, an unconventional perspective, and an open-mindedness, all of which is to say a lack of fear of difference. In *Illness as Metaphor*, Susan Sontag observes, "Any disease that is treated as a mystery and acutely enough feared will be felt to be morally, if not literally, contagious . . . Nothing is more punitive than to give a disease a meaning—that meaning being invariably a moralistic one. Any important disease whose causality is murky, and for which treatment is ineffectual, tends to be awash with significance."[3] Sontag goes on to compare the stigma of leprosy with that of AIDS. The fear and ignorance surrounding both diseases was—and, to a certain extent, remains—profound, and is best overcome by the intimate knowledge of knowing someone who suffers from the disease. As a teenager, Stewart benefitted from such a knowledge. In juxtaposition to the world inside the leprosarium, Stewart attended school in a small town called St. Gabriel, about ten miles away. Stewart witnessed firsthand how common perceptions of leprosy differed from the reality.

The Butler family had moved to Carville, Louisiana, where Stewart's father took a job at the US Public Health Service Hospital for Hansen's Disease in 1942. Leprosy, as it was known then, had been in Louisiana from the earliest years of colonization. By the 1780s, leprosy was so widespread in New Orleans that Spanish governor Esteban Miro established a hospital for people with the disease on Metairie Ridge. By the time Louisiana gained American statehood in 1812, leprosy was thought to have been eradicated, but such was not the case. There were more than fifty cases of leprosy in New Orleans alone by 1888—enough for the *New Orleans Medical and Surgical Journal* to recommend the establishment of a new hospital for lepers. In 1894, with authorization from the state legislature, Dr. Isadore Dyer leased land in present-day Carville for just such a hospital.

Carville, situated in an oxbow curve of the Mississippi River near Baton Rouge, occupies the ancient hunting and fishing grounds of the Houma, a Native tribe indigenous to southern Louisiana. In 1857, sugarcane planter Robert Camp built a 395-acre plantation there, which was eventually abandoned after the Civil War.

It was on this site in 1894 that Carville's first seven patients arrived and found shelter and refuge after being banished from New Orleans when a newspaper reporter outed them as having the dreaded disease. They lived in the old home alone for two years, their decrepit bodies a living reflection of the dilapidated and ruined structure that housed them, until four Catholic Daughters of Charity of St. Vincent de Paul arrived in 1896 to care for them. In 1905, the state purchased the property and turned it into the first home in the nation for leprosy patients. In 1920, the federal government bought the complex and turned it into the "National Leprosarium." According to researcher Kristy Christiansen,

> The site transformed into a sprawling complex, housing 450 patients in buildings linked by covered walkways. By the 1940s, it was a self-sustaining community with a power plant, an extensive drainage and sewer system and a 70-bed infirmary. There was a church and a theater, a golf course and a ballroom. Many patients spent hours fishing and gambling by the man-made lake, and everyone looked forward to the annual Mardi Gras parade.[4]

At Carville, these outcasts, feared and shunned by society, made the most of their often-involuntary quarantine and created a sustainable community with a culture unto themselves. Today the site is the location of the National Hansen's Disease Museum. When the Butler family moved to Carville, leprosy was still a misunderstood and feared disease. According to Carville researcher Marcia Gaudet:

For leprosy patients in the early twentieth century, however, admittance to the institution at Carville was tantamount to imprisonment. Because leprosy patients in the United States were subject to legal quarantine for more than half of the twentieth century, they were "sentenced" by law in most states to exile in Carville. It was not a real quarantine since patients were regularly given passes to visit their families, and many left illegally "through the hole in the fence." The diagnosis of leprosy, however, was a traumatic and life-altering shock. New patients at Carville not only took on sudden stigmatization, but they were also likely to lose much of their former identities, including their names. Often, not even the staff knew their real names. No identification papers were necessary to enter and often even the hometown was kept secret so the shame and ostracism would not extend to their families.[5]

As the material and maintenance officer and part-time pharmacist, Stewart's father was responsible for purchasing medical supplies as well as supplies for the vegetable garden and dairy and water plants. By the time Stewart's father had taken a job in Carville, medical research had yielded major breakthroughs in treatment for Hansen's disease, particularly sulfone drug therapy. The crippling effects of the disease along with the accompanying social stigma would soon enough be lifted. Public perceptions of leprosy, a disease feared and misunderstood for two thousand years, would gradually begin to shift. Ignorance would transform into understanding. It was in this environment that Stewart Butler would come of age.

Bertha June Perry married Stewart Harrison Butler on February 27, 1928, in Franklin, Mississippi. The couple met at the US Marine Hospital in Key West, Florida, where they both worked. After being graduated from the University of Mississippi, Stewart's father moved to Sonora, Texas, and secured a job coaching basketball at the local high school before returning to Oxford, Mississippi, to become a pharmacist. Bertha and Stewart moved to Mobile, Alabama, shortly after they married.[6] Stewart's parents both lived into their eighties. Bertha died at age eighty-four in Vermont of hypothyroidism and perhaps complications from Alzheimer's disease. Stewart's father died at age eighty-five, also in Vermont. At age seventy, Stewart Sr. was diagnosed with prostate cancer, but treatment was successful, and he lived another fifteen years. Near the end of his life, he became depressed and disinterested in life. He refused to eat and probably died of starvation. Bertha and Stewart produced two children. Stewart Perry Butler was born on August 21, 1930, at the US Marine Hospital in Mobile, Alabama, where his father worked as a pharmacist. In 1932, he was transferred to the US Marine Hospital in New Orleans.[7] A year later, Suzanne was born on October 9, 1933, in New Orleans.

The young family settled into life in New Orleans in a comfortable home on Tchoupitoulas Street, which runs parallel to the Mississippi River and, at the time, was a gravel road. The hospital where Stewart's father worked was a short, two-block walk away. Audubon Park was nearby, and mother Butler would often take Stewart and Suzanne there. The park featured a zoo, a merry-go-round, a snack shack, and a swimming pool. Once, at a contest at the pool, Stewart was named "cutest little boy." Stewart's sister Suzanne describes Audubon Park as

> a wonderful environment to explore and enjoy. Many wonderful hours were spent there. In addition to the pool there was an impressive zoo with monkeys, elephants, and giraffes, to name only a few. There was a baseball field where local teams could have playoffs and a merry-go-round which younger children enjoyed. Additionally, there was a small swimming pool for the younger children. Then, of course, there were the giant oaks with their ethereal hanging moss providing an acrobatic playground for the entertaining gray squirrels displaying their antics for their casual audience.[8]

Stewart—or Perry, as he was called growing up—was a curious child and loved to explore.[9] Sometimes, when he and his sister were not playing with their dogs, a fox terrier named Dixie and another terrier named Rusty, he would climb the gate in the front yard and walk to the corner store. On one such occasion he was struck by a passing car, but he was not badly injured. When Stewart misbehaved, which was often, his father would discipline him with a switch. When he was eight, the family took a vacation to Monterrey, Mexico, where they stayed at the venerable Gamma Monterrey Gran Hotel Ancira.[10]

Stewart attended La Salle Elementary School on Perrier Street, where he developed a habit of collecting newspapers. He also sold subscriptions to the *Ladies' Home Journal* and the *Saturday Evening Post*. This was during the Great Depression, and every penny counted.

At their home in Carville, the Butlers had an African American housekeeper named Minnie. Stewart and Suzanne were taught to respect her and came to think of her as a sister. According to Suzanne,

> Minnie was the offspring of the black negro housekeeper/cook at the Butler Household in McCall Creek, Mississippi, and a white schoolteacher, who lived and taught within the environs of this small rural

community. Because she had a lighter skin tone, her older siblings teased and made fun of her. This response moved Fanny, her mother, to take young Minnie to work with her where she soon began to sleep overnight more and more until she no longer slept at her own home. This was the beginning of her lifelong association with the Butler family.[11]

Racism was not tolerated in the Butler household. Their parents forbid Stewart and Suzanne to say the n-word. The values of tolerance and respect for different races stayed with them for the rest of their lives.[12] Minnie eventually married a man named Edward, and Stewart's parents served in her wedding party. On Minnie's fiftieth wedding anniversary, the Butler family, with the exception of Stewart's dad, who was suffering from Alzheimer's disease, returned to New Orleans to participate in a renewal of vows ceremony in the same church in which they were married. Stewart kept in touch with Minnie's daughter, Barbara, who once told Stewart, "Please know that although Minnie suffered for years, the pain of being given away or taken away from her mother or whatever the circumstances of separation was, she truly loved you all. You were her family and I know that you loved her also."[13]

The unique environment in which Stewart grew up not only shaped his ultimate worldview but also fostered his innate sense of curiosity. From an early age, he displayed a social consciousness, an awareness, of the world around him. In 1942, at the age of twelve, Stewart kept a scrapbook of newspaper clippings about World War II.[14] His sister Suzanne recalls:

When on vacation from school, whether from St. Gabriel or the Gulf Coast Military Academy, GCMA, he developed activities that focused on the actions of the military forces in Europe. He had a large oak table in the bedroom where all of his paraphernalia was laid out. He worked there for hours on end, keeping track of the movement of the military forces and developing a keen interest in collecting stamps and understanding the geographical features of far off places.[15]

In the margins of the scrapbook, he wrote personal commentary and raised questions about the content of the articles he saved. Stewart remembers first learning of the Japanese bombing of Pearl Harbor during their weekly Sunday evening gatherings around the radio. After the Normandy invasion, Stewart "plotted on a huge map the advancement of the Allied troops in Europe in France."[16] Later, Stewart cried when he learned of President Roosevelt's death.

Growing up, Stewart attended the Methodist church before beginning high school at the Gulf Coast Military Academy in Gulfport, Mississippi, and completing his last two years at Baton Rouge High School. After graduation, Stewart spent the summer in Idaho working for the US Forestry Service. There he developed a fascination with the West that would stay with him the rest of his life. Stewart remembers:

Frank Houston, a friend about whom I remember absolutely nothing except that he was good looking and was my companion that summer. We took the train to northern Idaho to work for the Forestry Service for $1.00 an hour and room and board. Room consisted of but a tent for six or eight. However, board was quite another thing in that it consisted of absolutely delicious fare, of which the portions were so large that a quarter of a 10" pie was not out of proportion to the rest of the meal. To my meager weight of 120 or 125 pounds, I added another 15, all of which went into my legs, the effects of which still show in my calves. All of this occurred in the brief six or so weeks I worked for them before I was fired. However, I managed to get a job with the local railroad section gang but quit in about three weeks to return to Louisiana with Frank when he left the Forestry Service.

Not having enough money to do otherwise, we hopped first onto a railroad oil tanker car's narrow wooden walkway, duffel bags in hand. I cannot remember if it was before or after we managed to transfer to the safer framework under the sloping end of the coal car when we crossed the continental divide high up in the Rockies. In either case, it was truly scary clinging on for dear life as we skirted along the edge of an almost straight down drop of perhaps a thousand feet. Some time after that, while stopping to change from coal to electric or vice-versa, the freight conductor came along and instead of throwing us off said, "You boys would be safer in a freight car," as he led us to an empty car and opened the door for us. By evening time, having gone only hundred-plus miles and being drenched in coal dust, we decide to try hitchhiking. We managed to make it to Ruston, in north central Louisiana, where we spent the night with a friend. We still had just enough money to buy bus tickets to Alexandria in the center of the state where my parents met us and gave us a ride the rest of the way home. We were exhausted but I'd had a seventeenth summer to remember![17]

That summer in Idaho was the beginning of a lifelong love affair with the West, an area he was drawn to and to which he would eventually move.

The expansive wilderness, the untapped potential, the natural beauty, and the unlimited possibilities all appealed to Stewart's sense of adventure and destiny. His parents had instilled in him a sense of purpose.

In 1947, the same year his father was transferred to Long Island, New York, Stewart enrolled as a freshman at Louisiana State University. He pledged a fraternity, Theta Xi, and worked part-time at the Goalpost, a popular eatery on the edge of campus. He made friends easily and became involved with a number of extracurricular activities. During his time as an undergraduate, Stewart served as a cabinet member of the YMCA and was a member of Phi Kappa Tau. He also served as Campus Services chairman. It was at LSU that, along with his friend Lawrence Baker, Stewart cultivated a hobby he had developed in childhood and would keep for fifty years—stamp collecting.

While at LSU, Stewart became friends with a fellow student, Wilds Bacot, who came out to him as gay. He recalls:

> I didn't think I was gay, but I didn't have any problem with the fact that this guy whom I was already friends with came into my room one night when my roommate was gone. He's crying because he just broke up with his boyfriend and he told me. In other words, he came out to me. And I had no problem with accepting him. He used to try to tell me I was gay, and I would say, "ah you're kidding me."[18]

It is unclear what precisely tipped Bacot off about Stewart's sexual orientation; he was not effeminate or "obvious." Bacot's intuition was correct, of course, and can be chalked up to what is commonly referred to as "gaydar." Stewart would later say he did not know he was gay at this time. It is easy in the twenty-first century to dismiss this claim as denial, and there may be some truth to that, but denial is a complicated phenomenon, one that is greatly influenced by environment. Surely Stewart knew he was attracted to guys, but in 1950, there were no cultural reference points for young people discovering their sexuality. Modern conceptions of sexual orientation were decades away. If homosexuality was ever mentioned, it was either in a cold, clinical, medical sense (homosexuality was still considered a mental disorder at the time) or in a pejorative sense, suggesting criminality or moral depravity.

The latter was certainly the case in the fraternity Stewart and Wilds were in at LSU. For example, Stewart recalls an incident involving a member of the fraternity who was suspected of being gay. So serious was this suspicion that the fraternity brothers convened a secret meeting without this member present to discuss the matter. One student in attendance at the meeting proposed they try to entrap the suspect. The plan was for the best-looking guy in the fraternity to invite the suspect to a movie and then take him home to see what would happen. The suspect did indeed make a pass at his friend—an act of treachery that was breathlessly reported to the larger group in yet another secret conclave. As they debated the situation, Wilds Bacot remained silent as member after member cursed the suspect and suggested they throw him out of the fraternity. Stewart was the only one who spoke in defense of the guy, arguing he should not be kicked out. But Stewart's pleas were ignored. It would be another fifteen years before Stewart would come out. First there would be the army, and then a ten-year odyssey in Alaska.

Coming out of the closet is never a one-time event. For many, coming out is long, gradual process laden with self-loathing, denial, incredulity, confusion, hypocrisy, pain, and ultimately, for the lucky ones, self-actualization and freedom. Life in the closet is a life of quiet violence, the despair of which not all escape. For those who do, extraordinary courage is required. Finding that courage can take years. Such was the case with Stewart. Once out, an entire world of possibilities and potential is unleashed. Stewart's coming out journey was a long one and eventually led to a life of consequence.

During the summers of his time at LSU, Stewart traveled. In 1948 he worked with the US Forest Service in Clarkia, Idaho, and one week on a railroad section gang before hitchhiking back to New Orleans. The following summer he journeyed to Valley Stream, New York, to visit his father.[19]

The summer of 1950 was Air Force ROTC summer camp at Fort Sam Houston/Kelly Air Force Base near San Antonio, Texas. Stewart provided an intimate glimpse into life on the base that summer in a letter he wrote to his friend Wilds Bacot:

Dear Wilds,

Well, this makes two Friday nights straight that I've stayed in camp. Last week I was broke, and the reason I'm staying in tonight is the same reason that I'm writing this letter on a typewriter. That is I'm CQ (Charge of Quarters). I have to stay in the sqdn. orderly room for 24 straight hours—the only thing that I can leave for is to eat and shit and to perform other duties such as pick up the mail, post material on the bulletin board, and run errands. I also have to answer the damn phone.

Things here really aren't too bad, but we sure do go through a long day. Up at 5:30; breakfast at 6:20; some tour, drill, or physical ed from 7:25–11:25; lunch at 12:00; class from 12:45–4:20; retreat at 4:50; and supper at 5:00. After that we have intramural sports on some days.

But in spite of the heavy schedule we, or at least I don't have too hard a time. In fact I rather enjoy it in a way. San Antonio's motto is "where life is different." Truer words were never spoken. Not only is San Antonio different, but the camp and the way things are run are not only different, but also even interesting. We have our good times. You couldn't ask for better recreational facilities—swimming pool, four bowling alleys, gym, weightlifting room, four softball fields, volley ball courts, barber shop, laundry, PX, soda fountain, handball courts, and last but far from least, the ROTC Cadet Club, where beer is sold for 15 and 20 cents a can and where there are slot machines, a juke box, a horse-race machine, and a piano. It has nice lounge chairs and writing tables. The only thing we have in the barracks is a bunk, a foot-locker, and a clothes rack.

I seem to be getting into fair shape from the few various and assorted ball games in which I participate and from the physical ed. But when I have the money I spend most of my time over at the club. When I got here I had a dollar in my pocket, 60 cents of which went for a haircut. Then everyone got their May checks, that is, everyone except me—mine was temporarily misplaced. But I wasn't too bad off, since Bill had a little money left from home. So he bought me beer the first two nights in camp. Then he went broke, but he got his May check and loaned me $5.00, $4.50 of which it didn't take me long to lose in bouray {sic}. I had the worst damn luck. We'd be playing upstairs in one of the two more or less private rooms (three cadets to each one), and I'd finally be ready to rack up with four trumps, when three big pieces of brass come up. Well, immediately the game is broken up, and I'm left holding the bag. So I was broke again. So last week-end Bill was once more my benefactor.

Saturday we went to see the Alamo; then we started to look for a nice cool bar, but they don't have such things in San Antonio; all they have are a bunch of joints which can only sell beer and most of which are in the Mexican District. However, we found a fair place and had a couple. Then we looked for a Mexican food place. We found an ideal one, the Casa Rio, which is partly outdoors on a plaza. There is a canal running by the plaza. Pretty good food too—more than I could eat for a dollar. Then we fell in with four others from LSU and went to the Tropic Club. 75 cent cover charge for the cruddyist floor show I've ever seen. Sunday afternoon we went out to Fort Sam Houston to see a boy who lives close to Bill and who is in the hospital there with TB. After that we went to see "The Reformer and the Redhead." It was an above the average comedy—in fact, it was pretty damn good. After supper we came on back to camp.

Wednesday, we got our travel checks, and Thursday I got my May check which had been forwarded home. I'm enclosing it endorsed. I want you to please put it in the Phi Kappa Tau checking account at your earliest convenience and get those checks to Co-Op and Victoria Press. But at any rate, since I was now fairly loaded, I had my share of the beer Wednesday and Thursday nights. Surprisingly enough the place was pretty quiet Wednesday night considering the fact that everyone had money. It wasn't anything like the first two nights, the first one of which they sold out of beer. That first night was really a wild one. Not many boys from LSU though. Altogether, there are about 900 of us from 24 different schools—all the way from Minn. And St. Thomas in St. Paul, Kansas State, Kansas State Teachers, Ark. Okla., Okla. A&M, Texas Tech, Texas U., Texas A&M.[20]

As an undergraduate at LSU, Stewart proved to be a classic academic underachiever. In May 1949, the dean of students wrote him a letter informing him he had been placed on attendance probation for excessive class absences. He managed to skate by for two years, earning mediocre grades at best, all the while keeping his parents in the dark about his lack of progress. In addition to academic underachieving, Stewart also managed to get into disciplinary trouble for stealing a civil defense tape recorder. In a 2017 interview for OUTWORDS, Stewart recalled:

Then I was indefinitely suspended for stealing a civil defense tape recorder because they were in the same building where our fraternity colony met. I noticed they never locked their room. Supposedly there was top secret chemical, maybe biological, warfare information on it. So they conducted a search like crazy. I just put it up in my closet. My motivation was because someone else was there and had one and he was playing jokes with it all the time. I thought I should have one.[21]

In March 1951, the university mailed Stewart's parents his mid-semester grade report, which indicated four Cs, one D, and one incomplete.[22] In a stroke of bad timing, the report arrived shortly after a request from Stewart to buy a recording device. His father responded with a tersely worded letter:

You are either dumb or don't give a damn . . . This I consider a disgrace . . . When you can pay for a wire recorder with your own money it will be your privilege to buy one, but not with the money I have earned . . . I am quite disappointed in you and never thought you would piddle around to the extent you would fail to graduate.[23]

By the spring of 1951, it was clear he would, in fact, not graduate. His grades were less than stellar, and his attendance record was abysmal, but worst of all, he had gone into debt with the university. Leaving his undergraduate career in ruins, he spent the summer of 1951 with his parents in New York and in October of that year joined the army. The Korean War had broken out the year before and Stewart was in no hurry to go to the front lines, but he figured he should join before being drafted. Also, there was the added advantage of getting his parents off his back.

He completed his basic training at Fort Dix in New Jersey and eventually became an officer in the US Army Medical Service Corps. He attended Officer Candidate School Fort Riley in Kansas, from which he was graduated on October 11, 1952. While at Fort Riley, Stewart developed a crush on an Irish Catholic farm boy and, in an effort to emulate him, decided to become Catholic. Nothing ever became of the crush, and the two enlisted men eventually went their separate ways. And while Stewart's "conversion" to Catholicism was less than authentically spiritual, it was not the last time his romantic feelings for another man would influence his spiritual journey.

During this time, he began to consider the next step in his military career. He narrowed his choices down to Medical Field Service School or Army Finance School. He chose Medical Field Service School and underwent medical service basic training in New Jersey. Stewart remembers, "Our company was pretty undisciplined. Our captain was, well, I forget his name, but he had to go away to some kind of school for however long there, so I was the commanding officer for the whole company, acting, brand new fresh First Lieutenant."[24] Realizing that Stewart was long in character yet short in physical stature, those under his charge dubbed him "Little Jesus."

After graduation, Stewart accompanied his parents back to New York and visited his sister Suzanne at the University of Connecticut, where she was in her second year. He was then commissioned as a second lieutenant in the army reserve corps and assumed active duty at Fort Sam Houston in Texas, where he was initially assigned to the demonstration section of the HQ Detachment of the Medical Field Service School before enrolling in the Medical Field Officer School, which lasted until February 1953. There, Stewart fell under the mentorship of Donald James McCormick, whom he greatly admired. He lived in a corner barracks, which he described as "not even as good as Riley." In a letter to Wilds Bacot, he acerbically observed, "This is really a stupidly run place even for the Army."[25] It was during this time that Stewart took a trip with a friend to Mexico, visiting Monterrey and Del Rio. He had first visited Mexico when he was eight years old on a family vacation. There would be future trips to Mexico in later years.

It didn't take Stewart long to tire of military life and begin thinking of what lay ahead for him after the army. He became somewhat depressed, not uncommon among those with restless minds and free spirits, and the rigidity of military life no doubt added to his dissatisfaction. The spring brought some relief when he was transferred to Camp Pickett in Virginia, where he served as a basic training officer. His duties also included teaching, which he at first enjoyed but eventually considered "a pain." In a letter to his friend Bill Finn, Stewart wrote, "In July I had the first of a series of run-ins with Col. Bullis, the Regiment Commander. So I got kicked off the faculty and started doing two months of straight troop duty, including two weeks as Company Commander."[26]

His lifelong penchant for being ornery began to manifest and is evident in the letters he sent home. In one he describes the battalion adjutant, First Lieutenant Brooks, as "one of the few people around here who knows what the hell he's doing."[27] Of another officer, he writes, "What have I done to necessitate my having to put up with him?"[28] He was ultimately removed from the faculty for "not going by the book." He was transferred to another company, which he felt had been treated too easily. He recalls, "I really had to crack down on them." Little Jesus could put his foot down when he had to.

But in addition to being strict and rude, he could also be generous and empathetic, as evidenced in this passage from a letter he wrote home from Camp Pickett:

> Starting yesterday morning at 10:00am I started a rifle inspection in the 3rd Platoon. The rifles were really poor due to the lack of care throughout the cycle. But I started sitting down with each man and showing him what was wrong and how to clean it. I showed quite a few how to take apart the trigger bolt and clip latch release. They'd never been showed before. Surprisingly enough, from what I could gather, the men didn't resent my presence or my requiring them to clean their rifles beyond the extent necessary for the ordnance inspection. Instead, they seemed, for the most part, to appreciate my interest, which was not in just their rifles, but rather in them too.[29]

Stewart was twenty-one years old when he joined the Army, and like many young men, especially those who are closeted, he began to struggle with depression, a condition that would plague him intermittently for the rest of his life. He revealed his depression vaguely in letters to his parents but less so in a letter to Wilds Bacot, the friend who had come out to him at LSU and told Stewart he was gay too. In that letter, Stewart writes, "The past several weeks I've been very upset. I wonder if I'll ever find happiness. I don't think I would by being like you, but on the other hand I doubt if I will anyway."[30] Writing from his home on Governor Nicholls Street in the French Quarter, Bacot's response strongly suggests Stewart was resisting the reality of his sexuality. The reply letter from Bacot contains the warning: "Read in Private." Bacot writes, "I hope the last two days have shown you what you wanted. And if they are what you want, face it, accept it, or forget it."[31] He goes on to reference "that person in North Carolina and who did you get to the wheat fields with."[32] Further, Bacot explicitly states, "I am not h-------- for the reason of s—primarily. I desire love, affection, and company, and because except in extremely rare cases, which I do not want, find it necessary to 'go all the way.'"[33] Also given the fact that Bacot mentions Stewart went on only two dates with women at LSU, it is reasonable to assume Stewart was beginning the often-painful process of coming to terms with his homosexuality. Coming out is a gradual process that begins with coming out to oneself. But this was the 1950s, and Stewart was not quite ready to do that. That would take another twelve years.

He achieved the rank of first lieutenant just prior to his discharge in 1954. Before Stewart was discharged, he began thinking about how to write the next chapter of his life. He knew he wanted to finish his degree, but he wasn't sure where to do it. He had already inquired about correspondence courses from Iowa State College and had considered returning to LSU to finish his degree. His parents tried to persuade him to enroll at the University of Connecticut, as his sister had done, but Stewart was not interested in going East. By late 1953, Alaska was on his mind. In that year, he requested a catalogue from the University of Alaska and subscribed to a magazine about the great territory. He also subscribed to the *Anchorage Times* newspaper; furthermore, he began writing letters inquiring about employment opportunities there. He eventually decided to drive up to Alaska in the summer of 1954, and by the fall of 1953, he was actively looking for a travel companion to join him.

Chapter 2

TERRITORIAL POLITICS

I would like to be in a position where I could influence man's thinking along
international lines. This is the only way that war is not going to wipe us out.
I'm against McCarthy, high tariffs, nationalism, totalitarianism, and the
things that go with them. I'm for the U.N., Esperante, capitalist Socialism
and the things that go with them.

—STEWART BUTLER

DAVE EATON MET SUZANNE BUTLER AT A FRATERNITY "GET ACQUAINTED
dinner" while they were attending the University of Connecticut. The two hit it
off, began dating, and ultimately married. Eaton met Stewart for the first time
when he was visiting the Butler parents in Valley Stream, New York. Stewart
had come to New York on leave from Officer Candidate School at Camp Pickett, Virginia. Eaton recalls that Stewart came across as "a very reluctant soldier."[1]

On January 30, 1954, Stewart traveled to Valley Stream, Long Island, New
York, to serve as an usher in his sister Suzanne's wedding. Sixty-six years later,
Eaton recalled the wedding day:

> Sue and I married in a well-attended wedding in the Protestant cha-
> pel on the UCONN campus in Storrs. The wedding was somewhat
> marred by several details that bear repeating. First I slammed the door
> on Susie's finger on my father's Plymouth station wagon we had bor-
> rowed for our truncated overnight honeymoon. We got as far as the
> first, reasonably well-lit motel with an attached restaurant, in Wellesley
> Mass. The first problem there was that we couldn't get champagne.
> Susie wasn't old enough. Finally, you might call it anti-climactic, my
> frenzied attempt to close the curtains against the curious, ended in
> only opening them wider. In my haste, I was pulling the closure cord
> in the wrong direction, opening the curtains instead of closing them.
> This was the worst possible time to make that particular error.[2]

At the wedding reception, during which Stewart had several cocktails, he remarked, "I'll drive to Alaska if I have someone to go with." Almost immediately, Bob Pattison, a friend of Dave Eaton's from Connecticut and the other usher at the wedding, declared, "I'll go."

The spontaneity suggested in Stewart's account of how he ended up in Alaska is a bit misleading. Alaska had been on his mind since his time at Camp Pickett, and he had already written Bob Pattison about joining him on the trip. Pattison was a good friend of Stewart's sister's fiancé, Dave Eaton. Eaton and Pattison had not known each other before they were assigned to be dormmates their freshman year at the Fort Trumbull branch of the University of Connecticut in New London. According to Eaton:

> Bob was recognized by the State of Connecticut as handicapped in that his vision was severely impaired by a birth defect. The State offered supplemental services to impaired students. One of those services was to provide a paid "reader" to read assigned texts to the handicapped person. The reader in this case was Bill Benedict. Bill, Bob, and I were very close by virtue of the proximity of our homes, similar schedules and interests, and a pervasive sense of good fellowship. It seems now to have been a natural for me to choose Bob as an usher at my wedding in January of 1954.[3]

Stewart and Bob Pattison had a lot in common and would become fast friends. Bob had a BS degree from the University of Connecticut in geological engineering and worked, sometimes, as a carpenter. He would have joined the army, but his poor eyesight prevented him from doing so.

Stewart remembers, "We didn't want to leave before April, when the snow would be gone. In order to save money, we decided to camp out and sleep in the station wagon during the thousands of miles we'd be traveling and during the time it took us to find jobs."[4]

They loaded up Stewart's 1950 Chevrolet station wagon and left New York on May 8. They removed the rear seats from the vehicle and installed a piece of plywood to, in effect, enable bunk beds in the wagon. They bought two air mattresses and a two-burner Coleman Camp Stove, which they often used to cook C ration meals Stewart had left over from his time in the army. The long sojourn across the continent took them through New Jersey, Pennsylvania, Ohio, Indiana, Illinois, Iowa, South Dakota, Wyoming, Montana, Alberta, and the Yukon Territory.

Stewart remembers the division of labor along the trip:

At any rate, Bob Pattison didn't see too well, so I was doing some of the driving, but we got on the Pennsylvania Turnpike and I said, "Now if there is any place he can drive, he can drive here." Then we came to a tunnel and I said, "Look out for the tunnel there." He said, "What tunnel?" I said, "Take your hands off that steering wheel and let me have it." We managed to get through the tunnel, and I took over the driving and he never drove one more mile. I drove the whole way. He took charge of all setting up camp every morning, preparing breakfast every morning and setting up camp in the evening and fixing supper.[5]

Leaving New York, they took the Pennsylvania Turnpike and drove all the way to Columbus, Ohio, where they spent the night at the home of Butler family friends Bill and Merna Benedict. Stewart recalls the Pennsylvania countryside being "pretty" but described eastern Ohio as "pretty shabby." The following day, a cold and rainy Sunday, they drove to Bloomington, Indiana, and spent the night with more family friends—Dr. and Mrs. Lenoir. Jim Lenoir had been Stewart's father's roommate at the University of Mississippi and was now a professor. Next, they drove through Illinois and Iowa before reaching South Dakota, where they visited the Badlands, the Black Hills, Mount Rushmore, and Wind Cave National Park. After spending the night in Moorcroft, Wyoming, they visited Yellowstone before driving to Gardiner, Montana, just south of Helena. From there they headed north and reached the Canadian border on May 13. They spent their first night in Canada about 150 miles south of Edmonton before they headed northwest and briefly cut through British Columbia. The road was lonely and desolate, and accommodations were few and far between. One evening they camped out at an abandoned road labor camp. They reached the Yukon Territory on Saturday, May 22, before arriving in Fairbanks, Alaska, on May 25 and Anchorage on May 29. To celebrate their arrival in Fairbanks, they bought some groceries and a pint of Walker's De Luxe whiskey.[6]

It was a grand road trip that deeply affected the rest of Stewart's life. Stewart recalled as much forty years later in a letter to Bob Pattison:

Dear Bob,

It is with hope that you will be as glad to hear from me at this time as I would be to hear from you were our roles reversed that I'd take pen in hand to write this.

Even though for whatever reasons we have not communicated with each other over the years, the news my sister gave me on the phone a couple of days ago regarding you hit me pretty hard and I felt that I did indeed need to write you right away. I do now wish I'd kept in closer touch but there is not much other than this letter that can be done about that now.

Whether or not you realize it, you had quite an impact upon my life. I shudder to think how perhaps tragically different things might have turned out for me had you not been so quick to seize upon the opportunity presented to you at Sue & Dave's wedding to join with me on that grand adventure to "the Last Frontier," now more than forty years ago.

I have such vivid memories of so much of that journey—beginning with your basic but rather clever concept of building across the entire rear of my old 1950 Chevrolet station wagon a shelf upon which to place our air mattresses and sleeping bags. I recall how underneath we had two wooden army footlockers, which, by the way, I still have, one on each side upon each of which we stored a two-burner Coleman stove. In one we had our cooking gear and in the other our food. Between the footlockers were five-gallon cans of water, kerosene, & gasoline.

Along with your carpenter tools we also brought an axe & a shovel, thinking I suppose that the Alcan Highway might be so primitive that we might have to somehow construct some sort of makeshift bridge across stream beds. If that recollection is correct, what a laugh it'd have been had we had to carry through with that notion—but on second thought, I rather suspect your skills and resourcefulness would have carried us through.

I remember how we thought that if there was any place you could safely drive it would surely be on the Pennsylvania Turnpike—that is until you entered a tunnel and told me you couldn't see. "Just follow that truck," I replied, but when you said, "What truck?" and I had to from the passenger seat steer us through the tunnel we realized that I'd have to do the rest of the driving. But you more than made up for it by staying awake during those endless hours to keep me company. And on top of that you felt you should assume full responsibility each day for making and breaking camp as well as all the cooking and cleanup. I never had it so good.

I remember spending the night with my Dad's old Ole Miss room-mate, who was a law professor at the University of Indiana, and I remember your riding "shotgun" through the Dakota Badlands. Of course there was Yellowstone and Glacier Park, where we had to rid ourselves of the roof rack so its legs wouldn't puncture the top of the station wagon, leaving behind whatever we couldn't otherwise stuff inside, stripping down covered wagon style so to speak.

And there were those monster Yukon mosquitoes that we could hear saying to each [other] that they should eat us on the spot rather than hauling us back to the swamp where the big ones would take us from them.

And I remember the economic shock of the dollar or two it cost us for toast and coffee at a Fairbanks restaurant to celebrate the completion of our journey—that is except for backtracking to Anchorage. I think that was the only restaurant food we indulged ourselves with the whole time.

I'm sure there were other highlights of the trip that you recall and I've forgotten, but so much for that for now. By any chance, are you still in touch with Bob Chapman? I wish I still had his address if he's still alive and kicking.

I hope your life has been as good to you as mine has been to me, thanks in part to you. I feel as though I've been blessed in so many ways that I sometimes wonder what terrible price I might have to pay in the future to make up for it all. I wouldn't be surprised but were I to wind up a lonely old man in some sort of home not having the slightest idea as to what might be going on.

But whatever the future holds, I hope that the powers that be will direct that we meet again if for nothing more than the sharing of memories. But beyond that, I do believe we'd enjoy each other's company.

In any event, I must take my leave for now while sending you

Best Wishes,
Stewart
Or did you think of me as Perry
I don't remember
Stewart Perry Butler[7]

Upon arriving in Alaska, Stewart and Bob immediately began looking for work. They applied at a wide range of places including the Alaska Railroad, the Alaska Road Commission, two coal mining companies, Alaska Freight Lines, the Arctic Plumbing and Heating Company, a fish company, Northwest Freight Lines, Standard Oil, a sawmill, and a real estate concern called Smiling Irishmen. The job market was tough. At every turn, prospective employers told them business was bad and that no one was hiring. The Territorial Employment Office informed them there were over 4,000 unemployed men in Anchorage alone. Government jobs were scarce because of budget cuts. The Laborers Local Union told them there were already 750 men on the waiting list for jobs. Making matters worse was a plumbers' strike, which had just ended when Stewart and Bob arrived; in addition, the carpenters union was on the verge of striking. But instead of getting discouraged, Stewart and Bob kept at it, and their diligence finally paid off. Bob took a food service job at Whittier, about sixty-five miles south of Anchorage. Stewart found work as a storekeeper for a concern called Universal Food Service at the Elmendorf Air Force Base in Anchorage.

Universal Food Service was a private company that fed construction workers working on government projects. Stewart worked in the office of the mess hall, doing administrative work such as keeping timesheets, analyzing food costs, and managing the inventory and ordering. The nine-hour shifts lasted from 5:00 a.m. to 3:00 p.m. and paid a salary of $104.50 per week, $94.00 after deductions for room and board.

During his time working on the base, Stewart began considering finishing college. He took night courses in geology three nights a week and explored other educational opportunities such as the local community college, mining school, and correspondence courses from LSU. In one of his letters home, he mused, "Maybe I could study mining engineering or geology. However, I am coming closer and closer, I think, to business. I might do a little amateur study of geology on the side. It seems as though I don't put my spare time to good use."[8]

Stewart did a lot of thinking during his first several months in Alaska in the second half of 1954. He was twenty-three years old and had tried his hand at college and served in the army. He had a keen interest in geology, as well as politics. Weighing in at 160 pounds, he was in good shape, and his health was generally good. His whole life was ahead of him, and he began to wonder what to do with it. He missed Louisiana and thought about returning home, but he also considered exploring and settling somewhere out West. But Alaska had a hold on him. In a letter home, he stated, "I like this country here because I believe in it, that it has a great and promising future."[9] Without realizing it, he was projecting his own future onto his newly adopted home.

In 1954, Anchorage was a decent-sized town with a population of fifty thousand. It boasted two television stations and was growing rapidly. Founded in 1914 as a tent city near the mouth of Ship Creek for the Alaska Railroad, the settlement grew steadily until World War II, which created something of an economic boom for the town. Stewart fell in love with Alaska. The territory was perfect for a bright, energetic young man with a thirst for adventure. The untapped wilderness of the territory appealed to Stewart's love of geology, and the territory's growing sentiment for statehood afforded him a chance to get into politics.

In another letter home, he waxed introspectively that he wanted an "eventful life" and to "make a contribution to the betterment of mankind."[10] He further wrote: "I would like to be in a position where I could influence man's thinking along international lines. This is the only way that war is not going to wipe us out. I'm against McCarthy, high tariffs, nationalism, totalitarianism, and the things that go with them. I'm for the U.N., Esperante, capitalist Socialism and the things that go with them."[11]

By this time in Stewart's young life, he had already formed a solid worldview and a very distinct political ideology. In letters to friends, he writes of his disdain for the myth of American exceptionalism. Of Colonel Robert R. McCormick and his "For America" organization, he writes:

> What type of fools be these who think Americans are better than anyone else and therefore deserve more? I think that this is a type of American totalitarianism and imperialism. I think it is time for Americans to give up this myth before it gets too strong a hold on them. If there is to be peace in the world, I think that the only means by which we will be able to attain and maintain it will be through a single world government.[12]

While Stewart's political consciousness was fully developed by this time, his sexual consciousness was woefully underdeveloped. In this regard, he was a product of his times. The term *coming out* was not then in use, and our current understanding of sexual orientation was nonexistent. Little is known of the gay scene in Fairbanks during Stewart's time there. If there were gay bars or other gay spaces, Stewart did not seek them out. He was not out to himself then, but during his Alaska years, the national homophile movement, which set the stage, so to speak, for Stewart's later activism, was in its nascent stage.

Henry Gerber founded the Society for Human Rights in Chicago in 1924. The Society for Human Rights is generally credited with being the first LGBT+ rights organization in the United States, but it was not the first voice in the country advocating for gay rights. The first public advocate for gay rights in the United States was a pastor in New Orleans, of all places. Reverend Carl Schlegel, a German immigrant, preached from his pulpit at a German Presbyterian church in 1906 that gays and lesbians and bisexuals deserved equal treatment under the law. His idea that homosexuality be decriminalized was influenced by the Scientific-Humanitarian Committee, an organization in Germany that also inspired Gerber to establish the Society for Human Rights. Schlegel was defrocked and dismissed as "queer." In 1950, Harry Hay founded the Mattachine Society in Los Angeles, which grew steadily until the Stonewall uprising in 1969. In 1955, Del Martin and Phyllis Lyon and another lesbian couple organized the Daughters of Bilitis in San Francisco. But while these important organizations were finding their way, the nation was in the midst of the "Red Scare." Conservative politicians like Senator Joseph McCarthy linked homosexuals with communism. In 1953 President Eisenhower issued an executive order that homosexuals employed by the federal government be fired. It was the 1950s, and the white patriarchy was obsessed with the threat of Communism. And although focused on the USSR, the establishment could see out of the corner of its eye African Americans beginning to agitate for their rights; the last thing it needed to deal with was a small group of pesky sodomites. The white, heteronormative patriarchy had bigger fish to fry, and its response to any group that challenged its authority was to label them communist. And the last thing Alaskans wanted was to run afoul of the federal government; after all, they desired statehood terribly, and that meant not antagonizing Congress.

In December Bob Pattison returned stateside, but Stewart decided to stay in Alaska.[13] In January 1955, Stewart enrolled in the University of Alaska, just north of Fairbanks. He would later write his parents that he enrolled in the university because he intended to stay in Alaska and wanted to make contacts.

Located on a ridge one hundred feet above the floodplain of the Tanana Valley and four miles from the center of Fairbanks, the University of Alaska was the last traditional land grant college established in the US. Incorporated in 1917 as the Alaska Agricultural College and School of Mines, the school opened in 1922. In the distance to the southwest, Mount McKinley (Denali), the tallest peak in North America, is visible from the campus. Three thousand years ago, the site of the campus was a campground for the indigenous Athabaskan people.[14]

As an undergraduate, Stewart indulged his love of geology, participating one summer with a geological field engineering party hired by the U.S. Steel Corporation searching for magnetite in the Percy Islands off the southern end of the southeastern Alaska panhandle. Stewart was on a four-man team, the other three workers being from Cal Tech. Because of twenty-foot tides, their cabin was elevated by pilings. There were no amenities on the island— no electricity, no running water, no plumbing, no automobiles. The days were long, and by night the men read by lantern light or wrote letters. A mail boat came once a week. The men showered by way of a five-gallon barrel with holes drilled into it. The water took about a minute to drain, which meant thirty seconds for soaping up and thirty seconds for rinsing off. Because the islands had not been named, the crew was afforded that privilege. Stewart named one island Ursula after a family friend in Long Island he briefly dated.

Other summers included similar expeditions. As was the case during his time at LSU, he made friends easily and quickly became involved in a wide variety of extracurricular activities: he was vice president of the Mining Society and coeditor of the campus newspaper; he was a member of the Joint Athletic Committee, the Finance Committee, the Legislative Council; he cofounded the Young Democrats Club; and he was elected president of the student body. He continued to work throughout his college career, often as a carpenter.

During his first year, he was elected to the student council as a representative from Merlin Hall. When asked why he ran, he said, "I was naturally drawn to politics."[15] In his second year, he was elected student body president. And in his third year, he chose not to run for reelection so he could become the editor of the student newspaper, the *Polar Star*.

As engaged as he was with campus life and making friends, he had a less than engaging attitude toward his coursework. He dropped several courses, and his grades were less than stellar. His transcript is filled with Cs and more than a few Ds. As was the case at LSU, academically, he was a classic underachiever. And he was not immune to disciplinary trouble. While serving as the president of the student body, the university adopted a strict no alcohol on campus policy. The first person to get caught violating the policy was Stewart.

The alcohol ban was the result of an annual event that got a little out of hand in the fall of 1956. Since its inception, the Mining Society's Starvation Gulch Dance had earned a reputation as a wild party and a cherished campus tradition. According to *The Cornerstone on College Hill*, a book on the history of the University of Alaska, after the announcement of the alcohol ban, hundreds of students gathered in front of Constitution Hall and buried an empty beer bottle in a grave with a marker that read, "Here Lies Tradition."[16] This marker quickly became known as the Tradition Stone. During the mock funeral, the students sang a parody of "The Old Rugged Cross" and reenacted a scene from Shakespeare's *Julius Caesar* where Marc Antony buries the slain leader. Later, when the administration ordered the Tradition Stone removed and destroyed, it was stolen. Despite a few periodic reappearances, its permanent location remains a mystery.

Probably in an effort to make an example, Dean William Cashen, whose office was next to Stewart's, disciplined Stewart by ordering him to move off campus. When Stewart complained he had no chance to defend himself, Cashen responded, "Look, Stewart, we're not trying to run a court of law here, just a university." Stewart did not put up a fight, but he did get the last word. At the alumni dinner that year, Stewart spiked the punch bowl and poured the last bit of it into Cashen's martini glass.

Thirty-five years later, in 1992, when he was firmly established back in New Orleans, Stewart received a letter from Henrik Wessel, then the president of the Associated Students of the University of Alaska, soliciting financial donations for the Tradition Stone Scholarship Fund. In response, Stewart wrote:

Dear Henrik:

Your letter . . . brought back to me a flood of memories. The fact that I was President of the ASUA during the 1956–57 school year, an eventful one to say the least, certainly played a big part in these memories.

The burial of the Tradition Stone was an outgrowth of then President Ernest Patty's banning the consumption of alcoholic beverages on campus. That was his response to what was perceived by some to have been an uncommonly roudy [sic] Starvation Gulch staged by the Mining Society.

As I recall, the campus exploded in a fury—the lead story of the next issue of the Polar Star began, "Prohibition, which heralded one of the wildest eras in the history of the United states, struck the University of Alaska campus without warning last week." It also contained a petition which, lifting language from the proscribing edit itself, in part stated that, "The following undersigned students of the University of Alaska do not understand that in drinking we are necessarily harming either ourselves or the University, and we are wondering to what extent the University feels it would be better off without us." It was signed by a significant portion of the student body including prominent graduating seniors and teetotalers.

Towards the end of the first semester, I was one of the first two students reported for drinking on campus and was thereupon denied campus housing for the second semester. When I complained to the Dean of Students William Cashen, who was a legend in his own right, that I hadn't been confronted with the evidence at any kind of hearing (I was actually innocent), he looked up at me and in a tired voice said, "Look, Stewart, we're not trying to run a court of law here; we're just trying to run a university." Later in the year he was reassigned to the math department because he'd been too sympathetic to the student point of view. I suppose that was because of his having been involved in some antics of his time as a student back in the 30s.

That was also the year of the Giant Volcano Hoax—another grand story that those of us who were present will never forget but that I won't now go into.

Least [sic] you conclude it was all play and no work in those days, allow me to state that most of us managed to go on to become responsible citizens. In my own case, I received two bachelors degrees at the '58 commencement, assisted Dr. Patty in lobbying the First Alaska State Legislature in 1959, and worked for the Fairbanks City Engineer's Office and was active in Democratic Party politics until I left Alaska, first in 1963, and finally in 1964, to attend Hastings College of the Law in San Francisco.

Some who may remember me from those earlier days might wonder why I never returned. I can assure them that it was certainly not for a lack of love for Alaska. Rather, it was because of the fact that while outside I discovered that I was gay and felt at the time that most of those I knew would reject me if they knew—and that it would be impossible to keep it a secret in Alaska.

Since 1980 I've been active in the gay and lesbian community here in New Orleans. I am presently serving as one of three Co-Chairpersons for the Host Committee for the Twelfth Annual International Convention of Parents & Friends of Lesbians & Gays to be held in New Orleans over next Labor Day weekend.

The enclosed $600 credit card authorization is due to the generosity of Alfred M. Doolittle, my life mate of very nearly 20 years. Kindly list the contribution in both our names.

It is my hope to be able to pay an extended visit to Alaska and the University in the not-too-distant future. In the meantime, I extend my best wishes to you, the student body, and the university for a successful future.

Sincerely yours,
Stewart P. Butler[17]

At the time of the incident, Stewart's positive attitude about the ordeal was not lost on the dean. In a letter written to Stewart's father concerning the incident, Dean William R. Cashen observed, "He has a broader outlook on things, and I find him able to see problems from the administration's point of view as well as from the student's viewpoint."[18]

This reasonable and pragmatic attitude was also reflected in his dealings with other students. In November 1957, he wrote to his parents describing an incident of which he was rather proud. While he was working for the school newspaper, a new student had come aboard the editorial staff. Stewart wrote, "He is a typical Southerner, prejudiced but not radical. About two weeks ago I introduced him to a Negro—it was the first time Ken ever shook hands with one, but he did it."[19] Growing up, Stewart's attitudes toward race relations were not horrific but typical of someone raised in the South. His parents were not racists, but the society in which he grew up was. Such an environment inevitably has an effect on children, and Stewart was no exception. Reflecting on the issue of race, Stewart recalls that whatever "soft racism" he harbored was eradicated in the army: "One thing the Army taught me that broke down my tendency towards discrimination, having been brought up in the South, so that was very much of a plus from being in the Army. Of course, that was important in a lot of ways."[20]

After being refused dormitory housing for violating the campus's new no-alcohol policy, Stewart and three of his friends rented a house on the edge of campus in a neighborhood called the Flats. Stewart and his crew nicknamed themselves the Flat Rack Flat. No longer burdened with a prohibition policy, the Flat Rack Flat began brewing beer in the bathtub of their rented house, which was consumed at the frequent parties they hosted. On one occasion, one of the boys obtained a pornographic film and suggested they have a "stag party." Stewart borrowed a film projector from Dean Cashen, explaining to him he wanted to watch a "wildlife film," and the party was on. The only problem was that the Flats was a Nazarene community and the neighbors were nosy. One of the Nazarenes called Dean Cashen and complained some of his students were having a wild party that involved alcohol and pornography. What was the university going to do about it, this neighbor demanded. "Nothing," Dean Cashen told him. Cashen called in Stewart to his office, but Stewart talked his way out of trouble. The dean told Stewart to be careful and mindful of the neighbors.[21]

For recreation, Stewart and his friends would often go bowling or to the movies. When not taking daytrips to Valdez or other outlying areas, bingo and blackjack were occasional pastimes. His taste in movies went against the grain. He was not too fond of blockbusters such as Cecil B. DeMille's *The Ten Commandments* or David Lean's *The Bridge Over the River Kwai*, but he did enjoy Stanley Kubrick's *Paths of Glory*, a film about the French Army in World War I, because "the moralists failed to triumph." Bing Crosby in *White Christmas* didn't bore him, but he "didn't think it was much of a movie," and *The Best Years of Our Lives* was "pretty good." His musical tastes included the likes of Burl Ives, Hank Williams, Webb Pierce, Sammy Kaye, and Count Basie. While working in Juneau, he became a regular at the Red Dog Saloon and very much enjoyed the ragtime performances of Hattie Jessup, also known as the Silver Dollar Lady. He spent a good amount of time reading as well. His literary fare included Ernest Hemingway and George Orwell, the local newspaper, and *Time Magazine*. Eating was apparently another favorite pastime; in his first five months in Alaska, he gained fifteen pounds.[22]

During his time as an undergraduate at the University of Alaska, Stewart developed an interest in the stock market. He bought stock in the Alaskan Oil Company, U.S. Steel, Studebaker-Packard, and North Canadian Oil.

Stewart spent the summer of 1956 on the Point Barrow peninsula working with an airport surveying crew. Point Barrow is a few miles south of the farthest northern point in North America. The peninsula juts into the Arctic Ocean and divides the Chukchi and Beaufort Seas. When Stewart arrived in May, the sun neither rose nor set. A constant haze hung in the frigid air, with temperatures in the high twenties and low thirties. The ocean was still frozen for several miles off the shoreline. The main camp consisted of six hundred men. Along the coast, every forty miles or so, there were smaller camps that housed twenty-five to seventy-five men. For living quarters, Stewart shared the laundry drying room with two other men. The small, framed structure stood alone behind the laundry and was sparsely furnished with a few bunk beds, an oil stove, and a clothesline.

Stewart worked in the chief engineer's office for a man named Don Eyink, like Stewart, a former president of the student body at the University of Alaska and a former engineer for the City of Fairbanks. His main duties were estimating steel and concrete requirements for the air strip, but he also performed other jobs such as operating the blueprint machine, "bluetopping" airstrips, assembling antennas for the towers, and drafting plumbing fittings. A typical workday lasted nine hours. For recreation, the camp showed four movies a week, and the workmen played softball with inhabitants of the nearby villages. Not far from the camp, there was also the Arctic Research Laboratory, which investigated a wide range of subjects, including electronics, botany, wildlife, biology, permafrost, and anthropology.

Stewart returned to school in September, enrolling in seventeen hours: Geophysics 461 (prospecting), Geology 421 (ore deposits), Geology 423 (mineralography), Civil Engineering 341 (hydraulics), Business Administration 331 (business law), and Business Administration 461 (personnel management).

During his last semester at the university, Stewart became actively involved in Alaskan territorial politics. As student body president, he had sent out letters to student government associations across the country, urging them to lobby Congress on behalf of Alaskan statehood. His efforts were later the subject of an article in *Alaska History Journal* in 2009, which noted the letter campaign ingratiated Stewart to local politicians.[23] He had worked as a page in the territorial legislature and was also involved in the Technical Engineers Union. These experiences enabled him to make a lot of political contacts. In the spring of 1958, he was elected to the Fourth Division Democratic Committee, which was chaired by Lou Dischner, whose nephew Johnny Balestere was, for a time, Stewart's roommate. After graduating in 1958 with a BS degree in geological engineering and a BA degree in business administration, Stewart lived briefly with the Dischner family. Dischner would become something of a mentor to Stewart and encouraged him to get involved in politics.

The US had acquired the territory of Alaska in 1867. Secretary of State William Seward had purchased the vast area from Russia in 1867 for just over $7 million, and Alaska was called "Seward's Folly" until gold was discovered there in the 1890s. There was not much interest in admitting the territory into the union as a state, despite a halfhearted attempt in 1916, until after World War II. During the war, Japan bombed Dutch Harbor and actually occupied two Aleutian Islands, Attu and Kiska, for fifteen months. The Japanese occupation, as well as the discovery of oil on the Kenai Peninsula in 1957, illustrated Alaska's military and economic strategic value to politicians in the lower forty-eight, who until then viewed the territory as too sparsely populated and too dependent to be a state.

The move toward statehood was well underway when Stewart arrived in the territory. In November 1955, in an effort to show Congress they were ready to be admitted to the union, fifty-five elected delegates met at the University of Alaska in Fairbanks to draft a state constitution. Stewart was in his first semester at the university, and there is no evidence he participated in the constitutional convention, although he followed the proceedings with great interest. Two and a half years later, on June 30, 1958, Congress voted to admit Alaska into the union. President Eisenhower signed the bill on January 3, 1959.

Prior to statehood, the Alaska Territory was divided into four political subdivisions. The first included the southeast and the panhandle, the second included Nome and the Arctic coast, the third encompassed Anchorage and the southern coast, and the fourth covered Fairbanks and the central interior. Senate seats were divided into two-year terms and four-year terms.

By early 1958, Stewart had considered running for the territorial legislature in the Fourth District but decided against it. One of his professors, Dr. Moberg, and a few friends persuaded him to reconsider. Stewart filed as a candidate for the Democratic nomination to one of two four-year terms in the territorial senate. Bob Longwith, the business agent of the Technical Engineers Union, of which Stewart was a member, asked him to run as a third-party candidate as a member of the new Alaska Party, but Stewart declined and ran as a Democrat.

He was a newcomer to politics and somewhat naïve. Shortly after his decision to run as a Democrat, he mentioned his candidacy to the office secretary of the University Engineering Office, who in turn asked him if he had told Alex Miller, the Democratic National Committeeman, of his intention to run. No, Stewart replied. This woman then urged him to inform the State Central Committee, of which her father was a member, of his candidacy, which he did. At the State Central Committee Meeting, each candidate had an opportunity to say a few words in hope of securing support. One candidate, Dick Greuel, the Speaker of the territorial house of representatives, simply said, "You know me so I don't need to say anything."[24] Stewart followed and opened by saying, "You don't know me so I need to say . . ."[25] He went on to explain his platform's chief plank, which was his belief that the district did not need to hire out-of-town part-time summer workers, which he called "fair weather workers."[26] The headline on the front page of the local paper the next day read, "Butler Blasts Fair Weather Workers."[27]

In the Democratic primary, he faced two formidable opponents—James Doogan, a Fairbanks city councilman, and Dick Greuel. Two of these three candidates would be selected to face off against two Republican candidates in the general election. The two Republicans were Dr. Paul Haggland, who had previously served in the Senate and was now serving as the mayor of Fairbanks, and John Coghill, who had served several terms in the House.

Of all five candidates, Stewart was the least experienced and least well known. He was the underdog in the primary and knew it; nevertheless, he waged a vigorous campaign. He opened the campaign with this statement:

> It is my belief that I possess qualifications that would be an asset to the citizens of the Territory and of this Division, although I have never held or been a candidate for public office before. Most important is an extensive educational background in government, engineering, economics, and business administration at the University of Alaska and Louisiana State University. I am a candidate for degrees in geological engineering and business administration in May of this year. Since entering the University of Alaska in January 1955, I have always been active in student body activities and was President of the Associated Students of the University of Alaska, Inc., last year.

As to political beliefs, I am not the representative of any interest group, large or small. I feel we must find ways and means of discouraging the exploitation of the Territory by summer workers. In regard to the Territory's bonding authority, I believe that there are far more advantages than disadvantages to be gained by its utilization for worthwhile projects. Finally, I think more consideration should be given to the welfare of the citizens living in our villages and outlying areas. I hope that they, as well as the citizens of Fairbanks, will write me at Box 584, College, concerning their ideas and suggestions as to our ills and needs. I realize that these are generalizations and, therefore, propose to go into further detail as the campaign progresses.[28]

He was a better campaigner than speechwriter, and his appeal to rural voters worked, although it would take three months for the vote totals to be verified. During that time, votes from far-flung, rural precincts would trickle in and the lead mercilessly alternated between Butler and Duncan every few days. On the day the US Senate voted to admit Alaska to the union, Stewart won the Democratic primary by one vote. Stewart was the Labor candidate, and Labor leaders had sent word to the rural areas to vote for Butler. Years later, Stewart recalled:

Initial returns from Fairbanks indicated a tie between me and another candidate. The tie remained when the absentee votes were counted a few days later. Because the district extended to the Bering Sea and covered thousands of square miles, the final tally wasn't made until 90 days after election day in order to allow time for the bush to get its vote in. The lead see-sawed back and forth as the press daily reported the vote of each village as it came in. Finally, the big day arrived. I had won 949 to 948, a margin provided by the illegal vote of Rosaduik, still then a Canadian citizen. But the long-anticipated results were buried on one of the back pages of the edition of the *Fairbanks Daily News-Miner* that headlined the granting of statehood to Alaska, an action that nullified my ill-gotten nomination. Now if that's not poetic justice, I don't know what is.[29]

Statehood rendered the election results moot and effectively served as a reboot. Although he was not seated, the election proved to be a valuable experience for Stewart. Elective success was not in Stewart's cards, but developing relationship-building skills was. He befriended and mentored Democratic

National Committeeman Alex Miller's son, Terry Miller, who was eventually elected lieutenant governor of the state.

Later that year, Stewart decided to run for the Democratic nomination to the state house of representatives but withdrew to run as an Independent for the state senate. On the Friday before the November 26 general election, Robert McNealy, who had run unopposed in the primary for the Democratic nomination for the at-large Senate seat, created a stir by endorsing a split ticket and alleging that Dick Greuel was backed by organized crime. In the US Senate race, McNealy endorsed Republican Mike Stepovich over Democrat Ernest Gruening. Democratic officials were furious and persuaded Stewart to drop out of the House race and run for the Senate to stop McNealy. Stewart ultimately withdrew from the race and eventually took a job as a staff member in the first session of the new state legislature.[30]

He remained active in Democratic Party politics by serving on the party's divisional committee. The 1959 Divisional Democratic Convention was particularly contentious. When state senator Hugh Gilbert was appointed to a superior court judgeship, a vacancy in the state senate was created. Governor William Egan, a Democrat, would appoint someone to fill the senate vacancy. The Democratic divisional committee chose to send three names to the governor as recommendations to fill the seat. At the convention, nine candidates emerged.[31] After a series of balloting, Stewart's name and two others were sent to the governor, who ignored the recommendations of the division committee altogether and appointed Bob Giersdorf, a state representative, to the seat. Stewart was disappointed but looked forward to running for the house of representatives in the upcoming election.

While in Alaska, Stewart made friendships he would maintain throughout the course of his life. In addition to Balestere and Dischner, there was Larry Brayton, Niilo Koponen, and Ken Gain. And, like so many closeted gay men of that era, he married a woman.

In 1959, while a student at the University of Alaska, Stewart met and began dating Sophie Ondola, who was majoring in business administration. Of Athabaskan heritage, Sophie grew up in a small village about thirty miles east of Anchorage. Stewart was twenty-eight years old and felt it was time to get married. On August 28, 1959, a week after his twenty-ninth birthday, the two wed in the Anchorage Gospel Tabernacle, a nondenominational church to which Sophie belonged. The date of the wedding was scheduled to coincide with a visit to Alaska Stewart's parents had already planned.

Stewart's parents were somewhat surprised at news of the wedding but had long since realized their son was strong willed and capable of surprising them. Sophie took immediately to her in-laws, and they to her. The correspondence between them suggests a warm bond. After Stewart's parents returned to New York, the young couple settled into married life in Fairbanks. The couple had two pets, a dog named Tuffy and a kitten named Martini (a gift from Sophie's brother, Carl). Stewart and Sophie occasionally went to movies or plays when they weren't working. They also joined the city employees' bowling league. Stewart remained devoted to union work and state politics while working in the Fairbanks city engineer's office. Sophie took a job as an administrative assistant at the state Veterans Affairs office.

But a happy married life, at least with Sophie, was not to be. Stewart was consumed with politics. The political arena was his real passion, and his dedication to it came at the expense of his marriage. In addition, sexual intimacy, or the lack thereof, became an issue. By February, just six months after the wedding, Sophie moved out and began living with another man, who, incidentally, was a political friend of Stewart's. In fact, before their divorce was finalized a year after they married, Sophie moved back in with Stewart when he ran for a house seat in the legislature so as to avoid a political scandal. Her boyfriend even endorsed Stewart. Their divorce was mutually agreed on and not contested in court. The two remained friends and kept in touch.[32]

Stewart had not accepted the fact, or perhaps even understood, he was gay at the time of his marriage, but claims he did not marry Sophie in an effort to hide or disguise his homosexuality. He remembers, "I can't say I had a passionate, romantic feeling for her." The marriage was consummated, but the two had a less than satisfying sexual relationship. Sophie noticed more than once that Stewart had an eye for good-looking young men and even asked him about it on one occasion, to which he responded by playing dumb, nonchalantly replying, "Who? Me?"

Stewart's parents were "disturbed and hurt" by news not only of the divorce, but also by the fact it was Sophie and not Stewart who informed them of the separation. They told him, "You are being very hasty in this matter, just as you were in getting married." In response, Stewart blamed most of the divorce on Sophie's drinking and spending. There is some evidence that this may have been the case, although Stewart downplayed his own role. The two were $2,000 in debt, and neither one of them was a teetotaler with regard to alcohol. At the same time, he also knew the real reason for the breakup—he simply was not in love with her.

In a letter to his parents, Stewart writes, "The separation has been what might be called friendly. Neither of us are bitter. We've talked about it a good deal. I'm quite sure she loves me, and I feel that I must love her, but not with the intensity she desires and requires. Naturally, we are both sorry it had to happen this way."[33]

Sophie echoed these sentiments in her own letter to Stewart's parents: "He has been very good to me regardless of the fact that he told me on several occasions that he did not love me. I just keep on hoping that he will tell me different someday. Also, for the time being, I am tired of politics and unions. It got so that I felt I married a bunch of guys rather than Stewart."[34]

Stewart's sister, Suzanne, who was living in Waterville, Maine, with her husband and three children, perhaps put it best in a letter to her parents: "Perry's attitude seems to be, at this point, that it is just easier to quit trying. It looks as though he hardly tried at all. The first year of marriage is hard enough to adjust to without all the tension of so many meetings. Perry seems so afraid of missing something and before he knows it, he's going to have missed everything that means something."[35]

Despite the split, the two remained friends and kept in touch with each other. Ondola would go on to remarry and live a full life, often crediting Stewart for her commitment to civil rights:

> We had a unique and loving relationship—though long-distance. I admired him and his drive to help everyone he came into contact with. I am an Athabascan Indian from Alaska, and I have been involved all of my life in civil rights due to Stewart's influence. I was part of the first civil rights demonstration in Anchorage (1968 or so) and one of the first members of the Alaska Civil Rights Union. Now, I am married to a Hispanic, who was very involved in civil rights.[36]

The divorce did not deter Stewart from his political ambitions. Shortly after the divorce, he filed for the Democratic nomination for the House of Representatives. He had recently been elected vice president of the local union and was a member of the Democratic divisional committee. He faced thirteen opponents, including five incumbents: Dick Greuel, Bob Giersdorf, Speaker Warren Taylor, (?) Chapador, and Bobby Sheldon. The centerpiece of Stewart's campaign was "the Butler Farm Program." The primary election was held on Tuesday, August 9. Stewart finished sixth in a field of thirteen candidates.

From 1958 to 1963, Stewart worked for the City of Fairbanks in the city engineer's office as a civil engineer. His duties included supervising draftsmen, designing subdivisions, public relations, general office management, and "computing." He also worked part-time from 1961 to 1963 as the business manager for the American Federation of Technical Engineers, Local 189. His work for the union involved keeping the books, preparing financial reports, conducting personnel interviews, managing public relations, engaging in contract negotiations, and lobbying the legislature.

In 1962 and 1963, Stewart took a long, three-month vacation. He traveled first to Virginia to visit his parents, who had recently retired. In Washington, DC, he met with several members of the Alaska congressional delegation in order to lobby on behalf of the Technical Engineers Union in Alaska. He then went to Puerto Rico and planned on flying to the Virgin Islands, where he planned to catch a tramp steamer on the way to the Panama Canal. But the flight to the Virgin Islands was canceled. Upon returning to his guesthouse in Puerto Rico, he found a letter waiting for him from an Alaskan friend who was in Lima, Peru, inviting him to visit there. In Lima, Stewart indulged his suppressed sexuality by visiting a notorious cruising area and procuring the services of a sex worker. He then traveled to Guadalajara, Mexico, to surprise yet another Alaskan friend who had moved there, but the friend had passed away. Although sad to hear of his friend's death, Stewart took the opportunity to explore the city's underground gay scene. He was finally beginning to explore his sexuality, at least under the safety of the anonymity that comes with being a stranger in a foreign city.

While he was in Puerto Rico, Stewart took the exam necessary to be admitted to law school. Law school had been on Stewart's mind since his days at LSU. He had applied for the Law School Admission Test as early as 1950. There were no law schools in Alaska in 1963, and if he was to pursue a legal career, he would have to leave his adopted state. Two of Stewart's friends from his time as a surveyor, Dietrich and Judy Strohmaier, suggested Hastings College of the Law in San Francisco. Stewart applied and was accepted. He was California bound, but he planned on returning to Alaska after earning his JD. Fate had other plans.

On March 27, 1964 (Good Friday), the largest earthquake ever recorded in North America (and the second largest ever recorded in the history of the world) struck Alaska. The 9.2 quake's epicenter was only seventy-five miles from Anchorage and wreaked destruction on the city. One hundred fifteen Alaskans died in the earthquake, and the property damage was estimated at over $300 million, close to $3 billion in today's economy.

Seismic shifts were also occurring in Stewart's life. In 1964 he would meet a man, fully realize he was gay, and move back to New Orleans.

Chapter 3

PRYTANIA STREET

For me, being homosexual is as natural as being heterosexual is to a heterosexual. It was the period of my life when I thought I was straight that I was
acting in an unnatural and perverse manner.

—STEWART BUTLER

STEWART ENDED HIS NEARLY TEN-YEAR STINT IN ALASKA IN AUGUST 1963
when he moved to San Francisco to attend law school. The next few years
would be a pivotal time in Stewart's life. A law degree was not to be. And
although he had entertained the notion of returning to Alaska, that was not
to be either. Rather, a sexual awakening was on the horizon, one that would
lead him back to New Orleans. It was during this period that he would also
begin a lifelong love affair with marijuana.

Stewart entered the Hastings College of Law in the fall of 1963. His interest in the law was not new. As early as 1950, when he was an undergraduate
at LSU, he applied for the Law School Admission Test. Upon arriving in San
Francisco, he took a room at the Broadmoor Hotel before doing the same
at the YMCA. Eventually, he settled into a sixth-floor apartment on Steiner
Street with a panoramic view of the San Francisco Bay and Oakland in the
distance. By April 1964, he was living at 620 Post Street, just twelve blocks
from the law school campus.

San Francisco was the perfect place for a closeted man to explore his
sexuality. If Stewart explored San Francisco's gay nightlife, he never talked
about or mentioned it in his letters; however, it is safe to assume he did. He
had cracked his closet door open in Mexico, and it is reasonable to assume
he nudged it a bit more open in San Francisco, especially since he knew no
one there. As with New Orleans and other port cities, San Francisco's queer
roots are deep. Stewart once told a researcher he did not begin going to gay
bars until the mid-1960s, but he did not specify if this was in San Francisco
or New Orleans. In the same interview, he did say he had been to a gay bar

once in 1952. This would have been during his time in the army. In 1952, he attended Officer Candidate School at Fort Riley, Kansas, and then Medical Field Service School in New Jersey. Given the lack of a gay bar scene in Kansas in 1952, it may be reasonably assumed he visited a gay bar in New York City while he was stationed in New Jersey.

In an excellent study of the city's queer history, historian Nan A. Boyd demonstrates that San Francisco's attitude of sexual permissiveness dates back to its earliest days as a frontier town after Spanish colonists founded the settlement in 1776.[1] The city experienced a population explosion during the gold rush of 1849, with 95 percent of the new arrivals being young men from a plethora of ethnic and cultural backgrounds. After the Civil War and into the early twentieth century, the political establishment began tightening morality laws, which had the effect not of eradicating queerness but rather of corralling it into gay spaces, specifically bars. What we would now think of as an LGBT+ community first coalesced in the 1920s and 1930s. Other than a military crackdown on gay and lesbian bars during World War II (one raid at the Rickshaw bar in Chinatown in 1943—twenty-six years before Stonewall—ended in a riot when two lesbians fought back), the queer community in San Francisco grew steadily. By 1964, the year Stewart arrived in town, *Life* magazine declared San Francisco the "Gay Capital of America."[2]

Stewart initially intended to return to Alaska. His ties there in union work and politics were strong, and he had purchased a duplex in Fairbanks in November 1962. He even reapplied with the City of Fairbanks to get his old job back in the city engineer's office. His priorities gradually shifted, and he never completed law school. He was becoming more comfortable with his sexuality, and if he returned to Alaska he faced a dilemma—go back into the closet or risk losing the friendships he had forged there.

On a Christmas visit to Waterville, Maine, to surprise his sister, he met on the bus a young man named Gregory Manella. Of English and Italian descent, Manella was seventeen years old at the time and had been hustling in San Francisco before deciding to return to New York to live with his father and his father's gay lover. Stewart and Gregory got along well on the long bus trip, and when the last leg of journey was interrupted by a snowstorm in New Jersey, the two took a room at the YMCA. Stewart and Gregory parted ways in New York and lost contact after the trip until the following year, when they ran into each other in San Francisco. Butler recalls,

> Gregory spotted me in the Tenderloin walking from school to my residence club and he came running out of this coffee shop and jumped on my shoulders. I started seeing a good bit of him, trying to get him

to quit hustling and smoking pot. In the fall I started seeing so much of Gregory that I fell way behind in my studies. During semester break, which started in early December, Gregory took a bus trip with me to Guadalajara, Mexico. I decided that if I was ever going to try marijuana that was the place to do it. I liked it, and we took perhaps three ounces of cleaned pot back with us. When this woman I'd been seeing found out about it, she went into a hissy fit of jealousy and threatened to call the FBI.[3]

Gregory had left New York and returned to San Francisco because his father's lover had "put the moves on me." Gregory was not gay but had turned to sex work as a means of survival. And while Gregory instinctively knew Stewart was attracted to him, he did not exploit the relationship because he appreciated Stewart's "big-brotherly" concern for him. Gregory needed a friend more than a client. Nevertheless, the two did "fool around." Stewart and Gregory were hanging out in Stewart's apartment one evening drinking beer when Gregory's experiences hustling came up in conversation. At one point in the conversation, Stewart said, "I've always wondered what that would be like. Why don't you show me?" Gregory stood up, closed the blinds, and took off his clothes. The two then engaged in mutual oral sex. The experience exhilarated and haunted Stewart for days. For the next week, Stewart mulled over the terrifying question, "Am I gay?" After several days of intense soul-searching, Stewart concluded the answer was *yes*, and thus he came out to himself. He then told Gregory he wanted to do it again, but Gregory confessed that he wasn't gay. At this point, Gregory unofficially became Stewart's "little brother."

Stewart and Gregory's friendship was cemented over Christmas 1963, when the two took a bus trip to Guadalajara, Mexico. Prior to that trip, Stewart had never tried marijuana. One evening, after attending a bullfight, Stewart told Gregory he was willing to smoke some weed. Gregory's response was reluctant, and he finally told Stewart, "Well, I'm not getting it for you." Never one to be deterred, Stewart discreetly asked around and was referred to a cab driver, who procured the marijuana. Stewart loved it and bought more to bring back to the States. Gregory and Stewart smuggled the pot across the border by sewing cellophane bags to the inside of Stewart's coat. It wasn't the last time Stewart smuggled weed.

The marijuana created a problem back home. At the time, Stewart was dating a woman named Denise and seeing another one on the side. Dating may be too strong a word. Denise, a woman of French/Swiss descent, served as the housekeeper. While she was on vacation in Hawaii, Stewart was having sex with another woman, all the while fantasizing about Gregory. Although Gregory and Stewart were not an official couple, Denise, with whom Stewart was sexually active, perhaps sensed the sexual tension between the two men and was disturbed by it. It was the other woman who flipped out over the marijuana they had brought back from Mexico. Her reaction set in motion an epic road trip, the kind about which movies are made—and one that would ultimately influence the future LGBT+ New Orleans.

When the woman, whose name has been lost to time, threatened to turn them in, Stewart and Gregory decided to get out of town. Stewart needed to bring a new Buick Electra to Riverside for a side job he was working, and this provided not only a good excuse to leave town but also a means of escape. Unfortunately, Stewart fell asleep while driving, as had Gregory while riding, and Stewart wrapped the new car around a telephone pole. Although the car was totaled, neither man was badly injured, but Gregory was brought to the hospital because he had a seizure shortly after the police arrived. In the aftermath of the accident, before the police arrived, Stewart hid their stash of marijuana in the bushes on the side of the road, which he later recovered. Greg was released the following day, and the two then took a bus the rest of the way to Riverside. Once there, Stewart bought a used 1959 Ford.

Stewart now had a choice—return to San Francisco or go somewhere else? He had become disengaged with his studies and was flunking out of law school. Returning to Alaska was not a very attractive option since he was coming to terms with his sexuality. Too many friends and familiar faces up there to be out. It was time for a change. It was time for a homecoming. He and Gregory decided to move to New Orleans. Destiny was whispering: Go east young men.

By the time they reached New Mexico, they had run out of cigarettes. Stewart found a grocery store and attempted to steal a pack but was caught and arrested. Stewart used his one phone call to call Dr. Jim Lenoir, Stewart's father's friend with whom he and Bob Pattison had stayed in Indiana on their way to Alaska ten years earlier and who was now on the faculty at New Mexico State University. Lenoir paid the twenty-five dollar fine and housed Stewart and Gregory for the evening. He also gave Stewart fifty dollars for the rest of the trip.

In Mississippi, Stewart became worried they might be mistaken for civil rights workers because of the California license plates. Earlier that summer, three civil rights activists—James Chaney, Andrew Goodman, and Michael Schwerner—had been kidnapped and murdered in Neshoba County. But the Ku Klux Klan left Stewart and Gregory alone. In Mississippi, they visited Stewart's uncle Powell, a bisexual man, who assumed Stewart and Gregory

were lovers. Powell told them of the gay bar scene in New Orleans, specifically mentioning Wanda's, a gay bar in the French Quarter. They then traveled
to Baton Rouge, where they stopped to visit some of Stewart's relatives before
continuing to New Orleans.

In New Orleans, Stewart and Gregory lived together intermittently until
1967, when Gregory returned to California to be near his mother and her
family. Stewart had fallen in love with Gregory, and although Gregory did
not identify as gay, Stewart stubbornly clung to the fantasy of a romantic life
with him. In a letter dated March 1969, Gregory wrote, "Stewart I do hope
we are still friends after this winter. I tell you things have changed one hell
of a lot for you and myself. You always will be my big brother and friend if
you'll just let it be that way."[4] Stewart and Gregory's relationship was more
emotional than sexual. Stewart felt sympathy for Gregory, who in addition to
the various hardships of his life also suffered from epilepsy. The two developed a deep friendship and maintained a robust correspondence, much of it
detailing Gregory's inability to get settled in California and Stewart's various
romantic interests. In the mid-1970s, Gregory moved to Ocean Springs on
the Mississippi Gulf Coast because a friend of his lived there. In Mississippi,
Gregory fell in love with and married a woman, Connie Lacey, in 1989. Every
few months, Stewart and his partner would drive to the coast to have lunch
and spend the afternoon with Gregory and Connie. Gregory died in 1999 at
the age of fifty-three. His widow kept in touch with Stewart until his death,
affectionately referring to him as "Mom."

Emotionally, the return to New Orleans was a distressing time for Stewart.
His newfound sexuality, financial insecurity, and lack of a clear life direction
all agitated his obsessive need for control and order. He had always possessed
a sense of purpose, but his life was in transition and his destiny was unclear.
Adding to all of his anxiety was the lack of a support network. His parents
were rigid and traditional, and while they were steadfast, they provided little
emotional support. His sister Suzanne lived across the country and was busy
with her career and family. There was Gregory, but he too had his own emotional needs. The one person in his life he could turn to was Minnie. Years
later, in 1989 before she died, Stewart told her, "I'll forever be in your debt
for the non-judgmental support you gave me back in 1965 when I returned
in such great distress after many years away . . . I know those were days that
were among the most difficult ever encountered by my parents."[5]

Back in New Orleans, Stewart lived from pillar to post for a few years.
From 1965 to 1968, he lived in a total of twelve different places, including five
in the French Quarter, four along Esplanade Avenue. In addition to Gregory,
several other roommates came and went. During this time, he worked various

odd jobs as a busboy, a waiter, and a draftsperson for three land surveyors. He eventually found secure employment as the office manager for John E. Walker, a civil engineer whose offices were in the historic Cotton Exchange building in the central business district. There Stewart consulted with clients, conducted personnel interviews, did title research, drafted legal descriptions, oversaw payroll and billing, handled correspondence, and did some engineering drafting. This job afforded him financial security, but working conditions were apparently less than ideal, for by 1970 he was actively sending out resumes in search of other employment.

Upon his return to New Orleans, Stewart also reconnected with Wilds Bacot, his friend from LSU, who was living in the French Quarter at the time. Stewart had come a long way from his days at LSU fifteen years earlier. He was much more sexually experienced with men by now, and he had familiarized himself with the gay subculture of the time and its conventions. He had grown comfortable in his own skin, comfortable enough to take the huge step of coming out to his parents in a letter. Alarmed, his father traveled to New Orleans to do what Stewart describes as an intervention. His father suggested he see a psychiatrist, a man who happened to be a relative. This was the uncle in Mississippi Stewart and Gregory had visited in 1964. He was quite relieved when this man told him, "Don't worry about being gay. I am too." Stewart's sister was supportive from the start, and his parents eventually came around as well, sort of, until 1972, when they were "born again." After her conversion, Stewart's mother wrote to him urging him to accept Christ. In one particularly emotional letter, she criticized Stewart for not caring about the family's feelings and being "blind, blind, blind."[6]

In response to his parents' constant requests that he "find God," Stewart wrote a poignant letter to them and stated:

> I readily acknowledge that I have problems, but I fail to see how becoming an active participating Christian heterosexual will automatically remove them . . . For whatever comfort it might give you, I consider myself to be a Christian even though I don't regularly attend church and am not a student of the Bible. Moreover, I'm sure I'm a stronger Christian—and have more love for my fellow man—than many who loudly—but falsely (be it consciously or unconsciously) embrace God and Christ—at least I'm not a hypocrite—and I hope I'm not vain.[7]

Stewart had always maintained what might be called a progressive spirituality—a sense of social justice and equality informed by reason and intellect that manifested itself in his treatment of others. Fundamentalist dogma never appealed to him, and although he underwent a conversion of sorts in 2008, it is fair to say his religion was essentially his relationships with other people.

Whatever faith he had did not suppress the urge to explore his sexuality. He sought and found many lovers. In an age before social media and dating apps, when society kept most gay men deep in the closet, one might think finding sexual partners was especially challenging, but this was not necessarily the case in the French Quarter. There was a plethora of gay bars in the Quarter catering to a wide variety of tastes. Café Lafitte in Exile was a popular cruise bar that featured "a blow job corner." Hustlers could be found down the street at the Caverns (later the Bourbon Pub), Wanda's, and a few other bars as well. Sometimes when barhopping, Stewart deployed a trick to lure young men to his home. After a potential trick caught his eye, Stewart would have a friend extinguish a cigarette in the young man's drink. The mark would naturally become upset, at which time Stewart would step in and buy the man another drink before saying, "Why don't you come with me and I'll fix you all the cocktails you want." The promise of weed would often sweeten the deal. In addition to the bars, a gay salon society also flourished among well-heeled "Friends of Dorothy." And for the deeply closeted, the men's restroom at D. H. Holmes on Canal Street saw its fair share of action. And if none of those venues worked, there was always the public restroom at the French Market.

For Stewart, college campuses were apparently fertile cruising grounds; Stewart's personal collection of correspondence contains more than a few letters and notes from former lovers thanking him for good sex. Some tricks turned into emotional investments. In 1971, Stewart fell in love with a man named Barton. In a letter to Gregory describing his feelings, Stewart confessed, "I'm so hung up on Barton that I think of little else."

Stewart and Barton lived together for a while before Barton took a job in Chicago. At one point in their time together, Barton stopped having sex with Stewart, which caused him no small amount of anxiety. Stewart confided his dilemma to an old friend from his LSU days named Pat. The letters exchanged between Pat and Stewart are fascinating not only for their subject matter, which included a lengthy dialogue about Stewart's curiosity and apprehension concerning sadomasochism and bondage, but also for Pat's blunt style. In one letter, for example, Pat chastised Stewart for being sentimental and unrealistic in viewing both Gregory and Barton through "rose-colored glasses" and even likened Stewart to "a fickle teenage girl."[8] Another friend, Annie Garza, echoed these sentiments, warning him in a letter that "Greg isn't going to change gay and just gay alone . . . I doubt very much if he'll ever change."[9]

During the day, Stewart escaped his from his romantic troubles by devoting himself to his job. Although he was making decent money, his salary was $8,000 a year, and despite having a nice office in the old Cotton Exchange building, Stewart gradually grew tired of being an office manager. He had started the job in August 1965, and by 1968, he had saved enough money to try law school again. Always restless, he was ready for a change. To that end he began renting a home at 2115 Prytania Street near the Garden District in Uptown New Orleans. Here he would live for ten years. The home, one of two adjoining residences, was built after the Civil War by Boss Tweed of Tammany Hall for his two daughters who had married two brothers in New Orleans.[10] Stewart recalls responding to the rental ad:

The ad under "Furnished Apartments" read "Cool spacious apartment on fringe of Garden District, $65 a month including utilities. No Pets." I called and made an appointment to see it. I took with me my best friend at the time, Trudy Starke, a straight woman probably in her early fifties, and my cute little mixed breed terrier, Jocko. The entry hall was big enough to accommodate a 12 foot long house trailer with room to spare. On the left side was a double parlor separated by large double doors which slid into the wall on each side. Similar doors at the end of the entry way entered into a humongous dining room with a large screened-in porch on the left which opened onto a fairly large yard. At the other end of the dining room was a serving door into a serving room with built-in glass doored cabinets filled with linens and dishes. It was large enough for a single bed. The spacious kitchen had plumbing that was probably installed in the 1920s or earlier. There was a walk-in pantry that had been turned into a comfortably sized small bedroom. To reach the bathroom one had to go through the second parlor, which wasn't otherwise part of the rental. Neither was the entry-way even though its use was allowed. The house was the family home of Mrs. Edna Conley, an only child, who guided us through all the above. She was an extremely nice and friendly lady of good up-bringing. She was rather taken by Jocko—no surprise. So when we sat down to discuss things, I asked her if I could keep him if I gave her an extra deposit, she responded that she didn't think that would be necessary. I then told her, "There was one more problem." "And what's that?" she said. "I have a cat." "Well bring it along. I suppose it's part of the family." As things turned out, Mrs. Conley, who lived in another house she owned right around the corner on Jackson Avenue, started walking Jocko on the days she came into her office.[11]

Settled into Prytania Street and enjoying a modicum of stability, Stewart successfully completed his first year of law school at Loyola University. He enrolled in nine hours of evening classes while working full-time. But then he ran out of money. Despite two attempts, he would never earn a law degree.

There would, however, be a lot of lovers. As if making up for lost time, Stewart explored his sexuality voraciously. Some lovers moved in with Stewart, but none stayed for very long. Most of these relationships were not that serious, but a few were. The most heartbreaking example was Gandhi, for whom Stewart developed very strong feelings. One day, Gandhi just disappeared, leaving only a crucifix on the bedpost. Others he kicked out, as was the case with a man named Vincent. Stewart frequented the bar scene in the French Quarter regularly and became a fixture at several bars. One night, on his way home from an evening in the Quarter, he picked up a young hitchhiker on Lee Circle. The two became pot buddies and would often buy pounds of marijuana for seventy or eighty dollars at a time and sell "lids" (ounces) to their friends. The business relationship didn't last long and ended when Stewart's partner disappeared after Stewart gave him the money to re-up on their supply.

Marijuana had become integral part of Stewart's life, and it would lead to several brushes with the law. In 1968, he received a letter from Greg Manella containing this curious passage:

> One night last week, Mother and I where [sic] and she said something to me that interested me. She said that when Bill was still alive the sheriff came to him and asked him if he knew where you were. She also said it was about the time when we had our mail coming here. Yours and mine together. What bugs me is—why would they trace your mail—and then send the sheriff out to see Bill. What did we do wrong Stew?? Was it because of the pot? Did they find it? And you just never did tell me. Bill also said—the sheriff said you had better never set foot in California again if you knew what was good for you.[12]

One trick that turned into a lifelong friend was Steven Duplantis. The two were barhopping in the French Quarter during the 1973 Carnival season when a young man, cold and shivering in the rain outside a bar, caught both their eyes. The kid was new in town, running low on cash, and feeling depressed. The kindness of strangers for which New Orleans is known was about to work its magic. Stewart's life would never be the same.

Chapter 4

ENTER ALFRED

Beloved Pope John Paul, God has given me the thrones of Russia, USA,
India, Islam, but the French are too sexy for me. Love, King Alfred, Caesar
—ALFRED DOOLITTLE

AS STEWART TURNED FORTY YEARS OLD, HE COULD LOOK BACK ON HIS
life with some measure of accomplishment. He had served in the army, graduated from college, been politically active, and finally accepted his sexuality. At the same time, there were regrets—namely a failed marriage and a
closeted youth.

He was in fairly good health despite being a drinker and a smoker. Stewart would smoke on and off his entire adult life until he finally gave up the
habit for good in 2002. In 1970, he weighed 160 pounds; stood five feet, eight
inches tall; and had brown hair (slightly receding) and blue eyes. Physically,
he had what has been described as "a presence," a characteristic no doubt
aided by a keen intellect and amiable personality. He had been employed for
five years at the same job and owned a 1960 Pontiac. A pet, a mixed-breed
terrier named Jocko, and the marijuana he grew on the second floor of his
home made life on Prytania Street more than comfortable.

The only thing he really had to complain about was the fact that he had
been somewhat unlucky in love. The few men who did capture his heart did
not return his romantic affections, at least not in a long-term, committed
way. After Gregory and Barton, there was Steven Duplantis. Stewart met
Steven at Café Lafitte in Exile during Carnival in 1971. Twenty years his
junior, Steven had come to New Orleans with a group of friends. He had
somehow separated from his group and found himself at Lafitte's about to
run out of money. He had already caught Stewart's eye, and Stewart decided
to make a move. He persuaded a friend to extinguish a cigarette in Steven's
drink so that when Steven became upset, Stewart could walk over and "save
the day." Stewart told Steven, "Why don't you come back to the house, and

we'll smoke a joint, and I'll fix you up all the cocktails you want."[1] They had sex and became somewhat romantically involved, but in a familiar pattern, the love affair turned into a friendship. Duplantis recalls, "We used to make a hobby of going out and seeing how many we could pick up and bring back to Prytania Street."[2]

But Stewart's record of unrequited love would change for the better in 1973. During Carnival season of that year, Stewart and Steven were barhopping in the French Quarter when they noticed a good-looking young man standing outside a gay bar on Iberville Street called Gertrude's. It was raining that day, and the young man was wet and shivering. In *Tinderbox*, a book about the tragic Up Stairs Lounge fire, Duplantis recalled remarking to Stewart how beautiful he was.[3] Stewart approached Alfred and invited him to join them in the bar. After a while, the trio then went to Café Lafitte in Exile, the city's oldest gay bar. The venerable old watering hole, located at the corner of Bourbon and Dumaine Streets in the French Quarter, was packed. At one point, Alfred whispered in Stewart's ear, "You can fuck me and I'll suck you." Stewart was smitten. "He looked just like Prince Valiant," Butler recalled. The two left Lafitte's and made their way back to Stewart's home on Prytania Street in Uptown New Orleans. It was a night that would change both their lives.

Years later, at the age of seventy, Stewart recounted the fateful meeting in a letter to Ann Landers:

> Late on a drizzly night ten days before Mardi Gras in 1973 I was sitting in a rather crowded gay bar in New Orleans when I noticed a Prince Valiant look-a-like. Before long he was coming on to me in an aggressive manner that I found irresistible. On the way to my car, I wondered what I was getting into this time when he said, "You'll probably throw me out tomorrow like everyone else does."
>
> But I didn't and Alfred stayed. After all it was party time and I was renting the downstairs of a large 1860s rundown mansion just a block from the main parade route. So there was a full cast of local and out of town guests.[4]

Thus began one of the strangest and most consequential relationships in queer New Orleans history—a relationship marked by insanity and a political legacy that lingers still today.

Alfred McLaughlin Doolittle was born into a prominent San Francisco family on June 16, 1936. His father was a gold miner, and his mother came from a family of meat-packers. Plagued by severe schizophrenia for all his adult life, he found respite, and his soul mate, in Stewart. The road that led Alfred to New Orleans was long and filled with twists and turns. By the time Stewart had moved to San Francisco to attend law school, Alfred had already left California on a bizarre sojourn that led him to New York and Paris before he found his way to New Orleans.

Alfred was named after his maternal grandmother's husband, a doctor who died of tuberculosis soon after the 1906 earthquake. Alfred and his sister Jean were born nineteen months apart and were very close, growing up in a comfortable home on Union Street near the Presidio in San Francisco. The family spent summers in Lake Tahoe. As a child, Alfred demonstrated a talent for creativity. At the age of five, he sketched the San Francisco skyline. The drawing still hangs in what was Stewart's bedroom.

As with millions of others at the time, this idyllic childhood was interrupted by war. After Pearl Harbor, there was a common fear was that the Japanese would bomb San Francisco next. In fact, two days after the December 7 attack, the *San Francisco Chronicle* ran the headline "JAPAN PLANES NEAR S.F.—4 RAID ALARMS." Although the raids turned out to be false, the Doolittles took the alarms seriously and left town during alerts.

Alfred's father, Jefferson Doolittle, joined the air force two days after Pearl Harbor at the age of thirty-eight. Dredging at La Grange halted, and its equipment was used in the war effort. Jefferson trained in Florida, then went to England as a supply specialist in the Eighth Army Air Force. He was later transferred to the Ninth for the Normandy invasion. His service in the European theater earned him the Bronze Star. Jefferson returned home on Christmas Eve 1944, a changed man. Alfred's sister Jean remembers she and Alfred were afraid of him. Father Doolittle was given to bursts of rage and would often fill the house with his loud, angry voice.

Years later, during the McCarthy hearings, the Doolittle family was accused of being communists. The FBI discovered that Jeff had written a paper as an undergraduate at Berkeley about China, which had turned Communist in 1949. Alfred's maternal grandmother Emma Moffett's feminism and work with the World Affairs Council undoubtedly also raised eyebrows with the bureau. During a visit to the Doolittle home, FBI agents noticed a copy of *Das Kapital* on the family bookshelf. When questioned about it, Jean (the mother) replied, "I believe we should know the enemy in order to fight it."

Decades later, in an email to Stewart in 2008, Alfred's sister Jean recalled the harrowing war years:

War transformed our lives. As children we were assigned dog tags with our name, address, telephone number. There were submarine nets across the Golden Gate. Searchlights combed the skies. Black cloth covered our windows; no light could escape. Everyone joined in the war effort; an uncle, a famous pilot, moved to L.A. to train pilots and test planes, younger relatives became belly gunners or parachutists on B-17s, mothers and grandmothers sewed and knitted; we saved aluminum from gum and candy to be recycled.

Before the war we had been rich. Now Mother had to live on a First Lieutenant's salary. The servants disappeared, both because of the war effort and because they could find more remunerative jobs. Our maternal grandmother became more important in our lives. She may have helped mother financially, but she certainly told her what to do, because she saw she was quite overwhelmed. Grandmother was a widow, a feminist and an intellectual. She had worked with diplomats and British Governor Generals in the Pacific to try and resolve some of the problems with Japan. Now she took control of our lives. She decided that we should go to camp in the summers to relieve Mother. I survived, as well as my older brother who ran away. As a good looking twelve year old, he was approached sexually by some of the teachers. My younger brother, seven, and I, nine, were sent to a camp for the deaf where we worked in the summer heat growing vegetables half naked. My grandmother and her friends believed that nudity in the California sun would help children and adults thrive. Three of us could hear, my brother and me and my roommate, who was the daughter of the person who ran the camp. Unfortunately, my brother did not have this saving grace. He went there summers for the balance of the war. I am afraid his schizoid genes began to kick in with this trauma.[5]

After the war, Alfred attended a private elementary school, the Town School, and was kept back a year. In 1951, upon completing middle school, Alfred was enrolled in the prestigious St. Ignatius High School, which had been founded a hundred years earlier in 1855. Highly intelligent, Alfred excelled in school, earning almost exclusively As and even taking Greek as a sophomore. In addition to excelling academically, he also proved to be proficient in athletics, particularly tennis and cross country. He was also a member of IRC (a social club), CSF (California Scholarship Federation, which encouraged community service in high schools throughout California), and Sodality (a spiritual student group). His high school resume also boasted roles in two school plays. One of Alfred's classmates at St. Ignatius was future California governor Jerry Brown, who served as president of the Debate Club. When he graduated, Alfred was named a Latin and Greek Scholar.

For college, Alfred was eager to explore the world beyond California. He applied to and was accepted at Yale and Princeton, but his father insisted he attend the University of California. At Berkeley, he studied the classics and eventually earned a BA degree. Academics came easily to Alfred, as did nighttime roistering and the shenanigans for which undergraduates are sometimes noted. He was suspended in his sophomore year for participating in a "panty raid," a disciplinary action that infuriated his father. He would resume his studies, but in the interim, he stayed with his grandmother for six months.

His academic career was not without hiccups. He joined a fraternity (Zeta Psi) in his freshman year and became president of his pledge class. In addition to drinking and carousing, hazing was a part of Greek life, and Alfred's pledge class was hazed severely, specifically with what is now called waterboarding. Alfred was the only pledge in his class not to flunk out in his first year as an undergraduate. It was during this time that Alfred's mental illness began to manifest.

In the 1950s, schizophrenia was still a misunderstood disease. Based on the psychoanalytic theories of Sigmund Freud, many psychiatrists at the time believed schizophrenia was caused by unresolved childhood conflicts in the subconscious mind. Although not accurate, this belief represented an advance from earlier beliefs that mental illness stemmed from demonic possession. Decades later, medical advances such as brain imaging, genetic studies, and antipsychotic medications demonstrated that schizophrenia has a strong biological basis. According to Dr. Neel Burton, "The term 'schizophrenia' was coined in 1910 by the Swiss psychiatrist Paul Eugen Bleuler, and is derived from the Greek words 'schizo' (split) and 'phren' (mind). Bleuler had intended the term to refer to the dissociation or 'loosening' of thoughts and feelings that he had found to be a prominent feature of the illness."[6]

While at Berkeley, Alfred met an Episcopal priest named Father Morse. There is evidence the two had at least one sexual encounter. According to Stewart, Jean once told him that Father Morse confessed to her and Alfred's mother on her deathbed that he had sexual relations with Alfred at Berkeley. But the relationship evolved into a lifelong friendship. Father Robert Morse eventually married and even met Stewart once in the 1980s when they brunched with Alfred and Stewart on a trip to California. Soon after Alfred's death in 2008, Stewart wrote to Morse informing him of Alfred's passing. Morse replied with a letter of condolence, describing Alfred as a "good and loyal friend."[7]

Alfred exhibited a religious streak early on and, as he became older, felt drawn to the priesthood. As an undergraduate, he developed friendships with a few other gay priests and, after graduating, wanted to become a priest. His application to seminary was rejected twice by the Episcopal bishop of California, the controversial James A. Pike. Alfred was greatly discouraged by the rejection but maintained a religious devotion for the rest of his life. In lieu of seminary, Alfred went to graduate school and earned an MA in creative writing from San Francisco State University.

Alfred graduated from Berkeley at the age of twenty-two and worked a couple of jobs in San Francisco before graduate school, but they were short lived. In 1963, Alfred indulged his love of traveling by spending nearly a year in Europe. He spent nine months in Paris and also visited England, Spain, Monaco, Germany, Denmark, San Marino, Sweden, Netherlands, Switzerland, and Italy. As a classics scholar and a man of means, it was perhaps inevitable that Alfred would spend time in Europe. In London, he was thrilled to meet the archbishop of Canterbury. And in Paris, his love of writing and general creativity flourished. There he lived briefly in the fabled Beat Hotel, where he met Allen Ginsberg, Peter Orlovsky, Brion Gysin, Ian Sommerville, Gregory Corso, Harold Norse, and William S. Burroughs. He had an affair with Norse, who gifted Alfred a few of his famous acid drawings.

In 1966, Alfred's great-aunt Henrietta died and left him a sizable inheritance. Two years later, his maternal grandmother died and bequeathed him a portion of the ranching fortune her branch of the family had acquired. Alfred decided to use the money to travel. After living briefly in Hollywood, he moved to a large apartment on Fifth Avenue in New York City. In New York he met and socialized with composers Sam Barber and Gian Carlo Menotti, and theater producer Roger Englander. He also befriended designer Gilbert Ireland and photographer Reed Massengill. And he resumed his acquaintanceship with Gregory Corso and Allen Ginsberg, whom he had met in Paris three years earlier.

Years later, in 1994, Alfred wrote a letter to Allen Ginsberg:

Beloved Allen,

I met you in Paris a long time ago. I was Harold Norse's lover. I am the connection to heaven on earth, I live in the sacred place by the Most High, God Almighty. I am new Buddha also I feel that Zen Buddhism is the worship of the Japanese.

Ginsberg did not reply.

After his European sojourn, Alfred returned home broke. While he was in New York and Paris, his sister Jean was married with four kids and taking care of sick in-laws. She complained that Alfred was wasting time and money and suggested he find a job. In response, Alfred described her as "plebian" and said he didn't need to work because creative people need to be supported. He took up residence in the basement of the family home and committed himself to writing.

His schizophrenia was worsening, but he stubbornly refused psychiatric help. There were a few psychotic episodes in which his mother had to call the police. One such episode occurred late in 1972 when his father died. Alfred was living at home at this time and was in his room drinking beer when he learned of his father's death. He became hysterical and began throwing beer bottles against the wall. Because he was so agitated, his family called the police. When they arrived, Alfred, cool as a cucumber, received them standing on the landing of the stairwell and greeted them politely by saying, "Good evening, officers. What can I do for you?"

After this incident, Alfred's family had him committed. He agreed to participate in a psychiatric evaluation program at Stanford University, but once there he changed his mind. Alfred left—some might say escaped—the program and came to New Orleans. Upon arriving, he checked into the Hotel Monteleone in the French Quarter and began exploring the city and its gay scene. There were several gay bars within a block of the Monteleone, including Wanda's, the Safari Lounge, Gene's Hideaway, the Midship, the Up Stairs Lounge, and Gertrude's.

Stewart recalls the early days of their relationship:

It didn't take long to discover Alfred was from a rather financially well-off San Francisco socialite family and would not be a financial burden. Now it didn't take long to realize he was also schizophrenic. First, he kicked in the TV, cutting his leg. Soon thereafter he broke the mirror over the water-bed, causing a minor flood. I never knew what to expect when I came home from work. Often the stereo was blaring forth Greek music, Aretha Franklin, Bob Dylan, Gregorian Chants, Beethoven, or whatever. We took my shaggy dog Jocko in my old convertible for evening runs in the park and dined at fine restaurants. At the same time, I had to avoid going by hospitals, police stations, or cemeteries which caused him to become hysterical. Sirens were impossible to avoid.

Some three years later, after being awakened in the middle of the night by his hitting me in the face with his fists, I reluctantly determined

I had to have him committed. I was frightened he'd become a vegetable or turn upon me, but he took it in stride and began taking medicine, which was only marginally effective at best in those days.

Many years later, though six years my junior, he legally adopted me for tax purposes and we thus acquired some of the lesser benefits of marriage, such as hospital visitation. Ironically, though a marriage can be dissolved, our commitment in the form of an act of adoption, is irrevocable.

Today's anti-psychotic drugs, though much improved, are still not perfect. Ironically, we've found out that music causes Alfred to hear voices, but we do watch TV. I've just turned 70, we're both in good physical health, we have the loving support of both blood and extended families, we love each other more than ever and look forward to many years of peace and fulfillment.[8]

On Prytania Street, Alfred settled into a somewhat regular routine. While Stewart was at work during the day, Alfred would burn incense and listen to music. His musical fare was wide ranging and included Aretha Franklin, Gregorian chants, Greek music, the Rolling Stones, and Bob Dylan. In the afternoons, he enjoyed drinking coffee from a fancy demitasse cup. In the evening, he liked to read or watch television, as long as the shows contained no guns, violence, sex, or horror. He would also watch the news sometimes, but he didn't like news stories about violent crime. His favorite shows were situation comedies like *Sanford and Son* and *All in the Family*. Alfred was cold natured, but he liked to air out the house when the weather was nice. Alfred had always loved dogs. In San Francisco he had a springer named Bo Bo and a beagle named Sissy; on Prytania, he and Stewart had Jocko and Putz. He insisted on feeding Jocko and Putz from expensive china he inherited from his grandmother. His love of animals was not universal; he was terribly frightened of spiders, snakes, bats, and vultures. He did, however, love it when Stewart would pretend to be a monkey, scratching and picking and eating fleas. According to Stewart, Alfred was very affectionate, an excellent speller, a good backseat driver, and he loved Greek sculpture, especially the discus thrower. Occasionally, Alfred attended mass at St. Louis Cathedral and then lingered in Jackson Square to watch the brass bands.

Stewart's friends found Alfred fascinating. For his part, Alfred easily slipped into Stewart's social orbit. Former romantic interests did not seem to bother Alfred, and jealousy, at least in the early years of their time together, was apparently not an issue in their nonmonogamous relationship. Gregory would occasionally drift into and out of the scene. Whenever Gregory slipped into a seizure, which was not uncommon, Alfred would nonchalantly say he was "seeing the stars." In a letter from Gregory to Stewart in 1977, Gregory, who was living in Las Cruces, New Mexico, writes: "The letter from Alfred I must say was something different. It did get me down to the library."

A frequent visitor at the home on Prytania was a friend of Alfred's from San Francisco, Freddie Lavre, also known as "the Mad Russian Countess." A career chef and sometimes waiter, Lavre made his mark in the hospitality industry at legendary restaurants such as the Paper Doll and Gordon's, institutions in the Bay Area. Lavre was an extended part of Stewart and Alfred's family and would visit New Orleans a couple of times each year. Once, while Stewart was at work, Alfred and Lavre transformed the front veranda of the house into a scene from *A Streetcar Named Desire*. Stewart recalled the scene in a letter he wrote to Lavre shortly before his death in 1998: "There you were, with your feather boa, playing the part of Blanche herself smashed, so to speak, to the tits. What an opening!"[9]

Letters to Stewart from Alfred's mother and sister during the early years of their relationship demonstrate they were not only supportive but also grateful and appreciative to Stewart for the stability he offered Alfred. Stewart communicated with them regularly and kept them abreast of how Alfred was doing. In so doing he earned their confidence. For example, in one letter from May 1974, a little over a year after Stewart and Alfred met, Alfred's mother asked Stewart if Alfred had opened any of the letters she had sent him. In two other letters written to Stewart the following year, she provides Alfred's social security number and financial trust information, comments on Alfred not caring about his eyes, wonders if he would see her if she visited New Orleans, references his "deep resentment" about being put in a mental institution, comments on his desire for a swimming pool, muses "I think Alfred has always wanted more 'elegance' than we ever had," and notes "He always wanted things done in the grand manner."[10]

In 1974, Alfred's sister Jean wrote to Stewart informing him of recommendations for psychiatrists in New Orleans she had secured from the Penn State Hospital. A few months later, she wrote again asking Stewart if he thought Alfred could be bribed into seeking psychiatric treatment at Stanford University. But Alfred was resistant to psychiatric help and hospitals in general.

For recreation, Alfred and Stewart liked to go barhopping in the French Quarter. Among their favorite haunts were Café Lafitte in Exile, the Roundup, Wanda's, and the Up Stairs Lounge. Sometimes while drinking, they would fight. One fight in particular in 1975 led to a lifelong friendship. The two were at Lafitte's when they fell to arguing. Stewart became so angry, he abruptly left to go home, leaving Alfred at the bar. Steve Willey, who worked at Lafitte's at the time, drove Alfred home to Prytania Street, and upon arriving, Alfred invited Willey inside. Willey recalls the house as being "very large" with a huge center hall.[11] Stewart had known Willey superficially from being a patron at the bar, but now the two would become lifelong friends. Willey would be a regular at the annual holiday gatherings Stewart and Alfred would host and later served on the LAGPAC (Louisiana Lesbian and Gay Political Action Caucus) board of directors. Willey would visit Stewart and Alfred often and have to call Stewart ahead of time to ask what color clothes to avoid; different colors on different days would trigger Alfred's neurosis. Willey recalls another memorable incident from a few years later, after Stewart and Alfred had moved to Esplanade Avenue. Stewart always kept a wad a cash stuffed in his file cabinet for emergencies and to help friends in need. He bailed more than one person out of jail over the years and used to give twenty dollars to a downtrodden neighbor on a regular basis. After an especially heated argument over something none of the parties involved could remember, Alfred raided the stash of cash and went to Wanda's, a hustler bar, and started handing out fifty-dollar bills to all the boys. He then brought several of them back home. Stewart was not amused.

Sometimes, when Alfred was out barhopping alone, he would call Stewart and request money. By the time they bought the Faerie Playhouse, they had opened a joint checking account, and Alfred was happy to let Stewart handle the cash they kept on hand at the house with the understanding he would give him whatever cash he needed from time to time, which didn't amount to much usually. One memorable exception occurred when Alfred was drinking at the Wild Side, a notorious dive bar in the French Quarter owned by the flamboyant Lee Featherston, better known as Miss Fly (who also owned the Corner Pocket a block away) and managed by Fly's good friend Ms. Do, a former prizefighter. Stewart remembers:

> Out of the blue, he decided he wanted $400 to buy a gown. I raised cane, but really had no choice. So off he went to Maison Blanche. Not much later he's calling me for another $100 for a $500 gown. He was at The Wild Side, a bar that was better known as Ms. Do's, the manager. When I told him "NO!" he responded by telling me he'd be spending the money drinking the night away with Ms. Do and Ms. Fly, the owner of a bar on the next corner. Both were known to be heavy boozers. So I immediately dropped everything, grabbed $100 and got down to Ms. Do's. I went with him to Maison Blanche to make

sure he bought the gown, which he wore out of the store to go back to Ms. Do's to show off his new gown to Ms. Do and Ms. Fly. They were both enthusiastic in their compliments telling him how great he looked. One of them told him there was a drag queen contest the next weekend in the courtyard of the Mississippi River Bottom, another bar in the French Quarter, and Alfred ought to enter it. When Alfred told them it would be too cold for him, one of them said, "Why you just get your husband to take you to buy a fur coat." That's when I said, "It's time for us to go home," which we did. It occurred to me I might be able to snatch back the gown and return it for a refund but by the time I got to it, he'd cut the neck out.[12]

Occasionally on the weekends, Stewart and Alfred were joined by Steven Duplantis, who would drive in from his base in San Antonio when he could steal away. The weekend of June 22, 1973, was one such occasion. As Sunday afternoon languished into Sunday evening, Steven prepared for the eight-hour drive back to San Antonio. Stewart suggested they have one more drink before Steven left town, so the three of them went to the weekly Beer Bust at one of their regular stops—the Up Stairs Lounge.

The Up Stairs Lounge was a gay bar on the edge of the French Quarter that occupied the second floor of a building at the corner of Chartres and Iberville Streets. Owner Phil Esteve opened the bar in 1970 and strove to make the place a relaxed, family environment. Despite the general seediness of Iberville Street, the atmosphere at the Up Stairs was markedly different from the other gay bars in the immediate area; these other bars, notably Gertrude's, the Midship, Gene's Hideaway, and Wanda's, catered to hustlers, rough trade, and their clients. Within a block from the Up Stairs were two adult-themed bookstores, and nearby was Exchange Place Alley, a notorious cruising strip. Not far away, along Decatur Street were several "Greek sailor" bars.

But the Up Stairs Lounge was different. Not only did it forbid hustlers to ply their trade, it also allowed Black people and women in at a time when most gay bars were firmly segregated, both racially and by gender. Manager and bartender Buddy Rasmussen went out of his way to make all the regulars feel welcome. The regular crowd consisted mostly of working-class gay men, many of whom were members of the newly founded Metropolitan Community Church of New Orleans. According to Up Stairs Lounge fire researcher Clayton Delery, "Butler believes that the difference in tone between the Up Stairs and most other bars—especially the other bars on Iberville—had a lot to do with the presence of the Metropolitan Community Church."[13] For a while, the MCC actually held Sunday services in the bar. Stewart often took his dog, Jocko, to the bar, who, much to the delight of the other patrons, liked to drink vodka and milk out of a bowl.

When Stewart, Alfred, and Steven arrived at the bar that night, the Beer Bust was well underway. Everyone was in good spirits with the exception of a troubled young man named Rodger Nunez. Nunez, a street hustler who lived in a flophouse next door to the bar, was highly intoxicated and generally annoying. Most tried to ignore him, but one regular, Mike Scarborough, had had enough and punched Nunez. He had already complained to Rasmussen that Nunez had been harassing him in the bathroom, but Nunez kept badgering him. As he was being escorted out of the bar, Nunez threatened to "burn you all out."

Steven Duplantis heard the threat and had a bad feeling about it. He immediately warned Stewart and Alfred that they needed to leave. But Stewart, who was chatting with his barber, another regular named Horace Broussard, didn't think much of it and said he wasn't ready to leave. Alfred, however, heeded Steven's warning and told Stewart he wanted to leave. But Stewart dismissed the idea, figuring Alfred was just being paranoid. Steven tried to persuade Stewart again, but Stewart wasn't budging. Frustrated, Steven told them goodbye and began the long trek back to Texas. Several minutes later, Alfred insisted they leave the bar, and Stewart reluctantly agreed. He was not happy about it, and the two got into an argument on the stairwell leading to Iberville Street. They then walked a block down to Wanda's bar, which was on the corner of Royal and Iberville Streets. Also on that intersection, across the street from Wanda's, was a Walgreens pharmacy. As Stewart and Alfred walked past the pharmacy, they had no idea Nunez was inside buying a can of lighter fluid. It was just after 7:30 p.m.

Minutes later, back at the Up Stairs, the buzzer in the bar rang, which usually meant a cab had arrived. Luther Boggs, a regular at the lounge, opened the door to the stairwell to be greeted by roaring flames. As the fire spread, panic ensued. Denny LeBouef was in the bar downstairs with her boyfriend when she heard what sounded like a stampede. She looked up at the ceiling and said, "That's an odd dance step. It sounds like everyone's just running across the room."[14] Bartender Buddy Rasmussen led about twenty people through a rear fire exit, which was not clearly marked. Many dashed for the windows, but the windows had burglar bars. A few were skinny enough to squeeze through the bars, but the others were doomed. Katherine Kirsch was on her way to buy cigarettes around 7:45 p.m. when she smelled smoke at the corner of Iberville and Chartres. She opened the stairwell, saw the flames, and immediately ran to the Midship bar next door to call the police. Fire trucks arrived about two minutes later. They were met by a grizzly, horrific scene.

The lifeless body of Bill Larson, pastor of the local Metropolitan Community Church, was wedged in the window, his face and right arm protruding stiffly over the sidewalk. Buddy Rasmussen saw his boyfriend, Adam Fontenot, knocked off his feet with a blast from a fire hose while he flayed around on fire. George Mitchell escaped the fire but ran back in to rescue his boyfriend, Louis Broussard; their bodies were found intertwined, thereby occupying in death a position they saw often occupied in life. Many of the dead were burned beyond recognition but were ultimately identified through the dental records of local dentist Perry Waters, who also perished in the fire.

At Wanda's, Stewart and Alfred heard the sirens and immediately walked outside to see what all the commotion was about. Stewart ran back up Iberville to the Up Stairs, but Alfred, who had always abhorred violence, remained at Wanda's. The scene Stewart encountered was horrific. Word of the fire had spread quickly, and a throng of people gathered in the streets as mayhem ensued. Steven Duplantis learned of the fire over the radio on his drive back to San Antonio. Upon hearing the news, he pulled over near Houston and cried uncontrollably. He tried to call Stewart's home from a pay phone, but Stewart and Alfred had not made it home yet. In *Tinderbox*, Duplantis recalled, "That was the hardest drive I've ever had to go through, from Houston to San Antonio."[15]

The next morning, Stewart went to work determined to hide the heavy emotional burden he was carrying. He was not out at work (although the office secretary knew his secret) and, like many other survivors of the fire, feared he would lose his job if his employer knew he was gay. "It was a hard, hard thing to do and not show any reaction," he later recalled.[16] The fire was all his coworkers could talk about, sometimes crassly.

Later that evening, Steven Duplantis finally reached Stewart by phone. His relief quickly turned to anxiety when Stewart implored him to return to New Orleans and tell the police what he heard in the bar. Steven didn't want to report what he knew because he was already under investigation for being gay back at the base in San Antonio. He apologized to Stewart and explained his dilemma. Duplantis remembers, "Stewart begged me to come back over and talk to the police. I said, 'Stewart, if I do that, my military is finished.'"[17] Nunez was never arrested; the case was never officially solved.

A few days later, Stewart received a letter from his parents saying they were relieved he was safe. Stewart had called them to let them know of the news on Sunday night when he returned home.

Thirty-one men and one woman died as a result of the arson. Nunez committed suicide the following year. Some believe Nunez killed himself because he was so filled with remorse. Stewart theorizes Nunez did not intend to kill anyone but was rather acting out—"I don't think he had any idea or notion whatsoever that what he was doing would have that kind of outcome. What a terrible cross he must have borne!"[18] Initial media reports and the police response to the fire were less than sympathetic. According to Stewart, "The fire chief didn't have any respect for gay people." Some family members of the deceased refused to claim the ashes of their "loved" ones. Radio commentators joked the remains should be buried in fruit jars. The *States-Item* described the aftermath of the fire in graphic language: "Workers stood knee deep in bodies . . . the heat had been so intense, many were cooked together." On the issue of identifying the victims, Major Henry Morris, a detective with the New Orleans Police Department, said, "We don't even know these papers belonged to the people we found them on. Some thieves hung out there, and you know this was a queer bar."[19]

While the media reaction was cruel and the police were nonchalant, the religious establishment's reaction was downright hateful. Church after church refused the use of their facilities for a memorial service. Father Bill Richardson (himself a closeted gay man) of St. George's Episcopal Church, however, believed the dead should have a service and graciously allowed, over the protest of many parishioners, the use of St. George's sanctuary for a prayer service on Monday night, which was attended by roughly 80 people. He was subsequently chastised by his bishop and received no small amount of hate mail. Days later, a Unitarian church also held a small memorial service. A larger service was held on July 1 at St. Mark's United Methodist Church, which Stewart and Alfred attended, on the edge of the French Quarter. Reverend Troy Perry, founder of the Metropolitan Community Church, officiated the service at St. Mark's along with Methodist bishop Finis Crutchfield, who would die fourteen years later from AIDS. After the service, Reverend Perry pointed out a side entrance for those who wished to avoid the television cameras that waited outside the main entrance. Of the estimated 250 people in attendance, no one took his offer.

The Up Stairs arson attracted gay activists from all over the country to New Orleans. Reverend Troy Perry and others criticized the gay community of New Orleans for its apathetic attitude and general lethargy regarding the gay liberation movement so much in vogue in other American cities at the time. Local bar owners concerned about how all the attention might affect their businesses and prominent gay men who had grown comfortable with their place in the order of things responded by calling Perry and the other activists "carpetbaggers" and "outside agitators."

Some have likened the arson to a "southern Stonewall," claiming it was the touchstone of the gay rights movement in New Orleans, but the comparison is not entirely accurate. On the thirtieth anniversary of the fire, a memorial plaque was placed in the sidewalk in front of the entrance to the Up Stairs Lounge, which reads in part: "At this site on June 24, 1973 in the Upstairs Lounge, these thirty-two people lost their lives in the worst fire in New Orleans. The impact went far beyond the loss of individual lives, giving birth to the Lesbian, Gay, Bisexual, and Transgender Rights Movement in New Orleans." Although the fire did raise awareness and spur a few efforts at organizing, these efforts were short lived. Whereas the Stonewall uprising resulted in long-term, tangible results—notably liberation marches and later Pride parades—the fire in New Orleans forced the gay community to retreat deeper into the closet.

Years later, in 1991, after Stewart had completely come out and become a gay activist, the Louisiana State Museum sponsored an exhibit at the Presbytère on Jackson Square called "Historic Fires of New Orleans." Stewart and his friend and fellow activist Rich Magill attended the opening of the exhibit and were incensed that there was no mention of the Up Stairs arson. It was, after all, the deadliest fire in New Orleans history—a distinction it retains today. In an interview with researcher and author Robert Fieseler, Stewart remembers telling Rich, "We've got to do something about this shit. So we started bitching and complaining."[20] Museum officials replied they had no artifacts to display but did put out a placard for the remaining duration of the exhibit.

The museum incident illustrates that by the early 1990s, attitudes regarding homosexuality in New Orleans were far from ideal, which is to say indifferent if no longer hostile. The city would come a long way in the following decades in terms of embracing tolerance and diversity. This shift in attitudes was rooted in events that occurred during the 1970s.

The Up Stairs Lounge fire occurred early—a few months after they met—in Stewart and Alfred's relationship. In retrospect, it is clear that in a very real sense, Alfred probably saved his and Stewart's lives by insisting they leave the bar just minutes before it was set ablaze. What is not so clear is how the intense trauma of that experience affected their feelings for each other in deeper, more nuanced, perhaps even unconscious ways. Stewart and Alfred had an immediate connection from the first time they met. That connection, or "chemistry" as it is sometimes called, can only have been strengthened by such a distressing ordeal.

Within a year or so, Stewart and Alfred's relationship had reached a level of trust most relationships take years to achieve. And although their love for each other was strong, it was far from perfect. Alfred could be violent during his occasional psychotic breaks, and sometimes he would disappear for days on end. One such incident occurred in November 1974, when Alfred seemed to vanish off the face of the earth. To no avail, Stewart called hospitals and jails. After a few days, Stewart received a letter from Alfred's mother informing him that Alfred was in Paris. He had called his mother to request money. Alfred had gone to Paris on a whim because he wanted a French-tailored suit. It never occurred to him to tell anyone he was going. Although he was not fluent in French, he could speak enough to "get by."

The following year, Alfred returned to Europe with Stewart. In September 1975, they visited both Amsterdam and Paris. Paris brought back a flood of memories for Alfred, including the Crazy Horse Saloon. The legendary cabaret had opened in 1950, and Alfred had been captivated by the show he saw there years earlier. Shows at the Crazy Horse featured nude female cabaret dancers as well as mimes, magicians, and other live performers. Initially, Stewart told Alfred they couldn't afford to go because of the price, but their hotel clerk clued them in on some insider, local tips on how to experience the Crazy Horse without spending a fortune. Thirty-three years later, Stewart still remembered the show, "Bourbon Street was nothing compared to this! That was one of the highlights of the trip for me."[21]

Mexico was another favorite vacation spot. Stewart and Alfred visited Acapulco twice, once in 1973 and again in 1975. And on holidays, they would sometimes travel north to visit their families. Alfred's sister Jean was living in Pennsylvania, and Stewart's parents were in Vermont. The couple could afford to travel because not only was Stewart working full-time, Alfred was receiving $700 a month from the Emma Moffett McLaughlin Trust, one of four trusts that ultimately benefitted Alfred. Alfred's family also had stock in Eastman Kodak. This financial security enabled Alfred to purchase the home on Prytania Street in 1976. His primary motivation to buy the property was his desire for a swimming pool. He had proposed the idea of a pool to Stewart previously and was disappointed when Stewart informed him that a pool was impossible because he didn't own the home. The couple also had other investments. For a brief while, they owned an antique store on Magazine Street, and in 1979, Alfred formed the Bar Angel Recording Company. These businesses were short lived.

When not traveling, Stewart and Alfred enjoyed the gay nightlife of the French Quarter and were regulars at several bars. Police raids of gay bars were still common at this time, and Stewart kept a list of phone numbers in his shoe in case he was ever arrested. The list almost came in handy during Halloween 1976 when the Loft, a bar on North Rampart Street that featured drag shows as well as a leather bar, was raided. Alfred was supposed to meet

Stewart at the bar, but he never showed up. It was not uncommon for Alfred to agree to go somewhere and then change his mind at the last minute.

By the 1970s, Stewart had come out to himself—the first step in what is sometimes a long, gradual process. The social mores of the times would not permit him to be out at work, but socially, he was as out as he could be. He had already come out to his parents in a letter, but unlike Alfred's family, who were fairly liberal and had no problem with his sexuality, Stewart's parents, who had always been conservative (his mother once wrote to him expressing her opinion that welfare recipients were "lazy" and that she thought George McGovern was a phony and that she planned on voting for Nixon), had a problem with Stewart's gayness. Exacerbating the issue was a "born again" experience his mother had undergone in 1972. She pleaded with him to devote his life to Christ and become straight, but when it was clear Stewart would not change, each of his parents wrote him a letter in response. His mother wrote:

> In spite of my love and concern and in spite of the fact that I do enjoy seeing and being with you, Perry, I just cannot cope with your friends and see no reason to meet Alfred. I am sure this will hurt you, but this life was your choice and I just cannot join in in a social way. It has always bothered dad for me to try to accept them. I did try when I was there before, but it tore me apart—hence the liquor and phenobarb. You must not misunderstand me as to my feeling for them. They are so bound that they do not even know it. We (your friends and I) have absolutely nothing in common. Nothing would please me more than to be able to reach out my hand and open their eyes to their bondage, and to free them of this tortuous life. No use to go on and on. I can only hope and trust that this "confession" will in no way change our relationship in any way.[22]

In the same envelope was a letter from his father, who wrote:

> Perry, I have read June's letter regarding the life you lead and the company you keep. I have nothing in common with or for the people you associate with and call friends. I am bored and depressed when in their company. Perry, we love you and accept you as our son and want you to understand it is not to hurt your feelings or displease you, but this is the way it has to be. We hope to see you as much as possible, while in the South, but in the proper environment.[23]

"No reason to meet Alfred," "this life was your choice," "bondage," "tortuous life," "bored and depressed," "proper environment"—these words had a profound impact on Stewart. They were words he would remember years later when he became involved in PFLAG (Parents and Friends of Lesbians and Gays). Such words also reflected the attitudes of many at the time and would strengthen his resolve to change those attitudes. His parents did eventually, as they say, "come around," which is to say they were not as hostile as the content of the aforementioned letters suggests. By the mid-1970s, Stewart's parents had both retired and moved to Ocean Springs, Mississippi, where they attended St. John's Episcopal Church. A friend of the Butlers, and a fellow congregant at St. John's, describes them as "quiet, dedicated Episcopalians."[24]

The year 1978 would be pivotal in Stewart and Alfred's life. In that year, Alfred decided he wanted to move back to California. Stewart, who had been wanting to quit his job for years, recalled:

> We were still living on Prytania, and the house was in Alfred's name. He put it on the market without telling me, because he wanted to move to West Hollywood and get a Corvette and relive his youth. We went out and bought a place there. He messed up on the parking portion of his driving test, and he gave up. He could have taken the test over, but he gave up. We came back after eight months and returned to New Orleans in '79. That was one division in my life. Before we moved to California, I said that if I was going with him, I wasn't going to work anymore. He agreed. When we got back, I got active in the community.[25]

Whatever his motivation for wanting to return to California, Alfred agreed to Stewart's demands about retiring, and the couple hired a moving van, although Alfred and Stewart made the cross-country trek in Stewart's 1969 Volkswagen minibus. In late July, they headed West. They bought a house 1307 North Orange Drive in Los Angeles near Hollywood Boulevard and Santa Monica Boulevard. There the two enjoyed frequenting the gay "chicken" bars and a restaurant called By the Numbers, where the young male waiters wore football jerseys as serving uniforms. Alfred bought a Jaguar convertible but could not obtain a driver's license because of his inability to parallel park. After eight months in California, Alfred was bored, and he and Stewart decided to return to New Orleans. Alfred wanted Stewart to become a full-time activist; for his part, Alfred agreed to begin seeing a psychiatrist on a regular basis. Back home in New Orleans, the two purchased a house at 1308 Esplanade Avenue. The house would eventually become known as the Faerie Playhouse and inspired Alfred to write the following song:

The Green Tree

There is a very green tree in the Garden of Paradise with
emeralds for leaves, deep green jewels, and there is a rainbow above the tree and a crown of twelve stars.

There are rubies, deep red rubies for flowers on the tree, and
flashing diamonds and brilliant topazes and pearls for flowers, and the sweet incensing of frankincense and myrrh on
the tree, there are cold pears and blackberries, and red cur-
rants, and cool peaches, and green grapes.

And there are also shiny silver leaves, pink rainbowed golden
leaves, and green and black tasty olives.

The top of the tree is pure gold, the middle is silver, and the
trunk of the tree is brass.

Around the tree is the lamb, the lion, and the bee on the lion's
tit. The lamb is at the feet of the lion and there is peace
beneath the mountain and the hill and the green emerald
tree. Also, the eagle flies around the very green emerald tree
above the calf.

And there is a drum, a harp and a diamond and brass trumpet
under the very green emerald tree.

The green tree lives in the Garden of the Paradise of God.

Stewart and Alfred found a paradise of sorts in each other—a paradise
that would be lived out for the rest of their lives in the Faerie Playhouse.
The Creole cottage had been built by a free woman of color in 1842 and for
a time was one of a series of four identical cottages. For a brief period, the
cottage was divided into two residences, but by 1979, it was a single-family
unit. In that year, Stewart and Alfred bought the home with a loan from
Alfred's mother.

When Alfred and Stewart bought the home, the backyard was a mess. They
cleaned it up and planted a few citrus trees, along with a fig tree, a maple
tree, and a pear tree. Eventually, the backyard would also house the memorial garden. They also repaired and renovated the dependency at the back
of the lot. Well, Stewart at least supervised the renovation, which included
an overhaul of the electrical system, the installation of barge boards and a
glass chandelier, as well as general cleaning and painting. Stewart did not
bother with obtaining permits to complete the repairs. Once completed, the
Cottage, as it came to be known, became home to many colorful characters
over the following years.

Life at the Faerie Playhouse was made possible by Alfred's financial security. Alfred was the beneficiary of four trusts as well as his parents' inheritance.[26] In addition, La Grange, the family dredging company, was paying monthly dividends. In 1988, the issue of money became a point of contention, not between Alfred and Stewart, but between Alfred's mother and Stewart. Originally, the Faerie Playhouse was in Alfred's name; in 1988, Alfred wanted to add Stewart as a legal owner, but Alfred's mother disapproved. She had also stipulated that Alfred was to be the only recipient of the trust she had established for him. To circumvent these obstacles, which could have been avoided if same-sex marriage had been legal, Alfred legally adopted Stewart. Alfred's mother was upset about the adoption, and for the first time in Stewart and Alfred's then fifteen-year relationship, Stewart felt he had to defend his relationship with Alfred in a letter to Alfred's mother.

Financially secure, Stewart and Alfred were free to pursue their interests. For Stewart, that was activism. For Alfred, it was writing. In addition to love letters, poetry, and plays, Alfred wrote dozens of letters to world leaders, both real and imagined. He would occasionally write equally bizarre letters to his friends. Consider this letter, probably written to Alfred's friend Freddy Lavre, "the Mad Russian Countess," but also possibly to Empress Frederika (1840–1901), the daughter of Queen Victoria who married Prince Frederick of Germany:

Beloved Empress Frederika,

I will extol you, O Empress, and will bless your name forever and ever.

Everyday I will bless you, and I will praise your name Empress Frederika forever and ever.

Great is the Empress, and greatly to be praised; and her greatness is unsearchable.

One generation shall praise your works to another.

I will speak of my glorious knowing your majesty.

They shall speak of the glory of your kingdom, and of your power, to make known to the sons of men the glorious majesty of your kingdom.

Love,
Tzar Alfred[27]

Jack Sullivan observes, "If you were lucky enough to ever get a letter from Alfred however, it was a thing worthy of framing, including the envelope."[28]

Sometimes, usually in the midst of a psychotic episode, he would pen random scribblings:

I was asleep and a golden spoon came to my lips. It was full of pink strawberry ice cream and I tasted of it. It tasted of deep substantial love. It was thick like thick love. Substance of love, substance of love. Love, love, love, love, love, love, love, the substance of love was spreading graceful, graceful love, graceful love, graceful love. I was high for three days without any bad effects, expanding to my friends brotherly love, brotherly love. I tasted of love.

If the grip of mania was especially tight, his handwriting would become completely illegible. Alfred filled dozens of yellow legal pads with visions and songs, all of which Stewart saved. While Alfred was indulging his love of language by transcribing his visions, Stewart was reclaiming his love of politics and activism. As the two settled into life at the Faerie Playhouse, Stewart reinvented himself at the age of fifty and became involved in LGBT+ activism, then just emerging in Louisiana.

Chapter 5

SETTING THE STAGE

Apparently the French Quarter of New Orleans has an atmosphere which
appeals to these people, who are an undesirable element in our community.
—POLICE SUPERINTENDENT PROVOSTY A. DAYRIES

AS STEWART AND ALFRED SETTLED INTO A LIFE TOGETHER IN THE MID-
1970s, social and political changes were stirring in New Orleans. Stewart's
passion for politics, so evident twenty years earlier in Alaska, had seemed
to fade, giving way instead to sexual exploration and his newfound love. But
Stewart was a political animal, and his political instincts could never truly
be suppressed. Throughout the 1970s, he assisted in voter registration drives
and attended a political meeting here and there, but for the most part, his
political drive had retreated into a gestation period in order to be born again
in 1980. The womb was 1970s queer New Orleans.

The New Orleans to which Stewart returned in 1964 was still very closeted.
Police raids of gay and lesbian bars were common, and discrimination against
queer folk was widespread in housing and employment. Age-old sodomy
and crimes against nature laws from the colonial period and nineteenth
century effectively made being gay illegal. Stewart would play a pivotal role
in kicking the closet door open in New Orleans. To understand just how
tightly shut that closet door was, this chapter offers a brief historical sketch
of queer New Orleans.

Long before the French aristocracy renamed Bulbancha New Orleans
and long before La Salle claimed Louisiana for France, there was something
queer about the Native trading post on the sharp bend in the Mississippi
River where the French Market now stands. Sixteenth-century European
explores were shocked to discover gender-bending Natives as they sailed
up the Mississippi River from the Gulf of Mexico. "Two-Spirits" were men
with feminine mannerisms and who performed work traditionally reserved
for women. Even more shocking to these European explorers was that these

Two-Spirits were highly regarded by their tribes. In 1751, Jean Bernard Bossu wrote of the Choctaw tribe, "They are morally quite perverted, and most of them are addicted to sodomy."[1]

The first recorded instance of homosexuality in New Orleans dates to 1724.[2] In that year, just six years after the city was founded, a sex scandal involving a ship captain and his cabin boy rocked the fledgling city. Captain Beauchamp of the *Bellone* was discovered to be having a sexual affair with his cabin boy. When word of the romance reached the French Superior Council (the governing authority at the time), the council reprimanded Captain Beauchamp by having the boy reassigned to another ship, *La Loire*. But the amorous captain would not be denied the object of his affection. Under cover of darkness, Beauchamp stole the boy away from *La Loire*, brought him back to the *Bellone*, and set sail down river for the Gulf of Mexico. The French Superior Council dispatched a skiff to give chase, but the *Bellone* was the quicker vessel. Beauchamp and his boy escaped as far as Dauphin Island off the coast of Alabama near Mobile, where the *Bellone* sank.

Captain Beauchamp's initial sentence, having the cabin boy reassigned to another ship, constituted little more than a slap on the wrist. Such a light sentence provides a glimpse into the sexual mores and attitudes of French New Orleans. During the American period, Captain Beauchamp would have faced life imprisonment for his sexual peccadilloes. Although sodomy was technically illegal in seventeenth-century France, the Crown rarely enforced laws against it. Sexual depravity was common in the royal court of Louis XIV and rivaled the most heralded excesses of ancient Rome. The Sun King's brother (who had a fondness for cross-dressing) and at least one of his sons were notorious for their sexual escapades with men. The son even joined what would now be called a gay orgy club. New Orleans was born out of this libertine milieu. The Church of course frowned on all of this, but the early colonists in Louisiana generally ignored the moral teachings of Holy Mother Church that they found inconvenient.

In 1805, two years after the Louisiana Purchase and drawing on English common law, the new American government outlawed "the detestable and abominable crime against nature." But what, precisely, is a crime against nature? In later decades, the vague wording and lack of a clear definition became the cause for a number of legal challenges as well as efforts by the state legislature to clarify the matter. Despite the legal ambiguities, the general consensus, at least among law enforcement officials, was that any sexual act that did not involve a penis penetrating a vagina was a crime against nature. It was on this pretext that homosexual acts were deemed illegal. In 1998, gays and lesbians filed a lawsuit challenging the sodomy statute's constitutionality on the grounds that it unfairly targeted the queer community (that case is discussed in detail in a future chapter).

Despite the invisibility of queerness in the nineteenth century, the literary and historical record does provide a few glimpses into that closeted world. Two writers in particular drew inspiration from the city's gay vibe. The lesbian bar scene circa 1850 is referenced in Ludwig von Reizenstein's *The Mysteries of New Orleans* (1854),[3] and Walt Whitman, who lived in New Orleans in 1848, drew poetic inspiration from the city's multitude of erotic imagery. Literary scholar Robert K. Martin has noted that New Orleans "had an important impact on his conception of male love."[4] Some have theorized that John McDonogh, the generous nineteenth-century philanthropist, was gay, and Christina Vella, biographer of the fabled Micaela Almonester de Pontalba who constructed the buildings that flank Jackson Square, was convinced Micaela's son, the artist Gaston Pontalba, was gay.[5] Other LGBT+ notables in New Orleans from the nineteenth century include religious figure Mother Mary Bentivoglio, piano master Tony Jackson, and gay brothel operator Miss Big Nelly.

In the early twentieth century, some of the brothels in Storyville (a red-light district on the edge of the French Quarter) featured women who specialized in "French love acts," which was code for lesbian sex. And from the 1920s to 1940s, the "Million Dollar Dolls," a group of "Black transvestites," were a regular feature on the streets each Carnival season. In 1931, the Zulu King created a bit of a stir when he chose as his Queen a female impersonator whom folklorist Robert Tallant called "Corrine the Queen."[6]

It is important to remember that prior to the mid-twentieth century, homosexuals as a class of people did not exist in the mainstream consciousness. Some people of weak moral character may have committed homosexual acts, but those acts did not constitute a defining identity or orientation. So the thinking went—homosexuality was a verb, not a noun. When gay identities began to emerge and homosexual communities became visible, the straight mainstream became alarmed. The development of gay identities and communities in the 1950s represented a significant, and, to some, disturbing, paradigm shift in society.

The existence of gays and lesbians, and—more to the point—their visibility and subsequent agency, was too much for straight society to bear. The illumination of queer spaces was perceived by many to be an act of violence in that it encroached on heteronormative spaces. Complicating binary notions of sexuality and gender was threatening to the hegemony. This was certainly the case in New Orleans. Reinforced by the homophobic teachings of Christianity and feeling threatened, the straight power structure that ran the city responded defensively and viciously. Consequently, police harassment of gay folk rose dramatically.

Another motivating factor to suppress gay visibility was the fear that such visibility would scare off tourist dollars. The current tourism industry, which brings roughly eighteen million visitors to New Orleans annually, has its modern origin in the late nineteenth and early twentieth centuries with the rise of leisure tourism. The creation of a middle-class resulting from the Industrial Revolution along with the mobility afforded by planes, trains, and automobiles enabled travel not just for business but also for amusement and recreation. When Storyville, the city's notorious red-light district, closed in 1917, many of the district's sex workers relocated operations to the upper Quarter. As World War I heated up, hotels and other commercial concerns pitched New Orleans as "European" and marketed the city as a safer, cheaper alternative to war-ravished Europe. The popularity of the French Quarter as a tourist destination coincided with the rise of Bourbon Street as an entertainment district. Richard Campanella describes the opening of Count Arnaud's Maxime Supper Club on January 13, 1926, as "the birthplace and birthday of modern Bourbon Street."[7]

By the mid-1950s, the tourist market consisted primarily of white, male conventioneers. That began to change in the 1980s when college students began forgoing the beach for Bourbon Street. The 1980s also witnessed more and more families coming to New Orleans, especially after the 1984 World's Fair and the opening of the Audubon Aquarium of the Americas in 1990. The spending power of the queer community—and its desirability as a tourist market—would not become evident until the late 1990s when Southern Decadence began attracting tens of thousands of queer revelers (and dollars) to the French Quarter every Labor Day weekend.

But in the 1950s, the closet door was still firmly shut. In 1951, the *Times-Picayune* ran a story entitled "Curb Advocated on Homosexuals: Crackdown to Save Young Persons Demanded."[8] In 1955, police superintendent Provosty A. Dayries publicly proclaimed that homosexuals were the city's "Number One vice problem," adding, "They are the ones we want to get rid of most."[9] Jacob Morrison, a prominent citizen (he was Mayor Morrison's half-brother) and cofounder of the Vieux Carré Property Owners and Associates, led an effort to have the Starlet Lounge's liquor license revoked because it catered almost exclusively to gay men.

In 1958, the New Orleans City Council established a Committee on the Problem of Sex Deviates. An initial report of the committee proposed a "climate of hostility" be adopted toward homosexuals. As its chairman, the council appointed Jacob Morrison. Morrison had been a thorn in the side of the gay community for years, often attacking gay bars through legal channels.

Before the city formally resolved to create a "climate of hostility" for gays, the climate was already pretty hostile. Widespread ignorance and familiar stereotypes of gay people were prevalent, especially the notion that homosexuals were predatory and looking to recruit teenagers and children. In 1951, the *Times-Picayune* reported:

> A warning that homosexuals in the French Quarter are at work corrupting high school boys and girls was made Friday by Richard R. Foster, chairman of the Mayor's Committee on the Vieux Carre, in an address before the Civic Council of New Orleans. For that reason, he said, the homosexual problem is one of the city's most serious. "In several instances, parents have come to police begging them to save their children," he asserted. "High school boys and girls enticed into places habituated by homosexuals often see an obscene show or something of that nature as a starter," he added. The homosexuals are, he said, "continuously recruiting" and there at least four "places" in the Quarter which cater to almost no one but homosexuals. "It almost seems as if youngsters who develop homosexual tendencies in other Southern cities are put on a train and sent to New Orleans," he said.[10]

About a month earlier, the *Times-Picayune* had run another article along the same lines with a new twist. At a meeting of the mayor's advisory committee, Chairman Foster argued that the city should develop a strategy for discouraging "perverts" from coming to New Orleans, claiming most homosexuals in New Orleans were "out-of-towners." That gay people lived in New Orleans was either incomprehensible or too distasteful to bear. The level of denial revealed in the article rivals the level of bigotry and hatred permeating straight society at the time. One man recalls, "We never flaunted our sexuality then because we were so afraid."[11]

Four events occurred in 1958 that made it a seminal year in the history of queer New Orleans: the creation of the Committee on the Problem of Sex Deviates, a lawsuit regarding a gay bar, the murder of a gay man in the French Quarter, and the birth of gay Carnival.

As one of its first orders of business, the Committee on the Problem of Sex Deviates turned its attention to Tony Bacino's, a gay bar located at 738 Toulouse Street. In the summer of 1958, the manager and staff of Tony Bacino's were arrested six times. They were charged with violating a city ordinance that prohibited "immoral" people, including "sexual perverts," from working in bars and restaurants. Amazingly, the ordinance was not repealed until 1993.

In the 1950s, it was common for gay bars to routinely pay off the police to leave them alone. But Roy Maggio, the manager of Tony Bacino's, was apparently not so inclined. Instead of making the customary "protection" payments or folding under the pressure of police harassment, Maggio and the two bartenders, Louis Robichaux and Amos McFarlane, both of whom had previously worked at the Starlet Lounge, applied for, and were awarded, a temporary restraining order against the police.

The city attorney responded by arguing the plaintiffs had obtained the temporary restraining order under false pretenses. In a brief arguing the temporary restraining order should be dissolved, the city argued the bartenders had committed the following "lewd acts": they "kissed," "embraced," and "fondled" patrons of the bar; they addressed male patrons as "Darling," Sweetheart," and "Doll"; they proposed "unnatural sexual intercourse" to navy sailors; and they encouraged patrons to "conduct themselves in a lewd and preverted [sic] manner."

Transcripts from the subsequent legal proceedings reveal a McCarthy-like investigation into the lives and characters of the bartenders. A sampling of some of the questions assistant city attorney Raoul Sere peppered the plaintiffs with include the following gems: "Have you at any time kissed or embraced other males in the place known as Tony Bacino's?" "Have you ever kissed them on the mouth?" "Now when attending bar at Tony Bacino's how are you attired?" "Do you use false eyelashes?" "Do you wear earrings?" "Do you wear bracelets?" And on it goes just like that for over one hundred pages of court proceedings transcripts.[12]

Roy Maggio, Louis Robichaux, and Amos McFarlane eventually lost their case and abandoned their fight on appeal. The case of Tony Bacino's is significant not only in that was an early attempt to have discriminatory laws based on homophobia ruled unconstitutional but also in that it was a perfect example of the "climate of hostility" toward the LGBT+ community the city of New Orleans actively encouraged. Not unexpectedly, violence ensued as a result of the city's attitude.

While Matthew Shepard's murder in 1998 was a touchstone in the national fight for equality, Shepard was not the first gay person killed just for being gay. In fact, the gay community in New Orleans also has a martyr who predates Shepard by forty years. In 1958, Fernando Rios was savagely attacked and murdered by three homophobes in the heart of the French Quarter.

It was September and the fall semester at colleges and universities was underway. At that time, a common recreational activity among fraternity brothers at college campuses across the nation was to "roll a queer." This homophobic ritual essentially consisted of two to five fraternity brothers going to the "gay" section of town, or a gay bar if the town had one, and beating up someone they perceived to be gay.

In New Orleans, that meant the French Quarter and Café Lafitte in Exile, the oldest gay bar in the city. And so one night, three fraternity brothers from Tulane University (John Farrell, Alberto A. Calvo, and David P. Drennan) decided to "roll a queer." The three homophobes went to the Quarter in search of a victim. After carousing a few hours, Farrell went to Café Lafitte in Exile at about 1:30 a.m. while Drennan and Calvo waited outside. Surveying the bar for potential victims, Farrell settled on Fernando Rios, a twenty-six-year-old tour guide visiting from Mexico City with a group of doctors and their wives.

The two sat next to each other in the bar and chatted for a while before they decided to leave together. As Rios and Farrell were walking back to Farrell's car, they entered a narrow alley adjacent to St. Louis Cathedral, where Calvo and Drennan were lying in wait. The three undergrads then attacked Rios, beating him repeatedly in the head and kicking him in the stomach several times.

After the attack, the three gay-bashers returned to campus bragging about the assault and showing off Rios's wallet, which they had stolen. Rios, barely conscious and unable to move, was not discovered until the next morning. His face bloody and swollen, he was rushed to Charity Hospital where he died.

During a routine autopsy, the city coroner discovered Rios had an unusually thin cranium, and this revelation played a key factor in the subsequent murder trial. Farrell, Calvo, and Drennan were arrested and went to trial on murder charges on January 21, 1959. The defendants admitted to the beating, citing what is now called the gay panic defense, which essentially argued that the attackers didn't want to beat Rios but were compelled to because he made a pass at them. They further argued Rios died because of his "eggshell cranium," not because of their attack. Tortured logic aside, this defense made perfect sense to a homophobic, all-male, all-white jury in 1959, and the three students were easily acquitted by the jury after it deliberated a mere two hours and fifteen minutes.

The acquittal and press coverage of the trial provide a glimpse into the highly homophobic public attitudes of the time. When the not-guilty verdict was announced, the courtroom erupted in cheers and applause. The *New Orleans States-Item* pictured on its front page a picture of the defendants smiling broadly next to a boxed joke entitled "Today's Chuckle," which read, "Overheard in a nightclub: ordinarily I never chase a man, but this one was getting away." Also, a deluge of letters poured into the editorial offices of the city's newspapers, the overwhelming majority of them supporting the homophobic defendants and urging the city to "clean up the Quarter." The few letters in support of Rios were often backhanded. One incensed reader argued the police should leave the gay bars alone so the "perverts" wouldn't feel compelled to mingle with "normal" people.[13]

It was also in 1958 that a group of gay men formed the first gay Carnival krewe. The Krewe of Yuga grew out of the annual Krewe of Carrollton parade-viewing party hosted by Doug Jones at his home, which was on the parade route. Other founding members included John Dodt, Jim Schexnayder, Jerry Gilley, Tracy Hendrix, Otto Stierle, Carlos Rodriguez, Bill Wooley, John Henry Bogie, and Jo Jo Landry. On Mardi Gras, this group of friends wandered the French Quarter, with Dixie's Bar of Music as a base of reveling operations. Miss Dixie affectionately referred to her gay regulars as "the cufflink set."

The annual Yuga party grew in popularity, and within a few years the krewe needed a new venue to host its ball. The 1960 ball was held at a jazz club on Lake Pontchartrain. In 1961, the krewe moved its tableau to the Rambler Room, the dance recital hall of a school in Metairie. The ball, and venue, was a success, and the krewe chose the same place for its ill-fated 1962 ball.

On Saturday, February 24, 1962, the Jefferson Parish Police Department raided the Yuga ball and arrested nearly one hundred men, most of whom were in drag. About fifteen minutes into the tableau, policemen with bullhorns burst into the room and announced, "No one is to leave this room!" Among those arrested was Carlos Rodriguez, who, a week earlier, had been presented as the first Queen of Petronius in the same hall. Escaping arrest were Bill Wooley and Elmo Avet, two founding members of Petronius who would go on to shape the phenomenal development of gay Carnival. When news of the raid reached the French Quarter, Dixie Fasnacht, owner of Dixie's Bar of Music, gave Carl Escovitch, who was sitting in the bar at the time, a wad of cash and told him to go bail out all those who had been arrested at the ball.

The Krewe of Yuga folded as a result of the ensuing scandal, but the idea of gay Carnival persisted. Several Yuga members had also founded the Krewe of Petronius in 1961; the first Petronius ball was held in 1962. Under the leadership of Bill Wooley and Elmo Avet, Petronius obtained a state charter and became an incorporated Carnival Krewe. The Krewe of Amon-Ra was founded in 1965 by six friends, some of whom had been Petronius members.[14] Two years later, four friends founded Armeinius in 1968.[15] In 1970, Olympus was founded. Many who were around then have noted that the first Olympus ball (1971), whose theme was Camelot, represented a departure from previous gay krewes' bal masques in that it elevated the tableaux from humorous satire to serious art. This was a pattern other krewes would follow.

By the early 1970s, meeting space became an issue for the growing number of gay krewes. Many locations were already reserved for the mainline nongay krewes. Other venues could no longer accommodate the crowds that gay balls were attracting. Still others chose to turn a cold shoulder to the gay krewes in light of the increasing visibility of the national gay rights movement. A few krewes held their balls in Black union labor halls. The civic center in Chalmette became home to several krewes' balls.

In 1976, Bill Wooley broke away from Petronius and founded the Krewe of Celestial Knights (KOCK). Wooley was not the first, nor the last, member to break away from one krewe to form another one. In 2000, longtime Petronius captain Mickey Gil and several others left to form the Mystic Krewe of Satyricon. Gil had joined Petronius in 1985, just as many krewes folded because their ranks had been decimated by the AIDS epidemic. Many credit Gil with reviving Petronius and, by extension, gay Carnival in that dark period. The Lords of Leather hosted their first ball in 1984 and remain the only leather-oriented Carnival krewe in the world.[16] The Krewe of Mwindo, a predominantly African American krewe, was founded in 1998 by several friends.[17]

In addition to the various krewe balls, another immensely popular feature of gay Carnival in New Orleans is the Bourbon Street Awards. In 1964 the owner of the Clover Grill wanted to drum up business for his diner and inaugurated a Mardi Gras costume contest. This event evolved into the extravaganza it is today. Over the years, the Bourbon Street Awards have garnered the attention of the international media. Another popular gay Mardi Gras event is the Krewe of Queenateenas Gay Mardi Gras Bead Toss from the balcony of the *Ambush* mansion. Begun in 1987, the bead toss is an excellent opportunity to see drunken male revelers exposing themselves. The Krewe of Queenateenas also names an annual King Cake Queen and hosts a coronation party each Carnival season.

The history of gay Carnival in New Orleans is a rich and vibrant tapestry about which volumes could be written.[18] At their height, before the AIDS epidemic took so many krewe members and shifted the focus and resources of the gay community, there were close to two dozen krewes, including the only lesbian krewe, the Krewe of Ishtar. Today there are nine gay krewes: Petronius, Amon-Ra, Armeinius, the Lords of Leather, Mwindo, Queenateenas, Rue Royale Revelers, Narcissus, and Apollo.[19] An additional krewe, Stars, was founded by two gay men and is gay friendly but does not identify exclusively as a gay krewe.[20]

During the golden age of gay Carnival in the 1970s, as gay men in New Orleans were building an infrastructure for the expression of their creative and artistic talents, lesbians were organizing as well, but not socially, per se. Rather, they were organizing politically. Second-wave feminism arrived in Louisiana in the 1970s. Statewide, there were a number of organizations advocating on behalf of women's issue. Not the least of these were the Baton Rouge and New Orleans chapters of the National Organization for Women (NOW) and the Louisiana Women's Political Caucus (LWPC). In New Orleans, many feminist activists were lesbians, which was not necessarily the case in other parts of the state.

But it would be misleading, if not inaccurate, to say this was an area of lesbian activism. Many of the lesbians in the feminist movement are quick to point out that they were feminists first and lesbians second. Clay Latimer has said that "the ERA and other concerns that applied to ALL women were priorities, and that other topics (such as lesbian rights) could be addressed after we succeeded in the broader areas. I felt that I was discriminated against more often as a woman than as a lesbian."[21]

In terms of lesbian activism, Vicki Combs and a few other lesbians formed a local Daughters of Bilitis chapter in the late 1960s. Historian Janet Allured writes: "The New Orleans chapter, headed for many years by Sharon Dauzat, offered safe space for lesbians in an intellectual, political, non-bar environment. In a chapter of 30 to 40 members, mostly in their twenties, anywhere from six to ten were African American, and three were of Asian descent. The New Orleans chapter continued into the 1980s, more than twenty years after the national organization had become defunct."[22] And one of the earliest efforts at gay political activism in New Orleans occurred in 1970 when Lynn Miller, a graduate student at Tulane University, and David Solomon, founder of the New Orleans Metropolitan Community Church, formed a local chapter of the Gay Liberation Front (GLF), which was born from a split in the Mattachine Society in the wake of Stonewall. The national Gay Liberation Front had been founded in New York in 1969 a few weeks after the rebellion at the Stonewall Inn. At that time, the major voice for gay rights was the conservative Mattachine Society, whose response to the Stonewall riot was a call for gays to settle down and work within the system to bring about change. This conservative, measured response angered some within the Mattachine Society who felt the time had come to give up on traditional and gradual reform. When the leadership of the Mattachine Society denounced the group's public support of a Black Panther rally, several members abandoned the Mattachine Society to form the Gay Liberation Front. This break represented a new way of thinking about gay rights. Instead of slowly gaining acceptance within the existing society, the radicals who formed the Gay Liberation Front called for the creation of a new society.

In January 1971, the New Orleans GLF (roughly seventy-five people) marched on city hall and staged a demonstration protesting police harassment. The group made three demands:

> One, an immediate end of all hostility, brutality, entrapment and harassment by the New Orleans Police of gay men and women and of their places of gathering; two, the formation of a Governor's Panel empowered to conduct a complete and thorough investigation of the police methods and actions against gay people. On this panel shall sit one gay man and one gay woman; and three, the immediate suspension from duty of Police Superintendent Clarence Giarusso and Vice Squad head Soule, until the Governor's Panel has completed its investigation. Should the panel find against these men, they shall be terminated immediately.[23]

The demonstration and the protestor's demands received some coverage in the *Times-Picayune* but were, for the most part, generally disregarded. They did not go unnoticed, however. Straight New Orleans was shocked not only at the visibility of gay people but also, perhaps more so, at the alarming fact they were demanding things.

Because of the chauvinism within the GLF, Lynn Miller grew disillusioned and left the group. The New Orleans chapter of the Gay Liberation Front disbanded shortly thereafter. From the outset, the group had been plagued by an issue that would eventually play out on a national scale. Lesbians felt the group was too preoccupied with the concerns of gay men. This split between lesbians and gay men was emblematic of tensions throughout the movement. As second-wave feminism began to gain steam, many politically minded lesbians devoted their efforts to women's liberation. In her landmark 1995 work, *Virtual Equality*, Urvashi Vaid offers a critical survey of the gay and lesbian movement since Stonewall, and drawing on the work of historian George Chauncey, Urvashi Vaid observes:

> The first fallacy—that oppression based on gender and sexual-orientation discrimination is not connected—is evident throughout our movement. Gay male leaders talk about a coalition with the women's movement as if it were something separate to begin with. Conversely, the mainstream women's movement has retreated from its critique of gender itself to the less threatening critique of gender inequality.

Lesbian activists who bridge both movements are handicapped by the sexism of the former and the homophobia of the latter and have been unable to make either acknowledge the value of accepting both movements as subsets of one common movement.[24]

The fallacy Vaid describes is essentially what caused the breakup of the New Orleans GLF, but during its short existence, the New Orleans GLF did publish the first locally gay-identified magazine (really more of a newsletter), called *Sunflower*. The first edition featured testimonials from several men, of whom one was straight, who were harassed, beaten, and arrested while in or near Cabrini Park in the French Quarter. The group also staged a "gay-in" at City Park. Soon after the group fizzled out, some members went on to establish the local Metropolitan Community Church.

The issue of lesbian inclusivity in the women's movement was nowhere more evident than in the Louisiana Women's Political Caucus. When president Pat Denton's proposed amendment to add the phrase "sexual orientation" to the mission statement was vetoed, she resigned in protest.

This GLF split and the tension within the women's movement between straight and lesbian feminists illustrates a unique predicament for lesbian feminist activists. They were not only fighting the patriarchy within the gay and lesbian community, they also had to contend with homophobia from within the women's movement. These pressures and how they affected lesbian feminists' priorities are often lost on gay men.

Barbara Scott made history in 1969 when she founded *Distaff*, the longest-running feminist newspaper in America (1969–1982). *Distaff* was a women's journal that featured biographical sketches, illustrations, cartoons, essays, poetry, short stories, reviews, and, of course, political commentary. It was the only feminist newspaper in the South. Scott edited the paper for the first year or so before Mary Gehman assumed editorial responsibilities.

Barbara Scott made history again in 1972 by being the first openly gay political candidate from New Orleans. She ran for the state house of representatives on what was then considered a radical platform: she opposed discrimination against women in the workplace, she was for equal pay for women, for decriminalizing homosexuality, and for the reform of marijuana laws.

In addition to promoting feminism, Scott was also a strong advocate for the French Quarter. She helped defeat the Riverfront Expressway (an ill-conceived proposal that would have positioned the I-10 overpass that is currently over Claiborne Avenue instead behind the French Market and Café du Monde opposite Jackson Square). Furthermore, Scott won an award from the Vieux Carré Commission for restoring 509 Burgundy Street. And from 1967 to 1972, she co-owned the Fatted Calf, a restaurant and bar popular among the Quarter's gay and lesbian denizens at 727 St. Peter Street.

After her unsuccessful campaign for the state house in 1972, Scott moved to Eureka Springs, Arkansas. There she bought an old Victorian-style hotel called the New Orleans. Scott billed the place as the nation's first "feminist resort." Shortly after it opened, a feminist newswire wrote a story on the hotel, which was picked up by over two hundred newspapers across the nation, including the *New York Times* and the *San Francisco Chronicle*. Soon feminists as well as battered women from around the country with no other place to go were flocking to Eureka Springs. Scott opened the doors of her hotel to them and offered them sanctuary.

Scott's success in Eureka Springs is also credited with helping that resort town become the "Gay Capital of the Ozarks." For a time, Eureka Springs was the only city in Arkansas to have a registry of domestic partnerships, and it is the only city in that state to provide employee health insurance coverage to domestic partners. The city has a disproportionately high LGBT+ population and celebrates that distinction each year with a lively Pride celebration and several Diversity Weekends. A gay mecca in Arkansas might not have happened if Barbara Scott had won her House race in 1972. New Orleans's loss was Eureka Springs's gain.

Counterintuitive to some, many lesbians in the women's movement were very involved in advocating for battered women. The initial primary challenge was to prove that domestic violence even existed. Yet another persistent hurdle was the question, "If it's such a problem, why doesn't the woman just leave?" As more and more women spoke up, the need for shelters took precedence. Advocates such as Jan Logan, Clay Latimer, Nikki Alexander, Betty Spencer, Virginia Ellis, and Millie Charles worked tirelessly to raise awareness about the issue of domestic violence.

Sexual assault was yet another concern of the women's movement. Several high-profile cases of sexual violence against women gave rise to the anti-rape movement in the mid-1970s. The Louisiana Coalition Against Domestic Violence sponsored an annual Take Back the Night March in Baton Rouge. In New Orleans, most of the march organizers were lesbians.[25]

One of the proudest—and most significant—achievements of the women's movement in Louisiana was the repeal of the state's "head and master" law. This statute guaranteed a husband's legal right to have the final say regarding all household decisions and jointly owned property without his wife's knowledge or consent. This law was repealed in 1979 and replaced with what became known as the "equal management" bill. Many women worked toward the repeal of the head and master law.[26]

At the same time lesbians in New Orleans were spearheading the women's movement, gay men in the city were still grappling with the aftereffects of the Up Stairs Lounge arson. The Up Stairs Lounge fire had motivated a handful of activists to form the Gay People's Coalition (GPC). The GPC launched a publication, *Causeway*, and established a Gay Crisis Phone Line. *Causeway* was edited anonymously by Bill Rushton, then a student at Tulane University, who also edited the *Vieux Carré Courier*. An editorial from the January 1974 edition of *Causeway* declared, "There are enough gay men and women in N.O. who are able to do anything they wish—be it swinging an election or electing a gay city councilman."[27] This clarion call, while certainly true, fell on deaf ears. As the embers of the fire cooled, so did the ire of the gay community. In what was to become the dominant pattern of gay activism in New Orleans, the GPC, and *Causeway*, eventually faded away. Former Baptist minister Mike Stark formed the Gay Services Center, located on Burgundy in the Marigny, in 1974. Initially the group enjoyed a flurry of activity, including the publication of a newsletter, the *Closet Door*. But the group's promise was never fulfilled; in a familiar pattern, the newsletter and the group were soon moribund.

The Up Stairs Lounge fire was a seminal moment in the history of gay New Orleans, the significance of which was even noticed by the arch-conservative *Times-Picayune*. A month and a half after the fire, the paper published a weeklong series of six articles, all written by Joan Treadway, concerning homosexuality, the first of which was titled, "Gay Community Surfaces in Tragedy of N.O. Fire." The tone of the article is surprisingly objective, and Treadway even quotes local gay activists who succinctly summarized the multitude of dilemmas facing gay New Orleanians: police harassment, job and housing discrimination, and general societal alienation. In addition to forcing straight New Orleans to acknowledge its gay community, the fire also, in a sense, forced the gay community in New Orleans to confront itself.

The second article in the series, "Independent Route Taken for Personal Objectives" offered various gay persons' views of how the newly created New Orleans Gay People's Coalition would affect their lives as gay New Orleanians. The third article, "Homosexuals Disagree on Behavior's Sickness," explored the debate within the psychiatric community over whether homosexuality should be removed from the American Psychiatric Association's list of mental disorders. A year later, in 1974, the APA finally voted to no longer consider homosexuality an illness. The fourth article, "Psychiatric and Clerical Views— A Wide Spectrum," elaborated on the debate within psychiatric circles and included the views of a Baptist pastor, which were predictably ludicrous—"If preachers condone homosexuality, they're anti-Christs, enemies to God in clerical garb." The next article, "It's Not Illegal to BE Gay—Certain Acts Are Criminal," enumerated the legal prohibitions against gay sex (a $2,000 fine and five years in prison) and detailed how law enforcement attitudes were in the process of changing. The final article, "50s 'Climate of Hostility' to Gays Gone—What Now?" surveyed how attitudes had shifted from hostility to begrudging tolerance over the previous decades. As one might expect, the series elicited a wide variety of responses, both positive and negative, from readers. This fair and balanced treatment represented a colossal paradigm shift in the print media's treatment of gay issues. Two years later, Gail Shister, reporter for the *New Orleans States-Item*, would become the nation's first openly gay lesbian working for a major daily newspaper.[28]

Southern Decadence began in 1972 with a group of friends who playfully called themselves the "Decadents."[29] All were young, mostly in college or recently graduated, and counted among themselves male and female, Black and white, and gay and straight. Many people are aware Southern Decadence began as a going away party, but what is not as well known is that there were actually two parties. The Decadents met regularly at a home in the Treme, which they dubbed Belle Reve after the plantation Blanche DuBois lost in Tennessee Williams's *A Streetcar Named Desire*. This home was owned by two of the Decadents, David Randolph and Michael Evers. Sunday night Bourré (a popular card game in South Louisiana) and croquet games were a staple of the Decadents' social life, as was gathering at Matassa's bar before a night of carousing in the Quarter.

As Labor Day 1972 approached, Randolph, who was roughly ten years older than Evers, had to leave town on family business. Fellow Decadent Frederick Wright was returning from Chicago to visit his good friend Evers. Maureen Block, a new arrival, kept complaining there was nothing to do. School would be starting soon, and an end of summer party was in order. The Decadents planned a costume party for the Sunday before Labor Day. It was a fun party marked by spiked punch and a lot of drug use, especially marijuana and LSD. A few weeks later, Evers left to join Randolph in Michigan. Robert Laurent designed and sent out invitations that encouraged all to come dressed as their favorite Decadents to another party to say goodbye to Evers. About fifty people attended the party.

In 1973, the Decadents decided to have another party on the Sunday before Labor Day. Laurent suggested they all meet at Matassa's and "parade" back to Belle Reve. This was the second Southern Decadence but the first parade. The party continued in 1974 with one notable change. The Decadents chose Frederick Wright to lead the parade. This was the beginning of the grand marshal tradition.

By 1980, the focus of Southern Decadence had shifted from the house party to the parade. In 1981, the grand marshal's parade began at the Golden Lantern, a tradition that continues today. After the advent of the internet in the 1990s, Southern Decadence grew exponentially in both participants and visitors, as well as in terms of economic impact. Over three hundred thousand revelers attended Southern Decadence 2019.

In 2018, Southern Decadence had an estimated economic impact of $275 million, a number that has grown steadily since records began being kept. Traditionally, summers are slow in New Orleans, especially in the tourism industry. Service industry workers are accustomed to scraping by through the summer; therefore, the influx of hundreds of thousands of gay people (with all their expendable income) to New Orleans over Labor Day weekend is a welcome respite from the doldrums of summer. Southern Decadence is significant historically in that it demonstrated the spending power of the gay community. Money may not buy acceptance, but it certainly buys a lot of tolerance. This truth played no small role in shaping citywide attitudes toward homosexuality.

Some have described Southern Decadence as New Orleans's version of Pride while others call it Gay Mardi Gras. Both of those descriptions are inaccurate. Southern Decadence is a time of revelry like Mardi Gras, but the Labor Day extravaganza falls well outside the Carnival calendar, and unlike Pride, Southern Decadence has no political agenda and is anything but a moveable corporate trade show. Southern Decadence is hedonism for hedonism's sake. And in its early years in the 1970s, Decadence was nowhere near the huge event it is today.[30]

While Southern Decadence was slowly growing in the mid-1970s, queer activism in New Orleans was coming of age as well. Despite the efforts at gay organizing in the wake of the 1973 arson at the Up Stairs Lounge, the first significant demonstration on behalf of gay and lesbian rights in New Orleans occurred in 1977. When it was announced in that year that Anita Bryant, the nation's leading homophobe at the time, would be coming to New Orleans to perform two concerts, local gay activists Alan Robinson and Bill Rushton must have thought to themselves, "Oh, hell no!"

The popular homophobic singer, and former Miss Oklahoma, had made quite a splash in Miami earlier in the year when she led a campaign to repeal Dade County's recently passed antidiscrimination ordinance that granted legal protection to gays and lesbians. She called her campaign "Save Our Children" and argued, "What these people really want, hidden behind obscure legal phrases, is the legal right to propose to our children that theirs is an acceptable alternate way of life. I will lead such a crusade to stop it as this country has not seen before." She was also quoted as saying, "As a mother, I know that homosexuals cannot biologically reproduce children; therefore, they must recruit our children," and "If gays are granted rights, next we'll have to give rights to prostitutes and to people who sleep with St. Bernards and to nail biters." Bryant went on to found Anita Bryant Ministries, which claimed to "cure" homosexuals by "deprogramming" them—a forerunner to the gay conversion camps that proliferated in the 1980s and 1990s.

Robinson, who was a gay activist while studying at the University of Illinois, had arrived in New Orleans two years earlier. He met Rushton while volunteering at the Gay Services Center, a community outreach facility in the Marigny. Rushton, a student at Tulane University at the time, had been involved with the Gay People's Coalition (GPC) and edited the organization's publication, *Causeway*. The two activists began dating, and one night over dinner they, along with Ann Gallmeyer, founded the Gertrude Stein Democratic Club, which eventually became the Gertrude Stein Society.

Upon learning that Bryant would be coming to town, the Gertrude Stein Society reached out to several local gay organizations and progressive groups and formed HERE (Human Equal Rights for Everyone). The group's purpose was to plan a protest against Bryant's concerts. HERE eventually grew into a coalition of fifteen different groups.

In response to Bryant's upcoming visit, HERE contacted Rod Wagner, a board member of the New Orleans chapter of the American Federation of Television and Radio Artists (AFTRA), and impressed upon him Bryant's virulent opposition to gay rights. The New Orleans board of AFTRA then unanimously passed a resolution asking its members to not air the Bryant concerts.

Wagner is quoted as saying, "They were afraid, and our board agreed, that her appearance could set up even more of a climate for violence here than we're already experiencing. And we are having our troubles. For instance, several older gay men have been stabbed to death in the French Quarter in the past few weeks, and I understand the suspect has said, 'Jesus doesn't like gay people.' What also concerns us are the reports of violence in the Miami area." He goes on to cite a bumper sticker popular in Miami at the time that read, "Kill a Queen for Christ."

The second prong of HERE's attack was a rally to be held at Jackson Square, followed by a march through the French Quarter to the Municipal Auditorium, where Bryant was scheduled to perform. In the weeks before that rally, Robinson and Rushton flooded the French Quarter with flyers announcing the rally. Because Byrant was the official spokesperson for the

Florida Citrus Commission, many gay bars in the French Quarter stopped serving Florida orange juice.

On the day of the rally, June 18, Robinson, Rushton, and the other organizers were astonished and delighted by the turnout. They had hoped for a couple of hundred people to show up. Crowd estimates at the time peg the attendance at 2,500 to 3,000 people. After the speechmaking, the crowd sang "We Shall Overcome" and began marching from the square to the site of the concert. James Welch, who attended the rally, remembers,

> I recall that the first few speakers were hard to hear and were not particularly exciting, I was sorry to say. But after a while, a small, stout woman from New York with a strong Brooklyn accent took the podium. I do not remember her name but she represented a lesbian group from New York. The first thing she said was that it was time for gays to realize that the criticisms against them were "bull shit" (as she said in a booming voice), and that seemed to get everybody excited. Then, she said that for years, gays had been teachers, marriage counselors, social workers, policemen, firemen, military members, cooks, janitors, and business people. And that gays were aunts, uncles, brothers, sisters, cousins, parents, and "most of all, we are their children! And the closet is no place to keep your kid!" I had never heard someone express what I supposed I had known all along. But it was absolutely riveting, and I felt a thrill inside of me. The crowd went pretty crazy after that.
>
> Then, Leonard Matlovich spoke. He said that he had been drummed out of the army for being gay, and for wanting to love men rather than kill them. He said that he had at first believed that he was sick, but then, he realized that it was Society that was sick. While I don't think we should blame Society for all of our problems, it never hurts as a crowd pleaser. By then, people were so excited, and I think that everyone thought there had been a sea change in our own beliefs about ourselves. It was evident in the enthusiasm of the group that something big had happened.[31]

In his landmark book on Southern gayness, *Rebels, Rubyfruit, and Rhinestones*, James Sears describes the march: "Supporters on wrought iron balconies wrapped with banners cheered. The march extended four blocks from sidewalk to sidewalk . . . Marking one of the largest civil rights demonstrations in the city's history, thousands of protestors arrived at the North Rampart Street Municipal Auditorium Entrance. Gertrude Stein was elated:

'The reaction within the ranks was explosive, euphoric, and pure; the silence of the past is ended.'"[32]

The success of the rally energized the LGBT+ community in New Orleans and also served as a harbinger of the shift in public attitudes toward homosexuality. Similar protests were held in other cities where Bryant performed, and the backlash against Bryant's bigotry caused the Florida Citrus Commission to drop her as its spokesperson. Her popularity among fundamentalist Christians further plummeted in 1980 when she divorced her husband, Bob Green. She married her second husband, Charlie Hobson Dry, in 1990 and attempted to resurrect her singing career, but in 1997, the couple filed for bankruptcy in Arkansas. They would do the same in Tennessee in 2001.

Robinson would go on to cofound LAGPAC and eventually buy FM Books, an important institution in the LGBT+ community. In 1977, Tom M. Horner, a former Episcopal priest, had two things on his mind—finishing his book on homosexuality in the Bible and opening a gay and lesbian themed bookstore. By 1978, *Jonathan Loved David: Homosexuality in Biblical Times* was published by the Westminster Press and Horner signed a lease on a space for a bookstore at the corner of Frenchmen and Chartres Streets in New Orleans.

Horner opened FM Books (Faubourg Marigny Books) with less than a hundred titles. At the time, the gay publishing industry was in its infancy. Ten years earlier, gay activist Craig Rodwell had opened the Oscar Wilde Memorial Bookshop in Greenwich Village, but it wasn't until after Stonewall that gay themed presses and bookstores began to proliferate in order to accommodate the growing number of gay titles. Glad Day opened in Toronto in 1970, followed by Giovanni's Room in Philadelphia in 1973 and Lambda Rising in Washington, DC, in 1974. Then came other, legendary gay bookstores such as People Like Us in Chicago and the Walt Whitman Bookshop in San Francisco. Glad Day became a chain, as did Lambda Rising and A Different Light. By 1994, there were forty-five gay and lesbian themed bookstores across the nation. Of these, only a handful remain.

Horner ran FM Books for ten years before retiring to California. Well-known New Orleans gay activist Alan Robinson then took over the store and ran it for the next sixteen years. Robinson had demonstrated an acute political consciousness as an anthropology student at the University of Illinois and became active in the local gay rights scene after he moved to New Orleans in 1975. For a while he worked at the Gay Services Center (a short-lived community outreach effort) before cofounding the Gertrude Stein Society with Bill Rushton and Ann Gallmeyer. The Gertrude Stein Society succeeded in assembling a mailing list, publishing a newsletter (*Gertrude's Notes*), and hosting a variety of social and political events, perhaps the most amazing of which was New Orleans's first gay TV talk show—*Gertrude Stein Presents*. In one memorable episode, Rushton interviewed Christine Jorgensen, whose sex change operation in 1951 had shocked the world.

At the bookstore, Robinson brought in more titles and hired a staff. He also began hosting signings for gay and lesbian authors visiting New Orleans. Johnny Townsend (author of *Let the Faggots Burn*, a book about the Up Stairs Lounge fire), who worked part-time at the store in the late 1990s, recalls:

> I remember Patricia Nell Warren, and Barbara Peabody (who wrote *The Screaming Room*, an AIDS memoir), and Vito Russo of *The Celluloid Closet*, and Aaron Lawrence (who wrote two books about escorting). I read my one solitary porn story, set in the bookstore and published in *Indulge*, at a reading while wearing my leather. Alan always had plenty of refreshments for all his signings, though I doubt he made very much money from any of them.[33]

In addition to promoting queer authors, Robinson also founded, along with Uptown bookseller Mark Zumpe, the New Orleans/Gulf South Booksellers Association. By the early 2000s, Robinson was not in the best of health and moved to Texas to be with his family. In 2003, M. K. Wegmann, the owner of the building that housed FM Books, approached Otis Fennell and asked him to help her find someone willing to run the store. Fennell took over the lease in July 2003.

Fennell changed the name of the store to FAB: Faubourg Marigny Art and Books. In addition to bringing in art, he also began stocking books about New Orleans and creating window displays. When he took over the store, Fennell had no experience in bookselling. "I had no experience, but I wanted to save the institution. Six months later I asked myself what the fuck have I done?"[34] Fennell came to the store with a business background, having earned an MBA at LSU and having served as the director of research for the New Orleans Chamber of Commerce in the 1970s.

Fennell has a keen sense of history, and preserving LGBT+ culture was extremely important to him. Part of that impulse to keep LGBT+ heritage alive was an awareness of the role the bookstore has played in its forty-plus year history. Culturally, FAB is significant not only because it was the only predominately gay themed bookstore in New Orleans but also because it is one of just a few independent gay bookstores in the nation that has survived in the internet age. Before the internet transformed the way everyone lives, gay bookstores functioned as spaces that fostered community building and served as an alternative to bars and porn shops.

Suzanna Danuta Walters, writing about coming out in Philadelphia in the 1970s, says of patronizing gay and lesbian bookstores, "Perhaps we were 'buying gay,' but I think the patronage of those bookstores felt more like 'being gay' in a world in which the spaces for that openness were severely limited."[35]

In 2018, Fennell was in failing health and sold the bookstore to his longtime friend David Zalkind. Zalkind, who is straight, has renovated the store and expanded its inventory while still maintaining an LGBT+ section. He has long been an ally to the LGBT+ community.

Before the advent of lesbian and gay bookstores, the world of queer letters was primarily relegated to organizational newsletters and underground newspapers. Gay journalism traces its roots to the 1960s and originally manifested itself in the form of bar bulletins and organizational newsletters. In those pre-internet, pre-Stonewall, highly homophobic years, the notion of a gay media was an alien concept because gay communities, if we can even call them that (perhaps gay subcultures is a better description), were essentially rendered invisible by the monolithic heterosexual society. *The Advocate* was founded in 1967 in Los Angeles as a local publication, but it soon thereafter went national. As gays, lesbians, and feminists began claiming a stake in the cultural revolution of the 1970s, gay political organizations proliferated across the nation and, with them, organizational newsletters and local newspapers.

New Orleans had its share of organizational newsletters—*Sunflower*, *Causeway*, *Gertrude's Notes*, and others—but these were as short lived as the organizations that produced them. There were a few other periodicals, but these did not enjoy long runs either. Rich Magill published the *Big Easy Times* in 1988 and 1989. There were a few entertainment guides such as *Headlines* and *This Week*, and for a while there were the *Whiz* and the *Rooster*.

Sustained gay journalism in New Orleans began in 1977 when Roy Letson and Gary Martin founded *Impact*. *Impact* differed from other publications in that it was not an organizational newsletter but rather a general newspaper. Throughout its twenty-two-year run, *Impact* went through several phases. In 1998, Kyle Scafide, who had acquired the paper, sold *Impact* to Window Media, a publishing concern based in Atlanta. A year and a half after the sale, the paper folded. Shortly after the sale, longtime writer and former editor of *Impact* Jon Newlin wrote,

Nevertheless, LimpAct has reinvented itself before and may well do so more than once again—reinvention usually had to do with what time Miss Letson had gotten up that particular day, thus the paper had its highbrow periods and its hard news periods and its arts-and-leisure periods and its scandal-sheet-tabloid periods, sometimes more than one at once.[36]

After *Impact* folded, Newlin would go on to write a column for *Ambush Magazine* for eight years.

Ambush was founded in 1982 by Rip Naquin and Marsha Naquin-Delain. Originally, the magazine covered Baton Rouge and north Louisiana, but it was expanded to include New Orleans when they moved to the city in 1985. *Ambush* now serves the Gulf Coast from Houston to Pensacola. Reflecting on the history of the paper, Rip recalls:

> Our first publication was the *Zipper*, distributed in Baton Rouge and lasted a year. The following publication was the *Alternative* distributed in Baton Rouge, Lafayette, Lake Charles, Alexandria, Monroe, Shreveport, and Houma, Louisiana, which was going into its sixth anniversary when we sold it to go into a straight bar business in Hammond. The person we sold it to ran it into the ground, and it closed within a year. When we left the straight bar business, we decided to do a publication reaching the whole state, including New Orleans. A group of our friends from across Louisiana came to our home in Baton Rouge to brainstorm for the publication. On the last night, we got cocktailed and tried to come up with a catchy name, and our dear friend Victoria Windsor, a famous drag queen from Monroe (weighing in at over four hundred pounds) better known as Queen Victoria, said "Ambush," and we all agreed, it'd catch attention.[37]

Still in publication, *Ambush* is one of the oldest remaining LGBT+ themed publications in the United States. The long tenures of both *Ambush* and *Impact*, especially in contrast to the short-lived organizational newsletters of earlier years, suggest that for gay publications to succeed, they must emanate from a business model rather than a strictly political or ideological orientation, which is to say that while some people may want "hard news," they also want lighter fare such as entertainment, gossip, and party pictures. In this regard, the gay media is not much different than the straight media.

The same subculture that gave rise to the gay rags also gave rise to the gay bars. Well into the 1970s, New Orleans was much more homophobic than recent generations can possibly imagine. Despite New Orleans's penchant for tolerance and its laissez-faire attitude, gays in New Orleans have faced a considerable amount of homophobia, especially from police. Although police harassment of gay bars now is mainly a thing of the past, it was, nonetheless, a very ugly past. Many bar owners paid the police to leave them alone. Such was the case at Café Lafitte in Exile. In the 1960s and early 1970s, a police officer would come in each week, like clockwork, and collect an envelope stuffed with cash. Tom Wood stopped making the payments when he took over the bar and eventually obtained a restraining order against the police because of their harassment. Nevertheless, the vice squad would, on occasion, either raid bars or send undercover cops (almost always young and good-looking ones) into the bars to make arrests. This practice continued well into the 1970s. Bartenders customarily slapped a wooden board on the bar to warn patrons they were getting too touchy-feely. Arrests were often accompanied by a beating and pressure to name other "perverts." Anyone unfortunate enough to be arrested for "crimes against nature" or "committing a lewd act" had his or her name and picture published in the local papers. This often resulted in family alienation, the loss of a job, and, in some cases, the loss of a place to live.

Gay bars as we know them today in New Orleans did not exist until the mid-twentieth century. Prior to that, drinking gays were relegated to a handful of straight bars that did not forbid their patronage but were a little less than welcoming. At the turn of the century in New Orleans, Tony Jackson, the famous gay pianist, used to hang out at a saloon called the Frenchman's (at Bienville and Villere Streets); the bar is also referenced by jazz historians as allowing cross-dressers. There was also the Golden Feather on St. Bernard Avenue and the Dream Castle on Frenchmen Street. And during Prohibition (1920–1933), there was, reputedly, a speakeasy in the lower Pontalba Building. All of these drinking establishments were predominately straight but somewhat gay-almost-friendly.

The oldest gay bar in New Orleans is Café Lafitte in Exile. In 1933, Tommy Caplinger, Harold Bartell, and Mary Collins opened Café Lafitte at the corner of Bourbon and St. Phillip Streets. They were accepting of and welcoming to their gay clientele. (Collins was a lesbian, Caplinger was straight, and Bartell's orientation is unknown). Although the bar could not be classified as a "gay bar" as we think of that term today, it was as gay friendly as the times would permit.

Throughout the 1930s and 1940s, Café Lafitte was a trendy nightspot. Robert Kinney mentions the bar in his classic 1942 book, *The Bachelor in New Orleans*, suggesting, "If the bartender is passed out, go behind the bar and mix your own drink!" In a city known for its bars, Café Lafitte was a must stop for visitors and a mecca for celebrities, including Lyle Saxon, Tennessee Williams, Frances Benjamin Johnston, Enrique Alférez, and Robert Ruark.

In 1951, the owner of the building that housed Café Lafitte (currently Lafitte's Blacksmith Shop) died. After his estate was settled, the building was sold by his family, and the new owner told the owners of Café Lafitte that they could keep their bar but that the queers would have to go. Caplinger made the decision to relocate the bar down the street on the next corner. The words *in exile* were added to Café Lafitte to refer to the bar's gay patrons who were "in exile" from the former location. Café Lafitte in Exile opened its current incarnation at 901 Bourbon in 1953. The grand opening was celebrated with a costume party. To avoid being discovered and thus raided, the front door was barricaded with sandbags and barbed wire. Those in the know had to enter through a back door.

At the dawn of the 1950s, Lafitte's was one of a handful of French Quarter "queershops," a derisive term used by police to refer to what we now call gay bars. There was also the Starlet Lounge on Chartres Street and Tony Bacino's on Toulouse Street and a few others. These bars were frequented almost exclusively by gay men—women, even lesbians, were specifically not allowed. A few lesbian bars opened on Tchoupitoulas Street in the Irish Channel in the 1950s, but these bars were short lived. Alice Brady opened Mascarade in 1952 and would go on to open a few more lesbian bars in the following decades. Other lesbian bar owners included Kitty Blackwell, Rosemary Pino, Charlene Schneider, and Diane Dimiceli. Gays and lesbians finally had bars of their own; the era of gay folk having to "tone it down" in order to drink in straight bars was essentially over, although a few bars managed to successfully blur the line between gay and straight, the most notable being Dixie's Bar of Music, which relocated from the central business district to Bourbon Street in 1949. There was also the My-O-My Club on the lakefront that featured female impersonators but essentially catered to a straight clientele.

By the time Stewart and Alfred returned from their brief stay in California and purchased the Faerie Playhouse on Esplanade Avenue in 1978, a queer subculture had emerged in New Orleans, and a number of events in the 1970s made the 1980s ripe for activism. The early attempts at organizing in the beginning of the decade with the Gay Liberation Front had been derailed from within by male chauvinism. The lesbians who were given to activism turned their attention to the women's movement. The gay male community seemed content with their Carnival krewes, even more so after the horror of the Up Stairs Lounge fire. For those not interested in activism, there was the bar scene. The success of the Gertrude Stein Society and the

Anita Bryant protest in 1977 demonstrated that times were changing. While early attempts at activism were not sustainable, the groundwork had been laid for future efforts. Successful, sustained LGBT+ activism began in 1980 with the founding of LAGPAC. And amid all the social change of the 1970s, no one could see the specter of AIDS on the horizon.

Chapter 6

GETTING ORGANIZED

*After the shock and trauma of coming out in mid-years, I felt
there wasn't any place in the political world for me.*
—STEWART BUTLER

WHEN STEWART REGISTERED TO VOTE IN 1948, THE CLERK AT THE REG-
istrar of voters' office checked the box next to "Democrat." Stewart protested,
saying, "I didn't indicate that." The clerk responded, "Well, Sonny, if you want
to be the seventh Republican in this parish, I guess that's okay." Stewart would
remain a Democrat for the rest of his life. Decades later, after becoming a
gay activist, Stewart noted, "In general, the Republican Party is much more
homophobic than the Democratic Party. We've made more gains under the
Democratic banner."

ORIGINS OF LAGPAC

If the 1970s were a decade when the New Orleans LGBT+ community came
(or at least starting peeking) out of the closet, the 1980s were a decade of
political activism. Many have assumed the Up Stairs Lounge arson in 1973
sparked the gay rights movement in New Orleans, but such an assumption
is erroneous. The few efforts that were made at organizing after the fire were
short lived. Ed Martinez, a writer for the gay newspaper the *Vieux Carré-
Star*, summed it up perfectly in 1977, four years after the fire, when he wrote:

> Where are the gay activists in New Orleans . . . ? Where are all the
> organized groups that give gay communities in other cities their sense
> of community and sharing? After the fire at the Upstairs Lounge
> everything has returned to normal. Nothing to raise gay conscious-
> ness in this city has happened, and nothing very much is very likely to

happen . . . nothing could have given a gay community more reason
to band together than that horrible tragedy.[1]

With the exception of the gay Carnival krewes formed in the 1960s, the
formation of the Gertrude Stein Society (GSS) in the 1970s was the first
successful sustained effort at organization. The 1977 protest against Anita
Bryant demonstrated that the LGBT+ community was finally ready to assert
itself. In addition to being a social organization, the Gertrude Stein Society
also expressed itself politically—something from which the gay Carnival
krewes shied away.

In an unpublished thesis, scholar Jelisa Thompson notes:

The Gertrude Stein Society was formed by Alan Robinson, a University
of Illinois graduate and gay activist who settled in New Orleans in
1975. After participating in the gay night life, Robinson found that the
gay community was broken and that rather than having a uniformed
social life, that members of the community were sectioned off based
on their social class. For example, the participants of the Mardi Gras
Krewes remained sectioned off by themselves, while the gay men from
Uptown New Orleans went to private parties and refused to participate
in the "dirty" bar scene or the clubs and bars in the French Quarter (the
usual hang out for the gay men in the lower and middle classes). After
seeing this, Robinson believed that it was necessary to form an organization that focused on social aspects of the city's gay community, as
opposed to political issues like its predecessors. Thus, Robinson formed
the Gertrude Stein Society, which played up social gatherings for the
gay community, such as Salons and cocktail receptions and a newsletter
that was published and issued throughout the city.

Robinson and members of the Gertrude Stein Society understood
that it was very difficult for a political organization in New Orleans to
be accepted and gain members. As seen with the New Orleans chapter
of the Gay Liberation Front, members of the city's gay community did
not welcome organizations that focused on changing legislation that
negatively affected homosexuals. Thus, the members of the Gertrude
Stein Society felt that if they began as a social organization they could
gain larger membership, and eventually progress into a political organization. As they promoted themselves in the community, Robinson and
the Gertrude Stein Society were readying themselves and the city's gay
community to venture into the political realm.[2]

Stewart describes the Gertrude Stein Society as a forerunner to LAGPAC, a political action group that would become the driving force behind the gay rights movement in New Orleans throughout the 1980s and 1990s. In 1980, the political education committee of the Gertrude Stein Society attempted to elect gay-friendly delegates to the Democratic National Convention as part of an initiative of the Gay Rights National Lobby called the Convention Project. About 110 people attended the caucus, 13 of whom were gay or lesbian, including Stewart and Alfred. Activist Roberts Batson, who was a member of the GSS's political education committee, recalled the Democratic caucus, which was held in the New Orleans City Council Chamber, in an April 11, 1997, article in *Impact*:

I noticed two men sitting by themselves. They seemed to be looking at us. Then one of them pulled out his notice from GSS and held it where we could see. That was all we needed to know. I scurried over and introduced myself. The fellow with the notice stuck out his hand. "My name is Stewart Butler," he growled. "And this is Alfred Doolittle." And so began the remarkable service of Stewart Butler as a gay political activist.[3]

At the dawn of the Reagan era, Roberts Batson, Alan Robinson, and others recognized the need for an organization dedicated to fighting for gay and lesbian rights in the political arena. To that end, Roberts Batson and Matt Easley hosted a meeting in 1980 at their home in the Marigny. It was agreed that a political action group was needed. In July 1980, thirty-five men and women, led by Alan Robinson, Roberts Batson, and others, gathered and began drafting bylaws for a new organization that would be fully dedicated to using the political process to advance the cause of lesbian and gay equality.[4] A month later, on August 18, a group of roughly sixty people gathered at 1445 Pauger Street in the Marigny and adopted the bylaws and elected officers and a board of directors. Thus, Louisiana Lesbian and Gay Political Action Caucus—LAGPAC—was born. Stewart and Alfred were charter members.

Batson later recalled:

Becoming involved in politics, I believed was not an option for us; it was an imperative. We had two opportunities to inject our presence into the political process: By jumping into the trenches of party politics, and by launching our own political organization. We did both.

In 1979, we offered a candidate for the Democratic State Central Committee. Although he was not successful, a core group of activists gained valuable experience in the nuts and bolts of New Orleans politics. The race also served notice that gay people were demanding a place at the political table. The following spring, six gay delegates were seated as voting members of the 1980 Louisiana State Democratic Convention.

In August of 1980, over fifty lesbians and gay men founded the Louisiana Gay Political Action Caucus. Within a few years, concentrated gay political efforts began to pay off and New Orleans political writers were ranking LAGPAC as a first-tier political force, joining the old-line white political groups and he newer organizations that had emerged out of the black civil rights movement.[5]

LAGPAC dues were five dollars a year in 1981. Membership rolls were kept on a computer in an oil company office in the central business district where a LAGPAC member worked. For the next twenty-five years, LAGPAC became a powerful voice for the LGBT+ community and demonstrated to the gay community that it could, in fact, make a political difference. Stewart would not only be a driving force in the organization, he would also forge long-lasting, significant friendships during his work with the group.

Article II of the LAGPAC bylaws, which Stewart helped draft, reads: "The purpose of LAGPAC shall be to work through the political system to promote full equality and civil rights for all lesbians and gay men." Seven standing committees would each play a part in working toward LAGPAC's purpose: communication, development, membership, research, volunteer, law and legal issues, and voter development. LAGPAC benefitted not only from a sound organizational structure but also from the diverse demographics and background of its members, which included gay men and lesbians, Black and white people, the proudly out and the deeply closeted. Gender and racial tensions would eventually lead to fissures in the coming years, but the bedrock was solid—at least on paper. Membership was open to anyone who could pay the five-dollar annual dues. As chair of the membership committee, Stewart was tireless. Wayne Christenberry remembers Stewart constantly badgering him about renewing his membership. "We're going to take you off the mailing list," Stewart would gravely warn. Under his leadership, membership increased sixfold its first year, from sixty to over four hundred. At the end of 1981, LAGPAC had members in fourteen parishes and could reach over two thousand people by direct mail. Throughout its existence, LAGPAC averaged a membership of roughly three hundred people. And by 1989, the group's mailing list boasted over five thousand names.

Attorney Jack Sullivan recalls the intense labor involved in putting out mass mailings:

> For a long while—decades, twenty years anyway—if there was any organizing in the community, it was organized literally out of a cigar box in Stewart Butler's Faerie Playhouse in Stewart's and Alfred's home on Esplanade. He literally had a cigar box full of index cards where he would keep up with people's addresses and phone numbers, and I guess he had a couple hundred . . . LAGPAC would send out mailings before each election and interview candidates and send out mailings, and we would literally hand-stuff these things at Stewart's house, twelve volunteers or so, stuff these envelopes, label these envelopes, stamp these envelopes, seal these envelopes. And Stewart, a wonderful steward of money, always wanted to do everything as inexpensively as possible, so we'd sort them by zip codes. They'd be presorted and stuff for the post office so we could mail bulk rate. But it was a tremendous amount of piecework. I laugh about it now because it's something you could go to a mailing agency and they'd press a computer button and it's all done. But it would take—I mean I have to tell you, it was literally backbreaking. You'd sit at a table for hours and hours and hours and do the same repetitive movement. One person's putting the stamp on; one person's folding it; one person's inserting it; one person's—oh, it was crazy, but it's the way it was done.[6]

LAGPAC also benefitted from extremely committed members who succeeded phenomenally is establishing the foundation of the organization. Within months of its formation, LAGPAC could point to several accomplishments: establishing contact with national gay rights organizations such as the National Gay Task Force, the Gay Rights National Lobby, and the National Convention Project; participating in the 1980 presidential election; publishing a pamphlet on the legal rights of gay people; sponsoring workshops at the Southeastern Conference for Lesbians and Gay Men (SECLGM); commending Lindy Boggs for her vote against the antigay McDonald Amendment; lobbying elected officials; compiling a mailing list that could reach 1,600 Louisiana voters; and playing a decisive role in swinging a New Orleans City Council race.

From its inception, LAGPAC focused on electing candidates sympathetic to gay rights, regardless of party. Although most members of LAGPAC were Democrats, the organization made a conscious decision to be nonpartisan because, as Stewart recalls, it wanted to be able to lobby all officeholders and candidates, regardless of party. LAGPAC did endorse Republicans on occasion and even had several Republican members, chief among them board member and future co-chair Leonard Green.

Raised in New Orleans, Leonard Green moved to Washington, DC, in 1990 and made quite a splash as an ultraconservative Black gay Republican. His column, Gayocracy, in the *Capital Spotlight* aroused no small amount of controversy and earned him a feature story in the *Washington Blade*.[7]

During election cycles, LAGPAC members would interview all the candidates and make an endorsement. Initially, the notion that a group of avowed homosexuals wanted to interview and publicly endorse candidates took the political establishment by surprise, especially in cities outside New Orleans. One of LAGPAC's early victories occurred just a few months after the group was founded. In October 1980, Brod Bagert vacated his New Orleans City Council seat when he was appointed to the public service commission. Five candidates ran for the open seat, and LAGPAC members Este Armstrong and Bob Stuart interviewed all of them. The three major candidates were Peter Castano (D), Lambert Boissiere Jr. (D), (?) Moulet (R), and Frank Mule. Based on the interviews, LAGPAC decided it was comfortable endorsing either Castano or Boissiere but went with Boissiere because Castano was terrified of a public endorsement from LAGPAC and requested the endorsement not be publicized, even in the gay press. Conversely, Boissiere quipped that he wouldn't mind if the endorsement was on the front page of the *Times-Picayune*. LAGPAC endorsed Boissiere.

Stewart led the Boissiere campaign forces on the ground, coordinating distribution of yard signs and letter writing campaigns and knocking on hundreds of doors. Stewart concentrated his efforts on four precincts in the Marigny and two in the Bywater. On election night, the Boissiere campaign staffers and volunteers were at his headquarters watching the returns come in. When the vote totals from the four precincts Stewart had targeted trickled in, someone asked, "Hey, what's going on down there?" Jim Duffy, Boissiere's campaign manager, exclaimed, "LAGPAC strikes!"[8] Boissiere led the crowded field and landed in the runoff by less than a 60-vote margin with Frank Mule, who had responded least favorably to LAGPAC's questionnaire in the primary. In his speech on election night, Boissiere acknowledged and thanked LAGPAC for its role in the campaign. In the runoff, LAGPAC doubled its efforts. Boissiere won by 258 votes out of nearly 20,000 votes cast. Boissiere would serve on the city council until 1994, when he was elected to the state senate.

Baton Rouge attorney Glenn Ducote, an early board member of LAGPAC and its first secretary, recalls, "In New Orleans, the endorsement was usually highly sought after since the gay community constituted a small but significant voting block that could be counted on for contributions and Election Day effort. On several occasions in New Orleans politics, the gay vote was the swing vote between the Black vote and the white vote, and we often sided with Black candidates before that was universally accepted in New Orleans."[9]

Not everyone shared Ducote's viewpoint. *Times-Picayune* columnist James Gill wrote, "Politicians hereabouts would as soon declare a campaign contribution from Carlos Marcello as accept the endorsement of a homosexual organization." Indeed, some candidates expressly rejected LAGPAC's endorsement. One candidate for the Jefferson Parish School Board, Georgia L. Clesi, upon receiving the LAGPAC survey in the mail, threw it away saying, "For the area I represent, their endorsement could do nothing but ruin me." Judge Jules Hillery, who ran for Congress in 1992, responded to the LAGPAC survey by writing the following letter:

> There is no need of me taking your time in answering your questions. You know my answers! But you need to turn from your wicked ways—repent—clean up your act or God will allow you to be judged by your own actions. Turn to Jesus. He really does love you and He will give you the power to change and be that person He wishes you to be. If I can be of help let me know. Please keep in mind that I do not judge you. That is God's business.

Other candidates avoided LAGPAC altogether. The most glaring example of this occurred in the 1982 mayoral election. In the primary, incumbent Ernest "Dutch" Morial faced a field of five opponents: state representative Ron Faucheux, state senator William Jefferson, perennial candidate Rodney Fertel, and two Socialist candidates—Rashaad Ali and Leon Waters. Morial made the runoff with Ron Faucheux. During the primary, LAGPAC's endorsement committee interviewed every candidate except Faucheux, who refused to speak with anyone from LAGPAC, much less be interviewed.

In his first term, Morial made good on the promises he made to the LGBT+ community when he courted their votes in 1977. He issued a policy statement prohibiting discrimination against lesbians and gay within his administration. He worked with gay activists for police reform and instituted sensitivity training at the police academy. He appointed openly gay people to various committees and task forces. He was genuinely open to hearing the concerns of the LGBT+ community.

The 1982 mayoral election was more controversial than usual. Overshadowing the campaign were Morial's demeanor and, more significantly, his race. Morial was New Orleans's first African American mayor, and unlike his predecessor, as John Maginnis has noted, "was a throwback to the old-line city boss in the Bob Maestri mold," who "skips the Chamber of Commerce crap and commands respect with blatant political muscle." Many voters found Morial's style, as well as his penchant for effectively using race to stir the electorate, repugnant, but what really made people angry was his bid for unlimited terms. During his first term, Morial attempted to change the city charter to allow mayors to serve more than two consecutive terms.

LAGPAC endorsed Morial, who won the election. In a letter to the editor of *Impact*, an LGBT+ themed weekly newspaper, Stewart wrote, "To those of you who will base your vote on race, I say cast your anti-black vote if you must—but realize that it will be just as anti-gay—and don't complain about police harassment, discrimination, and oppression." After the election, Stewart proved adept at analyzing election returns. He wrote detailed letters to the editors of local publications explaining, through statistical analysis, precisely, precinct by precinct, how the gay vote influenced the election.

Despite Faucheux's silence and the predictable homophobic reactions to queer political visibility, the Boissiere election nevertheless proved that the gay vote could swing a close election. After the Boissiere victory, many politicians in New Orleans coveted the LAGPAC endorsement. Leonard Doty, who at one point co-chaired the New Orleans office, remembered, "We had a substantial voting block."

LAGPAC made recommendations in local elections as well as in statewide and federal races. The group endorsed Jimmy Carter in 1980. Stewart and several other members watched the returns on election night at the Golden Lantern. He joked with Gertrude, a man who owned Gertrude's Bar, because he was the only Republican in the bar. Even though Reagan won in a landslide, Gertrude didn't gloat.

In addition to endorsing candidates, LAGPAC also aggressively lobbied legislators concerning bills that affected the gay community. In December 1981, Jean Carr and Roberts Batson met with Congressman Bob Livingston concerning the Moral Majority–backed House overrule of the Washington, DC sexual reform bill. After the meeting, Livingston spoke out against the bill and also voted against it. And in 1986, LAGPAC was instrumental in persuading Congresswoman Lindy Boggs to cosponsor the national gay and lesbian civil rights bill. LAGPAC would often meet with politicians, informing and educating them on the needs and issues of the gay community and asking them where they stood.

In addition to lobbying congresspeople and endorsing state and local candidates, LAGPAC also worked to improve relations with the New Orleans

Police Department. In October 1980, LAGPAC officials met with New Orleans police chief James Parsons to discuss the issue of police harassment. In an effort to foster understanding and develop relationships, the group also participated in softball games between police officers and members of the gay community. LAGPAC was successful in ending the routine procedure of asking new hires if they were gay and in the creation of a police liaison to the gay community. Despite these efforts, attitudes on "the force" toward gays and lesbians were slow to change.

On the weekend of April 24, 1981, the New Orleans police conducted a massive "sidewalk sweep" outside of several gay bars, including the notorious Jewel's on Friday night and two lesbian bars—Diane's and the Grog—on Saturday night, and arrested over eighty people and charged them with "obstruction of free passage." In other words, they were standing on the sidewalk. The mass arrests aroused the ire of the gay community, and a protest rally was held at the Catholic Community Center, of all places. The director of the center at the time was a gay man. The arrests also led to the creation of the Crescent City Coalition (CCC), founded by John Ognibene, which focused on direct action and public education.[10] CCC founding member Roger Nelson recalls that the CCC "grew out of a feeling in our community with the surfacing of police harassment that we needed a more active and community accountable civil rights organization than LAGPAC had been to that date. We wanted more activism and not just backing politicians we HOPED would back our civil rights."[11]

On May 4, John Ognibene, Rich Sacher, and others met with Mayor Dutch Morial with questions and six demands: 1) that all the charges against those arrested be dropped; 2) that an independent investigation be conducted into the motivation of the arrests; 3) that disciplinary action be taken against the arresting officers for harassment; 4) that regular meetings be held between the police, the mayor's office, and the gay community; 5) that sensitivity training be included in the police academy; and 6) that the mayor make a statement regarding nondiscrimination in his administration. Most of the demands were met; however, an independent investigation was never completed, and no officers were disciplined. The meeting also led to a police training program. At LAGPAC's urging, the city council authorized the establishment of the Office of Municipal Investigation to examine allegations of police misconduct.

Another complaint against the New Orleans Police Department involved the use of field interrogation cards. These were index cards that beat officers would use in the field to gather information about individuals in an effort to fight crime. Several gay men complained that they had been detained by police at random while the cards were filled out. The cards had been used in New Orleans, and other cities, for years. According to superintendent of police Henry Morris, the cards had helped reduce crime in the French Quarter significantly and homosexuals were not being targeted. LAGPAC disagreed.

Despite resistance from the police department, LAGPAC not only kept the pressure on but also attempted to establish goodwill with the department. In the summer of 1983, LAGPAC and the Crescent City Coalition held a fundraiser that netted $2,100 for new bulletproof vests for the department.

While fighting local battles against the police in New Orleans, LAGPAC also kept an eye on the state legislature in Baton Rouge. During the 1981 session, state senator Joseph Severio introduced a bill that would have required all teachers in the Louisiana public school system to officially declare if they were gay or straight. Friendly insiders at the capital advised LAGPAC leaders that the best way to kill the bill would be to quietly lobby a few key senators without drawing attention to the bill. LAGPAC took this advice, and the bill never got out of committee.

While Stewart fully immersed himself in politics, the same cannot be said for Alfred. Alfred sometimes accompanied Stewart to meetings and events—for example, both attended the Anita Bryant protest—but more often than not Alfred was content to stay home and tend to domestic matters while Stewart attended board meetings and strategy sessions.

Sometimes, Alfred would go out barhopping at night by himself. Stewart recalls one evening when Alfred had been out and returned home to retrieve some of the cash he kept in a drawer in his dresser. Stewart gave Alfred a lot of space, but when Alfred kept coming home for money, Stewart tried to reason with him, but Alfred would have none of it. When Stewart physically intervened, Alfred punched him in the jaw. Stewart was tempted to retaliate but wisely did not, realizing a fight would lead to no good end. On the whole, Alfred had a gentle, playful spirit, but on rare occasions, when mania gripped him, he could be given to fits of violence if provoked. Stewart understood this and dealt with it about as well as anyone could be expected to.

On at least one occasion, their outings to the bars resulted in both of them being victims of violence. On March 10, 1989, Stewart and Alfred arrived at the Roundup about 10:30 p.m. The Roundup was a dive bar that catered to hustlers of the "rough trade" variety. There, Stewart and Alfred met up with acquaintances Wesley Little and Michael Lee, both about twenty-one years old. The four had met at the bar a month prior. As Stewart and Alfred prepared to leave around 1:00 a.m., Little and Lee asked them for a ride to the home of one of their mothers on Marconi Drive near City Park. On the way, at City Park, one of the boys told Stewart, who was driving, he had to pee. Stewart pulled over, and Little and Lee got out of the vehicle to relieve themselves. They then attacked Stewart and Alfred with a brick and stole the car (a 1984 Toyota Tercel). Stewart and Alfred, bloody and dazed, were picked up by City Park police and brought to Touro Infirmary. Stewart was treated and released that night; Alfred was released the next afternoon. Both required stitches. According to the police report, Little and Lee had been banned from Lafitte's, Gregory's, Rawhide, and several other bars.

In an era before ATMs, it was not uncommon for Alfred to run out of money. Once, after a night of carousing, he called a cab to bring him home and, having no cash, paid the driver with a gold-plated tea set he had inherited from his grandmother. The next day Stewart called the cab company in an unsuccessful effort to retrieve the tea set.

Although founded in New Orleans, LAGPAC was to be a statewide organization. In the course of its political activities, LAGPAC realized the need for networking. The effort to establish a statewide network was greatly aided in 1981 when the Southeastern Conference of Lesbians and Gay Men (SCLGM) was held in Baton Rouge. The Baton Rouge conference was hosted by LSU's Students for Gay Awareness. The president of the student group at the time was Robert Udick, who would later serve on the LAGPAC board from 1984 to 1987 before moving to Syracuse, New York, to earn a PhD.[12]

The Southeastern Conference at LSU led to the creation of the Louisiana State Conference, which eventually became known as Celebration. Writing for the LAGPAC newsletter in June 1990, Stewart recalled the origins of the conference:

> This year LAGPAC celebrates its tenth anniversary, and this month many of us will be attending the Tenth Annual Louisiana State Gay Conference. However, this is only the eighth year that the conference has been called Celebration.
>
> There is a connection between all of this and more that might be appropriately recalled at this time. In a sense, it all started back in 1980 when a small contingent of L.S.U. Students for Gay Awareness members journeyed to Memphis, TN, for the annual Southeastern conference for Lesbians and Gay Men. Included in the group was Robert Udick, who is still today a LAGPAC member even while attending graduate school at Syracuse University.
>
> Anyway, these students were so overwhelmed by their Memphis experience that they got the notion they could pull off the 1981 Southeastern Conference at L.S.U. How dizzy can you get?

In the meantime, the Spring of 1981 was a heady time for LAGPAC, then less than a year old. In particular, the mass arrests for obstructing a sidewalk contributed to a doubling of the membership from some 200 early in the year to over 400 in the Fall. It was during that Spring that the Gay and Lesbian community provided the handful of votes that so affected the outcome of the primary election for an unexpired District D New Orleans City Council Seat as to permit Lambert Boissiere to go on to win the seat, which he holds to this day.

It was against this backdrop that a number of LAGPAC zealots decided that the conference at L.S.U. might provide a golden opportunity to expand the organization into the hinterlands of the state.

As for myself, who had been a student there from 1947 to 1951, I was hardly prepared for the words of greeting from the representative of the Chancellor. My flesh tingled as he proclaimed, " . . . and we hope you are as happy to be here as we are to have you." Wow! And that was just for openers. That conference, which was keynoted by our very own Larry Bagneris, went on to blow me totally away—truly, it was like being born again—and I went on to become a conference junkie.

Anyway, it was that conference which inspired LAGPAC to sponsor the First Louisiana State Gay Conference, which was held at the Country Club on Louisa St. October 9–11, 1981. Although only some 65 or 70 persons attended, it was deemed to be enough of a success to repeat the effort the following year.[13]

The second conference, also sponsored by LAGPAC alone, was held on December 4, 1982, at the Emporium bar at 2183 Highland Road in Baton Rouge. Although an uncommon winter deluge produced such flooding as to prevent the attendance of many from New Orleans, those who did make it were treated to a total of thirteen workshops on such subjects as culture, education, music, religion, arts, self-image, health (including an early-on presentation regarding AIDS), and social concerns. It was also the occasion for the first public performance for the newly formed New Orleans Gay Men's Chorus.

But even though there was only one workshop dealing with "politics" in the specific sense of the word, it was determined that a number of people didn't go because they perceived it to be too political. In an effort to overcome this incorrect impression, a nucleus of LAGPAC members secured the participation of representatives of almost all the other then existing gay and lesbian supportive organizations on an ad hoc committee. Thus it was in 1983 that Celebration with its fireworks logo of exploding lambdas came into existence.

Because there had been no GayFest in 1982 and there was some doubt as to whether there would be one in 1983, Celebration decided to schedule the Third Annual Louisiana State Gay Conference on the first Gay Pride weekend.

The Friday night pre-conference cocktail party with a live Dixieland jazz band in the newly opened and spectacular Menefee's on North Rampart Street was a smashing success. The next day, some two hundred gay men and lesbians descended on the Jazz Complex in Armstrong Park to attend a wide variety of workshops, break bread, and play and celebrate in a manner many before had never imagined possible. Celebration was off and running. In 1986, Celebration cosponsored the Southeastern Conference for Lesbians and Gay Men, from whence it came into being, at Tulane University. The annual Celebration conferences enjoyed a twenty-two-year run. In 1990, during an awards ceremony in which he was honored, Stewart reminisced:

> That small band of L.S.U. students who set out for Memphis ten years ago could not in their wildest dreams have imagined that they would set off a chain reaction that would inspire and uplift so many hundreds of their sisters and brothers over the years to come. It is those brave few who ventured forth and dared to seize the day to whom I today express gratitude and pay tribute.[14]

The conference that so inspired the LSU students to whom Stewart referred in his remarks had been founded in 1976 in North Carolina. In 1975, Tom Carr was a graduate student at the University of North Carolina at Chapel Hill. At a time when gay rights were a fairly new concept, Carr persuaded the city of Chapel Hill to pass an ordinance that protected gays and lesbians from discrimination. Carr was very active in the Carolina Gay Association (CGA), which had been founded by Dan Leonard, Michael Grissom, and others at UNC in 1974 to increase gay awareness on the campus. Carr, Leonard, Grissom, and the other early members of the CGA probably had no idea how influential their efforts would become, but they did have a vision, and that vision has positively impacted millions of LGBT+ folk over the last forty years, especially in Louisiana.

In 1976, Carr, working through the CGA, coordinated the first Southeastern Gay Conference (the name was later changed to the Southeastern Conference of Lesbians and Gay Men). Held at Chapel Hill, that first conference attracted hundreds of attendees from all over the South. The annual conference, held in cities across the South (including New Orleans in 1986), grew not only in numbers but also in stature, relevance, and influence. Joshua Burford, director of outreach and lead archivist for the Invisible Histories Project, notes, "The

Southeastern conference for Lesbian and Gays was an important event both to the dissemination of education and activism, but as a Southern specific answer to the question of how Queer organizing would happen outside of coastal cities. The conference provided blueprints for a new, organized Queer South created and controlled by Queer Southern people."[15]

In 1981, the conference was held in Baton Rouge on the LSU campus. A glance at the conference program from that year offers an insightful look at the issues gay folk were dealing with at the time. Consider the following workshop titles: "Gay Switchboards: Forming and Operating a Referral, Information and Crisis Line," "Suicide Prevention," "Hidden People: Social History of Gay People," "Gay Health Issues," "Establishing a State Organization and Lobbying Office," and "Using Political Systems: The Time is Now" (which was conducted by LAGPAC cofounder Roberts Batson).

One of the keynote speakers at the conference was Larry Bagneris, who was working in Houston for an insurance company. Bagneris had grown up in New Orleans and began his career as a civil rights activist at the age of sixteen by picketing the Maison Blanche department store's Jim Crow policies. He was arrested several times as a teenager for similar demonstrations at other locations. Bagneris took a job in Houston after college and joined the Houston Gay Political Caucus and spoke about the importance of diversity in gay political organizing. At the conference, Bagneris met Roberts Batson and other members of LAGPAC, who in the next few years would make periodic visits to Houston to meet with Bagneris and learn about what was going on there. In addition to his work with the Houston Gay Political Caucus, Bagneris also helped found and organize Houston Pride. Bagneris would return to New Orleans in 1986 and get involved with LAGPAC. Batson convinced him to run, unsuccessfully, for the city council in 1990 and the state legislature in 1991 and 1995. Bagneris worked as the community affairs director for the NO/AIDS Task Force from 1990 to 2000 and also served in the mayor's office on the human relations commission, eventually serving as its chair.

The conference program is also telling in what topics were not included. HIV/AIDS was not yet a blip on the gay radar screen; marriage equality and, to a lesser extent, gays serving openly in the military were inconceivable. In an era before the widespread use of personal computers, much less the internet, the primary focus was on sharing information—very basic, fundamental information that we often take for granted today. Gay political organizing in the South was in its nascent stage then, and its chief obstacle was rampant homophobia—both externally throughout society and internally for the untold millions still in the closet.

The 1981 conference in Baton Rouge was the first of several Southeastern Conferences Stewart attended. That first conference was a homecoming of sorts for Stewart. When Stewart enrolled at LSU in 1947, the notion of a gay conference was inconceivable. As he walked the campus at the conference, he remembered his undergraduate days there thirty years earlier. He didn't even realize he was gay then. Years later, Stewart recalled, "I could not believe it. There was nothing like that when I was there. But there we were."[16]

Reflecting on the experience, Butler recalls, "It opened my mind to the secondary status of women." He further noted, "It established the seed for the Louisiana state conference, which was held at the Country Club in the Bywater later that same year (1981)."[17] Held in October 1981, the first annual state gay conference was organized by LAGPAC members Alan Robinson and Liz Simon and featured workshops, speakers, and social events.

The Second Annual Louisiana Gay Conference was held in Baton Rouge in December 1982 at a gay bar called Emporium. The keynote speaker was Dr. Marcus Conant, president of the Kaposi's Sarcoma Research and Education Foundation. The leading AIDS researcher spoke on AIDS. This was the first time Stewart heard of the disease. Rain affected attendance at the conference. It was also at this conference that the New Orleans Gay Men's Chorus debuted. Glen O' Berry, a member of the chorus, suggested to conference organizers that since the conference was sponsored by LAGPAC some people may have thought the conference was exclusively political and therefore stayed away. The organizers agreed and began to reach out to other nonpolitical gay groups to participate in the conference. They also changed the name of the conference to Celebration. Thus, the Louisiana State Conference morphed into Celebration in 1983 and was held at Armstrong Park that year. The Celebration gatherings, which lasted into the 1990s, featured workshops, keynote speakers, musical entertainment, and food.

In 1984, Celebration was held at Bayou Plaza (at Tulane and South Carrollton) and featured Reverend Troy Perry, founder of the Metropolitan Community Church, as a keynote speaker as well as Virginia Apuzzo, executive director of the National Gay Task Force. It had been eleven years since the Up Stairs Lounge arson, and the New Orleans Perry experienced in 1984 was much different than the one he encountered in 1973. Not only had the closet door been kicked off its hinges, the community was actually organizing and asserting itself.

Not unexpectedly, Celebration eventually drew protesters. In 1986, it was held at Tulane University in conjunction with SECLGM. About six hundred people attended the conference, including newly elected New Orleans mayor Sidney Barthelemy, on whom Stewart personally impressed the need for gay and transgender rights. The four-day series of over one hundred work-shops, seminars, and lectures included nationally known speakers such as Dr. Mathilde Krim, Lea Hopkins, and David Scondras. Covering Celebration for *Impact*, Patrick Shannon encountered a small group of protesters outside McAlister Auditorium carrying signs with homophobic messages. Shannon recalls being confronted by one of the protesters:

> "Hey, who the hell are you, anyway? Are you with a newspaper?"
>
> "Yeah," I responded, walking away, "I represent the national gay press. Who do you represent?"
>
> "None of your business, buttfucker!" he snarled.
>
> "By this time, several female attendees arrived and enclosed me in a sort of circle. I walked away with my escort of women, a brave wall of no-nonsense lesbians. Thanks again, ladies, we couldn't do anything without you."[18]

Stewart attended Celebrations and remained on the board until 1986, when he fell into a disagreement with some of the other board members over the inclusion of nongay attendees. Some wanted a no heterosexual rule, but Stewart had invited Johnny Jackson, a straight political ally on the city council to participate in the conference. After a particularly heated meeting, Stewart received a letter accepting his resignation from the board. Celebration would go on to last another nineteen years.

Stewart recalled the incident in 2011 during an interview with Mark Cave:

> But as time went on, you know, after '86, you know, it's time for me to go. I stay on the board of directors, but I didn't like the direction in which it was going, because we were always very, very open about it and could invite anybody we wanted, including politicians and all, but in this one year, because of two or three people who didn't want their homosexuality to come out, they said just lesbians and gays can come to this. And so whereupon I decided that I would invite Councilman Johnny Jackson [phonetic], who had been the point person on our eventually getting a gay ordinance passed in New Orleans. I'm not sure when that was. It was around 1990. So I invited Johnny Jackson, so when they found out I got a letter that says "We accept your res-ignation from the board." [laughs] And then they turned it into an all-female function, not that males couldn't go, but there was nothing there for males. I mean all the entertainment, all the speakers, all the workshops all had to do with lesbians. And then it petered out.[19]

Celebration is just one example of the conferences and efforts that were spawned by the SECLGM. The Southeastern Conferences had a profound effect on gay organizing all across the South. This was especially true not only in Louisiana but also in Alabama. In Birmingham, Ron Joullian had founded LAMBDA in 1977, which in turn led to the founding of the Alabama Conference, a gay sports league, and the newspaper *Alabama Forum*. LAMBDA also provided meeting space for the Metropolitan Community Church, a gay Alcoholics Anonymous group, and other organizations. When the AIDS crisis appeared, members of LAMBDA created the Birmingham AIDS Outreach and the AIDS Task Force of Alabama.

Joullian met Stewart at the 1983 Southeastern Conference in Atlanta, where Stewart conducted a workshop on the topic of internalized homophobia. Joullian was impressed and kept in touch with Stewart. Eventually, both Joullian and Stewart would serve on the SECLGM board of directors, and it was through their work on the board that the two cemented a close friendship. Joullian recalls, "We were neophytes, and Stewart was a mentor."[20]

Reminiscing on the conference thirty-two years later, Joullian observes, "It was quite an eye-opener for this little group of country bumpkins from Birmingham."[21] Joullian and his partner, Tim Angle, became friends with Stewart and Alfred and eventually moved to New Orleans. Joullian remembers the Memphis Conference, which drew over six hundred attendees:

At one point, the hotel wanted to back out of the conference but organizers persisted. Afterward, the hotel said that the attendees were probably the nicest to ever have a conference there. On Sunday morning, a group of "Christian" protesters came to the hotel and began signing hymns and were met by conference attendees on the opposite side of the driveway joining in with them. This was the first such conference for future Faerie Playhouse members Rick Adams, Tim Angle and Ron Joullian. We had become involved in the fledgling Lambda, Inc. of Birmingham founded in 1977. Journeying the back roads from Birmingham to Memphis we were awestruck by the Conference's size, the participation and energized by the conference attendees. This was the beginning of our future involvement in the Conferences, our meeting Stewart and our hosting the 1984 Conference where the Conference was incorporated. We also travelled the next year to the Baton Rouge conference, although we didn't recall meeting Stewart until the 1983 Atlanta Conference. It was there that we met Louisiana activist Blanchard "Skip" Ward with whom we later formed bonds of affection as a mutual friend of Stewart. There was a dramatic shift at the

Baton Rouge Conference with intense discussions concerning Lesbian, Feminist concerns. Although the issues needed to be discussed, I personally feared the intensity of feeling and emotions might jeopardize future Conference unity. I do recall meeting New Orleans' other Stewart friends Dr. Niki Kearby and her partner Betty Cardwell who made a calming and impressive presence there among the interchanges.[22]

Considering the social milieu in which the Southeastern Conference was founded, the phenomenal success of the SECLGM was inevitable. Butler, Joullian, and others who attended the Southeastern Conferences recall them fondly, often using adjectives like "energizing," "electrifying," and "inspiring." When once asked why the SECLGM was so significant, Butler looked at the interviewer as though he had just checked in from another planet and said, "The dispensation of sorely needed information." When asked the same question, Joullian responded, "We gays from rural areas got to meet other gays, and afterward we didn't feel so alone."

While LAGPAC was getting started, it enjoyed some surprising successes and not unexpected opposition, but one of its earliest threats came not from religious fanatics or right-wingers, but rather from within its own community. The issue of gender bias within LAGPAC first surfaced as early as 1981, when LAGPAC members Danny Frank and Wayne Denny made and carried a banner in the GayFest parade (a forerunner to Pride) that featured an image of Uncle Sam declaring "LAGPAC wants you!" Some lesbians found the banner sexist and offensive, and it was decided to feature the Statue of Liberty on the banner for the 1982 parade. But the issue of what we would now call cis-gay male privilege really reared its head when Rich Sacher and Henry Schmidt, representing Dignity (a gay Catholic organization) and another group called GLAD (Gays and Lesbians Against Discrimination) proposed to the LAGPAC board that it boycott Café Lafitte in Exile and the Bourbon Pub for their policies of not allowing women and African Americans into their bars.

LAGPAC appointed a "Select Committee on Discrimination Within the Gay Community." At a board meeting on February 21, 1981, committee member Syndie Reames reported the committee's recommendation that it join Dignity and GLAD in signing the following advertisement, which was to be published in *Impact*:

Are You a Bigot?
The time has come for the gay community of New Orleans to abolish the blatant sexist and racist discrimination practiced by some of our

bars. It is hypocrisy for us to demand our full civil rights from the straight political establishment while we ignore the harassment and humiliation of our fellow gay men and women suffer as their civil rights are violated at the door of the gay bar. We are taking a stand on this issue—will you? How about now?

Roberts Batson offered a minority report in opposition, citing that LAG-PAC's mission statement did not include racial or gender discrimination. The motion failed by a vote of 2–5. Melanie Miranda and Pat Denton voted in favor; Este Armstrong, Roberts Batson, Jean Carr, Alan Robinson, and Stewart voted against joining the boycott.

The board rejected the proposal, citing that its mission statement only covered sexual orientation. But this was only a guise; the real reason was more nuanced. Some felt that at this embryonic and fragile stage of its existence, LAGPAC should not wander into the controversy. Complicating the issue was the fact that the bar owners, Tom Wood (Café Lafitte in Exile) and Jerry Menefee (the Bourbon Pub), were members of LAGPAC (Menefee served on the development committee). The board's decision not to join the boycott almost destroyed LAGPAC. Years later, in a 1990 workshop at Celebration, Stewart acknowledged the decision was a mistake.

The vote caused a backlash among the general membership and some of the board of directors. Melanie Miranda and Pat Denton abruptly departed the meeting and subsequently resigned from the board. In her resignation letter, Denton chastised the board for its hypocrisy:

Having thought that this organization opposed and would stand against discrimination based on sex as well as that based on sexual preference . . . And being further led to believe that LAGPAC stood for full access to public accommodations as stated in its recently set goals, but finding that in actuality (by virtue of its refusing to take a stand against existing and blatant sexual discrimination being practiced by some gay bars—one in particular going so far as to publicly display a "Men Only" sign—it gives tacit approval to discrimination based on sex, I must conclude that the majority of this Board does not stand for full equality for all people.[23]

Denton's seat was filled by the appointment of Liz Simon to the board, but before Simon accepted, she had a few concerns of her own. Simon had earned an MA in social work from Tulane University and worked in private practice as a therapist for a primarily gay and lesbian clientele. Simon was not new to activism; she had previously served as chair of Women Against Violence Against Women and on the board of the YWCA Battered Women's Program. She had also been involved in the Gertrude Stein Society and was a founding member of LAGPAC. Simon agreed to join the board on the condition it conduct a weekend-long workshop on "oppression dynamics." Simon remembers,

> Many members of the Board were taken aback and resented my proposal. However, Stewart was one of the first main players who immediately supported me and thought it showed I would be a good asset in planning Political Strategy on lots of levels . . . I will always remember Stewart's immediate support, which never wavered in the 20+ years that followed where we worked closely on the grassroots level to promote the cause of LGBTQ+ freedom from persecution and less than honorable treatment.[24]

Simon also formed a lesbian-feminist caucus within the auspices of LAGPAC.

Despite the board's efforts to contain the damage from its controversial decision, several LAGPAC members also quit the organization over the issue, some writing excoriating letters. Stewart attempted to do damage control by reaching out to several disgruntled members with limited success. One wrote to him,

> Dear Stew, Thanks but NO thanks, and believe me I've "carefully considered" LAGPAC—and discover each time I have only feelings of CONTEMPT for it. I see its members running around changing everyone else's house—but nothing is done at home. I sincerely hope our rich and powerful Bar Owners support LAGPAC in every way—for staying out of their way . . . If your membership is down, I feel good. Try C.C.C.—that's what I tell people—especially if they are black or female. Sorry Stew, but like I said I have nothing but CONTEMPT for LAGPAC—PLEASE remove my name from your mailing list—and be thankful I stay away.[25]

LAGPAC received letters not only from its own members but also from other organizations encouraging it to examine its own prejudices and privilege. One such letter came from Louisiana Sissies in Struggle: "By setting goals that will predominantly benefit people of European origins and holding events in gay establishments that are openly racist (Bourbon Pub/Parade

Disco) LAGPAC is endorsing the institutions of white supremacists and white racism in America—if not in rhetoric, certainly in practice."[26]

If anything, the boycott controversy and the tangled web of race and privilege nerves it exposed revealed that there were sharp divisions withing the wider LGBT+ movement. In subsequent years, LAGPAC would make genuine efforts to overcome these divisions, but to a certain extent, they persisted. On the subject of race, Kenneth Mitchell remembers one particularly memorable LAGPAC meeting a few years after the boycott:

> At one of our well-attended meetings there was a lull in the discussion. Alfred blurted out a question, unrelated to the agenda but probably on the minds of at least a few others in attendance. I know it was on my mind. Alfred was sitting in the front of the room while I was sitting in the rear. Now mind you this was a pretty large-sized room. All the way in the back I heard Alfred ask in his loud and strong voice, "Where are all the Black people?" It seemed to have come out of nowhere. A period of awkward silence followed. I don't know if this was due to no one having an answer or was it due to people being stunned that, alas, someone had addressed the proverbial pink elephant in the living room. I do know that soon afterwards, the organization Langston/Jones Society, an offshoot of LAGPAC, for people of color, was started.[27]

Another important development in 1982 was the formation of the New Orleans Regional Chapter of LAGPAC (NORCO). The creation of this chapter in the spring enabled the state board to concentrate on developing chapters in other parts of the state. A Baton Rouge chapter (BRAGPAC) was founded in the fall. An Acadiana chapter would soon follow. In 1983, NORCO continued to flex its political muscle: out of the eleven candidates for public office endorsed by LAGPAC, eight won their races, including Mayor Morial and Miriam Waltzer—the first woman elected as a criminal court judge in New Orleans. Several members were active in the Democratic State Central Committee, and Co-Chair Jean Carr and board member Roberts Batson continued lobbying US Representative Bob Livingston and cultivating a relationship with the Louisiana congressional delegation.

In June 1983, Alan Robinson traveled around the state on a fact-finding and information-sharing mission. The weeklong statewide tour had been authorized by the LAGPAC board of directors, which charged Robinson with three tasks: 1) inform people around the state about LAGPAC; 2) learn the

issues, concerns, and potential of the gay community in various cities; and
3) establish an AIDS Lobby Network (ALN). Robinson traveled to seven cities
and, when he returned to New Orleans, wrote a report of his observations.

Robinson's report is fascinating in that it offers a unique glimpse into
LGBT+ Louisiana outside of New Orleans in the summer of 1983. In every
city Robinson visited, there was a tremendous need and desire for accurate
information regarding AIDS. In Shreveport, Robinson attended part of that
city's Gay Pride Week, which featured a Mr. and Mrs. Gay Pride Pageant, a
costume ball, a pool tournament and other bar events, and a picnic attended
by over one hundred people. Shreveport's Gay Pride Week had been organized by Joe Hutson and John Benson. Hutson and Benson had consulted
and worked closely with New Orleans native Larry Bagneris, who had previously organized Houston's Gay Pride.

Robinson made two contacts in Monroe, whom he did not name, and
left LAGPAC brochures at two gay bars—Twin City Landing and Apertif,
which he describes as "mixed." In Natchitoches and Alexandria, Robinson
made solid contacts for the AIDS Lobby Network. Alexandria boasted two
gay bars—Silly Sallie's and the Union Station. In Alexandria, Robinson met
with Debbie Salser, who led a religious group called the United Church of
Faith, which had something of a following around central Louisiana. Robinson noted that the local chapter of NOW in Alexandria had dissolved
and reported that even the League of Women Voters there was divided over
whether or not to support the ERA. In Lake Charles, he met with the owner
of a bar called Paragon, who viewed the bar as a communication center for
the area. He also reported that the Metropolitan Community Church and
Dignity were active in Lake Charles. Like Shreveport, Lafayette was having
a week of Gay Pride events when Robinson was in town. GayFest Acadiana
shared a lot of members with Acadiana MCC. Randy Chestnut, owner of a
bar called Fantasy, one of three gay bars in Lafayette, made his bar available
for LAGPAC meetings and expressed a willingness to get involved. And in
New Iberia, he met with two men who agreed to forms a LAGPAC chapter
there as well as work with the AIDS Lobby Network.

Working closely with the AIDS Project of the Gay Rights National Lobby,
the ALN focused its energy on lobbying Congress and the state legislature for
increased funding of medical research, financial assistance for medications
for those who had been diagnosed with HIV, and education. Active in the
network were the Gay Pride Committee of Shreveport, Acadian MCC, Le
Beau Monde in Alexandria, the Baton Rouge and New Orleans chapters of
LAGPAC, as well as individuals in Monroe, Natchitoches, and New Iberia.

LAGPAC eventually did expand to other cities throughout the state, including Baton Rouge, Acadiana, Alexandria, and Shreveport. Membership and activity fluctuated in various chapters; for example, the Acadia chapter was on and off every few years, despite the earnest efforts of hardworking volunteers.[28] BRAGPAC, the Baton Rouge chapter, perhaps because it was the capital city and also because of its size, was fairly strong in the early years of LAGPAC but suffered periodic bouts of dormancy in subsequent years. The New Orleans chapter, however, was consistently active.

LAGPAC's man in central Louisiana was Skip Ward. Central and north Louisiana are about as Deep South as it gets—land of Baptists and Pentecostals: a desolate cultural hellscape of ignorance, racism, and homophobia. It was, and, to some extent, still is, a very lonely place for LGBT+ people. Until recently, virtually all closet doors were cemented shut, and life behind them was hopeless and dark. But in 1971, Skip Ward came out of the closet and, in so doing, raised a beacon of light and hope to untold thousands.

Ward and his partner, Gene Barnes, began publishing a gay themed newsletter and formed Le Beau Monde in 1981. Le Beau Monde was an informal social group of gay people who met regularly to "explore the humanistic and spiritual aspects of being gay." As the CEN-LA chapter of LAGPAC fizzled, Le Beau Monde became something of an ersatz substitute.[29]

Spirituality had always been an integral part of Ward's life. As a child, his grandmother instilled in him a strong mistrust of organized religion, especially Christianity. Ward eventually became a lifelong Unitarian Universalist and went on to cofound the Unitarian Universalist Church's Gay Caucus. Ward became associated with the Radical Faeries (a national organization for rural-based gender and sexual nonconforming spiritualists) and in 1994, he and Barnes acquired twelve acres of land in north Louisiana and called it Manitou Woods. It became a retreat space for spiritual communion and meditation. In 1987, Ward wrote, "I'm not sure where we should be going with our new-found spiritual consciousness. We are walking forth upon new ground, watered by streams of paganism, faerie spirituality, shamanism, and a revival of berdache spirituality."[30]

The aforementioned quote is from a letter Ward wrote in response to a letter he received from a gay man in New Mexico who was curious about gay spirituality. This was just one of dozens of gay men who wrote Ward seeking advice. Ward took the time to respond to all of them, and his letters are beautiful expressions of wisdom and courage. Take for example the following excerpts. To a closeted man: "Still trying with women, you wrote. If it had worked for me, just screwing women, I'd not be gay today. Many have tried this. Sure, you can get married, have kids, etc., but you'll never cease to look longingly at certain people of your own sex."[31] To yet another he wrote, "I learned long ago that for me it is thoughtful, considerate, and kind to leave women alone. Why involve one of them in a hopeless relationship, doomed to incompleteness. Women deserve someone who can love them unreservedly, unconditionally. And so do men!"[32] And to a man who had just come out of the closet in 1983 and was fearful of the consequences: "How can ignorant, but maybe well-meaning people threaten or hurt us anymore? Together we have no fear to tangle with wildcats. And we can climb Everest too, because we are learning the rewards of courage with its concomitant of prudence."[33]

In all these letters of hope and encouragement, there are undertones of quiet confidence and profound wisdom delivered in a gentle fraternal spirit. In other letters, letters to politicians, Ward adopts a tone of moral indignation and challenges the bigotry and prejudice espoused by these politicians.

Skip Ward was a voice—often the only voice—for thousands of gay people in rural Louisiana (indeed, throughout the South) who had chosen silence and invisibility. In speaking on their behalf, he also challenged them to find their own voices. In this regard, Skip Ward was a visionary who offered courage to a people that desperately needed it. He was ahead of his time. When he died in 2009, part of his remains was buried in the memorial garden behind the Faerie Playhouse.

As LAGPAC entered its second decade in the 1990s, new leadership within the organization would rise. Among these leaders were Eddie Domingue and Chris Daigle. Christopher Daigle was a banker before he became a gay activist in the early 1990s. Educated at Loyola University, Fairfield University, and Dartmouth College, Daigle settled in New Orleans and took a job as the director of the Office of Lesbian, Gay, Bisexual, and Transgender Life at Tulane University. Daigle became involved in LAGPAC and led the organization for roughly ten years. He joined the board of directors in 1993 and became co-chair in 1994.

Daigle brought to LAGPAC an impressive array of experience: he co-chaired the 1993 Louisiana March on Washington Committee, was the principal organizer of the 1993 March on Mississippi, was the former director of the Lesbian and Gay Community Center in New Orleans, was a member of the HRC Steering Committee, was a member of the Gender Bias Study Group, was a member of Mayor Morial's transition team on HIV and AIDS issues, was a member of the New Orleans Regional AIDS Planning Council, and worked on numerous political campaigns. He ran unsuccessfully for the state house of representatives in 2005, finishing third behind Juan LaFonta and Michael McKenna.

In late 2004, the state representative for District 96 in New Orleans, Ed Murray, was elected to the state senate. A special election to fill the vacancy was held on January 29, 2005. Five candidates ran for the open seat, including Daigle, who was LAGPAC co-chair at the time. Daigle's decision to run was not without controversy. Several LAGPAC members strongly urged Daigle not to run, but he did anyway. This decision alienated some people. Daigle lost the election, finishing in third place. Juan LaFonta won the seat.

After the election, Daigle reported the LAGPAC computer stolen. This meant the loss of the extensive LAGPAC mailing list, which at the time contained over five thousand names. By this time, Daigle had been leading LAGPAC for ten years.

Daigle and his partner, Rick Cosgriff, lived a block and a half away from the Faerie Playhouse and became friends with Stewart and Alfred. Cosgriff, who was originally from North Dakota, worked on political campaigns in California, including Harvey Milk's race for the San Francisco Board of Supervisors in 1978, before moving in 1990 to New Orleans, where he became involved in AIDS activism as well as LAGPAC, serving on its board for much of the 1990s. In 2002, he served as the director of a homeless youth shelter.

Reminiscing on the evolution of LAGPAC's leadership, longtime member Glenn Ducote recalls, "Eddie Domingue bridged the gap between Batson and Daigle. After the Batson era, Chris became the energy force."[34] Like Daigle, Edward "Eddie" Domingue brought a lot to the LAGPAC table. Educated at the University of New Orleans, Domingue served as the operations manager for a New Orleans manufacturing firm. He joined the LAGPAC board in 1993 and became treasurer in 1994. Similarly, he had previously served on the board and as treasurer of the Lesbian and Gay Community Center of New Orleans. In addition, he was a member of the NO/AIDS Task Force, PFLAG, LEGAL, and the Forum for Equality, and he served on the mayor's advisory committee on LGBT+ issues. A member of the gay Carnival krewe Polyphemus, Domingue had run as an openly gay candidate for the Orleans Parish Democratic Executive Committee. In later years, Domingue would be involved with Project Lazarus and Halloween New Orleans.

Domingue served as treasurer of LAGPAC for nine years and as co-chair for three years. Remembering how he became involved, Domingue recalls:

My involvement started at the stuffing envelope level. I attended my first general meeting and knew that I wanted to help in some way. That original stuffing party happened at Stewart and Alfred's place. I met Chris Daigle at this stuffing party and we became immediate friends.

Over the next couple months Chris got me more and more involved with LAGPAC till eventually I ran for Treasurer. From the first time I met Stewart he came across as very dedicated and committed to the LGBT movement. I always found his knowledge of the history of the New Orleans movement to be very insightful. Alfred was nice but a bit unusual. I remember a night at Stewart and Alfred's when we stuffed envelopes for LAGPAC. Alfred actually showed up to stuff with no clothes on. Stewart got him to at least put on some shorts.[35]

In 2001, Domingue, along with Rabbi Edward Cohn, Deyette Danford, and Laurie Reed, was presented LAGPAC's coveted Community First Award. The annual Awards Gala had been founded in 1996 as a way to honor individuals who had significantly contributed to the LGBT+ community. At that time, Domingue observed:

I have to admit that my initial drive for volunteering was selfish. I started out volunteering for the NO/AIDS Task Force to meet people. Over time, I have grown to appreciate my mother's comments that when you give of yourself, you usually get back more than you give. Over the last 15-plus years, I have volunteered with various organizations within our community, and I have received more than I have given. The friends I have made, the feelings of accomplishment—I know one day I will leave this world a little better than when I came into it.[36]

In 1995, LAGPAC turned fifteen years old. To commemorate the anniversary, three events were held, the first of which was a party at the home of Andre de la Barre and Scott Gentry in June. In August, Arthur Roger hosted a reunion of members and candidates LAGPAC had endorsed over the years. The event featured an exhibit of memorabilia highlighting the group's accomplishments since its founding. And in October, on the eve of the Alliance of Pride parade, LAGPAC held an endorsement meeting where legislative candidates courted the group.

Sometimes LAGPAC-endorsed candidates who won their races ended up betraying the LGBT+ community. Such was the case in 1995 when a furor erupted during the gubernatorial campaign when former governor Buddy Roemer publicly attacked Lieutenant Governor Melinda Schwegmann (both of whom LAGPAC endorsed in 1991) for a program the Louisiana State Museum, the administration of which falls under the lieutenant governor's office, called "Pride in Our Heritage: Lesbian and Gay History in Louisiana." The panel discussion was the brainchild of Wayne Phillips, who at the time was assistant curator of exhibits and programs, and featured three panelists: Roberts Batson, Rich Magill, and Karen Trahan Leathern.

Roemer held a press conference and attacked Schwegmann for "being out of touch" and "not having her priorities straight." The attack took Schwegmann by surprise, and she initially responded by claiming not to know anything about the program. LAGPAC then obtained and publicized a letter from Schwegmann to museum director James Sefcik in which she wrote:

> Had I been consulted, I would have told you that I don't see this as an appropriate subject for the State Museum. While I don't believe government can effectively dictate lifestyle choices, such as sexual preference, I also don't believe we ought to exalt alternative lifestyle choices through programs such as this. I do not endorse this program. If the topic is "Pride in Our Heritage," I'm certain you could find many other, more fitting subjects to explore.[37]

LAGPAC took both candidates to task for their blatant homophobia. The public controversy ultimately helped promote the panel discussion; attendance at the event far exceeded all expectations. Phillips remembers, "The room was packed."[38]

In 2002, under the leadership of Daigle and co-chair Melinda Shelton, LAGPAC could point to several accomplishments. It had been instrumental in persuading the New Orleans City Council to pass an ordinance in September 2001 that extended health benefits to same-sex partners of city employees. It also had a deep influence in the recent citywide elections—it endorsed candidates in sixteen races, including the mayoral race as well as every city council race. Over 250 people attended its mayoral candidate forum, and LAGPAC conducted Election Day poll watching at a dozen precincts with heavy LGBT+ populations. And it had successfully worked with allies in Baton Rouge to provide LGBT+ focused sensitivity training to that city's police department.

In 2003, state representative (and future New Orleans mayor) Mitch Landrieu announced his candidacy for lieutenant governor. Randy Evans ran for the state house seat vacated by Landrieu. Evans had run unsuccessfully for the seat twice before in 1995 and 1999. In both of those races, LAGPAC had endorsed Landrieu. Some found this odd since Evans was not only gay but also a founding member of the Forum for Equality. He had helped steer the nondiscrimination ordinance to passage in 1991 as well as the domestic partners ordinance in 1993.[39] He was also a cofounder of the Lesbian and Gay Community Center and the Louisiana Log Cabin Republicans. When he sought LAGPAC's endorsement in 2003, he stated that he remained in the Republican Party because he believed in its philosophy of less government and that he wanted to provide an alternative to the Christian Coalition, which in the early 2000s was gaining control of Republican State Central Committees across the nation. With the exception of Daigle, Evans had an excellent, collaborative relationship with most of LAGPAC's leadership.

By 2004, LAGPAC had changed its name to Equality Louisiana. The leadership agreed a fresh image was needed. Membership and interest had declined. And times were changing too. The year 2003 witnessed tangible manifestations in a massive paradigm shift in the way most Americans viewed homosexuality: the Supreme Court's landmark decision *Lawrence v. Texas* declared all state sodomy laws unconstitutional, the popularity of *Queer Eye for the Straight Guy* took everyone by surprise, and the move toward same-sex marriage was picking up steam in several states.

In 2004, one of Equality Louisiana's leaders, local attorney Randal Beach, left New Orleans after it was discovered that the accountant at his law firm (one Gerard Beaudoin, whose name, it was later discovered, turned out to be false) was embezzling money from the firm. Beaudoin, who was also very involved in LAGPAC, eventually fled the country only to resurface recently in Oregon, where he was arrested for another fraud.

Beach had been a LAGPAC board member since 1995 and served as secretary in 1997. In addition, he had been an attorney and president of a life insurance company; a member of the governor's task force on local government finance in 1988; executive director of the Louisiana Conference of Mayors, 1987–1988; the chief administrative officer for City of Baton Rouge, 1984–1988; the state deputy commissioner of insurance, 1992–1994; a member of the Mayor's advisory committee on LGBT+ issues, and a member of the HRC's Federal Club.

In that year, Stewart, along with Dr. Jody Gates, received the Community First Award from Equality Louisiana. In his acceptance speech, Stewart said: "I strongly advocate that Equality Louisiana follow a policy very recently adopted by the HRC. I have not contributed to the HRC for almost a decade because they have supported non-discrimination legislation that was non-inclusive of discrimination based on gender identity or expression. I urge Equality Louisiana and all of its members to follow HRC's lead and exclude no one for political expediency."[40]

Spirits were high at the annual banquet, but few could foresee that Equality Louisiana's days were numbered. By 2006, the group was no more. LAGPAC fizzled out, according to Stewart, because Chris Daigle neglected membership and fundraising. Stewart had previously stepped back from being chair of the membership committee and the board of directors because the group was too identified with him. Also, he became more involved in PFLAG. LAGPAC/Equality Louisiana's death knell came on August 29, 2005, with the arrival of Hurricane Katrina, which scattered not only the membership but also several key leaders.

Reflecting on the decline of LAGPAC, as many still referred to it, Eddie Domingue theorizes:

> I believe that the decline of LAGPAC started with the loss of Chris Daigle's run for state legislator. All of us were highly invested in Chris's race and when he loss we all took it hard. We tried to continue our work but for me personally it was never the same. Soon after that loss my partner got real sick and passed away. I left LAGPAC to deal with him so I'm not completely sure what led to the final demise of LAGPAC. I know toward the end Chris Daigle had several health issues and he was the back-bone of LAGAPC.[41]

Throughout its existence, LAGPAC made many strides, its greatest singular achievement being the passage of the nondiscrimination ordinance in 1991. The group was incredibly successful at organizing, mobilizing, and raising awareness. Yet, the gains were gradual. Although LAGPAC did manage to open some hearts and minds, many more hearts and minds remained closed. Despite what can only be described as "baby steps" with the New Orleans Police Department, the force remained predominantly homophobic. The amount of time, money, and resources the city spent on trying to suppress homosexuality is truly amazing. Consider the case of the short-lived Decatur Street Bookshop.

In 1986, Larry Lingle and his partner Bill White opened a gay-themed bookstore on lower Decatur Street in the French Quarter. Although it was a legitimate bookstore (for a while, Lingle also owned the legendary Oscar Wilde Memorial Bookshop in New York City and LOBO in Dallas), the Decatur Street Bookshop also sold gay pornography. Almost immediately, the New Orleans Police Department began investigating the bookstore. Undercover agents began frequenting the shop, which was under police surveillance. In addition, the police department rented an apartment across from owner Bill White's residence on Royal Street so they could keep his comings and goings under twenty-four-hour surveillance. White was eventually arrested and struck a plea bargain before the case went to trial. White's lawyer estimated the New Orleans Police Department spent over $100,000 on the whole operation.

Public attitudes toward homosexuality in New Orleans would eventually begin to shift in the 1990s for a variety of reasons, not the least of which was the phenomenal growth of Southern Decadence after the advent of the internet. The annual Labor Day extravaganza had begun in 1972 with a house party and by the 1980s was focused around the traditional Sunday parade. Originally, Southern Decadence was not a gay event, although some of the founders and early participants were gay. The "gaying" of Decadence occurred in the 1980s and, until the late 1990s, was primarily a French Quarter event for locals in the know. After Rip and Marsha Naquin-Delain began promoting the event online in the mid-1990s, the festival grew exponentially. In 2018, an estimated three hundred thousand out-of-town visitors came to New Orleans for Southern Decadence and had an economic impact of over $275 million. As Southern Decadence grew, so did its economic impact.

LAGPAC had paved the way for LGBT+ activism in New Orleans by being the first organization to bring LGBT+ rights to the forefront of the city's political conscience. By the end of the 1980s, there were other political action groups as well as an entire network of organizations that arose in response to the AIDS epidemic. The vast array of political campaigns, legislative fights, discrimination lawsuits, and health challenges required extraordinary collaboration.

Chapter 7

WORKING WITH OTHERS

Stewart was very passionate, and he would go to battle for whatever
he thought was right, but sometimes you can get what you want without going to battle.
—RANDY EVANS

LAGPAC TURNED SEVEN YEARS OLD IN 1987 AND COULD LOOK BACK WITH
pride on what it had accomplished in its early years: it had mastered the art
of grassroots campaigning and getting out the vote; it had demonstrated the
value of its endorsement; it had effectively helped elect openly gay and lesbian
candidates to the New Orleans Democratic and Republican Executive Committees, State Central Committees, and the National Democratic Convention; it had been instrumental in achieving an ongoing dialogue between the
lesbian and gay community and the New Orleans Police Department; it had
sponsored the first two Louisiana State Conferences and cosponsored each of
the ensuing Celebration conferences, as well as the eleventh annual SECLGM,
which was held at Tulane University; it had been instrumental in persuading
Congresswoman Lindy Boggs to cosponsor the national gay and lesbian civil
rights bill; it had convinced New Orleans mayor Dutch Morial to issue a policy
memorandum banning discrimination in city employment based on sexual
orientation; it had been a principal cosponsor of the Sexual Privacy Project,
which challenged the constitutionality of Louisiana's "crimes against nature"
statute; and, perhaps most significantly, LAGPAC had raised the visibility of
the LGBT+ community across the state. Throughout all these achievements, it
had educated the public—both politicians and voters—about homosexuality.

Stewart, who had served on the LAGPAC board since 1981, was elected
secretary of the organization in 1987, a position he had held a few years earlier. Karen Button, who had been heavily involved with Celebration and, to a
lesser extent, the Metropolitan Community Church and the NO/AIDS Task
Force, and Roy Racca, who had served as statewide secretary and co-chair of

the Acadiana chapter, were elected co-chairs. The following years would witness more progress—voter registration drives, lobbying the state legislature as well as numerous candidate interviews and endorsements, opposition to Robert Bork's appointment to the Supreme Court, a protest of Pope John Paul II's visit to New Orleans, participation in the second National March on Washington for Lesbian and Gay Rights, a protest of the Republican National Convention, the Sexual Privacy Project, a lawsuit challenging the state's prohibition against sodomy, and the fight for more HIV/AIDS funding. These challenges and opportunities were far more than any one person or group could handle. Groups, and individuals, that did not necessarily like each other or see eye to eye on some issues had to work together.

Despite its successes throughout the 1980s, LAGPAC endured disappointments as well, chief of which were two failed attempts at persuading the New Orleans City Council to pass a nondiscrimination ordinance in 1984 and 1986. After the second time the ordinance failed to pass, some proponents in the community began to think that perhaps a different strategy was needed. LAGPAC had broken ground by being the first gay activist group to aggressively advance a sustained queer political agenda in Louisiana, but the group was, in many ways, not as effective as it could have been due to its lack of experience. LAGPAC was a grassroots organization, and many of its most passionate adherents did not come from political backgrounds, nor did they have deep, insider connections to the political establishment.

In 1989, Randy Evans, a Republican attorney with political ambitions of his own, gathered four of his friends to discuss the idea of forming a political action group.[1] The group met a few times and brainstormed and then held a larger meeting at the home of Dr. Brobson Lutz. One of the twenty-five or so people in attendance was Susan Clade, who expressed frustration over a failed attempt earlier that year to form a lesbian action group called Lesbian Agenda. Recounting the internal squabbles that prevented Lesbian Agenda from getting off the ground, Clade described their early meetings as a lot of "wasted energy."[2] After a productive meeting, the group decided to form a political action group with a realistic, no-nonsense approach. Practicality, not ideological purity, would be the organization's guiding principle. Thus, the Forum for Equality was born. Within the first month of its existence, Jim Wiggins alone recruited over one hundred members. Membership grew rapidly and consisted mostly of upper-middle-class professionals who had business and political ties. The Forum, as it was commonly called, offered the candidates it endorsed both volunteers and financial donations.

If LAGPAC was the radical revolutionary fueled by ideological rage banging on the city gates, the Forum was that member of the establishment already inside the gates who attempted to affect change from within. The Forum was conservative in nature and therefore much more amenable than LAGPAC to endorse republican candidates. As an ideologue, Stewart criticized the Forum because of its more reserved approach to politics. Years later, referring to the group's name, he recalled "not a word in the title about being gay."[3] He also criticized the Forum because they did not issue endorsements for president, a charge the Forum responded to by pointing out they were a local organization. The idealistic hippie in Stewart did not like the Forum, but being pragmatic, he grudgingly realized the value of their approach, even if he disagreed with it.

An example of the philosophical differences between the two groups occurred in the early 1990s when the state legislature was considering cutting HIV/AIDS funding from the state budget. While some LAGPAC members' first reaction was to stage a public demonstration and raise hell in the media, the Forum's leadership went to work behind the scenes. The Forum had endorsed Donald Mintz in the 1990 mayoral race. Mintz, an attorney and prominent Jewish lay leader, did not win the race but he did appreciate the Forum's support. At the Forum's suggestion, Mintz called in a favor from his friend, grocery magnate John Schwegmann. The favor? Lean in on Representative Bill Jefferson, who sat on the legislative reconciliation committee. Schwegmann, who had previously bestowed his coveted grocery bag endorsement to Bill Jefferson, did just that, and without fanfare, the proposed $20 million cut was restored.

Considering the differences between LAGPAC and the Forum, LAGPAC co-chair Eddie Domingue reminisces:

> We had a relatively rocky relationship with the Forum. While the Forum gave money to various candidates it was LAGPAC that did a lot of the leg work to get out our vote. There were several times that we could not agree on policy. One area that we disagreed quite a bit on was Transgender Equality. From an early part of the Transgender movement LAGPAC took an inclusive stance on adding Trans individuals to all LGB equality bills. There were many times that the Forum was willing to sacrifice the Trans Community if it meant we could get more votes.[4]

Attorney Larry Best, a former chair of the Forum for Equality and a member of Mayor Marc Morial's Human Relations Commission, sums up the differences between LAGPAC and the Forum for Equality this way:

While the two political organizations sought the same social justice for our community, they were in other ways dissimilar. I think of them as eternally opposing forces that made up the whole, sort of the yang and yen of our community. There was healthy competition of course and even occasional, if infrequent, collaboration. Each had its own agenda and approach to local politics. We did not always endorse and support the same political candidates. I do think, however, that each refrained from attacking the other in the interest of solidarity.

The stark differences between the two sprung from their roots. While I cannot speak authoritatively about LAGPAC since I was not a member, my impression of them at the time was that they were a grass roots political organization with an ethos rooted in the 60s civil rights movement and thus frequently focused on protests and demands, along with an uncompromising ideology.

In contrast, The Forum, founded later, was created by a base of professionals including doctors, lawyers, accountants, engineers, and business men and women among other occupations, who felt insufficient progress was being made in Louisiana gay rights and wanted to use a different and more pragmatic approach.

The Forum's formula was to support good government candidates who also understood and supported gay rights and progress. This support came in the form of political endorsement of candidates interviewed by our members, and in members' individual and discretionary campaign contributions. While other local mainstream political organizations "sold" their endorsements in exchange for cash support from a candidate, The Forum uniquely turned the tables.

Beyond that, it was our belief that more could be accomplished at City Hall, and even statewide, by a group of successful experienced professionals whom we expected would be viewed more favorably by the political establishment, because we were in some ways also part to the "establishment." We weren't so much demanding change as attempting to induce it. Our candidate interviews were carefully crafted to emphasize good government issues along with the LGBT issues we sought to educate them about through our questions, thus linking good government with decency and gay rights. We also reached out to build coalitions with other minority groups and the ACLU.

The formula gradually succeeded and resulted in the statewide organization that exists today and is able to support full time lobbyists in Baton Rouge during legislative sessions and beyond. Further, the organization has evolved well beyond its original founders, many of whom have moved on or retired. Its annual gala dinner fundraiser is well attended by both state and local level politicians and judges and also receives corporate sponsorship support.

The Forum was also intended to be bi-partisan and even non-partisan. LAGPAC in contrast was to my knowledge exclusively composed of democrats. I was a republican myself in the nineties when I still vainly hoped gay republicans could change the party from within. That hope has long since been abandoned and I have been a registered democrat for two decades.

The differences between the organizations did not preclude both from participating in important local or regional political endeavors and as well as public protests in which both participated. What was lacking was true collaboration and coordination. While Chair, I once even floated the idea of consolidation the two groups, but found no support within the Forum, and thus never explored the possibility of support in LAGPAC.

In summary, the Forum was the establishment group and LAGPAC was more counter-cultural. The members of each presented themselves accordingly. We were the starched shirts and suits while they were T-shirts and sandals. I expect The Forum may have been characterized in some quarters as a group of privileged elites, but its formula worked, and the organization prospered and contributed significantly to regional gay rights. It continues to do so today long after the demise of LAGPAC.[5]

Best's recollections of the differences between the Forum and LAGPAC are reminiscent of the differences between the conservative Mattachine Society and the more radical Gay Liberation Front, which broke away from Mattachine in the wake of Stonewall. It was perhaps inevitable in a very conservative state that gay Republicans would eventually organize. By 1993, there was a Louisiana chapter of Log Cabin Republicans, which shared a lot of crossover membership with the Forum.

The idea was to reform the Republican Party, not abandon it. After coming out of the closet and becoming involved in gay political activism, Larry Best considered switching parties from Republican to Democrat, but Evans urged him not to, saying they needed to try to change the party from within. This effort proved to be an uphill battle, but Evans was determined. In 1992, the chair of the Mississippi State Republican Party, Evelyn McPhail, spoke in Baton Rouge at a Republican Leadership 2000 meeting and offended many in the audience by making a homophobic joke. After her speech,

Evans confronted her and extracted a halfhearted apology from her, which he followed up with a formal letter sever days later, stating, "By belittling the individual rights of Gays, and their relationships with one another, you belittled our party, as well as the contributions of Gay Republicans to our party, and to our country."

Gay Republicans mystified and confused Stewart. He may not have understood them, but he did acknowledge their effectiveness. At one point, he considered whether LAGPAC and the Forum should merge into one organization. When he pitched the idea to Evans, Evans wisely told him that given the fundamental differences in personality between the two groups, it was probably best if they remained separate but still collaborate. The two groups maintained a good working relationship until Chris Daigle became co-chair of LAGPAC. Much to the frustration of many, Daigle viewed the Forum as a rival organization. This was a departure from the history of collaboration the two groups had forged. Evans recalled, "That resulted in a lot of missed opportunities."[6] Daigle was not as eager as previous LAGPAC leaders to share the credit for collective wins, and this attitude alienated a lot of people. When Daigle ran for the state house of representatives, out-of-town volunteers sent by the Democratic National Committee were shocked at how little local support he had. But for the most part, LAGPAC and the Forum worked well together. Evans cites his relationship with Jim Wiltberger as evidence of the collaborative nature between the leadership of the two groups. After serving as co-chair of LAGPAC, Wiltberger went to work for the Forum as its New Orleans political director.

The different natures and approaches represented by the Forum for Equality and LAGPAC in some ways was beneficial—the ethos of each organization enabled it to effectively reach audiences the other group would have little chance of successfully persuading—but in other ways the differences would lead to clashes on the local front and foreshadow a huge schism in the national movement over the issue of transgender inclusion.

In 1998, transgender activist Courtney Sharp and various allies from LAGPAC and PFLAG turned their attention to the state legislature. LAGPAC and its allies filed a nondiscrimination bill that included transgender protections. Simultaneously, the Forum for Equality, another political action group based in New Orleans, had a similar bill filed that did not include transgender language.

The two bills confused the New Orleans delegation to the state house of representatives. The delegation was generally sympathetic to LGBT+ causes, but the two bills revealed a frustrating lack of communication and coordination. The delegation called a meeting of both LAGPAC and Forum for Equality officials and chastised them for "not having their shit together."[7]

During the meeting, Tony Clesi, an attorney for the Forum, angrily asked, "Why in the hell are we talking about including transsexual people when we need to protect gays and lesbians?"[8] He did not know that Sharp, who was in the room, was transgender. Sharp was shocked at the remark and left the room to calm down and collect her thoughts. Upon returning to the meeting, she referenced Clesi's question and said, "This is why . . ." and then, after coming out as trans, excoriated the Forum for Equality for its hypocrisy. Years later, Dr. Jody Gates, a former co-chair of the Forum, summed up the issue of trans inclusion succinctly when she said, "The politicians were closed-minded to anything transgender. It became a question of do you sacrifice something or get nothing?"[9]

This episode foreshadowed the national controversy in 2007 over the issue of trans inclusion in ENDA (Employment Non-Discrimination Act). The first attempt at providing employment protections for gays and lesbians came in 1974 when Bella Abzug introduced a bill in Congress that came to be known as the Equality Act. The bill never made it out of committee. It was introduced again in 1975 with the same fate. The Equality Act differed from ENDA in scope in that it amended the Civil Rights Act of 1964, which extended discrimination protection to housing and public accommodations; ENDA focused specifically on the workplace. ENDA was first introduced to the 103rd Congress in 1994 and has been introduced to every Congress since then with the exception of the 109th Congress (2005–2007). In 1995, for the first time, ENDA came up for a vote on the US Senate floor and failed to pass by one vote. The House passed a controversial version of ENDA in 2007, but the bill never reached the Senate floor.

The 2007 version of the bill was controversial because, for the first time, it included protections for trans people. When House Speaker Nancy Pelosi realized she didn't have the votes to pass the bill, Representative Barney Frank took the trans-inclusive language out and also introduced a separate version of the bill with trans protection. When the *Washington Blade* broke news of Frank's strategy, many in the movement, especially the trans community, felt betrayed and responded with outrage. Nine national LGBT+ advocacy groups (PFLAG, the National Gay and Lesbian Task Force, the National Center for Transgender Equality, the National Center for Lesbian Rights, National Stonewall Democrats, the National Coalition for LGBT Health, Pride At Work, the AFL-CIO, and the National Coalition of Anti-Violence Projects) issued a joint statement sharply criticizing the strategy and affirmed that they would oppose any version of ENDA that did not include protections for transgender workers. When votes for the two bills were whipped, it became apparent that the trans-inclusive bill would not pass. After conferring with lobbyists from the Human Rights Campaign (HRC), who favored the watered-down bill, but not with any other activist groups, Frank pushed the bill to passage (235–184) in the House.[10] Writing in *Workers World*, journalist Leslie Feinberg captured the firestorm this way:

> Angry individuals fired off a barrage of letters and emails to congressional representatives.
>
> Activists set up 24-hour protests outside Pelosi's and Frank's offices on the West Coast and East Coast respectively. Pelosi was targeted by a demonstration outside her appearance as a feted guest of honor at the Human Rights Campaign national dinner on Oct. 6
>
> Within days, it was clear that HRC—which describes itself as one of the largest LGBT civil-rights organizations in the United States—was refusing to unite for transgender inclusion. Donna Rose, the only trans person on its Board of Directors, publicly resigned on Oct. 2 as a result. More resignations reportedly followed.
>
> More than 90 national and state LGBT groups signed a letter that was hand-delivered to congressional representatives on Oct. 1. These groups include the National Black Justice Coalition, International Federation of Black Prides, Mautner Project, National Youth Advocacy Coalition, American Institute of Bisexuality and BiNet USA.
>
> More than 150 organizations announced in an Oct. 15 news release that they'd formed United ENDA—a united front to win a fully inclusive ENDA bill, H.R. 2015.
>
> The National Organization for Women issued its own news release, stating that it joined with "hundreds of civil, women's and human rights organizations" to demand passage of the inclusive ENDA bill, H.R. 2015.
>
> Nancy Wohlforth, co-president of Pride At Work, summed up, "Transgender people face the highest rate of unemployment in our community and it would be unconscionable for us to sit idly by and see them stripped from this important piece of legislation."[11]

All the backlash took Barney Frank and other politicians like him by surprise. For his part, Frank responded to the criticism by resorting to pragmatism, arguing that something would be better than nothing, that proponents should settle for what was achievable and fill in the gaps later. But the LGBT+ community, with the notable exception of the HRC, felt differently.

Stewart, who derisively called the HRC the "Human Rights Champagne," and others in New Orleans had been calling for trans inclusion in the movement generally, and ENDA specifically, long before it was fashionable. He and Courtney Sharp had spearheaded the effort to make PFLAG (locally and nationally) trans inclusive in the 1990s (a major undertaking treated in a subsequent chapter in this book). Ten years before the 2007 firestorm over ENDA, he was lobbying the HRC to be trans inclusive. He, along with Charlene Schneider, Skip Ward, and Jim Kellogg, wrote a letter to HRC executive director Elizabeth Birch stating, "We find it mind boggling that an organization would have a mission statement so inconsistent with its very name. The solution is obvious. We demand that the mission statement be revised to include bisexuals and transgenders."[12] And in 1999, PFLAG New Orleans president Sandra Pailet wrote Barney Frank urging him to "reconsider your position on maintaining the current limited language within ENDA."[13] The year before, 1998, New Orleans became one of the first cities in the nation to pass an ordinance protecting transgender people from discrimination, largely due to the efforts of Stewart, Sandra Pailet, Courtney Sharp, and other local trans activists.

In a sense, the issue of transgender inclusion illustrated a fundamental difference between LAGPAC and the Forum for Equality, the difference being idealism versus pragmatism. Louis Volz, who had been heavily involved in both groups and even served as chair of the Forum in the early 1990s, recalls, "The Forum was more conservative than I would have preferred, but they were also more practical . . . Both groups had different perspectives, but we both wanted the same things."[14]

The difference in approach and sensibility of the two groups became starkly evident in 1987. Early in that year, the Vatican announced that Pope John Paul II would visit New Orleans in September. At a LAGPAC executive committee meeting, Magill noted that the pope's nine-day tour of the US had prompted activists in other cities such as Miami, Phoenix, Los Angeles, San Francisco, and others, to organize protests. The committee asked Magill to prepare a report exploring "the prospects for and ramifications of a social action during the papal visit." Magill's report recounted the theological conservatism of the pope, Archbishop Philip Hannan's fierce opposition to the nondiscrimination ordinance that the New Orleans City Council failed to pass in December 1986, and the Vatican's dogged description of homosexuality as a "disorder" and homosexual acts as sin. Magill's report concluded that LAGPAC take action but advised that the issue needed further study and that any action taken should be coordinated with other community groups. The result was something called the New Orleans Coalition on the Papal Visit.

As the public relations coordinator for LAGPAC, Magill issued in the fall a press release calling on anyone interested in protesting the papal visit to attend an organizational meeting. He subsequently received thirty harassing phone calls, which included death threats. Undeterred, Magill proceeded with the meeting, and when the pope's helicopter landed at Notre Dame Seminary on Carrollton Avenue, Magill was there with about a dozen other protesters holding signs calling for gay rights and reproductive rights for women. When the pope visited St. Louis Cathedral, Magill, along with Nathan Chapman, Roy Racca, and another person, distributed an open letter to the pope to the throngs of people waiting in line to see the pontiff. The letter took the church to task for opposing gay and lesbian rights and urged it to respect the constitutional principle of the separation of church and state.

Magill and others distributed the letter outside the cathedral as people waited in line to see the pontiff, a priest found Magill and handed him a stack of the letters, saying, "We don't want these." Magill recycled the letters and continued handing them out. Later, when the Popemobile rode down Canal Street, Stewart organized a protest march to follow it. "The four-person LAGPAC contingent with our sizable LAGPAC banner preceded by Robby DeJacimo, prancing along as if he were a majorette. I was a bit more discrete walking off to the side as if I were some sort of chaperone."[15] Leonard Green and Michael Thompson (whose mother would become president of PFLAG and a dear friend of Stewart's) carried the LAGPAC banner.

In the spring of 1987, LAGPAC began making preparations to participate in the second National March on Washington for Lesbian and Gay Rights. Stewart and Charlene Schneider were the co-chairs of the Louisiana delegation. Throughout the 1980s, Stewart and Charlene developed a deep friendship. Recalling their friendship, Stewart remembers: "I was very close to her. Celebration (a glbt conference) and LAGPAC were going on then. Charlene and her partner lived in back of her bar. It's the bar that's called John Paul's now, but back then it was called Charlene's. I had entry to her private living quarters in the rear, and on more than one occasion, we smoked a bowl together."[16]

The first March on Washington had taken place on October 14, 1979, and attracted over one hundred thousand participants, although fewer than a dozen were from Louisiana. The idea for a national march had been conceived in 1973 by Jeff Graubart in Urbana-Champaign, Illinois. Many national gay and lesbian organizations initially resisted the idea, and the march was postponed several years. The idea came up again in 1978, and a steering committee was formed but eventually dissolved because of internal bickering. Openly gay San Francisco board of supervisors member Harvey Milk, who had served on the steering committee, continued efforts to organize the march but was assassinated on November 27, 1978. His death, however, served as a catalyst for organizers, who assembled a national coalition and office that successfully organized the historic march.

By the mid-1980s, Steve Ault and Joyce Hunter, who had spearheaded the first march, began making plans for a second one. Prompted by the Reagan administration's cruel indifference to the AIDS crisis and the landmark 1986 US Supreme Court case *Bowers v. Hardwick*, which, by a 5–4 ruling, upheld the constitutionality of Georgia's sodomy law, Ault and Hunter began organizing.

LAGPAC co-chair Roy Racca and board member Leonard Green attended the South Central Regional Meeting (which included Louisiana, Texas, Oklahoma, and Arkansas) in Houston in April. Green led a workshop on minority outreach. In addition to his involvement with LAGPAC, Green, an activist and writer, was a member of the National Coalition of Black Gays and Lesbians, founder of M-PAC (Minority People Against AIDS Committee) and had been co-chair of the Langston/Jones Society. At the conference, Green and Racca were elected to the national steering committee, which met in Atlanta the following month. Stewart accompanied Green and Racca to Atlanta and helped organizational efforts in Louisiana.

In July, about fifty people attended an organizational meeting, and Stewart, along with Heidi Revels, was elected co-chair of the National March on Washington Committee.[17] Roughly five hundred people from Louisiana attended the National March on Washington in 1987, including Stewart. City councilman Johnny Jackson's participation was especially significant. In announcing his intention to travel to Washington, Jackson issued a statement that said, "Their issues are my issues." When asked about Jackson, Stewart said, "It adds legitimacy to the march because as a publicly elected official . . . when Johnny's up there and sees that crowd, it will give him some sense of self-empowerment . . . it makes a statement."[18] And when asked if the march might have a negative effect or some sort of backlash, Stewart said, "There is no redemption without the shedding of blood. And that's the tragedy of it all."[19] Green echoed Stewart's sentiments when he publicly stated, "The March is important in reference to our standing up and letting the nation see and understand that we are very serious about getting our rights as gay people and in particular as a person of color, it is equally important for the nation to see that people of color are involved in gay issues and that we do exist and that we insist upon our rights."[20] For his part, Jackson was especially moved by the AIDS quilt.

While in Washington, LAGPAC representatives took the opportunity to meet with Congresswoman Boggs, aides to six of Louisiana's other seven congressmen, and aides to both Senators John Breaux and Bennett Johnston. Senator John Breaux and Congressman Jimmy Hayes told LAGPAC lobbyists they had never taken the lead on AIDS issues because no one had ever asked them to do so.

On October 11, 1987, an estimated 750,000 people marched in the largest demonstration on behalf of LGBT+ rights in the nation's history. In addition to the march and rally, participants, over the course of five days, witnessed a spectacular sunrise ceremony in which the AIDS quilt was revealed, participated in a demonstration at the US Supreme Court (in which hundreds were arrested), saw thousands of same-sex couples partake in a ceremony affirming their unions, dedicated the final resting place of Harvey Milk, enjoyed over 250 bands, and held a gay veterans memorial service at the Tomb of the Unknown Soldier.

Those who attended the March returned home energized and hopeful and determined to continue the good fight. One woman, Jennie, a server at the popular restaurant Quarter Scene, said in an interview with *Ambush Magazine*, "I came back with a feeling that is hard to describe. It was almost a feeling a peace and serenity."[21] Many, however, were disheartened when the national media downplayed the historic march by underestimating crowd sizes and offering it minimal coverage. *Time, Newsweek,* and *U.S. News and World Report,* the nation's three largest weekly newsmagazines, ignored the march completely. About a month after the march, on November 20, the New Orleans March Committee and Dignity New Orleans held a "March Afterglow Gathering" at the St. Louis Community Center in the French Quarter. Cliff Howard, who was arrested at the Supreme Court building, shared his recollections of the march. John Wilson showed video footage of the march he had taken, and others testified about their experiences in Washington. In a sad commentary on society's widespread ignorance of the LGBT+ community, some airlines disinfected the planes that carried the marchers to Washington out of fear concerning AIDS.

The following year, LAGPAC and other groups from around the nation, including the Human Rights Campaign, the National Gay and Lesbian Task Force, and ACT UP (AIDS Coalition to Unleash Power), protested the GOP convention in New Orleans. Rich Magill organized GLITER (Gay and Lesbian Initiative to Educate Republicans), which held a candlelight vigil at Armstrong Park. Four hundred twelve candles were lit, that number signifying the number of people who would be diagnosed with HIV during the convention. Congresswoman Lindy Boggs spoke at the vigil as did Mayor Barthelemy, ACT UP cofounder Peter Staley, and others. A police officer assigned to the event was overheard asking another officer, "How did the fags get the mayor?"

In 1983, LAGPAC joined the Crescent City Coalition and the ACLU to form the Sexual Privacy Project (SPP). The SPP's objective was to bring a legal challenge to Louisiana's "crime against nature" statute, arguing it was unconstitutional because it violated the fundamental right to privacy. The suit also argued that the law was the legal foundation for discrimination against gay people. The plaintiffs further claimed that the law stigmatized all gay people as criminal, thus encouraging homophobic attitudes that caused gay people to hide their true identities. The SPP filed suit in federal court in New Orleans in 1984, but that suit was nullified in 1986 when the US Supreme Court upheld Georgia's sodomy law (*Bowers v. Hardwick*). Led by attorney James Kellogg (who handled a lot of AIDS cases) and Martha Kegel (executive director of the Louisiana ACLU), the SPP was at a crossroads after the Hardwick ruling. By the end of November 1986, Kegel had resigned her position with the ACLU and Kellogg was preparing to move to New York to take a position with Lambda Legal as its AIDS litigation director. Not wanting to let the SPP dissolve, Kellogg reached out to Leonard Doty and Carole Pindaro of the NO/AIDS Task Force and LAGPAC co-chairs Richard Devlin and Mary Russ in an effort to formalize the SPP as an organization and thereby ensure its future.

In July 1987, the ACLU of Louisiana, the NO/AIDS Task Force, and LAGPAC formalized the Louisiana Sexual Privacy Project. The project's stated purpose was to provide funding for law reform litigation relating to matters of sexual privacy, including AIDS-related discrimination.

Shortly after LAGPAC was founded, the primary factor shaping public opinion about gay folks was the AIDS epidemic. Along with lobbying for LGBT+-friendly legislation in both Washington and Baton Rouge, endorsing political candidates, conducting voting drives, and educating the public, LAGPAC, which already had a full plate, also did its part in the fight against AIDS. Early on it formed the AIDS Lobby Network, and many LAGPAC members also worked as AIDS activists.

In some ways, AIDS had the inadvertent effect of humanizing the gay community. As more and more people became sick, straight people began to have epiphanies—"Oh, I didn't realize my neighbor, coworker, etc. was gay." In this regard, AIDS, to some degree, put a face on—humanized—the label "gay." But for the truly closed-minded, it had the opposite effect. Religious leaders consistently preached that the dreaded disease was God's judgment on a wicked lifestyle. And in the minds of many, AIDS reinforced deeply entrenched, negative societal stereotypes about gay men, namely that they were promiscuous and sick and perverted and worthy of whatever punishment God or Nature might mete out.

Stewart did not consider himself an AIDS activist, though his work with LAGPAC and other organizations dovetailed with the larger fight against the disease. In his later years, Stewart once said,

> I was not an AIDS activist because so much of our resources were being devoted to that battle that our other needed organizations were being neglected. However, I had to work with AIDS organizations in conjunction with the things I was doing for LAGPAC, PFLAG, Celebration, and the SECLGM. I also participated in the annual March Against AIDS and was chairperson of the annual Candlelight AIDS Memorial March for one year.[22]

Stewart's claim that he was not an AIDS activist is odd given the fact he participated in AIDS-related events ranging from protests, vigils, and candlelight marches to legislative lobbying. He was even arrested with dozens of others during a sit-in on Loyola Avenue to protest the state's lack of funding for HIV treatment. His activism most certainly did include AIDS work, but it was not his top priority.

One member of LAGPAC who did make AIDS a top priority was John Ognibene. Originally from New York, Ognibene moved to New Orleans in 1978. Ognibene had earned a degree in fine arts and worked in New Orleans as an interior designer and painter before turning to activism. After the massive sidewalk arrests in 1981, Ognibene founded the Crescent City Coalition. When the AIDS epidemic hit New Orleans, he turned his attention to raising awareness, and money, to fight the disease. Ognibene was also involved in LAGPAC until he abruptly resigned in 1988. Circumstances surrounding his resignation are unclear, but his resignation letter states, "It was my understanding, apparently mistaken, that LAGPAC and NORCO were formed to encourage political activity within the Gay/Lesbian community. It now appears that such political activity is only desirable if it conforms to the beliefs of the majority."[23] He then became active in ACT UP before ultimately succumbing to the disease himself in 1990. Part of his remains were buried in the memorial garden behind the Faerie Playhouse.

As the AIDS epidemic unfolded in New Orleans, the community responded in a variety of ways. By the end of the decade, New Orleans was a model city for providing AIDS-related services, but at the beginning of the 1980s, the gay community in New Orleans, as in other cities, was shocked. Ignorance of the disease caused a lot of fear. Dr. Jody Gates, the administrator of a hospital at the time recalled, "The most important thing was to not let people panic."[24] Added to fear and panic was widespread despair. Will

Bennett, a longtime bartender who lost over one hundred friends to the disease, remembers:

> It was so bad you were afraid to answer your phone. I remember throwing away my address book because most everyone in it had died. It was horrible. No one knew what was going on and everyone was fearful. Charity Hospital had a separate floor for AIDS patients. Orderlies would set patient's meals outside the doors in the hall for fear of being in the same room with someone infected. And visitors were forced to wear masks and gowns. You'd go to the hospital to visit a friend and be shocked at how sickly they looked but also at how many other people you knew were also patients. After a while it took a heavy toll on me. I became cold.[25]

In 1985, no facility in Louisiana would provide long-term care for AIDS patients. Charity Hospital in New Orleans was only able to provide short-term acute medical care. Gay Lynn Bond, the director of Charity Hospital's social service department, wrote an editorial lamenting the challenges facing the hospital—a lack of finances, budget restrictions, an ever-increasing number of patients, and the inability to provide support and home health care for discharged patients still in need of long-term care.[26]

Charity Hospital was able to expand its services to AIDS patients when it received a grant from the Robert Woods Johnson Foundation. Dr. Michael Kaiser recalls how the Metropolitan AIDS Advisory Council (MAAC) was founded:

> I think it was 1986-ish when a group of us wrote a grant request to the Robert Woods Johnson Foundation. When awarded, it funded some of the HIV Outpatient Program at Charity (then known as C-100): community-based case management, mental health services, volunteer support, etc. RWJ required a community advisory board = MAAC. I chaired it. One of the MAAC sub-committees was responsible for fund raising and started calling themselves United Services for AIDS. United Services became more independent over time, especially when it started Art Against AIDS as a fundraiser. Eventually MAAC was replaced by the Ryan White Planning Council and United Services started providing emergency assistance.[27]

According to Dr. Catherine Roland, a clinical therapist, Community Relief for People with AIDS began in the back room of La Peniche, Al McNairn's popular eatery in the Marigny. Roland's friendship with Kaiser, McNairn, Rich Sacher, Bill Dailey, and others led her, along with Christine Franz and a few other lesbians, to found New Orleans Women Against AIDS (NOWAA). NOWAA raised money for the NO/AIDS Task Force by hosting sock-hop dances at Pino's, New Year's Eve parties, and other events. NOWAA even brought in nationally renowned lesbian entertainer Lynn Lavner on three occasions.[28] The group also helped bring the NAMES Project quilt to New Orleans. In addition to providing financial support, NOWAA members would visit patients at Charity Hospital and bring in the trays of food orderlies had left outside their doors.

In addition to editorials and letters to the editor written by health-care workers and AIDS activists, journalist John Pope covered the epidemic regularly and extensively. Pope addressed a variety of issues: background on the epidemic, information about AIDS transmission, the lack of effective treatment options, current research on treatments, efforts by the gay community to dispense accurate information, benefits and fundraisers for victims, the city's lack of an effective response, discrimination against AIDS patients, risks to the heterosexual population, case studies, the costs of treating AIDS patients, the lack of research funding, and the experiences of health-care workers. He also wrote a lot of obituaries. Pope's coverage was significant not only because of the information in his reports but also because it dispelled much of the ignorance surrounding the disease.[29]

By 1988, there was a local chapter of ACT UP in New Orleans. As in other cities, there was much to "act up" about in New Orleans. The disease had hit the French Quarter and Marigny neighborhoods especially hard. Unlike other cities, the gay community in New Orleans had been somewhat organized since the 1960s in the form of the gay Carnival krewes, albeit this organization was more social than political. The krewes were not immune to the virus, and at the peak of the epidemic, gay Carnival reached its nadir. For example, by 1992, Gary Martin, who had founded the Krewe of Polyphemus ten years earlier, had lost so many friends and krewe members to AIDS, he was ready to call it a day, and the krewe folded. Southern Decadence, the annual Labor Day weekend extravaganza that had begun in 1972 and was already an institution twenty years later, could not ignore AIDS. In 1992, Southern Decadence Grand Marshal "Rhie," (Harry Sherman), died before naming her successor. And Jamie Temple, owner of the Phoenix and Southern Decadence grand marshal in 1991, remembers, "The shift came after AIDS hit. We knew we couldn't just keep going with Decadence. We had to start fundraising to help our community. We never looked back."[30]

ACT UP had been founded in New York City in 1987 by Larry Kramer as a direct-action group to raise awareness about the epidemic and, more specifically, the lack of adequate funding allocated by the government to fight the disease. Unlike New York mayor Ed Koch, who essentially ignored AIDS, New Orleans mayor Dutch Morial met with leaders of the gay community and created a program of educational seminars. New Orleans ACT UP met weekly at the NO/AIDS Task Force headquarters.

ACT UP was aggressive and confrontational. This is evident in its statement of purpose, which in part reads, "We are committed to addressing AIDS within the context we find it—a homophobic, racist, sexist, classist society and profiteering medical industry. WE WILL NOT BE SILENT." This sensibility created friction between the New York–based national chapter and the local New Orleans group, which was informed by a less aggressive sensibility.

New Orleans ACT UP staged a protest at the Republican National Convention in New Orleans in 1988. Specifically, the group protested the fact that state funding for AZT (azidothymidine), the only FDA-approved drug for the treatment of AIDS at the time, was about to run out. Protesters formed what they called a "human billboard" at the entrance to the convention. Protesters held signs and panels from the national AIDS Memorial Quilt and distributed leaflets indignantly questioning why the state and city should spend $800,000 hosting the Republican convention and not spend a dime on AIDS. ACT UP New York sent a delegation to assist with the protest, but the out-of-towners did not get along well with local ACT UP members. In a 1992 interview Doug Robertson remembered, "ACT UP New York came down for the Republican convention and destroyed us."[31] The tactics of the New York group turned off the locals, and membership dropped dramatically.

In addition to a disagreement about tactics, money was also an issue. In 1989, the New York group had sent a fundraising letter to members of New Orleans ACT UP. This caught the local chapter, who had not been informed or consulted, by surprise. In response, the local chapter sent a letter to New York ACT UP protesting what locals felt was territorial usurpation and a lack of respect:

> Sending fundraising letters to our members, supporters and potential supporters, without the input, support or consent of our group communicates to us that you do not recognize our legitimate role in the fight. For all of us, funds are a scarce commodity. Your leadership has argued that you do the national work and therefore have a right to

gather funds nationally. However, assuming national responsibilities would require you to be accountable nationally. There are no mechanisms in place to provide accountability or to solicit participation. To decide unilaterally that New York's agenda is the only legitimate national agenda can only divide and split our movement.[32]

The local chapter also called attention to discrimination within the criminal justice system against people living with AIDS. There was a 1991 class action lawsuit against Sherriff Charles Foti alleging maltreatment of inmates in the parish prison, and in 1992, ACT UP held a press conference in front of the criminal courthouse to call attention to police brutality. Specifically, the press conference recounted the case of an incarcerated man who had been beaten by police during an arrest at his home on minor charges. In the course of the beating, the man, who was HIV positive, bled on one of the officer's shirts. The man was charged with attempted murder and booked into Orleans Parish Prison, where he was denied medical treatment.

This homophobic attitude permeated the criminal justice system. The district attorney's office had a policy of charging persons arrested for prostitution with the crime of knowingly transmitting HIV. Attorney Mark Gonzalez, who was a member of ACT UP, testified to the mayor's advisory committee on lesbian and gay issues in 1989 about a client of his who was the victim of this policy. Several police officers had barged into this man's French Quarter apartment, without a warrant, and arrested him on drug possession charges, even though police found no drugs at the scene. During the arrest, the police noticed a bottle of AZT and told him as they were taking him to jail "not to worry about the charges—you'll probably die of AIDS in jail."

In 1990, ACT UP, which then consisted of only half a dozen members, managed to stage a protest at city hall in which five hundred people participated. This was the protest in which city councilman Johnny Jackson was arrested along with Stewart. The group was protesting not only inadequate funding in general but also the state's plan to defund the pharmacy fund for people with AIDS. The arrest made quite a splash in the news, which irritated the politicians and bureaucrats in Baton Rouge. That night Johnny Jackson made a few calls to the capital city and let the powers that be know that if the pharmacy fund was dissolved, they would stage another protest and shut down the Mississippi River Bridge on a Friday at 5:00 p.m. The pharmacy fund was spared.[33]

Another memorable demonstration occurred at the Orpheum Theater, when international celebrity socialite Princess Radziwill was an honoree at some gala function. According to Rich Sacher, "We dressed as jesters, handed out roses and flyers to the arriving crowds, and told them the city was joking around with AIDS. At that time, there was zero support of any kind from city government for PWAs. I remember that Sidney Barthelemy was mayor, and he was embarrassed when Radziwill told the audience from the stage that she was shocked at the city's dereliction."[34]

ACT UP also waged letter-writing and petition campaigns to be sent to Governor Buddy Roemer and Department of Health and Hospitals secretary David Ramsey demanding $3 million worth of funding for Charity Hospital's C-100 outpatient clinic. In addition to letters, the group also flooded the governor's office with postcards depicting a coffin with the succinct message: "This is the alternative to C-100 full funding!"

Funding for research and treatment was not the only thing lacking. Ignorance of the disease and the lack of effective treatments created a real need for education and outreach in the early 1980s. Led by Ted Wisniewski, who as a resident at Charity Hospital saw the need firsthand, several medical professionals and others in New Orleans began meeting to discuss ways to address the crisis.[35] Out of these meetings, the NO/AIDS Task Force was born in 1983.

The NO/AIDS Task Force, now known as Crescent Care, began with a single telephone line. Gradually, additional services were added, including an information center and hotline, case management and mental health services, a meal delivery program, additional offices, and legal services. The agency grew robustly under the leadership of Jeff Campbell, who served as executive director from 1989 to 1994, increasing its staff from eight members to forty-five and increasing its budget from $450,000 to $2.5 million.[36]

Initially, the immediate need was to dispense information and raise awareness. To that end, on October 8, the NO/AIDS Task Force participated in the National Candlelight Vigil for AIDS by holding a vigil in Jackson Square. The New Orleans Gay Men's Chorus performed, and speakers included Mayor Dutch Morial (who served on the US Conference of Mayors AIDS task force) and representatives from the NO/AIDS Task Force, LAGPAC, and Crescent City Coalition.[37] In 1986, John Ognibene organized the first annual Memorial Service for AIDS. The service was held at St. Mark's Methodist Church in the French Quarter and followed by a candlelight march to the Moonwalk along the river. At the river, the candles were extinguished one by one to symbolize "the hundreds of lives that have been extinguished by this disease."[38] Partially funded by the Ryan White Act (1990), today Crescent Care offers a broad range of health and wellness services for anyone who is seeking health-care services in Greater New Orleans and southeastern Louisiana. Adequate funding was always a challenge. In the early 1990s, the task force hired Larry Bagneris to lobby the legislature on behalf of AIDS-related measures.[39]

In 1987, activist Judy Montz began lobbying New Orleans mayor Sidney Barthelemy to establish a "mayor's advisory committee on gay concerns."[40] In a letter to the mayor, Montz wrote: "It is more important than ever that your administration demonstrates an understanding of AIDS and its related problems. It is more important than ever that your administration have a real and useful line of communication with the gay community which is trusted, respected, and accepted." By 1995, Montz was director of the mayor's Office of Health Policy and AIDS Funding, which oversaw the allocation of $3.7 million for AIDS-related services.[41]

This money became available as a result of the Ryan White Act. The Ryan White HIV/AIDS Program was established in 1990 and works with local and state governments and community-based organizations, such as the NO/AIDS Task Force, to provide services to an estimated 536,000 people each year who do not have sufficient health-care coverage or financial resources to cope with HIV disease. The program is administered by the US Department of Health and Human Services.

Funding provided by the Ryan White Act to insurance companies to cover HIV/AIDS medications would later become the focus of a nationally significant landmark lawsuit that originated in New Orleans. In January 2014, John East received terrible news. His caseworker at the NO/AIDS Task Force called to inform him that his insurance company, Blue Cross/Blue Shield of Louisiana, would no longer accept payments from third parties. The news devastated East because without insurance his HIV and other medicines would cost him over $6,000 a month.

East had faithfully paid monthly payments to Blue Cross/Blue Shield of Louisiana since 1985, almost thirty years. In 2009, East's premiums became unaffordable when they were raised to $650 a month. On the day his insurance was set to expire, he qualified for insurance subsidies from the Ryan White HIV/AIDS Program. East breathed a sigh of relief. He was not going to die for lack of medication. East's financial crisis would not have been as dire if Republican governor Bobby Jindal had not rejected $1.65 billion, funds offered to the state as part of the Medicaid expansion provided for in the Affordable Care Act (Obamacare).

When Blue Cross/Blue Shield of Louisiana announced they would no longer accept third-party payments, Lambda Legal, a national advocacy group for LGBT+ rights, contacted East and asked him if he would be willing to be the chief litigant in a class action lawsuit against Blue Cross/Blue Shield of Louisiana and two other insurance companies (Louisiana Health

Cooperative and Vantage Health Plan). East was reluctant at first but ultimately agreed.

Recalling his decision to participate in the lawsuit, East observes, "Health trumps privacy."[42] Lambda Legal initially sent the three health insurance companies a letter urging them to reverse their policy of not accepting third-party payments. When the three insurance companies ignored the letter, Lambda Legal filed a lawsuit in United States District Court, Middle District of Louisiana on February 20, 2014, against the insurance companies on behalf of East and other low-income Louisianans living with HIV and won an emergency injunction to force the companies to accept the premiums until the case was settled. The Louisiana case caused the federal government to issue a regulation that insurance companies nationwide accept payments from the Ryan White fund.

When the lawsuit was announced, East said publicly, "No one should be made to choose between medications and keeping a roof over your head and food on the table . . . It is unconscionable, despicable and a humanitarian atrocity that Blue Cross and other insurance companies are dumping policy holders with HIV."[43] Blue Cross/Blue Shield of Louisiana officials claimed they decided to stop accepting third-party payments in an effort to reduce fraud but could produce no evidence of fraud with regard to the Ryan White fund payments.

Noel Twilbeck, CEO of the NO/AIDS Task Force, summed up the case's significance by stating, "John's willingness to share his story enabled Lambda Legal to draw great attention to unfair and harmful practices of BC/BS (and possibly other insurance carriers). If the unjust insurance practices had not been challenged, the trickle-down effect of other carriers following them could have meant that hundreds of individuals who needed assistance with premium payments in Louisiana would have been unable to access Marketplace policies."[44]

In addition to political groups like ACT UP and service providers like the NO/AIDS Task Force, living facilities for people living with HIV emerged in the early years of the epidemic. In the early 1980s, Father Bob Pawell noticed a number of black wreaths on doors as he walked through the French Quarter. He soon learned that someone had died of a strange new disease called GRID (Gay Related Immune Deficiency). Alarmed, he turned to prayer and meditation.

Father Bob had arrived in New Orleans in 1976 to establish the Tau House, a Franciscan outreach to people alienated by the Church. The ministry was located in a double-shotgun house in the 1000 block of Governor Nicholls Street in the French Quarter. He began making his rounds at bars, restaurants, and shops and soon developed a network of friends and acquaintances. Tau House quickly earned a reputation as a nonjudgmental place where regular sinners could seek spiritual services.

In 1984, a young man known as Robert H. was released from Charity Hospital after a nasty episode from what we now know was AIDS. Robert H. was homeless and penniless and had nowhere to go when a compassionate nurse called the Tau House and pleaded Robert's case. Father Bob gave the young man a place to stay, and soon the word spread that someone was willing to care for people with AIDS. This was rather remarkable at the time because most people with AIDS then were completely shunned. Even doctors and nurses treated them tepidly, with gloves and masks. Before long, the need was obvious and Father Bob along with Father Paul Derossiers of Holy Trinity Church in the Marigny approached Archbishop Hannan about the possibility of providing shelter to homeless AIDS patients. The archbishop immediately agreed it was necessary and right, and thus was born Project Lazarus. The home designated to house indigent AIDS patients was just around the corner from Holy Trinity Church in the old convent of the German Benedictine nuns of the nineteenth century. The first residents were Bob T., Leon G., and Ray G. At the time, the location of the house was kept secret for safety reasons. Tau House was the public face of the ministry.

Around this time, Father Bob met Jonathan Clemmer, a nurse at Tulane Medical Center who was getting involved in the emerging AIDS crisis. Both men joined the newly formed NO/AIDS Task Force, which would collaborate with Project Lazarus in offering AIDS-related services. A support team then came together, and by 1986, Paul Ploche was designated as a fundraiser and Katie Quigley was hired to provide twenty-four-hour assistance to the residents.[45] By the following year, the staff had grown to ten.[46] Also at this time, the famed Halloween Bal Masque annual fundraiser was founded.

In the early years, Lazarus House (as it has come to be known) essentially functioned as a hospice; it was a place to die. That began to change in 1996 when protease inhibitors became available. These antiviral drugs led to the AIDS cocktails that have enabled those infected with HIV to live much longer than before their advent. Because of this, Project Lazarus is not so much a hospice anymore as it is a transitional living facility. Its mission is to help heal and empower people living with HIV/AIDS by focusing on wellness, providing housing, and offering important support services.

In 1992, the Lazarus House was filled to capacity and another living facility was needed. In that year, with a federal HOPWA (Housing Opportunity for Persons with AIDS) grant from HUD (Department of Housing and Urban Development), David Mesler, Jan Vick, and Peter Drago purchased a modest home in the Bywater and then used their own money to renovate the home to house eight residents. Belle Reve opened its doors in 1993. Belle Reve expanded to include two more buildings and now, in addition to providing housing, also sponsors support groups and offers programming to help residents transition into independent living. Some of these programs included life skills classes, substance abuse counseling, and psychosocial support. Other services included twenty-four-hour personal care, medication adherence counseling, daily meals, social activities and recreation, and a weekly computer class. Because of federal budget and funding cuts during the Trump administration, the mission of Belle Reve has shifted to providing affordable housing to LGBT+ seniors.

Brotherhood Incorporated was established in 1995 with the mission of fighting the spread of HIV and alleviating the struggles of African Americans living with HIV and AIDS. Brotherhood Inc. opened a facility called Trinity House, which provides transitional and permanent housing to low-income individuals living with HIV/AIDS in a group home setting. In addition to providing residential services, the group also offers sensitivity training to African American community leaders. In recent years, the group began an outreach to African American transgender women living with HIV.

In 1988, the NAMES Project AIDS Memorial Quilt came to New Orleans and was displayed at the Rivergate convention hall. The quilt had its inaugural display eight months earlier on the National Mall in Washington, DC, during the 1987 March on Washington. By the time the quilt reached New Orleans, it had doubled in size and consisted of almost five thousand three-foot by six-foot individual panels. New Orleans was one of nineteen US cities on the NAMES Project tour.[47]

Funding for bringing the quilt to New Orleans was provided by United Services for Aids, which was the public relations and fundraising arm for the Metropolitan AIDS Advisory Committee. Founded in 1987, United Services was an umbrella organization for AIDS-related groups in New Orleans. Art Against AIDS was also founded in 1987 by a number of gallery owners to raise awareness and money. Gallery owner Arthur Roger remembers:

> Several galleries in New Orleans had a December benefit but it was immediately clear it looked like all other fundraisers. Bill Fagaly from NOMA suggested to me to organize an art ornament exhibition and we hosted the first collective of all galleries and artists participating at my Julia Street gallery and we billed it as a formal event. It was an immediate black tie success with collectors lined up to get in first when the doors opened. National artist such as Keith Sonnier, Lynda

Benglis, Peter Halley as well as New Orleans Ida Kohlmeyer, George
Dureau and just about everyone here participated. Each year was a
thousand artworks to display which was daunting as well as design-
ers constructed elaborate displays. I have great photo documentation
(even Noel running the auction) and dozens of friends volunteering.
I served with United Services For AIDS to help distribute the funds.
In our first year we received an award from the city of New Orleans
being one of the top 10 fundraisers in the city. We continued to host
the event for several years and grew as well as the AIDS benefit landscape evolved with and collectively decided the Contemporary Arts
Center was a better venue but the event lost its momentum. George
Lancaster stepped in and brought back a more formal event at Canal
Place and again made it a huge success. Later NO AIDS took the event
to NOMA and has remained with them.[48]

Originally sponsored by the Contemporary Arts Center and several local
galleries, Art Against AIDS was a series of events that lasted throughout the
month of November. The event has been held annually since then.[49] By the
end of the decade, New Orleans was considered nationally as a model city
for AIDS organizations and services.

In addition to fighting the disease itself, the need to combat ignorance and
discrimination persisted. An example of this occurred in 1988 when John
Blackstone, the manager of Van Gogh's Ear, a record shop next door to Café
Lafitte in Exile, started a public campaign against the Gay 90's carriage tour
company for its homophobia. Blackstone wrote, "On a daily basis in front of
my shop, I am hearing such comments as 'On the left we have a fag bar and
when we kill them off with AIDS, we send them across the street to the NO/
AIDS Information Center' or 'Don't shop or walk down here or you will catch
AIDS.'"[50] The bigotry surrounding AIDS wasn't confined to just the streets. In
2003, Cecil Little Jr.'s family filed a complaint with the state Department of
Health and Hospitals and in district court against six nursing homes claiming
Little was denied treatment and discriminated against because of his HIV-
positive status. AIDS discrimination was so prevalent that in the early 1990s
Ginger Berigan, then with the ACLU, appeared regularly on the open-access
television talk show *Just for the Record* to provide legal updates on HIV/AIDS
legislation and subsequent lawsuits. In 1994, President Bill Clinton appointed
Berrigan as a district court judge in the Eastern District of Louisiana.

In 1997, Dr. Michael Kaiser left New Orleans for Washington, DC, to
become the director of the pediatric AIDS branch of the Maternal/Child
Health Bureau in the Department of Health and Human Services. He had

previously established the Children's Hospital Emergency Room. He was an early volunteer with the NO/AIDS Task Force, spearheading early intervention services, and later served as its executive director. He also served as chair of the New Orleans Regional AIDS Planning Council, which had been established in 1993.[51]

Looking back on the early years of the epidemic, videographer Valda Lewis recalls, "The Angel of Death was sweeping through New Orleans and nobody gave a crap. They evaporated, giving themselves back to the universe. I remember thinking, 'I'm too young to know this many dead people.'"[52]

At the same time the community was mobilizing against the AIDS epidemic, political activists were also carefully preparing to challenge the state's crimes against nature law, commonly referred to as the sodomy statute.[53] In 1994, attorney John Rawls took an ad out in *Impact* announcing he was planning a civil lawsuit, with the request: "We would like to hear from the following groups of people as possible plaintiffs: people who have the courage to reveal their sexual orientation and fight openly in court for their rights."[54] Under the auspices of LEGAL (Louisiana Electorate of Gays and Lesbians), the suit was filed in Orleans Civil District Court on June 13, 1994, and listed ten plaintiffs: attorneys Larry Best, Lloyd Bowers, and John Rawls; Joan Ladnier, a city employee and a member of the governor's violent crime and homicide task force; registered nurse Kevin Besse; social worker and professor Jeanne LeBlanc; optometrist John Foster; Rhonda Leco, who was having difficulty being granted joint custody of her children; Johnny Baxley, who was being prosecuted for violating the sodomy statute; and Rick Cosgriff, Chris Daigle's partner and a member of several activist organizations who worked in the hospitality industry.[55]

Shortly after the suit was filed, Judge Robin Giarrusso issued a temporary restraining order barring enforcement of the sodomy statute. Ten days later, Judge Michael Bagneris converted the restraining order into a preliminary injunction and subsequently ruled that district attorney Harry Connick violated the injunction by proceeding with two prosecutions. Connick filed an appeal but later withdrew it.[56] The case was then assigned to Judge Carolyn Gill-Jefferson. On November 18, 1994, the case became a class action suit against prosecutors across the state. After much legal wrangling, the case went to trial on March 26, 1998.[57] The trial lasted five days and made headlines. The plaintiffs' case would consist of three chief claims: the sodomy statute is rooted in religion, homosexuality is natural, and the law's application is used to target the gay and lesbian community.

The law's religious origins were important because of its constitutional implications regarding not only the First Amendment, but also the right to privacy implied in the due process clause of the Fourteenth Amendment. The plaintiffs were specifically alleging that the Louisiana sodomy law violated the right to privacy enshrined in Article I, Section 5 of Louisiana's constitution. In his opening statement, John Rawls said he would prove that the very concept of crimes against nature was religious in nature and therefore unconstitutional. He called the statute "a religious idea introduced by a group of monks for political purposes in the 1100s and 1200s" and adopted into English common law by King Henry VIII to "prove he was more Catholic than the pope."[58] Mark Jordan, a theologian and professor of medieval studies from the University of Notre Dame, then testified to the law's religious roots. Referring to Catholic theology, he said, "Sodomites are often said . . . to be incurable. That is, there is nothing you can do except burn them at the stake."

To establish the fact that homosexuality is a naturally occurring phenomenon, Rawls called several expert witnesses. LSU medical center neurobiologist Dr. Cheryl Weill testified that homosexuality was biologically determined during pregnancy. Her testimony was corroborated by J. Michael Bailey, a genetics researcher, who testified that sexuality is biologically or genetically determined and not a choice.[59] Veterinarian Dr. Michael Scott Williams testified to the existence of homosexuality in the animal kingdom.

In order to prove the law was discriminatory, Rawls had to establish that gays and lesbians were a distinct group with an identifiable culture and history. To this end he called to the stand historian Roberts Batson, sociologist Joel Devine, and bookseller Alan Robinson. Batson provided the court a historical overview of how the law had been used to harass gays and lesbians. Plaintiff Jeanne LeBlanc explained how the law not only struck fear in the hearts of gays and lesbians but also had negative consequences: "I forced myself to date. I forced myself into affairs that were detrimental. I was not myself. I was playing a role. I felt like a fugitive. I felt hunted and furtive."[60] LeBlanc's testimony was followed by fellow plaintiff Johnny Baxley, who recounted the homophobic slurs and taunts of police officers as they arrested him for violating the statute. This testimony was followed by that of Gene Adams, owner of a bathhouse in the French Quarter that had previously been raided by police.[61] Larry Best took the stand and told the court how the law had harmed him by creating and propagating a "climate of intolerance."[62] Best recounted being outed at work, losing business clients, having to leave his law firm, and getting divorced from his wife.

In rebuttal to the claim that the sodomy statute unfairly stigmatizes gays and lesbians, the state argued that the law, which forbids oral and anal sex, applies to both heterosexual and homosexual couples; therefore, since the law does not specifically mention same-sex pairings, it is not discriminatory. But the plaintiffs refuted that claim by comparing the sodomy law to the bygone law that forbade interracial marriage. Proponents of the ban on interracial marriage used the same argument now being advanced by the state—that the law did not specifically mention Black people and was therefore perfectly fine. Rawls put on the stand a cultural anthropologist from the University of Southern California, Walter Williams, who said, "But by their presence in the law books, they served that precise function."[63] Williams then cited other countries that had repealed sodomy laws and testified about how different cultures throughout history have viewed homosexuality.

The state's attorney, assistant attorney general Charlie Braud, called only one witness to defend the statute on behalf of the state—a "Christian homosexual healer," who claimed homosexuals could be healed of their "sickness" through prayer. John Rawls called as a rebuttal witness Davis Eagle, who told the court of "the seven years he had been the victim of Christian healing programs to no avail."[64]

Judge Gill-Jefferson was persuaded by the plaintiffs' case and on March 17, 1999, ruled the sodomy law unconstitutional because it violated the right to privacy. The defendants appealed to the Supreme Court, which remanded the case to district court. The Fourth District upheld the judge's ruling. The case was then appealed to the state Supreme Court. On July 6, 2000, the Supreme Court handed down a ruling in a separate, criminal case that also challenged the constitutionality of the sodomy statute. This case involved a man who had been acquitted of rape but found guilty of engaging in oral sex with a woman. The Fourth Circuit ruled the sodomy statute unconstitutional in that case, but that decision was reversed by the Supreme Court. In a 5–2 ruling, the Supreme Court found that the sodomy law was constitutional and, in light of its decision in the Smith case, remanded the LEGAL case back to district court for reconsideration. Judge Gill-Jefferson noted, "The Supreme Court did not give a compelling reason why the state should control private, noncommercial, consensual sexual behavior between adult human beings."[65] On March 23, 2001, the Fourth District again, in defiance of the Supreme Court's decision in the Smith case, upheld Gill-Jefferson's original ruling. On March 28, 2002, the Supreme Court vacated the Fourth District's ruling. The sodomy statute would stand. For a little while, that is. The following year, the US Supreme Court handed down *Lawrence v. Texas*, a landmark case that invalidated sodomy laws nationwide.

Looking back with the perspective of twenty-five years, plaintiff Larry Best reflects on the case:

I was not at all confident about the outcome, but our team believed we had a good chance of winning in the trial court. Our win was a huge victory and vindication. Then we won again in the Court of Appeal. I began to think we just might win before the feared and notoriously conservative Louisiana Supreme Court. I attended the oral arguments before The Supreme Court and watched with anger and dismay as judge after judge dismissively challenged John Rawls' arguments and conclusions. Under this assault he eventually became angry, impassioned, and impolitic. The outcome was clear long before we later got the formal opinion overruling the lower courts and holding that no constitutional rights were violated by the law.

Because I knew one of the judges personally, Justice Chet Traylor, who was also close to my law partner, I had harbored hopes that he might intervene and do the right thing, but I was wrong. We were all crushed though we had known all along the odds were against us. All that effort, time and emotion for nothing; but it wasn't. The *Times Picayune* and several prominent local columnists publicly supported our cause and had urged the court to uphold the findings of the lower courts. So we had made a difference after all. John had laid out a meticulously crafted case to which there was no factual or legal defense and the public now knew it. We would later be vindicated in 2003 when The United States Supreme Court ruled in *Lawrence v Texas* that such laws were indeed unconstitutional. Sadly, those laws remain (to my knowledge) on our state's books despite efforts to have them repealed.

So our challenge was not in vain and was instead predictive of the zeitgeist slowly overtaking the nation on gay rights. I am so honored to have been a part of that effort and to have had the opportunity to speak up for myself and others against injustice from the witness stand in a court of law.[66]

Stewart was not actively involved in the lawsuit although he certainly followed it with interest. At the time, he was still volunteering for LAGPAC, but most of his time was devoted to PFLAG. By the early 2000s, the Faerie Playhouse was a de facto headquarters for many causes and throughout the day hosted many visitors, often unannounced, who needed to bend Stewart's ear or seek his advice. While Stewart was holding court, either in person or on the phone, Alfred was in his own world—writing, reading the Bible, listening to Gregorian chants, or having afternoon tea parties with the dogs.

Evenings were usually reserved for Stewart and Alfred to spend time together. At home, they would often read to each other and catch up on the day's events. Sometimes they would attend the theater or an opera. Occasionally Alfred would embarrass Stewart in public. Once when they were attending a performance of Richard Strauss's *Salome* at the Mahalia Jackson Theater for the Performing Arts, Alfred began taking off his clothes along with the lead soprano as she disrobed. Stewart sat nervously but said nothing (probably because they were in a box seat) as Alfred removed his shirt, but when he started unzipping his pants, Stewart told him to stop. For the most part, Stewart was incredibly longsuffering with Alfred, but there were times when his patience ran thin. During another opera, Alfred began running up and down the aisle, which prompted Stewart to leave the show during the intermission. He later felt somewhat guilty for "ditching" Alfred but chuckled the next day when he read a review of the performance in the *Times-Picayune*; the reviewer noted that the music was so moving, it inspired some in the audience to dance in the aisles. Stewart was quick to forgive when his patience boiled over. His activism was made possible, after all, by Alfred's benevolence.

Of all the collaborative efforts made by various political action groups and other organizations in the 1980s and 1990s, the most frustrating, and ultimately the most rewarding, was a nearly ten-year battle to persuade the New Orleans City Council to pass a nondiscrimination ordinance protecting LGBT+ people. Commonly known to veterans of that battle as simply "the ordinance fight," Stewart considered it one of LAGPAC's most significant achievements and personally one of his proudest moments.

Chapter 8

THE ORDINANCE

Stewart had a community, not a personal, agenda. Politicians took him seriously because he was not Uptown monied and he never kissed ass or gave a damn about being seen with the right people or going to the right parties.
—RANDY TRAHAN

IN 1986, CHARLENE SCHNEIDER CALLED HER FRIEND VALDA LEWIS AND told her that she and her girlfriend Loretta Mims needed to attend a city council meeting. The council was considering a nondiscrimination ordinance to protect lesbian and gay employees. A similar measure had been voted down two years earlier by the council, despite heavy lobbying from LAGPAC and other groups.

The nondiscrimination ordinance was not passed that day. Lewis was astounded at the misinformation and downright ignorance on display at the council meeting as the ordinance was being debated. Resolved to do something to clear up the prevalent misunderstanding of homosexuality, she and Mims began producing a television show called *Just for the Record.*[1] Lewis recalls, "We needed a better image." The first show featured Charlene Schneider and Johnny Jackson, who talked about their experiences at the recent March on Washington.

Just for the Record was a weekly cable access television show that aired from 1987 to 1993 and covered both local and national topics of interest to the gay and lesbian community. The shows ranged from thirty to sixty minutes. In addition, Lewis and Mims also published a monthly newsletter of the same title from 1989 to 1993. After the show's run, they produced another show called *Queer Street Live*, which ran for thirteen weeks.

Valda fell in love with the camera producing these shows and began recording other events relating to the LGBT+ community. A sampling of what she recorded includes four annual conferences of the National Gay and Lesbian Task Force Policy Institute, the second HIV/AIDS Regional Summit, the thirteenth National Lesbian and Gay Health Conference, the National Commission on AIDS "Sex, Society, and HIV" Hearings, several Bourbon Street Awards contests, Armeinius and Amon-Ra Carnival balls, Pride festivals, and just about anything else queer related that was happening in New Orleans. In all, Valda Lewis recorded almost eight hundred hours of living history. In 2019, she donated the footage to the Amistad Research Center.[2]

These recordings and their preservation are just one aspect of Charlene Schneider's profound legacy. Upon graduating from high school, Schneider landed a job as a cryptographer with a private company that subcontracted with NASA. Charlene worked at Michoud Assembly Facility, in New Orleans East, where she had a top-level security clearance. It was a great job, and she was devastated when she was fired for being a lesbian. She had been arrested in a lesbian bar, and in the early 1960s, this was grounds for dismissal in most jobs. The injustice of it all had a profound impact on Charlene, who resolved to fight for gay and lesbian equality. The consequences of that decision reverberate still today.

Being arrested in a gay bar usually meant the person's name and picture would appear in the next day's newspaper, which, in turn, often resulted in the person being fired or evicted or generally ostracized by friends and family. Charlene went on to be arrested in bar raids six more times. Typically, women in a lesbian bar would be charged with "lewd behavior" or sometimes even prostitution. Charlene later recalled, "You didn't get arrested if you had a purse, though."[3]

After leaving Michoud, Charlene took a number of jobs, including stints at Western Union and the *Times-Picayune*. She was working as the social director at the Country Club when Susan Landrum and Doddie Finley encouraged her to open a bar for lesbians. Charlene, always fearless, decided to take a chance. Having no experience in the bar business, Charlene called on Kitty Blackwell, who had opened the Grog on North Rampart Street in 1969, to help her set up the bar. (Blackwell would go on to own Ms. Kitty's on Burgundy Street, Mississippi River Bottom on St. Philip Street, and Kathryn's Upstairs-Downstairs in Metairie.)

Charlene's, located at 940 Elysian Fields, opened in 1977. Over the next twenty-two years, Charlene's would earn a prominent place in the pantheon of legendary New Orleans bars. Bars often take on the personality of their owners, and Charlene's was no exception. Saundra Boudreaux, a regular in the 1980s, recalls, "Charlene cared about her girls, they were family" and "She always made us feel loved and safe."[4] The notion of Charlene's being a "safe space" is a recurrent theme in many women's memories of the bar. At the time, Charlene once recalled that "women's bars were like boxing rings."

The late Toni Pizanie remembered, "She worked toward giving women a better space."[5] Charlene would often accompany patrons to their cars upon leaving the bar.

Her charisma was underscored by the care and concern she had for her guests. She would often sit with women at the bar and ask them about their lives and offer them encouragement or advice. "She genuinely cared about us," one regular recalls.[6] And whenever a new girl would come into the bar, Charlene went out of the way to make her feel welcome.

On such occasions, Charlene probably remembered her first time at a lesbian bar. In 1957, while still in high school, Charlene went to the Tiger Lounge (originally on Tchoupitoulas Street but later on Burgundy Street), which was owned by a former nun named Jo Jo. In an interview with *Curve Magazine*, Charlene once described going to the Tiger Lounge that night: "I felt at home, because finally, I knew where I belonged. It was wonderful seeing people like myself. I saw eight of the butchest women you've ever seen in your life. I fell in love with each and every one of them."[7]

In addition to providing a warm, safe space for lesbians, Charlene's was also a hotbed of political activity. Charlene fought tirelessly for equal rights and often held voter registration drives at her bar. She often invited LGBT+-friendly politicians to come to the bar to address patrons. Charlene was instrumental in working with LAGPAC, which often held meetings at her bar. She was one of the first members of the New Orleans chapter of PFLAG (Parents and Friends of Lesbians and Gays), and she helped start PrideFest. She had a leading role in the protest rally and march against Anita Bryant in 1977, and she participated in the National March on Washington for Lesbian and Gay Rights in 1979.

It was not uncommon for Charlene to grab the microphone at events at her bar and lecture the crowd on the importance of voting and being politically active. On closing night at Charlene's in 1999, Loretta Mims recalled, "I wouldn't have voted if it wasn't for Charlene."[8] Another regular, Bridgette, observed, "Charlene showed us how to get into politics." And Rebecca Stilley described the closing of Charlene's as "the end of an era for women in the city." Joan Ladnier observes, "I know there were others but for me, Stewart Butler and Charlene Schneider were the father & mother of the Queer activism in NOLA. I was honored to know them, learn from them and work alongside them."[9]

For her work on behalf of equal rights, Charlene Schneider was the recipient of the Human Rights Campaign Equality Award, the Forum for Equality Community Service Award, and the Gay Appreciation Award for Lifetime Achievement. Her bar also received the first Gay Appreciation Award for

Bar of the Year. Perhaps the best summary of Charlene's legacy came from Wayne Christenberry: "Charlene was a force."[10]

Linda Tucker, Charlene's longtime partner whom she met at the bar one Sunday afternoon in 1987, remembers, "A lot of grass roots came out of her club. She would be amazed today by how far we've come."[11] After Charlene's closed in 1999, Charlene and Linda enjoyed a quiet life in Bay St. Louis on the Mississippi Gulf Coast until Charlene's death in 2006. Reminiscing on their time together, Tucker said, "We had such a wonderful life together. She was a wonderful soul and our relationship was just magical."[12]

After the city council voted down the nondiscrimination ordinance in 1986, Charlene and her fellow LAGPAC members vowed to try again. Their strongest ally on the city council was Johnny Jackson, who had been elected with LAGPAC's endorsement, and who had sponsored and introduced the ordinance.

Johnny Jackson Jr. grew up in several New Orleans neighborhoods and became a community activist in the 1960s. After Hurricane Betsy in 1965, he worked on a cleanup crew at the Desire Community Center, and within a few years he was the directing head of the center. He also worked with Total Community Action and the New Orleans Jazz and Heritage Foundation. From 1972 to 1986 he served in the state legislature, where he became the New Orleans delegation's floor leader before being elected to the New Orleans City Council.

Johnny Jackson became an early ally for LGBT+ rights at a time when few politicians were willing to do so. The first politician in New Orleans to openly court the gay vote was Harry Connick Sr. in his first unsuccessful run for district attorney in 1969. Meeting with several members of the LGBT+ community, Connick promised an end to the longstanding practice of police raids of gay bars. At the meeting, which was mostly a question-and-answer session, a notoriously outspoken drag queen named Jo Jo Landry dared to ask the question that was on everyone's mind, "Let's cut the crap. What we really want to know is, are we going to jail if we get caught sucking dick in the bars?"[13] Connick answered yes, noting that public sex acts, regardless of who committed them, were still illegal. Despite this disappointing answer, most in attendance came away relieved that Connick was at least not aggressively hostile to them.

In 1981, Mayor Ernest "Dutch" Morial established a public education task force to look into problems in the gay community. Political activists from that era agree that Morial was the first mayor to demonstrate any support for the gay community and the first mayor to meet with the community. Attorney Jack Sullivan recalls the meeting, "Dutch gave a very supportive speech and the one line I'll always remember is him saying, 'As long as I'm mayor, no one will ever be discriminated against because of his sexual *affectation*.'"[14]

Connick and Morial are rightly remembered as early political allies of our community, but it wasn't until Jackson's election in 1986 that a true legislative champion for LGBT+ rights emerged. During his eight-year tenure on the council, Jackson was at the forefront of championing LGBT+ rights. In addition to leading the Louisiana delegation in the historic 1987 March on Washington for Lesbian and Gay Rights, Jackson also sponsored, and led the fight for, the nondiscrimination ordinance; he fought for adequate HIV/AIDS funding as well as advocated for extending health benefits to the partners of gay and lesbian city employees. He served on a council subcommittee to work with the city health department and local AIDS agencies, and, furthermore, Jackson was actually arrested in a sit-in on Loyola Avenue to protest a lack of proper funding to study AIDS and help AIDS patients. And in 1993, Jackson authored a proposal and voted with a majority of the city council to extend health insurance to the "domestic partners" of gay and lesbian city workers. When the mayor vetoed the measure, Jackson was one of only two votes to override the veto. Jackson's courage and vision are especially remarkable when one considers he represented a majority African American district with very few out constituents.

On the day of the nondiscrimination vote in 1986, Jackson gave a rousing twenty-minute speech in support of the ordinance. Unfortunately, it failed to pass, by a vote of 2–5. When the council voted the ordinance down, council member Joseph Giarrusso told gay rights advocates they had failed to prove they had been discriminated against. This comment gave supporters of the ordinance the motivation and focus they needed to try again. Disappointed but determined to not give up, advocates of the measure went to Charlene's for a party after the council hearing. It was there that Stewart met Rich Magill, who would become one of Stewart's closest friends, and a key figure in the next ordinance battle. Upon striking up a friendship, Butler warned Magill, "I'm a political animal." At Butler's urging, Magill joined LAGPAC.

Magill later recalled attending the Council hearing and being astounded at the sight of gay people standing up for their rights:

Council chambers were to the walls; you couldn't get in there. God, that was fun. That was such an exciting day. I had never been to anything like this in my entire life. I had never seen gay people stand out there in front of a city council and say, "We want this." Never. It was amazing to me. It gave me hope for the first time ever. Until then I had always been hiding, and I didn't think I had a choice.

Then all of a sudden I see these people in this city saying, "Nuh-uh. We want this. We want to have our jobs, our housing, and be able to go to a restaurant without fear." I was just astonished.

Everybody met over at Charlene's bar over on Elysian Fields after it was all over, and John and I went over there, and this was my first introduction to all these people who I thought were so sharp and smart. . . . Everybody else was a little down, and here I am, "Man, I can't wait till we get started again," and I spent the next five years working on it.

There was one council member, Giarusso . . . He said "You didn't prove your case today. If you had been able to prove to me that you are discriminated against, I'd vote for you, but you didn't do it." And he voted no.

And I'm sitting there thinking, "You know what? I think he'll come around." So that was my whole focus for the next five years, was him. "I'm going to make him change his mind."[15]

Born in St. Louis, Magill was reared in a military family and lived in six different places by the time he was graduated by Autauga County High School in 1964, in Prattville, Alabama. Afterward, he attended the University of Alabama and was graduated in 1968. He entered the United States Air Force and was honorably separated in 1972 at the rank of captain. After traveling through Europe, he entered the University of Florida to study building construction and was graduated in 1975. He worked in Fort Lauderdale, Florida; Montgomery, Alabama; Austin, Texas; and Seagrove Beach, Florida, building houses until spinal cord problems forced him to retire at age forty. Magill moved to New Orleans in 1986.

In addition to his work with LAGPAC, Magill was a member or supporter of Mensa, Disabled American Veterans, the Human Rights Campaign, NOW, PFLAG, the NAACP, Compassion and Choices, Beta Theta Pi, the ACLU, the NO/AIDS Task Force, the Sierra Club, and the Democratic Party. In 1988–89, he also published a short-lived newspaper called the *Big Easy Times*. Magill was a regular contributor to the *Big Easy Times*, as were Jerry Zachary, who founded the New Orleans Gay Men's Chorus in 1982; Shelley A. Hamilton, who served as pastor of what was then called the Vieux Carre Metropolitan Community Church; and Henry L. Phillips. The paper lasted a mere six months, but its fourteen issues provide an insightful glimpse into gay New Orleans in the fall of 1988 and winter of 1988–89.

Magill and his partner, John, who would eventually die of complications from AIDS, became two of Stewart and Alfred's closest friends. Magill first met Alfred in January 1987, a few months after meeting Stewart. Stewart suggested the four of them go to dinner together at the Quarter Scene—a popular local eatery among Quarterites. During conversation over the meal, Alfred remained unusually quiet and then at one point loudly blurted out, "Why don't you fuck me anymore?" Magill later recalled, "That was the first of many times Alfred made me very nervous. You were never sure what he might say or do."[16]

Alfred's penchant for taking people by surprise with completely inappropriate comments was a trait his friends learned to deal with. These comments usually came out of nowhere and, while funny, were still sometimes embarrassing. For example, once during a visit to California to visit Freddie Lavre, the three were at a swanky restaurant when Alfred rose from his chair and loudly announced to the entire dining room that he had once tricked with a man who was sitting at a nearby table.

In 1989, LAGPAC and other gay activists turned their attention once again to the antidiscrimination ordinance. The ordinance had been defeated twice before, first in 1984 and again in 1986.

In 1984, Mike Early, who was first elected in 1977 and reelected with LAGPAC's support, cosponsored the ordinance along with fellow council member Wayne Babovich. On January 17, 1984, Stewart and Roberts Batson met with ordinance coauthors Mike Early and Wayne Babovich to discuss the ordinance's chances of passing and to discuss strategy. Early was somewhat concerned about the growing media coverage and advised they adopt a low-profile strategy. A week later, Stewart, Batson, and Martha Kegel met with council member Singleton, who was upset LAGPAC had not endorsed him in his last election. When Singleton mentioned he had not heard from any of his constituents concerning the ordinance, Batson immediately made sure letters from voters were forthcoming, including some from clergy.

Opposition to the proposed ordinance was swift and fierce. When the council met to debate and vote on the measure, Babovich declared he would vote against it because of opposition from "the vast, vast majority of people throughout this city."[17] Much of that opposition came from the religious community, particularly the Temple of Faith in Babovich's district. Roman Catholic archbishop Philip Hannan informed the council that if the ordinance passed, "We would immediately circulate a petition to call for a referendum to repeal the ordinance." He further added, "We cannot compromise our principles in this matter."[18]

Supporting the ordinance were LAGPAC, Crescent City Coalition, the newly formed PFLAG chapter, the ACLU, and other groups. LAGPAC, CCC, and the Louisiana ACLU issued a report explaining the ordinance and refuting arguments against it. Citing a study conducted by Dr. Shelley Coverman, an assistant professor of sociology at Tulane University, the report provided statistics and examples of discrimination in employment, housing, and public accommodations against gay people. The report also clarified misconceptions of what the proposed ordinance did and did not do. It concluded with a long list of quotes from community, religious, business, and labor leaders in support of the ordinance.

But despite the best efforts of the ordinance's proponents, the city council rejected the ordinance. Brian Wagner and Joe Giarrusso, bowing to pressure from the Catholic Church, joined Babovich in voting no. Sidney Barthelemy, Johnny Jackson, and Lambert Boissiere voted yes. Jim Singleton avoided voting by being absent. After the proposed ordinance's defeat, the *New York Times* quoted Alan Robinson:

> Working in the gay political community, we are continually faced with people coming to us who have been thrown out of their apartments or fired from a job because of their sexual orientation. They ask us, "What can we do?" Our response is, "Nothing, it's perfectly legal to fire someone for being gay. Gay people are not a protected class." There is a definite need for such an ordinance. It is not enough but it's the only thing the city can do. . . . It's not a major defeat to lose it on the first vote. We're on a long-term agenda. We will work very hard to get rid of the councilmen who voted against it. In the next election, we'll get rid of at least one of them if not more. They stood up there and voted against the rights of 10 percent of the population of this city. Those people are not going to forget.[19]

Proponents of the ordinance vowed to try again. When the ordinance was introduced again in 1986, opponents rallied as well. Behind the scenes, Archbishop Philip Hannan leveraged the entire weight of the Catholic archdiocese against passage. But Hannan's resolve did not deter proponents of the ordinance. A LAGPAC delegation consisting of Stewart, Louis Volz, a Catholic brother, and a lesbian professor from Tulane met with Monsignor Robert Muench, executive assistant to Archbishop Hannan, to try to convince him to ask the archbishop to not actively oppose the ordinance. Volz, an assistant US attorney and a devout Catholic and former Catechism teacher, had become involved in LAGPAC after coming out of the closet. He and Stewart fell into a dispute over the meeting with Muench. Volz felt that it would be more effective if only Catholics attended the meeting and argued that the archdiocese would be more resistant to "outsiders." Stewart prevailed, but it probably did not matter. While Muench was polite at the meeting, he was not moved. Hannan had dug his feet in and would not budge.

When the ordinance finally came up for a vote, only Johnny Jackson and Dorothy Mae Taylor voted for it. Reaction among proponents of the ordinance was disappointment and anger. Some wanted to express their feelings by having a demonstration at city hall. Roberts Batson proposed a more reserved approach and suggested they show their gratitude to Taylor and Jackson by sending them roses. Rich Sacher made the arrangements and sent the flowers, recalling Jackson and Taylor each received "50 red roses by one of our friends, as a thank you for their efforts. They both were brought to tears."[20] Batson remembers Dorothy Mae Taylor calling him and asking, "What's going on? My office is filled with roses!"[21]

The 1986 defeat was particularly painful because one of the votes against it came from Council member Mike Early, whom LAGPAC had previously endorsed. In his first term, Early had introduced a resolution supporting GayFest (forerunner to Pride) and had mediated between the police and the gay community during times of harassment. So why did he vote no? Pressure from Archbishop Hannan. Early and Hannan had a long personal relationship. Early had spent twelve years in Catholic seminary and served two years as a priest at St. Jerome Parish in Kenner, Louisiana. Early eventually left the priesthood over the church's dogmatic and unrelenting position on contraception. He and Hannan remained friends, and in the lead-up to the ordinance vote, Hannan, through Muench, asked Early to vote no.[22] Many in the community viewed Early's vote as a betrayal.

Led by attorney John Rawls, LAGPAC organized a "Recall Mike Early Rally," which was held at St. Mark's Methodist Church on December 18. Emotions were running high, and the anger in the room was palpable. About fifty-five people attended the rally, which began with an impassioned speech by Rawls. This was followed by questions and comments from the audience. Roberts Batson and Lou Volz attempted to explain what a recall election involved. Nathan Chapman urged everyone in attendance to join LAGPAC. Mary Stuart, co-chair of LAGPAC, frustrated and tired, admonished the crowd:

It's up to you, not LAGPAC! LAGPAC is tired of bustin' its ass alone. The rest is up to you, even if you don't ever stand up and become visible! We will never get our civil rights unless we use the power of our dollar or our vote! When the rest of you get sick enough, you'll get off your tired asses and become involved! If I can do it, visibly and otherwise, from my middle-class Catholic background, then you can too! Just like in the movie, I'm sick and tired and I'm not going to take it anymore! We have simply been not visible enough![23]

At issue was not only Early's *no* vote on the ordinance but his reasons for voting no. During the council meeting, Early attempted to justify his vote by invoking the AIDS crisis. More specifically, Early claimed "the jury is still out" regarding how the virus is transmitted. This comment caused the NO/AIDS Task Force to also call for a recall election. On December 9, the task force issued the following press release:

In his statements before the City Council and a public forum, Councilman Early expressed opinions which clearly contradict the facts. In articulating his ill-informed impressions, the Councilman has further contributed to the "epidemic of fear" which leads to unnecessary anxiety in our community and mistreatment and the unreasonable and unlawful discrimination against those with AIDS and those at risk. We find this indefensible for any reason.

I have spoken with Councilman Early after sending him a copy of the Surgeon General's Report which clearly refutes his position. In his statement to me this morning, however, Mr. Early repeated his belief that "medical evidence is inconclusive regarding transmission of AIDS through other bodily fluids," and feels his statements last week were carefully worded and not inappropriate given what he considers a lack of "conclusive evidence."

While the AIDS virus has been found in tears and saliva, it must be emphasized that "no instance of transmission from these bodily fluids has been reported." (US Surgeon General)

Mr. Early's irresponsibility has jeopardized the health of this community and the effectiveness of medical professionals and AIDS service providers. In provoking unwarranted fear and possible reprisal against those with the disease and in contributing to the AIDS hysteria characterizing employment, insurance and housing provisions, Councilman Early has acted unconscionably. The Board of Directors of the NO/AIDS Task Force, representing some 300 trained community volunteers, hereby calls for the immediate resignation of Mike Early as Councilman for District C.[24]

But Early did not resign, nor was he recalled; nevertheless, the firestorm raged on. About a month after the vote, Stewart, Rich Sacher, Roberts Batson and others staged a protest at a campaign fundraiser Early held at the New Orleans Museum of Art. Sacher remembers:

> It was a cool December night as we gathered in the dark, by the lily pond at the entrance to the museum, and we were chanting slogans against Mike Early. I remember that I had a large chime which I would strike every sixty seconds, in memory of friends we lost to AIDS . . . and others in our group were handing out flyers to everyone who showed up for the fundraiser, accusing Early of being a Judas, deliberately spreading ignorance about AIDS, and warning people that he would betray them, too. It was a pretty bold, loud, in your face protest. I was surprised that most people took the flyers and carried them into the museum with them.
>
> About 15 minutes into our protest, a four piece jazz band which had been playing inside the museum was sent outside, with obvious instructions: play loud, and drown them out. We fell silent. We could not compete with the volume of their music. All of a sudden, Roberts Batson yells out, "We shall overcome!"
>
> Several people near him begin singing, and a young woman with a violin begins to play. (Who brings a VIOLIN to a protest?) More and more of our group take up the song, and before we are half-way through the first verse, every one of us is singing: "We shall Overcome . . . deep in my heart I do believe . . ."
>
> And then it happened: Those four African American musicians stopped playing! They would NOT play while our group of 50 or 60 white gay men and women were singing THEIR song of protest and liberation! At the end of each verse, Roberts would shout out the next line: "We are not afraid . . . we are not alone . . . we'll walk hand in hand."
>
> The atmosphere was electric . . . people inside the museum were pressed up against the doors, looking out at us . . . and those jazz musicians were absolutely still, almost standing at attention, as we sang verse after verse of We Shall Overcome. They would not play again until we finished singing, and when they did, it was a lighter, more joyful jazz. We had arrived at an unspoken understanding: now, they would play FOR us, and we would sing TO them, for several more rounds. It was extraordinary!
>
> I have often thought about that night. We had our protest, and we certainly got our message out; but what started as an angry demonstration against a vicious political betrayal became something else . . . something hopeful and uplifting. It was the respect and deference

shared between us and those four black musicians that helped all [of] us believe in the message: We shall overcome.

This was over 30 years ago, and to this day, I still do not know if Roberts Batson had planned to sing that night . . . or if it was his inspiration of the moment. Either way, it was brilliant.[25]

But despite the outrage of his opponents, Early won reelection.

Advocates for the ordinance regrouped and, with help from an even wider coalition, resolved to try yet again. The ordinance coordinating committee was formed in Dr. Brobson Lutz's living room in December 1989.[26] The committee began collecting data on the prejudice and discrimination gays and lesbians in New Orleans were experiencing. From June 11 through September 6, ten thousand copies of a four-page questionnaire were distributed and yielded four hundred responses. The logistics of distributing the questionnaire were a massive collaborative effort between several organizations.[27] At the conclusion of the survey period, Magill and Jim Wiltberger then spent a year analyzing the data. The results were not surprising; the report's conclusion stated, "Quite simply, our 1989 survey and subsequent study prove that homophobic hate-motivated violence and discrimination are serious problems for New Orleans."[28]

Exposing Hatred: A Report on the Victimization of Lesbian and Gay People in New Orleans, Louisiana by Rich Magill was published by LAGPAC in 1991 and offered a thorough look at the homophobia the gay community in New Orleans faced at the time. The comprehensive report examined everything from subtle forms of discrimination to overt acts of violence. It was the first study of its kind in New Orleans.

At the same time local activists were working on the next ordinance fight, the Louisiana Advisory Committee to the United States Commission on Civil Rights met in 1988 to hear testimony regarding "the administration of justice of homosexual persons in New Orleans." In addition to the conclusions found in the *Exposing Hatred* report, the data gathered by the commission would also bolster the case for the ordinance. On May 27, 1988, a daylong public forum was held in New Orleans. Louisiana assistant attorney general Glenn Ducote opened the forum by providing an overview of state laws that applied to gay and lesbian people. Twenty people then testified, including Stewart and several of his friends and fellow activists.[29] In his testimony before the committee, Stewart compared homophobia to a wheel, stating, "Homophobia is like a wheel—a homophobic wheel of evil—whose spokes interlock in an intricate web of cause and effect. The unequal administration of justice is only one spoke of that wheel, but it is impossible to discuss that spoke without discussing the others."[30] He went on to explain that the other spokes included the hysteria surrounding AIDS, the unconstitutionality of sodomy laws, youth suicide, violence and discrimination, and "a conspiracy of silence."

Proponents of the ordinance were optimistic that the third time would be a charm. Times were changing and public attitudes regarding homosexuality had begun to shift. This shift was the result, in part, of increased media coverage. In 1990, television personality Angela Hill devoted a show to PFLAG and later did a five-day series of gay-related programming. Also that year, the *Times-Picayune* ran a feature story on Kevyn Aucoin, a Baton Rouge makeup artist who had become internationally famous by working with celebrities Madonna, Whitney Houston, and Cher and fashion models Naomi Campbell and Cindy Crawford. Allies such as enormously popular local news anchor Andre Trevigne also helped dispel negative stereotypes. In addition, *Just for the Record* helped raise awareness. Increasing queer visibility gave activists hope.

Another factor affecting public attitudes that had been absent in the previous two ordinance fights was the recent gubernatorial election, which pitted former governor Edwin Edwards in a runoff with former Ku Klux Klan grand wizard David Duke. Because of Louisiana's unique open primary (the top two vote-getters proceed to a runoff regardless of party), incumbent governor Buddy Roemer, who was elected as a Democrat but then became a Republican while in office, tried to appeal to moderate voters but was squeezed out of the primary by Edwards on the left and Duke on the right. The race captured national attention, and many organizations threatened to cancel their conventions and conferences in New Orleans if Duke was elected. The threat of a boycott certainly resonated in New Orleans. The election, held a month before the ordinance vote, was fresh in the minds of everyone. Many who testified at the ordinance hearing, including several council members, referenced the gubernatorial election in their condemnations of bigotry and discrimination.

Then, in a stroke of good timing, the night before the ordinance hearing, popular journalist Connie Chung interviewed Magic Johnson on national television. The professional basketball star talked about being recently diagnosed as HIV positive and the widespread ignorance surrounding AIDS. The interview was a landmark moment in the nation's thinking about the epidemic. At the time of the interview, 75 percent of the people living with HIV, worldwide, were heterosexual, but in the US, the general public still considered HIV/AIDS a primarily homosexual disease. That began to change when Johnson went public.

Johnny Jackson, whose testimony as a city council member and a straight Black man bore a lot of weight, spoke about the hatred he personally experienced during the last ordinance fight: "People phoned my office, people phoned my home with all kinds of threats. My children were confronted, my wife, my family, even within my church, and by people from all segments of this community—not necessarily only the police, but whites, Blacks, religious people. People who heretofore had pronounced a commitment for the struggle of human rights approached me and my family in a manner which scared me."[31] But Jackson was undaunted.

Johnny Jackson continued to work closely with LAGPAC leaders and introduced the nondiscrimination measure again in 1991. During a strategy session before the vote, proponents explored the idea of including an exemption to the ordinance for churches and other religious institutions. Stewart became enraged when the idea was floated. Always an ideological purist, Stewart vehemently opposed the idea of compromising and even threatened to testify against the ordinance at the council meeting if the religious exemption was included. At that point everyone else had had enough, and Jim Wiltberger, who was co-chair of LAGPAC at the time, told Stewart, "If you do that I'll lay you out right there in the chamber!"[32] Stewart got the message, and Wiltberger did not have to punch Stewart.

Testimony at the hearing was sometimes heated, sometimes humorous, but for the most part methodical and streamlined. One opponent of the ordinance, Reverend Marie Galatus, testified that her contacts in the homosexual underground had informed her that New Orleans was the "target city" in a grand scheme to overthrow the federal government. When she claimed, "If passed, the population of New Orleans would skyrocket with homosexuals," the audience burst into laughter.[33] Most people who spoke against the ordinance opposed it on religious grounds, the primary witnesses being from the Catholic Church and a few fringe churches. But the religious arguments were deftly rebutted by Randy Evans, who quoted prohibitions against eating shellfish in Leviticus, the same Old Testament book so often quoted by homophobic preachers. Evans also cited an obscure document that Rich Magill had somehow located—the policy handbook of Associated Catholic Charities, which prohibited discrimination on several grounds, including sexual orientation. The hypocrisy of the Church was further illustrated by the fact it opposed the ordinance even with the religious exceptions. Many Protestant religious groups who had testified against the ordinance in 1984 and 1986 apparently felt satisfied with the exemptions and did not show up to testify in 1991. Evans then pointed to the recent gubernatorial election, thus raising the specters of Nazi discrimination and death camps for homosexuals. Rich Magill talked about the prevalence of not only discrimination against gay and lesbians but also hate crimes. Then state senator Marc Morial testified in favor of the ordinance, invoking the hallowed name of the Reverend Avery Alexander, who decades before had been forcibly removed from the very room they were meeting in because of his race.[34] And Maggie Tidwell refuted the accusations that gay men were child molesters by pointing to the growing pedophilia scandal in the Catholic Church, arguing it would be unreasonable to assume all Catholic priests are pedophiles just because of the actions of a few. Sandra Pailet talked about her two sons not having the same rights just because one of them was gay.

When the antidiscrimination ordinance came up for a vote before the city council, the *Exposing Hatred* report offered the council members the political cover they needed. Councilman Giarrusso finally had his proof and, after six hours of heated debate, voted to approve the ordinance along with Dorothy Mae Taylor, Jim Singleton, Johnny Jackson, and Lambert Boissiere Jr. Voting against the ordinance were Jackie Clarkson and Peggy Wilson. When the vote was taken, the roughly 130 people in attendance erupted in applause and celebration. Afterward, Jackson was quoted as saying, "I always had faith that people would get over their fears." Rich Magill said, "It was the happiest day of my life."[35]

As the vote was being taken, members of the council made remarks justifying or explaining their votes. While Wilson cited concerns over "moral standards" before voting no, Clarkson launched into a bizarre harangue claiming the ordinance would create more discrimination than it eliminated by exercising too much "regulatory control" over businesses—a point that no one had referred to in the long six-hour session of testimony. Clarkson's vote was especially troubling to many since her district included the heavily gay-populated neighborhoods of the French Quarter and Marigny. Eddie Domingue remembers:

> Troy Carter's race for City Council to remove Jacquelyn Clarkson was very important to us since Ms. Clarkson had backed out of her promise to support the Equal Rights Amendment in City Council. We worked our ass off to beat her and on election night when Troy Carter won by a little over 3,000 votes (LAGPAC had over 5,000 voters on its voter list) we could not have been happier. Troy Carter actually mentioned LAGPAC in his acceptance speech and recognized the work we did to get him elected.[36]

Clarkson went on to serve in the state house of representatives in 1994, serving two terms there before returning to the city council in 2002. Troy Carter eventually became a state senator before succeeding Cedric Richmond in Congress in 2021.

The passage of the nondiscrimination ordinance was the culmination of a long eight-year struggle. Many people from many different groups worked tirelessly for the ordinance's adoption, and it would be inaccurate to credit one group or one person with its success; it truly was a collaborative effort. Nonetheless, it should be noted that Stewart was the only person to serve on all three ordinance committees. The ordinance's ultimate passage was a singular achievement that demonstrated how effective gay activism could be when the LGBT+ community and its allies united and worked together to achieve a common goal. But such unity would not last long. The issue of transgender inclusion within the movement would soon shatter the illusion of unity. The battle for trans inclusion in nondiscrimination legislation, which came to the national forefront in 2007 over ENDA (Employment Non-Discrimination Act), was foreshadowed in New Orleans in the 1990s. The battleground was PFLAG.

Chapter 9

PUTTING TRANS RIGHTS ON THE RADAR

It amazed me that Stewart, a cisgender gay man who had
no skin in the game, would take up our cause.

—COURTNEY SHARP

IN 1992, ROY LETSON SOLD *IMPACT* TO KYLE SCAFIDE. SHORTLY AFTER
Scafide took over the paper, Stewart called him to arrange a meeting. Stewart was concerned about the paper's coverage of trans issues. He, Courtney Sharp, and a few other transgender leaders met Scafide and editor Jon Newlin at the 2601 bar, where Scafide assured them the trans community would be treated fairly under his tenure.[1] At the time, trans rights were not a high priority for anyone. Stewart was a visionary in his early and active support of the trans rights movement. In addition to his work with LAGPAC, Stewart also became heavily involved in the New Orleans chapter of Parents and Friends of Lesbians and Gays (PFLAG), which was founded in 1982, just two years after the founding of LAGPAC. Through PFLAG, Stewart would make his mark on the national trans rights movement.

The first PFLAG chapter had been formed ten years earlier in New York after Jeanne Manford's son Morty was physically attacked during a Gay Activist Alliance demonstration in New York. After the attack, Jeanne Manford wrote a letter to the *New York Post* declaring, "I have a homosexual son and I love him."[2] She then marched with her son in the Christopher Street Liberation Day parade (predecessor to New York City's Pride parade). During the march, she proudly held a sign that said, "Parents of Gays: Unite in Support of Our Children." The message resonated, and soon thereafter POG (Parents of Gays) held its first meeting at the New York City Metropolitan Church. POG evolved into PFLAG, which now boasts over two hundred thousand members in over five hundred chapters across the United States.

The phenomenal success of PFLAG has been nothing short of remarkable, and its contributions to the LGBT+ community's collective fight for tolerance and equality are immeasurable. PFLAG's national history is well documented, but what is not as well known is the New Orleans chapter's pivotal role in influencing the national organization. Specifically, the New Orleans chapter pioneered the effort to have trans people included in the national PFLAG mission statement. In addition, the local chapter's scholarship program became the model for the national organization's scholarship program. And as with LAGPAC, Stewart met people through PFLAG who would become an integral part of his life.

The New Orleans chapter of PFLAG was founded in 1982 by Dr. Niki Kearby and Betty Caldwell. Kearby says the chapter grew out of her dissatisfaction with her church's intolerance of homosexuality. One of Kearby's friends who had worked in the church's administrative offices was fired when she admitted to being gay. Kearby had grown up a devout Methodist and was a member of the Rayne Methodist Church on St. Charles Avenue. After her friend's dismissal, Kearby began attending the more gay-friendly St. Mark's United Methodist Church in the French Quarter.

In 1982, after seeing Mary Jo Webster tell a television news reporter that she was gay and had very supportive parents, Niki called her parents and recruited them; Molly and Doug Webster became PFLAG New Orleans's first sponsoring parents. Molly Webster would also serve as president and editor of the group's newsletter.

The earliest New Orleans PFLAG meetings were held at the St. Louis Community Center on Barracks Street in a very small room. About twenty people attended the first meeting in May 1982, half of whom had to sit on the floor. The conservative *Times-Picayune* initially refused to run an ad for the meeting, but after some string pulling, the paper's owner acquiesced and ran the ad. Attendance steadily increased, and the meetings were eventually moved to Mercy Hospital. In the early years, PFLAG meetings attracted thirty to forty people, including Father Bill Richardson, who was in his eighties. Richardson, who had angered his congregation at St. George's in 1973 by holding a memorial service for the victims of the Up Stairs Lounge fire, finally came out of the closet after his wife died and he was retired.

As chair of the LAGPAC membership committee, Stewart was a relentless recruiter, and other LGBT+ organizations provided fertile grounds for enlisting new members. Stewart was fond of saying, "Membership lists are the foundation of any organization," and he brought that philosophy to PFLAG as well. In 1997 alone, he recruited 210 new members. And every few months, Stewart would include an article in the monthly newsletter reminding people to renew their memberships. For decades, Stewart oversaw the PGLAG newsletter, *Banner*, which by 1995 boasted over 2,000 recipients. When a newsletter was ready to be mailed, volunteers gathered under the watchful eye of Stewart at the Faerie Playhouse, where he meticulously supervised the grouping of newsletters according to zip code. Once a volunteer correctly sorted a few sets of zip codes, Stewart would reward the worker with a joint. While supervising these meetings, Stewart also had the task of keeping Alfred fully clothed; it was not uncommon for Alfred to completely disrobe during the process of sorting envelopes. Randy Trahan observes, "Stewart was always the one to keep things on track. He believed in order."[3] Indeed he did. Those under his command in the army didn't call him "Little Jesus" for nothing. After Hurricane Katrina, the newsletter went digital.

In 1990, Rich Sacher approached PGLAG co-chair Sandra Pailet, who had joined PFLAG in 1984 after her son came out, with the idea of starting a scholarship fund for LGBT+ high school students who wanted to attend college. Begun with a generous donation from Rich Sacher and his partner Bill Dailey, the first scholarship was awarded in 1991. Since that time, the local chapter has dispensed over $500,000 to over 450 gay, lesbian, bisexual, and transgender students. Currently the program offers scholarships ranging from $1,000 to $10,000 to eligible students. Sacher recalls how the program got started:

> Sandra Pailet was P-FLAG president, and I suggested that we should start a scholarship fund to support graduating gay high school students as they began college. There was some hesitation concerning legal matters, so I wrote the first check to P-FLAG Scholarship Fund, for $1,000, and gave it to Sandra. That made the concept real to her, and soon the paperwork had been done, so fundraisers could be held. Needing a location that was free, we decided to use the site at American Aquatic Gardens for annual champagne receptions/fundraisers.
>
> The first five years, all annual fundraisers and awards were held at the Aquatic Gardens. The event grew constantly, and because we had minimum outdoor shelter, I always worried that we would be rained out, and the event would be cancelled. That never happened, but after five years, I told Sandra she had to find a larger, indoor venue.[4]

The local scholarship program, to which Stewart and Alfred donated annually beginning in 1993, was a tremendous success and eventually became the model for the national organization's scholarship program.

In a 2002 interview, Joe Melcher, who worked with the scholarship committee for decades, recounted how he became involved in PFLAG:

> I was aware of PFLAG for a number of years prior to my becoming a board member. I originally thought it was primarily for parents who were having difficulty accepting their gay and lesbian children. When PFLAG started having its scholarship receptions I attended those as a way of supporting their efforts and as a social event. Six or seven years ago I decided to fill out one of the slips that came with the *Banner* requesting volunteers. Niki Kearby, the scholarship chair, invited me to attend one of their committee meetings, and I decided that perhaps I could be of assistance to them. I had noticed in the past few years that there were few scholarship recipients from racial minorities, and since I worked at Xavier University, I thought that maybe I could help some of the African American students learn about the opportunity and encourage them to apply. The next year four students from Xavier were among the recipients. After I had served on the committee for a couple of years, Sandra Pailet, the president, invited me to serve on the board . . . For the 2000–2001 academic year, Niki, who was considering retirement, asked if I would serve as her co-chair and begin to learn some of the details of the committee.

The year 1993 was notable for the New Orleans chapter. Not only did it send a delegation to the 1993 March on Washington, it also hosted the national conference in New Orleans. Roughly 750 people from Louisiana attended the third March on Washington. The US Park Service estimated attendance at 300,000, but march organizers claimed attendance was closer to 1,000,000. The PFLAG delegation included Stewart and Alfred, Sandra Pailet and her son Devan, Betty Caldwell, and others. After the march, which took place on April 25, the New Orleans chapter of PFLAG spent the rest of the spring and all summer preparing for the national conference, which was held in New Orleans in September.

One of the more significant consequences of the 1993 March on Washington was the founding of the New Orleans chapter of the Lesbian Avengers. The national Lesbian Avengers had been founded a year earlier in New York City.[5] The New York group staged a Dyke March in Washington on the eve of the larger march. An estimated twenty thousand lesbians participated in the first Dyke March and returned to their respective states energized.[6] Margaret Coble and Charlotte Bahm and a group of their friends from New

Orleans attended the march and founded the New Orleans chapter a month after the national march and met weekly at the Lesbian and Gay Community Center.[7] The group lasted a little over a year and boasted a membership of about fifty. The group's goal was to raise lesbian visibility and advocate for women's issues. The Lesbian Avengers did not endorse political candidates, but they did put pressure on legislators from time to time; for example, the Avengers joined a coalition of other groups to lobby the New Orleans City Council when it considered an ordinance extending domestic partnership benefits to spouses of city employees. The New Orleans chapter also had social events as well, the most memorable of which was a huge Lundi Gras party at Charlene's bar in 1994.[8] The group was revived briefly in 1998 to stage another Dyke March.

The first week of September 1993 was a banner week in the LGBT+ history of New Orleans. On September 1, 1993, Rip and Marsha Naquin-Delain dashed down to city hall at 6:30 a.m. to be the first in line to register as domestic partners under the new city ordinance. Southern Decadence was also in full swing that week. On Sunday, September 5, the legendary Ms. Fly (Lee Featherston) led the twentieth Southern Decadence parade as grand marshal. Coinciding with Southern Decadence 1993, PFLAG held its national conference in New Orleans at the Sheraton Hotel on Canal Street. Local chairs Sandra Pailet (president of the local PFLAG chapter), Stewart Butler, and Billy Henry helped organize the conference.

The theme of the conference was "Celebrating Family New Orleans Style." In addition to featuring Gerry Studds (the first openly gay member of Congress) and Mitzi Henderson (national president of PFLAG) as keynote speakers, the conference also included a number of local figures. Local PFLAG founders Niki Kearby and Betty Caldwell welcomed attendees into their 1835 Creole townhouse. Local gay Carnival royalty hosted an exhibit of costumes previously worn at their krewes' bal masques as well as judged a costume contest. Local historian Roberts Batson offered customized tours for attendees, as did Tulane architecture professor Gene Cizek and his partner Lloyd Sensat. Among the dozens of workshops, several were led by locals. For example, Ms. Tracey, Honey, and Eloy led a session titled "What Is Meant by 'Drag,' Transvestitism, and Transsexuality." Rabbi Edward P. Cohn and Reverend Suzanne P. Meyer (Unitarian) led a session on "Religious Leaders in Support of Understanding." And Otto Stierle and Allen Lombard presented on "Gay Mardi Gras: History, Krewes, Queens, and More!"

Julie Thompson, longtime copresident of New Orleans PFLAG, recalls the 1993 conference fondly:

I was new to PFLAG, having joined in Feb. 1993. But, we all had to work to make the convention a success. We would meet on Saturdays to fill the gift bags and to be told what our jobs would be at the convention. My job was to be a tour guide on one of the buses that took everyone on a champagne tour of New Orleans. My son, Michael, was the bartender on my bus. We were the only mother-son team. It was so much fun! Everyone loved it! The workshops and speakers were wonderful. Very inspiring to a newcomer like me. The closing banquet was amazing. There was a Mardi Gras theme. People wore costumes and a krewe from a gay ball danced around the room in their fabulous costumes. The waiters paraded in with flaming desserts. What an amazing night! What an amazing weekend! People are still asking us to host another convention. I told my parents how excited I was to be part of such a wonderful group. And 25 years later, I am still a part of it.[9]

The national PFLAG conference presented a dilemma for Stewart. Attire for the opening reception was formal black tie and Stewart hated tuxedos. An additional stressor was the minor detail that Stewart was the master of ceremonies for the evening. Costumes were optional, however, and this option afforded Stewart the opportunity to make one of his most memorable public appearances. The conference was in September, but earlier that spring Freddie Lavre, a longtime friend of Alfred's from San Francisco whose drag persona was "the Mad Russian Countess," suggested Stewart go in drag as Dame Edna. Alfred's sister, Jean Henry, thought it was a great idea and enthusiastically proclaimed, "And I have the perfect gown for you—Alfred's grandmother's."[10] It seemed like a fun idea at the time, but Stewart didn't take it too seriously—until the dress arrived in the mail.

On the day of the conference dinner, Freddie Lavre and Robby DeJacimo, who occasionally performed in drag as "Savannah Summers," instructed Stewart to strip to his underwear and lay on his back on the floor of their hotel room at the Sheraton. They then helped transform Stewart into Dame Edna. Also witnessing the metamorphosis were some of Stewart's closest friends, including his sister Suzanne and his niece Alicia. Anticipation was high as Dame Edna and her entourage approached the ballroom because no one had any idea Stewart would arrive in drag. Conference co-chair Sandra Pailet announced the Dame's arrival with an ear-piercing shriek to a very enthusiastic and quite surprised crowd. Stewart recalls being perfectly comfortable in drag, except for the shoes, which were too small, "They made walking very painful on top of the difficulty in maintaining my balance in half-high heels for the first time."[11] Stewart's drag persona of Dame Edna was captured in a portrait by J. B. Harter.

The year 1993 was not the first time Stewart, or the local chapter, would make a splash at a national conference. In 1998, at the national conference in San Francisco, PFLAG, at the urging of its New Orleans chapter, became the first national gay rights organization in the country to include transgender people in its mission statement. Stewart Butler and Courtney Sharp led the charge.

The two had met in 1995 at the LGBT Community Center, which was then located on North Rampart Street. One afternoon, as Stewart was sitting on the center's stoop smoking a cigarette, Courtney approached the entrance to meet with Crystal Little, with whom she volunteered at the center. Stewart greeted her and then gruffly asked, "Who are you?" Her answer was followed up with, "Are you a Democrat or a Republican?"[12] The gruff introduction was the beginning of a long and warm friendship. Years later, reflecting on the early years of their relationship, Sharp remembered how amazed she was that this gay man, a man that had "no skin in the game" regarding trans issues, would champion the trans cause, especially at a time when no one else was.

Not long after their chance meeting, Stewart summoned Sharp and Little (both of whom are trans) to the Faerie Playhouse. As they sat at the kitchen table, Stewart had a notepad filled with questions and, as Sharp recalls, "he sized me up."[13] The purpose of the meeting had to do with getting transgender protections included in the upcoming New Orleans Home Rule Charter. Stewart was in recruiting mode; this would be his next fight, and he needed fellow soldiers.

Sharp was no stranger to the struggle. Her resume of activism would eventually boast stints as a board member of the Gulf Gender Alliance, the Lesbian and Gay Community Center in New Orleans, LAGPAC, and PFLAG (both locally and nationally). Sharp had also served on the mayor's advisory committee.

Transgender protections had not been included in the 1991 nondiscrimination ordinance passed by the New Orleans City Council. Efforts at transgender organizing in the New Orleans area date to the 1980s, but those efforts focused more on offering support and dispensing information rather than political activism. As Chloe Raub, head of archives and special collections at Newcomb College Institute, has observed, "All too often, trans history has been minimized or erased from the historical record."[14] Little had been involved with a group called the Gulf Gender Alliance, founded in 1987, serving as its president for four years before working with the Lesbian and

Gay Community Center of New Orleans. Attorney Jim Kellogg had offered legal assistance to trans people in New Orleans before relocating to San Francisco. These efforts were important, if not highly visible, and foreshadowed the advent of groups like BreakOUT! and Louisiana Trans Advocates in the 2000s.

After his meeting with Sharp and Little, Stewart enlisted the help of *Ambush* publisher Rip Naquin-Delain. Butler and Naquin-Delain then contacted two allies on the city council—Troy Carter and Roy Glapion—to discuss strategy. Carter had been elected in 1994 and succeeded Jackie Clarkson, who incidentally succeeded Carter when he was elected to the state house of representatives in 1992 before winning a state senate seat in 2015. Also elected in 1994, Glapion had served as president of the Zulu Social Aid and Pleasure Club from 1973 to 1988, during which time he led the effort to racially integrate the popular Mardi Gras parading club. At the time of his death on December 28, 1999, Glapion had been named King Zulu for 2000. According to Stewart, both Carter and Glapion "were on board immediately."

After conferring with a number of people, it was decided to adopt an "under the radar strategy." Although not an exact comparison, "home rule charter" may be thought of roughly as a municipality's "constitution." In 1995, an overhaul of the charter that had been adopted in 1954 was proposed. One of the more controversial amendments was the authorization of charter schools in Orleans Parish. The public debate over this issue was so great that trans advocates correctly calculated that they could quietly "slip into" the charter the term "gender identification" to be added to the nondiscrimination statute. Sharp remembers, "Everyone was so focused on the big picture, they didn't notice the details."[15]

It was a quiet victory, but a victory nonetheless. In that same year, calls to include gender identity in the national PFLAG mission statement had begun at the national conference in Indianapolis. Mary Boenke, who founded the Roanoke Valley, Virginia chapter of PFLAG in 1992, attended a transgender workshop at the conference but was disappointed to learn that her son's local PFLAG chapter would not be much help to her transgender son because trans people were not included in PFLAG's mission. After the workshop, Boenke and a handful of other attendees met and began brainstorming solutions to the dilemma they were facing. In the coming months they reached out to PFLAG chapters across the country in search of "transgender coordinators." Within two years, they successfully established a network of over two hundred transgender coordinators, each advancing the cause of transgender inclusion within their local chapters. The point person in Louisiana was Courtney Sharp. Sharp would eventually take the lead in the long campaign to persuade the national organization to include transgender people in its mission statement.

Like so many trans people, Courtney Sharp's journey to self-realization was a long one. Growing up, she knew she was different but couldn't quite put her finger on it. All she knew for sure was that she had better keep that difference secret. Her family was religious, and this was north Louisiana, after all. When her "difference" began to manifest, her family, which was Roman Catholic, steered her into traditional gender roles.

Sharp was born in New Orleans but had moved away as a child when her father took a job near Vidalia, Louisiana. While attending college at Louisiana Tech in Ruston (near the Arkansas border), she attended a talk on campus given by Christine Jorgensen—the first widely recognized trans woman in the US (she transitioned in the early 1950s). Most of the attendees came out of curiosity, but it was more than curiosity for Sharp. Sharp was looking for answers, a reference point, hope.

Sharp had dealt with her internal struggle by turning to academics as a coping mechanism. Incredibly bright, in 1976 she earned two degrees in chemical and biomedical engineering. She then landed a job with a chemical company in Lake Charles, where she worked for seven years before being hired by another company that relocated her closer to Baton Rouge.

When she anonymously asked the human resources department at the company what the policy on being transsexual was, she received no response. She then asked a lawyer to assist her in obtaining information, but still no response was forthcoming. Sharp kept working because she really enjoyed her job, but after a few years the struggle had become too intense to deny. When Sharp personally approached the HR department, she was told that she would be fired if she began transitioning. The excuse the company gave her was that it would create a "hostile work environment." Sharp later recalled, "I do not think anyone really understands what discrimination feels like until they confront it personally."[16]

Sharp then began seeing a psychiatrist at a gender clinic in Galveston in 1985. She kept working but gradually became depressed to the point of being hospitalized in 1992. Sharp eventually sued her employer in federal court, but her case was dismissed. Ultimately, she was terminated for long-term disability. Unemployed and on disability, she then began spending countless hours researching and educating herself on transgender legal issues. She regularly attended transgender conferences in Houston.

In 1993, Sharp moved to New Orleans. She had lost her career as well as her family, who rejected her when she began transitioning. She was lost, lonely, broke, and depressed. She considered suicide. But a nagging thought kept her from ending it all. She had learned of a statistic that haunted her. In her own words, Sharp recalls, "Forty percent of the kids in my community are killing themselves and I know exactly why. What am I going to do about it?"[17] The answer was to get involved with PFLAG and the community. She volunteered at the LGBT Community Center and also worked with LAGPAC. Sharp also served as the first transgender person on the mayor's advisory committee (MAC) and the following year joined the board of directors of LAGPAC.

In 2000, when a Louisiana Winn-Dixie grocery store fired Peter Oiler for cross-dressing when he wasn't working, he reached out to the LGBT Community Center for help and was referred to Sharp. Sharp met with Peter Oiler and his wife Shirley and helped organize a protest campaign consisting of thirty-eight different organizations. While a lawsuit was working its way through the federal court system, Sharp said, "The transgender community had demanded that Winn-Dixie institute a nondiscrimination policy for gender identity and expression and sexual orientation. We also asked them to institute sensitivity training. Those demands have not been withdrawn and were not dependent upon the legal case."[18]

In addition to battling politicians and corporations, Sharp also waged a subtler campaign within the LGBT+ community to foster greater under-standing and inclusion of transgender people. When she joined PFLAG, she asked why the group did not include transgender young people in its mission. The question caught the attention of the local chapter's leadership (Sandra Pailet, Julie Thompson, and Randy Trahan), and they took Sharp to dinner to discuss the matter further. Sharp emphasized to them that the path to understanding was education and then offered to educate PFLAG. And educate she did. Sharp began bringing other trans people to PFLAG support meetings and providing reading material to anyone who would accept it. Thompson remembers one book Sharp made her read about a trans person who ended up committing suicide. Thompson was so depressed by the tragic story, she told Sharp she didn't want to read anymore. Sharp replied, "You have to." Thompson, Pailet, and Trahan were receptive to Sharp's message, but the rest of the board, at least initially, was not.

Sharp had put transgender youth on the local PFLAG chapter's radar, but there was still much to do, namely convincing the local PFLAG board of directors that the trans issue was something the national organization needed to address. When the PFLAG board read a letter Stewart had published in the local paper that took the local HRC to task for ignoring trans people just before its gala fundraiser, they were incensed that Thompson, as president of PFLAG, was one of the signers. In 1995, neither Sharp nor Butler was on the PFLAG board. President Julie Thompson recalls the board, which consisted of fourteen members, being split about the transgender issue. Before the board meetings, Stewart would call Thompson and coach her on what to say and how to respond to objections. After board meetings, Sharp would call Thompson and ask her if the board "fussed" at her. "Yes," Thompson would reply. But ultimately, largely because of Stewart's and Sharp's efforts behind the scenes, the PFLAG board came around. Together they gradually persuaded the local chapter to lead the fight for transgender inclusion in the national PFLAG mission statement. Julie Thompson recalls the group first writing letters to the national office urging the inclusion of transgender people in their mission statement and not receiving a reply. But the local chapter would not be ignored.

The New Orleans chapter of PFLAG formally proposed that the national organization vote to include the word transgender in its mission statement. The resolution would be voted on by the national board at the national conference in San Francisco in 1998. The board required written arguments both for and against the resolution before they voted. Sharp wrote the argument for trans inclusion. The resolution passed and PFLAG became the first national LGBT+ organization to include trans people in its mission statement. Mary Boenke later remembered the vote:

> There were maybe about five hundred people at that conference. I was sitting at the back of the room, and I still get choked up talking about this because when it came to a vote on accepting the change in the bylaws, every hand went up except one fella across the aisle from me, and he just didn't vote. And there were no nays, there were nearly five hundred yays. And that's how PFLAG became transgender accepting. And at intermission, I talked to the fella [laughs] who hadn't voted for it and he goes "Well Mary, I'm not against it, I just think we've got our hands full trying to get people to accept gay issues and gay people." So it was alright, I could accept one.[19]

Boenke and Sharp had met through PFLAG's Transgender Network and forged a friendship during the long struggle to have the national mission statement changed. They both served at the same time as regional directors for PFLAG and were both appointed to the national board. In 2000, Sharp became the first transgender member of the national PFLAG board of directors. In 1997, Boenke and Sharp, along with Jessica Xavier, whom Sharp had met at a transgender law conference in Houston, wrote a booklet entitled *Our Trans Children*, which was published by the PFLAG Transgender Network.

In addition to leading the charge for transgender inclusion on the PFLAG front, Stewart also took other organizations to task for excluding transgender people. Chief among these groups was the Human Rights Campaign and anyone who supported it. The HRC was founded in 1980 by Steve Endean as a political action committee called the Human Rights Campaign Fund. For most of the 1980s, the HRCF endorsed and funded political candidates, but by 1989, it had evolved into a membership-based organization as well. By 1995, the group dropped the *F* and became HRC. In New Orleans, and nationally, the HRC is often criticized for being too rich and too white, a club of privilege unconcerned with those on the margins of the community.

When Stewart picketed the local HRC gala dinner in 1998 along with a group of trans women and other supporters, Randy Trahan remembers attendees at the dinner asking, "Why are all the drag queens picketing us?"[20] In addition to picketing, Stewart also sent letters to almost everyone. He bought an ad in the PFLAG newsletter, the *Banner*, explaining his reasons for boycotting the HRC dinner, which caused no small amount of controversy within the PFLAG board. "There he goes again," the thinking went. As a former recipient of the HRC award, he recruited other previous recipients—Jim Kellogg, Charlene Schneider, and Skip Ward—to write a letter calling for the withdrawal of financial support of the HRC until it included trans people in its mission statement and in ENDA (Employment Non-Discrimination Act). The letter reads:

Dear _____,

Because you have been and may continue to be a supporter of the Human Rights Campaign, we are writing to advise you that although we had hoped it wouldn't come to this, we feel that we now have no choice but to call upon you to join us in suspending financial support (be it in the form of donations, dinner tickets, or auction prizes) for the HRC until it includes transgendered [sic] people in its mission statement and in ENDA (Employment Non-Discrimination Act).

In order to give you some background on this issue, we are enclosing a copy of a letter we wrote HRC Executive Director Elizabeth Birch last year. Although no formal reply was received, an HRC team that was dispatched to New Orleans last fall sought to soothe troubled waters, to placate local organizations and to stonewall. They succeeded in convincing us that nothing short of an actual and massive withdrawal of financial support would ever move them beyond mere words to true action on this issue.

Although we arrived at our present position on principle alone, we have since become more concerned in that there is mounting evidence that if ENDA fails to include transgendered persons it will also unwittingly exclude lesbians and gay persons who, although not transgendered, display non–gender conforming feminine and masculine mannerisms or who dress in non–gender conforming ways. In order to give you some idea of what we are talking about in this regard you will also find enclosed a couple of handouts published by PFLAG's (Parents and Friends of Lesbians and Gays) Transgender Special Outreach Network.

Also enclosed is a list of community leaders who have agreed to endorse this letter.

We are sure there will be some who will be quick to charge us with creating divisiveness within the community. To them reply that it is not us, but the HRC that has created divisiveness with its policy of exclusion.

In closing, we would like to suggest that the more who join us now in this campaign, the sooner we will all be able to return to working together again for our primary goal of human equal rights for everyone.[21]

This letter was sent to over two hundred people associated with the local HRC gala and was published in *Impact* and *Ambush* magazines. The letter included the names of forty individuals as enclosures, including three PFLAG board members. Enclosed with the letter were two handouts published by PFLAG's Transgender Special Outreach Network.

Reaction to the letter was mixed but for the most part positive. Some people had already soured on the HRC for different reasons. Larry Best, a former recipient of the HRC award, responded by writing,

Politically I have come to the same conclusions for somewhat different reasons. I have already withdrawn my support for the Human Rights Campaign and terminated my membership in its Federal Club. This is because of the HRC's relentless and questionable support of democratic candidates, to the exclusion of republican candidates, irrespective of their support for gay, lesbian, and transgendered [sic] rights. Specifically, the HRC refused to even co-endorse Governor William Weld in his bid for the United States Senate. More recently they also failed and refused to endorse United States Representative Mobray of Southern California. Neither action was remotely supportable other than on purely partisan grounds. Accordingly, I resigned from HRC.[22]

Stewart was criticized for giving the impression that PFLAG supported the HRC boycott, which it did not. In fact, PFLAG advertised the HRC gala in its newsletter and purchased an ad in the gala's dinner program. Stewart caught so much hell for his crusade that he had to write a letter to PFLAG's membership explaining that he was not representing PFLAG's position.

Stewart's feelings were eloquently expressed in a May 22, 1998, letter to the editor of *Impact*, which he criticized for giving the HRC too much credit:

Dear Editor,

For one who started out claiming on the one hand to be in favor of the inclusion of transgendered [sic] persons in HRC's mission statement and in the Employment Non-Discrimination Act (ENDA), but on the other hand to oppose a boycott to achieve those goals, you have managed to become HRC's most public local apologist.

You said little if anything as to why transgendered [sic] persons should be included. Instead, you have taken the position that because HRC is the largest national gay and lesbian organization and has done a lot of good things, that it should be excused from doing what almost every other national gay and lesbian organization has done, i.e., recognized that transgendered [sic] persons are fundamentally as much a part of our GLBT community as are lesbians, gays and bisexuals.

Where did you get the notion that HRC had anything to do with Mary Landrieu's narrow victory over Woody Jenkins for a seat in the U.S. Senate? Do you really think a lousy $10,000 had anything at all to do with it? You write that they had "staff members from Washington assist in the campaign at the local level." A reliable source tells me they sent one inept bumpkin who had no idea as to what was going on. If any gay and lesbian organization was responsible for Landrieu's victory, it has to have been LAGPAC. They raised more money for Landrieu; they provided sign locations; they put people on the phones and on the street; they provided a mailing list of some 6,000—and they did it without any paid staff.

It was LAGPAC, not HRC, that secured both of Louisiana's two votes in the U.S. Senate for ENDA, giving us the distinction of being the only southern state that had both senators voting for ENDA. And it was LAGPAC, in conjunction with LEGAL, the Forum for Equality and local Log Cabin Republicans who won victories in our conservative state legislature. Just imagine what our potential would be if we were to take even half of what we export to HRC and put it toward local paid staff.

Maybe we need to rethink our priorities. And maybe we need to take a good hard look at the two-year old federation of statewide gay, lesbian, bisexual and transgender political groups being developed under the auspices of the National Gay and Lesbian Task Force and described in the April issue of OUT magazine as "an organization to watch as a possible rival to HRC."

If HRC was the source of your claims regarding the Landrieu-Jenkins race, as well as all the other things you claim HRC has accomplished, then I'd have to find these claims as suspect as well.

But, in any event, since you paint HRC in such glowing terms, I think it only fair to inform your readers of at least one HRC screw-up: When former Republican Governor William Weld of Massachusetts, who did more for GLBT youth in that state than has been done in any other state, ran against Democratic Senator John Kerry for the U.S. Senate, HRC totally ignored Weld's GLBT record, and, instead of staying out of the race or issuing a co-endorsement, endorsed Kerry alone on what must have been purely partisan grounds. The result? They succeeded in alienating almost every knowledgeable GLBT Republican in the country. As a generally wild-eyed liberal Democrat, I say that was stupid.

Now let's talk about strategy. HRC says that to include transgenders [sic] in ENDA would delay its passage into the indefinite picture because of the attacks that would be generated from religious political extremists. Well, in case you haven't heard, these attacks are already about as virulent as they can get. Even if, however, they did become more virulent I'd suggest that they could create a backlash that might work to our advantage.

As for the public in general, I don't believe they hold transgendered [sic] people in any lower regard than they hold gays and lesbians. But the bottom line is that HRC's strategy is flawed in that it's based, by their own admission, on expediency as opposed to principle. HRC's slogan "Working together for equality for all" is a lie, unless there is added the unspoken caveat "one at a time in the order that we determine."

In your May 8 editorial you state that the boycott "has not achieved its goal." Well, I for one did not expect instant tea. You go on to say "we are the only city in the nation that has chosen this method of objection." I think it would be far more accurate to say that we are the first city that has chosen this method. To paraphrase the early American Naval hero John Paul Jones, "The fight has just begun."[23]

Stewart was a tireless advocate for trans people. On more than one occasion, really any chance he had, he would tell fellow gays and lesbians, "Transgendered [*sic*] people need protections more than we do."[24] And this at a time long before trans rights were on anyone's radar. By establishing a model scholarship program and leading the fight for transgender inclusion, the New Orleans chapter of PFLAG played a large role in shaping the national organization and contributing to its extraordinary success. In this way, the gay community in New Orleans has made a significant contribution to the national struggle for gay rights. Stewart took a less active role in PFLAG in 2003 but remained involved with PFLAG for the rest of his life serving on its board of directors as an advisor.

PFLAG's overall influence and significance was evident in 1997. In that year, *Impact* commemorated its twentieth year of publication by running a series of articles, by Roberts Batson, highlighting significant events of each year. These articles were accompanied by a profile of an "honored citizen." Of the twenty people profiled, six were PFLAG board members and an additional five were heavily involved in PFLAG: Sandra Pailet, Laura Peebles, Billy Henry, Stewart Butler, Niki Kearby, Betty Caldwell, Regina Matthews, Alan Robinson, Mary Stuart, Joan Ladnier, and Roberts Batson.[25]

Stewart's involvement with PFLAG and LAGPAC not only won him awards and titles but also afforded him deep friendships, many of which evolved into what came to be known as the family. Stewart and Alfred never bore any children, but they did assume the roles of parents for a few wayward young men. In 1989, Frances Monnier, a man from Raceland, Louisiana, who occasionally made the forty-five-minute or so trip to New Orleans to attend PFLAG meetings, connected Stewart to a troubled young man he had met.

Pierre DeLancey, or Peter as he was commonly called, was seventeen years old, gay, dyslexic, epileptic, and alcoholic. Stewart's first impression of DeLancey was that he was "a total mess."[26] Indeed he was. Abused by his father routinely since the age of five, DeLancey ran away from home when he was fourteen and was placed in the Lafourche Parish Juvenile Justice Facility when he was fifteen. A guard there sexually assaulted him regularly. Rich Magill described his life as "sad and tragic . . . He had little education and was illiterate . . . he never held a job . . . and he never had a home of his own."[27] He worked periodically as a fisherman and factory worker and even appeared in a few pornographic films, but on the whole, stability eluded him. Nonetheless, he did manage to find some joy in living and maintained a remarkably positive attitude, expressing a desire to help homeless youth.

After being released from juvenile detention in 1987, he eventually found his way to New Orleans and took temporary shelter at the Covenant House, a residential facility for homeless youth. Although not legally, Stewart and Alfred essentially adopted DeLancey and gave him a home at the Faerie Playhouse. DeLancey lived with Stewart and Alfred on and off for ten years. When Peter's disease began progressing and he knew the end was near, he reached out to Stewart and Alfred and asked if he could come home to the Faerie Playhouse to die. Stewart said yes, of course, and upon arriving the two met with an attorney, and DeLancey gave Stewart power of attorney to handle his legal and medical affairs.

Due to complications from AIDS, the last six months of his life were spent in constant pain. Stewart, Alfred, a neighbor called "Skateboard," and other members of the family took turns looking after DeLancey. Stewart kept meticulous notes and records detailing DeLancey's medications, times they were taken, his moods, nap times, even the time duration of his groans from fits of pain. DeLancey died in 1998. His ashes, along with those of Stewart and Alfred's cocker spaniel, Adonai, were buried in the memorial garden behind the Faerie Playhouse. Rich Magill wrote a short memorial piece about DeLancey, which was published in both *Impact* and *Ambush*, noting:

> I met Peter in August, 1988. The GOP was coming to town and lesbian and gay activists were preparing for their visit. Having a construction background, I chaired a committee of one to build a platform in Armstrong Park from which our speakers would address an issue Ronald Reagan would not: AIDS. Our stage was small, 64 square feet. Behind it was a large pink triangle, eight feet tall. In the lake we would place 412 floating candles—the number of Americans to be diagnosed with AIDS during the four-day convention. We started construction in the early morning. Several people came out to help and cheer me on. Before noon, Stewart arrived to deliver a young man, strong and eager to help. This boy of 19, named Pierre Rene Delancey, said to me, "Call me Peter." He had blonde hair, blue eyes and was tall and lanky. He smiled and I thought to myself, I'm in trouble now. Before I could ask about his construction experience, he took my hammer and said, "Where are the nails?" We went to work, and in a few hours our stage was ready. I don't think Peter knew then he had AIDS. He was living at Covenant House and I think his political activities prior to this week in August were nil. In those few days, no group affected our community more than ACT UP/New York. Peter was affected by them too.

He was adopted by them and he adopted them. Everywhere ACT UP went, Peter was there, acting up . . . he had a big heart.[28]

After his death, Stewart received a handwritten sympathy card from Dr. Michael Kaiser, the former executive director of the NO/AIDS Task Force who had the year before left New Orleans for Washington, DC, to become the director of the pediatric AIDS branch of Maternal/Child Health Bureau in the Department of Health and Human Services. In part, Kaiser wrote, "One of the few areas where I have a sense of accomplishment is a new grant program that will target infected youth, age 13–19. Please know that Peter's story will impact this new national program."[29]

Stewart and Alfred had extended the same kindness to another troubled youth a year earlier. Like Peter, Anthony "Robby" DeJacimo had grown up in a dysfunctional family in a small town. When he was seventeen, his family kicked him out of the house upon discovering he was gay. DeJacimo recalls:

As I mentioned my family threw me out when I came out over Christmas and then all my acting out they just couldn't take it any-more. I contacted PFLAG and they put me in touch with Stewart and Alfred. A friend of theirs, Roy Racca, drove from Lafayette and picked me up and took me to his house and then drove me to New Orleans the next day. I decided to stay with Stewart and Alfred instead of the lesbian couple Betty and Niki that lived on Decatur Street. I have never regretted my decision, but I do wonder if my life would have been different if I had come to different conclusion about that, but hindsight is 20/20.[30]

While both Stewart and Alfred loved DeJacimo, Alfred adored him while Stewart was more of the disciplinarian. DeJacimo was one of the few people in the extended family that Alfred never banished from the Faerie Playhouse, a fate that was always temporary but dramatic nonetheless. DeJacimo struggled with alcoholism and at times could be a handful. Several people have noted that Alfred derived no small amount of devious pleasure living vicariously through DeJacimo's shenanigans.

Stewart liked to think of me and Peter as their kids, but they never acted much like parents in the traditional sense. However, they did love us and showed us that in the things they did for us. They also tried to guide us to make what they felt would be better decisions but ultimately they knew" we would make our own decisions and most of the time they were there to pick us up. In hindsight, that might not have been the smartest thing for them to do but it was how they showed they cared, and I think it was born out a true sense of responsibility.[31]

DeJacimo maintains, "Stewart played a bigger role in developing my sense of responsibility to myself and my community. And I am also a better person for having him in my life. I believe he really wanted to see me self-sustaining before he died. I am not sure if he took in any comfort in my ability to do that but I have."[32]

DeJacimo eventually found sobriety and, for a while, achieved some notoriety as a drag performer in California. He eventually returned to New Orleans but would from time to time take jobs in other states. Career stability eluded him while medical issues did not. Money and financial support were also consistent stressors in Stewart and DeJacimos's relationship. In 2016, the relationship fractured beyond repair. DeJacimo's mother, with whom he had reconciled, was dying, and DeJacimo quit his job to return home to care for her. DeJacimo remembers,

> Stewart thought I should not have quit my job to take care of her. I disagreed and was quite offended by such a thought. It was ultimately the crack that continued to get wider and ultimately made my decision to leave and strike out on my own easier. I never resented or got angry with him because of that decision because it was in line with Stewart's philosophy as it had related to me.[33]

DeJacimo wrote Stewart a farewell letter, which Stewart misinterpreted as a suicide note. Those closest to Stewart chose to let him believe that, concluding the relationship had run its course anyway. The disagreement over DeJacimo's decision to quit his job and care for his mother illustrates a flaw others have noted in Stewart—stubbornness: "He could be very judgmental if he felt you weren't doing what he felt was right. I know many times I would have been better listening to his advice that doesn't fundamentally change that flaw in my opinion."[34]

Stubbornness was a flaw others saw, but what most people didn't see was that much of his stubbornness was a façade tempered by a willingness to listen and compromise. This side of his personality he showed only to those closest to him. Bill Hagler, who lived with Stewart after Alfred's death, recalls, "If I had a problem, he would genuinely listen and try to change his behavior."[35] Longtime friend Ron Joullian echoes this sentiment: "It was his saving grace."[36]

In terms of friends passing away, 1998 and 1999 were *anni horribilis* for Stewart and Alfred. In addition to DeLancey, Freddie Lavre, Alfred's friend from California also died, as did friend Cliff Howard. John Foster (Rich Magill's partner) committed suicide when living with AIDS became untenable, and Gregory Manella succumbed to lung cancer in the fall.

There was, however, one bright spot in that dark time. In 1998, Stewart was publicly recognized by the LGBT+ community by being selected co-grand marshal of PrideFest, a forerunner to New Orleans Pride. Stewart and co–grand marshal Toni Pizanie led the parade by riding in a mule-drawn carriage throughout the French Quarter. PrideFest 1998 was held at Armstrong Park on the weekend of September 26–28. In addition to Stewart and Pizanie, two honorary grand marshals were named—legendary bar owners Dixie Fasnacht and Andy Boudreaux, who had recently passed away.[37]

In 1978, the Pink Triangle Alliance hosted the first gay Pride rally ever held in New Orleans. The Pink Triangle Alliance was the public face and political name of the Louisiana Sissies in Struggle—a group that came out of the Mulberry House Collective in Fayetteville, Arkansas, when Dennis Williams, Dimid Hayer, Stacey Brotherlover, and Aurora relocated to New Orleans.[38] The Sissies had grown out of the back-to-the-land movement advocated by Milo Pyne and served as sort of a forerunner to the Radical Faeries. The Louisiana Sissies in Struggle were short lived, but while they lasted, they not only advocated for queer issues but also protested non–gay specific issues such as racism, police brutality, and socioeconomic inequality. They also helped edit *RFD*, a quarterly magazine founded in 1974 for rural folk that aimed to raise queer consciousness. After the Pride rally sponsored by the Pink Triangle Alliance in 1978, a small group of people met to discuss a Pride event the following year. The Pink Triangle Alliance members in attendance argued that more was needed than a parade. They decided on a festival.[39]

The first GayFest, which would evolve into Pride, was originally to be held at Jackson Square, but when the Roman Catholic archdiocese learned of the event, Archbishop Philip Hannan went to work behind the scenes with his contacts at city hall and had the venue nixed.[40] Organizers were not happy at having the venue pulled, but GayFest found a suitable location at Washington Square Park not far away in the neighboring Marigny neighborhood. In subsequent years, the money raised for the community center mysteriously vanished. A lack of financial resources was a constant problem. By 1994, Pride was on the verge of bankruptcy when co-chairs Robert Brunet and Joan Ladnier asked Stewart and Alfred for help. Stewart wrote a check without hesitation.[41]

The archdiocese's opposition to gay visibility in front of its landmark Cathedral was ironic considering that one of its own facilities—a church and building complex that had once been a cloistered convent for nuns on the corner of North Rampart and Barracks—was being used as a de facto gay community center. When Richard O'Connor, Charlene Schneider, Mark Gonzalez, and others organized GayFest in 1979, part of the idea was to raise money for a community center. Prior to the founding of the Lesbian and Gay Community Center of New Orleans, the St. Louis Community Center in the French Quarter served as a gay friendly meeting place for various LGBT+ organizations such as PFLAG, a gay Alcoholics Anonymous group, Dignity, Crescent City Coalition, LAGPAC, and a few other LGBT+ groups. This was made possible because of the tolerance of a gay priest who ran the facility. Rich Sacher observes, "For a few years, before the Catholic Church in Rome swung to far right conservatism, this location was practically a gay community center . . . When Pope John Paul II was elected, we were all told to leave."[42]

The idea of an LGBT Community Center in New Orleans had been around since the late 1970s, years before many community centers in other cities grew out of the HIV/AIDS organizations that sprang up around the country to address the HIV/AIDS crisis. The history of the community center is a study in the age-old dichotomy of the ideal versus the reality. From its inception, the community center has embraced the noble vision of unifying the various subgroups of New Orleans's LGBT+ community; conversely, the reality is that the center's history has been marked by sharp division within its leadership, poor financial management, lack of widespread community support, and unrealized potential. Historically, the center's board of directors has been prone to coup d'états from within, and throughout its nearly thirty-year history, the center has gone through numerous directors. And yet, the center survives, which is something of a miracle considering all the challenges it has faced.

In 1989, Leo Watermeier visited the LGBT Community Center of New York, which had been founded in 1983. After touring the facility and meeting with its director, Watermeier was convinced New Orleans needed such a facility. Back in New Orleans, Watermeier took out an ad in *Ambush Magazine* announcing a public meeting for those interested in exploring the idea of a community center. About a dozen people attended the meeting, and this group became the first board of directors. Watermeier remembers the debate over what to name the center. Various names were suggested, including "Pride Center" and "Rainbow Center," but someone said, "We're not going to be in the closet in our own building." They ultimately decided on "Lesbian and Gay Community Center of New Orleans."[43]

Watermeier, who worked for the city as the manager of Armstrong Park on the edge of the French Quarter, had entered into a lease/purchase agreement for a property across from the park. The building at 812–16 North Rampart Street was a traditional Creole cottage. Watermeier lived in the residential attachment at the rear of the property and leased the main cottage to the community center. The main building was ideal because a previous tenant, the artist Joey Bonhage, had modified the interior into a large open space to use as a gallery.

In 1992 the Lesbian and Gay Community Center of New Orleans began with a group of friends who believed the local LGBT+ community needed a central organization and location to dispense information, provide resources, and offer meeting space.[44] From the very beginning, there were tensions. One early board member recalls, "My own impression has always been that there was a significant class element to our failure. I believed the 'uptown queens' did not want to associate too closely with the 'downtown queens.' The uptown crowd had most of the money."[45] These socioeconomic differences would give rise to other fractures along racial and gender identity lines. Over the years, some felt the center was "too Black," or "too trans," although they would not use those specific terms. For his part, Stewart, who felt the center should be all inclusive, did not help matters with his stubbornness. More than a few early board members remember meetings degenerating into "shitshows" when Stewart would launch into one of his seemingly endless harangues. His obstinance was never more clearly demonstrated than when the board voted unanimously, with the exception of his vote, to not allow NAMBLA (North American Man Boy Love Association) to hold meetings at the center.

By the mid-1990s, the center's board began considering the possibility of a permanent home. In 1995 and 1996, co-chairs Rip Naquin-Delain and Rene Parks led a fundraising campaign that raised over $30,000 for a building fund. These funds were placed in two certificates of deposit. In 1996, the center entered into negotiations for the purchase of a Creole cottage at 2020–22 Royal Street in the Marigny but withdrew its offer "due to the unpredictable and fickle actions of the seller."[46] Complicating matters was "an outstanding lawsuit with an adjacent property owner, who appears to be at odds with the lesbian and gay community."[47]

The problem of finding a permanent home for the community center appeared to be resolved when, in 1999, Niki Kearby and Betty Caldwell, who had cofounded the New Orleans chapter of PFLAG in 1982, graciously offered the community center the use of a building they owned at 2114 Decatur Street just off Frenchmen Street in the heart of the Marigny. Kearby and

Caldwell renovated the space and charged the center a very modest rent with the understanding that as the center grew, the rent would gradually increase in order to offset the cost of the renovations. Kearby and Caldwell even expressed their intention to bequeath the building to the community center on the condition that it demonstrate it was stable and sustainable. None of this was in writing; Kearby and Caldwell made the arrangement in good faith and expressed their desire to eventually bequeath the building to the center. The money raised for the building fund began to be diverted and used for operational expenses.

By 2009, the center was on the verge of closing due to lack of adequate funding, a sad note that *Ambush* columnist Toni Pizanie (a center cofounder and former board member) recognized in her column, Sappho's Psalm. Citing the board's arrogance, Pizanie wrote, "The blame falls directly on the Center Board, and the non-business like or non-organized attitude that has caused the Center to fail . . . they have been unwilling to take advice or direction from anyone." This criticism hit a nerve, and as a result, the entire board (Mary Griggs, Dave Haynik, Shawn Johnson, and Charlotte Klasson), with the exception of Crystal Little, resigned in protest. Little, a longtime volunteer, pleaded with them to not resign and argued that Pizanie's criticism was constructive, but they didn't want to hear it.

Ambush publisher and editor Rip Naquin-Delain, who had spearheaded the building fund campaign, also weighed in on the controversy, writing in a scathing editorial:

> The Lesbian & Gay Community Center of New Orleans Board is attempting to rape the Center Building Fund. In a letter signed by Co-chair Crystal Little and Treasurer Linda Bush, " . . . the reason for the Building Fund no longer exists by virtue of Dr. Kearby's generosity and intent to bequeath us her building, the Board of Director of the Lesbian and Gay Community Center requests that you consider re-directing your Building Fund Contribution." We find it odd that a letter of this magnitude was not signed by Co-chair Michael Olivas. Does this perhaps mean that Olivas did not endorse this plan of destruction?
>
> With vision and farsightedness, the Building Fund was set up by the 1995–96 Center Board of Directors explicitly and could only "be used for the purchase of a building, or to renovate a structure donated to the Center as its permanent home." The fund was placed in yearly cds and all interest earned was to remain in the Building Fund in order for maximum growth potential. If the Center should close, all funds were to be returned to individual donors and businesses who donated the funds. . . .

Since 1996, subsequent Center boards have diverted the Building Funds' interest payments into the General Fund, supposedly to borrow against until the funds could be replaced. Obviously, these funds have never been replaced. The 1998 Center board even went so far as to hire a paid executive director bankrupting the General Fund, the very funds needed to keep the Center's doors open. This same board also ran off one of the best volunteers it ever had who was responsible for keeping the Center's doors open 7 days a week 6–8 or more hours per day....

We urge all Building Fund donors to keep the Building Fund intact, the '95–'96 board's vision for the future. It is time for the community and Center members to demand better accountability and stop the current and future Center Boards from raping its Building and General Funds.[48]

When the building housing the center suffered extensive water damage during Hurricane Isaac in 2012, Kearby and Caldwell's adopted daughter (who had assumed management of the property) told the community center board that it would have to pay increased rent to cover the repairs; the board (which never paid the increased rent they agreed to in 1999 to cover the initial renovations to the building) decided it could no longer stay there.

Despite the aforementioned issues, the community center did manage to achieve many of its goals. The center regularly hosted various types of support groups and social events.[49] In 2000 the center received a federal grant and launched the Hate Crimes Project, which tracked hate-based crimes against LGBT+ and other groups targeted by discrimination. In 2003 the center began hosting an annual Trans Day of Remembrance to commemorate the lives of transgender people murdered every year. After Hurricane Katrina, the center hosted a meeting of the Community Coalition, a collective of LGBT+ and allied organizations that met to share information and collaborate during the initial recovery period. And in 2011 the center established a program called Safe Space for LGBT+ and questioning youth.

In 2013 the center moved into a small administrative space in the ArtEgg Studios on South Broad Street and established a new mission statement. The current mission of the community center is to provide resources and advocacy that foster community development and social and economic justice efforts to strengthen the collective power of gender and sexual minorities and their allies in the Greater New Orleans area. The vision of the center is to create a Greater New Orleans area where gender and sexual minorities are equitable and empowered. Although the center's future is uncertain, one thing can be said about its history: it is a prolonged study in untapped potential. In that regard, the center is a truer reflection of our local LGBT+

community than the center's critics would like to admit. In 2014, community center director Sebastian Rey wryly observed, "Asking for LGBT unity is like asking for world peace."[50]

The Butler family home in Carville. Courtesy of the Estate of Stewart P. Butler.

Stewart as a young man with friends. Courtesy of the Estate of Stewart P. Butler.

Alfred as a boy. Courtesy of the Estate of Stewart P. Butler.

Stewart when he was stationed at Fort Riley. Courtesy of the Estate of Stewart P. Butler.

Stewart and Bob Pattison during their road trip to Alaska. Courtesy of the Estate of Stewart P. Butler.

Stewart (standing, left) with coworkers in Alaska. Courtesy of the Estate of Stewart P. Butler.

Stewart with Sophie Ondola on their wedding day with Sophie's parents. Courtesy of the Estate of Stewart P. Butler.

Gregory Manella. Courtesy of the Estate of Stewart P. Butler.

Stewart and Alfred in March 1973. Courtesy of the Estate of Stewart P. Butler.

Alfred with Stewart in Jackson Square, 1973. Courtesy of the Estate of Stewart P. Butler.

Stewart at his home on Prytania Street. Courtesy of the Estate of Stewart P. Butler, Steven Duplantis photographer.

Bill Hagler and Ron Joullian at the 1987 March on Washington. Courtesy of Invisible Histories Project.

Johnny Jackson, Stewart Butler, Charlene Schneider, and Rich Magill. Courtesy of the Estate of Stewart P. Butler, Tyronne Edwards photographer.

Ron Joullian, Stewart, Alfred, and Rich Magill at the plaque ceremony at the Faerie Playhouse. Courtesy of the Estate of Stewart P. Butler.

The Faerie Playhouse. Courtesy of Ellis Anderson, *French Quarter Journal*.

Courtney Sharp. Courtesy of Courtney Sharp.

Charlene Schneider and Stewart. Courtesy of the Estate of Stewart P. Butler.

Stewart, seated, as Dame Edna, at the 1993 PFLAG Conference, with Freddie Lavre, Cliff Howard, unknown man, Ron Joullian, Suzanne Eaton, Gary Griffin, Jeff (last name unknown), and Robbie DeJacimo. Courtesy of the Estate of Stewart P. Butler.

Alfred and Stewart. Courtesy of the Estate of Stewart P. Butler.

Stewart at his desk. Courtesy of Larry Graham.

Chapter 10

LION IN WINTER

*After lecturing me on how I needed to settle down at my age, the judge
sentenced me to six months of home incarceration and I was thereupon
outfitted with a monitoring anklet—a new life experience at age 69.*
—STEWART BUTLER

THE 175-YEAR-OLD CREOLE COTTAGE AT 1308 ESPLANADE AVENUE IS
familiar to many in New Orleans. Reddish pink with big hearts attached
to the façade and a rainbow flag proudly flying on the rooftop, the Faerie
Playhouse is located on the edge of the historic Treme neighborhood just a
few blocks beyond the French Quarter. Behind the home is a small backyard,
at the edge of which is a small dependency, formerly the slaves' quarters.

On the front of the house is a plaque that reads:

The Faerie Playhouse

This Creole cottage became the home of Stewart Butler and Alfred
Doolittle in 1979 and was the site of many organizing meetings in the
LGBT civil rights movement during the late 20th Century and early
21st Century.

The garden behind the home contains the cremains of many significant leaders in the struggle for equality, including Charlene Schneider,
John Ognibene and Cliff Howard, as well as artist J. B. Harter.

Over four decades, the Faerie Playhouse would become the center of an
amazing array of lives. Much of New Orleans LGBT+ activism of the late
twentieth and early twenty-first centuries would take place there. It would
become the gathering place for an ever-evolving group of friends called "the
family." At various times, it would also be a "plantation" (plantains, cotton,
avocados, sugar cane, peppers, and potatoes), an orchard (kumquats, limes,

grapes, and pears), a youth refuge, a guesthouse, a wildlife refuge (squirrels, rats, mice, geckos, turtles, and several cats and dogs), a memorial garden (hosting the cremains of nearly two dozen people), a bird refuge (sparrows, cardinals, blue jays, pigeons, hummingbirds, crows, and bumble bees), a meeting house, a winery, a spa, an art gallery, and a wedding chapel. But most of all, it was the home of Stewart Butler and Alfred Doolittle.

The Faerie Playhouse derived its name from a play that was once performed there. On Saturday, June 20, 1992, the summer solstice, a few dozen people, mostly gay men, gathered in the early evening in the backyard for the world premiere (and only production) of *Peter Puck*, an original play written by Alfred Doolittle. The smell of marijuana was strong, and almost everyone in attendance, including the actors, was very, very high.

The performance was in honor of Doolittle's fifty-sixth birthday. Doolittle, who billed himself as "Alfred the Elf, Friend and Counselor to the Elves," directed the play and reveled in the fact that his friends had joined him in realizing his creative talents. The actors included Lenny Frank, Karl Ezkovich, Rich Magill, and John Foster, with Stewart as narrator.

Peter Puck was a comedy in one act that featured the son of a conservative rabbi who falls in love with the daughter of their next-door neighbor, a liberal professor of Greek classics. At one point, Professor Doolittle tells his daughter, "Don't have anything to do with that mama's boy next door. He's probably as religious as his father, the rabbi. The Jews ruined Greece with their religiosity. Athens and Jerusalem can never come together." For his part, the rabbi gives his son Peter a similar warning, "You'll end up like that sex fiend next door." But the two children do meet and, not unpredictably, get married.

Although *Peter Puck* would not win any theatrical awards, its premiere at the Faerie Playhouse embodied the essence of what can only be described as a magical love story—the love story of Stewart and Alfred, soul mates whose relationship not only spanned a pivotal era in the history of queer New Orleans but also helped shaped it. When *Peter Puck* premiered, Stewart and Alfred had been together nineteen years, thirteen of which played out at the Faerie Playhouse. By 1992, both men were advancing in age—Stewart was sixty-two, Alfred fifty-six; nevertheless, age did not deter Stewart's social activities. He and Alfred continued to regularly frequent the gay bars in the French Quarter and host holiday gatherings at the Faerie Playhouse throughout the year. And Stewart, always introspective, began thinking about the remarkable twists and turns his life had taken. He reached out to long-lost friends and began reconnecting with his roots.

In July 1996, Stewart returned to Alaska to attend the University of Alaska (Fairbanks) Alumni Association reunion. He and Alfred spent a week there,

staying in a university dorm room, and although none of his former classmates were in attendance, Stewart did enjoy getting reacquainted with former
friends Bruce Halderman and Judith and Dietrich Strohmaier. It was the
Strohmaiers who had convinced him to enter Hastings College of the Law
in San Francisco thirty-three years earlier, a move that eventually led Stewart
back to New Orleans.[1]

He made summer visits to Alaska from 1996 to 2001, and on one of these
visits reconnected with LeVake Renshaw, who had served as Stewart's best
man at his wedding. In 2006, Renshaw wrote Stewart to inform him he had
run into Stewart's ex-wife Sophie at a cocktail party. Sophie and Stewart
had lost contact in 1963 and Renshaw hoped to put them in touch with each
other. The two chatted, but when Renshaw asked where she lived, Sophie was
evasive. Then in 2007, Renshaw noticed in the obituaries of the *Anchorage
Daily News* that Sophie's daughter died. Renshaw, an amateur historian and
sleuth, did a little digging and was able to provide Stewart an address for
Sophie. Stewart wrote her and provided his phone number. The two played
phone tag for a few days but eventually connected and spent an hour on the
phone catching up. Stewart then wrote a letter to Renshaw thanking him for
making the reunion possible, a sentiment echoed by Sophie in a note she
penned to Stewart, "One of the nicest happenings in my life was to meet
you and then to continue our friendship after an absence of 46 years. I will
always be grateful to LeVake for 'reuniting us.'"[2] Stewart and Sophie kept in
touch periodically until his death.

The annual trips to Alaska allowed Stewart a chance to reconnect with
other friends as well: Frank Chapados, Alex Miller, Sumner Weed, Niilo
Koponen, Jude Hengler, Ken and Joanne Gain, Johnny Johnson, Pete Weimer,
Robert and Virginia Taylor, Rod Graham, and Larry Brayton.[3] In February
2003, Stewart and Bill drove to Palm Springs, California, to visit Lou Dischner, his political mentor in Alaska, who died later in the year.[4]

A lot had changed in the preceding five decades since he first went to
Alaska. Stewart, given to pensiveness, appreciated the perspective, that
invaluable gift afforded by time and experience, of it all.

On one of his trips to Alaska, he was busted for possession of marijuana.
In 1999, he was detained at the New Orleans International Airport for having
thirty-nine joints hidden in a baggie in a sock. Reporting the incident in his
annual newsletter, Stewart wrote:

> It happened during our pre-boarding search on our then annual trips
> to Alaska in 2000. I'd gotten away with it previously, but this time I
> had an ounce in each sock. This time their search wand was set off

by the foil in a legitimate cigarette pack in my pocket. Thereupon the searcher ran her hands down my left leg and found the pot in my left sock. For whatever reason, she failed to search my left leg . . . Praise the Lord! She asked me to step aside and I was able to throw the other bag of pot behind a table. When the deputies got there they decided to give me a summons and release me instead of throwing me in jail.[5]

When I told the United Airlines clerk we missed our flight due to a seizure she said there'd be no charge to book us out the next morning and we managed to arrive in Anchorage in time for a planned get together with friends to attend The Whale Fat Follies, a musical that matches anything here in New Orleans, at the Fly-By-Night Club. After a few days in Anchorage, we drove the beautiful 360 miles or so up to Fairbanks, where we attended my fourth in a row University of Alaska in Fairbanks Alumni reunion. Every year we meet one or two or more old friends and acquaintances I haven't seen for 35 or 40 years, even as we meet new friends. It's a grand and rewarding experience.[6]

Stewart did manage to bring some pot to Alaska. Before heading to the airport the day after being detained, friend and neighbor Skateboard rolled up an ounce or so into joints and taped them around Stewart's waist.

As for the drug charges, Stewart later pleaded guilty to misdemeanor possession. Years later Stewart recalled, "After lecturing me on how I needed to settle down at my age, the judge sentenced me to six months of home incarceration and I was thereupon outfitted with a monitoring anklet—a new life experience at age 69."

It was also in 1996 that Stewart began sending out his annual *Faerie Playhouse Newsletter*. By the time of his death, there were 210 names on the mailing list. Initially sent at the end of the year and later on Valentine's Day to honor Alfred, the newsletters related life at the Faerie Playhouse: memorable parties and other events, the illnesses and deaths of various people in Stewart's orbit, recipes, and even news of the Faerie Playhouse's resident pets:

Those of you who received Christmas cards from us in 1995 will perhaps recall Putzy, our then new English Springer Spaniel, who graced its cover. Well, let me tell you, over the course of the next fifteen or so months he was more than a handful. He ate everything . . . not just mundane things like the morning newspaper, slippers, shoes, books, upholstery, and chair legs and such, but everything. I mean he ate the bedroom carpet and our boxspring and the baseboard molding.[7]

For Stewart's seventieth birthday in 2000, Anthony DeJacimo organized a surprise birthday party for Stewart at the Mint. As he entered his eighth decade, Stewart could look back on twenty years of robust activism in New Orleans on behalf of LGBT+ causes. He and Alfred, who turned sixty-four the same year, had enjoyed twenty-eight years together. Many of their friends, including some from Stewart's activist years, attended the party, and proclamations from the mayor and city council honoring Stewart were read.

In attendance at the birthday party were a group of friends of Stewart and Alfred's that would eventually become known as "the family." This group would gather for holiday meals and other social events at the Faerie Playhouse, and some would even live in the backyard dependency ("the cottage"), thus becoming "resident players." One of the resident players was Bill Hagler. Hagler's role in the family would eventually evolve into that of Stewart's caregiver, but early on his relationship with Stewart and Alfred was fraught with tension and drama.

Hagler first met Stewart and Alfred in 1987 in Washington, DC, during the second National March on Washington for Lesbian and Gay Rights. Stewart and Alfred hosted a dinner at a DC restaurant for about twenty of their friends, including Ron Joullian and Tim Angle. Stewart and Alfred had met the couple in the early 1980s through the Southeastern Conference. At that time, Joullian and Angle lived in Birmingham, Alabama. Stewart and Alfred would often stop in Birmingham to visit the couple during their trips to Vermont to visit Stewart's family. Joullian and Angle would eventually move to New Orleans and become two of Stewart and Alfred's closest friends.

Hagler accompanied Joullian and Angle to the dinner. Stewart got along well with Hagler and invited him to stay at the Faerie Playhouse for Mardi Gras the following year. In 2000, Hagler moved to New Orleans and stayed briefly with his friend Paulette, who had once lived next door to Bill and his partner in rural Alabama outside Birmingham and who had since moved to New Orleans and was living in an apartment Stewart and Alfred owned on Magazine Street.

In 2001, Stewart and Alfred were renting the dependency behind the Faerie Playhouse to a man named Joey. After Joey's drug addiction forced Stewart and Alfred to evict him, Stewart offered the apartment to Hagler. At first, Hagler was a perfect fit at the Faerie Playhouse compound, and handy too. Stewart recalled, "His talents as a carpenter and electrician came at a good time as we were in the midst of improving our energy efficiency with new attic insulation and by replacing our aged central air and heat units . . . his talents also include plumbing, painting, gardening, sewing, computer expertise, and traveling companion."[8]

In 2001, Hagler began decorating the exterior of the Faerie Playhouse for Christmas, a task performed by longtime friend and neighbor Stephen "Skateboard" Samuel from 1997 to 1999. Hagler's work earned the Faerie Playhouse the neighborhood association's award for best door and window decoration. In 2002, as a political comment on the US "War on Terror" and looming invasion of Iraq, he added a message that read "Peace Not War" along the roofline. As Christmas turned into Carnival season, he replaced it with "Beads Not War." Later, Hagler added other political messages such as "Peace Through World Domination?" and he once hung fake money from the tree in front of the house with George W. Bush's face in the amount of $9.11. And because Valentine's Day was Alfred's favorite holiday, Hagler attached red hearts to the front façade of the home. The hearts made the perfect background for the bombs he hung from the eave of the house, which were featured on the local CBS news affiliate.

In addition to helping out around the Faerie Playhouse, Hagler would often accompany Stewart to social and political functions when Alfred refused to go, which was often. Eventually, Hagler, a self-professed hermit, grew tired of accompanying Stewart to these events and stopped. Around this time, Stewart developed an unhealthy fixation with Hagler—obsession is not too strong a word. For example, Stewart monitored his comings and goings and would constantly ask Alfred what Hagler was doing. Eventually Alfred, who was more annoyed than jealous by the situation, had enough and told Stewart that Hagler had to go immediately. Stewart told Hagler he had to vacate the premises that day and offered him $5,000 cash to help him relocate. Initially Hagler agreed to go but refused the money until Rich Magill convinced him to take it. Magill thought what Stewart did to Hagler was completely wrong and unfair and became so angry, he didn't speak to Stewart for a year. Stewart later described the incident as a "fit of total madness" and acknowledged in his annual newsletter, "I've harmed and brought grief to the other remaining family members . . . and I remain devastated by the harm I've caused our ever-diminishing family."[9]

Hagler would eventually forgive Stewart, and the two would reconcile but not before Hagler went to Florida for about six months to work and be near family before returning to New Orleans. Back in the city, he stayed with Rich Magill on and off before moving in with Joullian and Angle. After another year and half stint away after Katrina, Hagler returned to New Orleans in 2007. By this time, Paulette was living behind the Faerie Playhouse. Stewart had invited her to move into the apartment in the hopes that Hagler would come around. After Alfred's death in 2008, Hagler would move into the Faerie Playhouse to become Stewart's caregiver.

Hagler, Joullian, and Angle were the core of what became known as the Alabama branch of the family. Other Alabama family members included Rich Magill, Paulette Picket, Ron's sister Cindy Joullian, and Terry Carter. Carter had met Joullian at the University of Montevallo and later socialized with him in Birmingham. Not long after Joullian and Angle moved to New Orleans in 2002, Carter followed suit and became a part of the Faerie Playhouse orbit. According to Joullian, there were also

Joey King and Shane Dyess (spouses), Bruce Ivey and Robert Jason (partners), Bruce Stewart, Brian Smith, Douglas Hogge, Poula Skip who visited with Ron and Tim. Terry often accompanied Ron and Tim in their later trips to N.O. and shortly afterward returned to New Orleans a previous home after college. Rick Adams, a close friend to Bill, Ron and Tim often came down for trips with Ron and Tim with plans to eventually move here after retirement which ultimately much to everyone's regret did not occur . . . I often noted that the "Alabama Gang" often constituted a majority at particularly the bar night outings.

It was through Carter that Charles Paul and Pete Pietens also became a part of the family. Carter had met the couple at a French Quarter bar called Le Roundup and he and Paul became close friends. After a year or so of getting acquainted at the bar, Carter invited them to the Faerie Playhouse. Paul recalls:

I think it was in 2012 around Southern Decadence the first time he took us to The Faerie Playhouse. This was the "test" run to see if we would be accepted or perhaps be acceptable. Terry had also invited Jason Benvenuti aka "drunk Jason." My first direct interaction with Stewart was him asking me "who is Terry's sloshed friend?"

After that, we became regulars at the larger events, but had not yet been pulled into the "circle of friends" . . . That would be another year or so.

I think we gained Stewart's attention in 2014. We attended the Easter celebration there on 04/20/2014. It was during Memorial Day or another event when he talked to me and asked me about my work, my clients, etc. . . . It interested him that the focus of my practice is nonprofit organizations and that I discount the fees as a way of helping them and giving to society.

He called Terry and asked about us. It was during Decadence 2014 that Terry told me that we had impressed Stewart and that I was to expect a phone call from him. The call happened in typical Stewart fashion with him running the call. It was what I call "the interview." He asked about the charities I work with, to whom I contribute, what Pete did for a living, etc. and then gathered our phone numbers, address and personal information. At this point, we were in his orbit, although the junior member orbit.

Over the next five and a half years, I would receive the occasional phone call which became more regular, I also became someone who advised him on finances and sometimes we (Stewart, Pete, Bill and me) would just chill and chat.[10]

In December 2015, shortly after the US Supreme Court ruled same-sex marriage constitutional nationwide, Paul and Pietens, who had been together twenty years at the time, were married at the Faerie Playhouse. Carter officiated the service.

Another member of Stewart's inner circle was Charlotte Aitken. Like Paul and Pietens, she was casually introduced to the family. After being displaced by Hurricane Katrina, Aitken found herself living uptown in the Carrollton neighborhood where she met Paulette Picket, who lived in the same building. Picket's daughter lived across the street, and the two of them enjoyed regular visits from Hagler, Joullian, and Angle. Aitken found them all interesting and during their visits gradually became better acquainted with them. Picket eventually moved out of the building in 2007 but subsequently ran into Aitken and invited her to "bar night." Aitken remembers:

I went to the bar, not sure which, a few faces were familiar Bill, Ron, Tim and Paulette. Everyone said hello and wanted to know who I was, Ron made a lot of the introductions, one thing that I found very interesting it was all men and there was this old guy, much older than anyone else, yet everyone was fussing over him, and greeted him with a kiss.

I was introduced to Stewart Butler, he offered me a seat. The first thing he asked: "was I a lesbian?" The next: did I know all these men were gay.

I had a wonderful evening, interesting topics, funny stories, what a diverse group of people. It may sound strange, but it was wonderful to be able to talk without the sexual pressures and hang ups of straight men.[11]

Bar nights were Wednesday and Saturday and usually consisted of anywhere from half a dozen to a dozen people. The tradition started back in the 1990s, and the regular attendees, and bars, changed over the years. One of the early "home bars" was Chet's, owned by family member Chet Robin. Joullian recalls, "It was and remains one of the most elegant bars I've ever visited. Not just the wonderful decor, stage and piano for entertainment but Chet himself who added to the ambiance."[12] Other bars over the years included the Golden Lantern, Grand Pre's, and Cutter's. In addition to bar nights, another tradition was holiday potlucks at the Faerie Playhouse. These attracted a larger attendance, usually around forty people. Aitken remembers her first potluck:

> My first pot-luck was Christmas 2008 at The Faerie Playhouse, this was even a bigger, more diverse group, straight, gay, lesbian. So many walks of life joining together, some for the gay connection, others in the same Mardi Gras Krewe etc. Everyone brought food drinks, and a few helped with clean-up which made the day very enjoyable. Start time and end time was very regimented, it ended at a certain time and Stewart was not shy about telling people to leave.[13]

Another member of the family was Paul Orfila, who served as a house-keeper at the Faerie Playhouse for several years. After his life partner, Jack Gentry, died in 2000, Orfila's addiction to crack cocaine worsened and he left the Faerie Playhouse orbit in 2003 and passed away in 2004.

One family member who met a tragic end was J. B. Harter. On March 13, 2002, John Burton Harter was found murdered in his home in the Gentilly neighborhood of New Orleans. Investigators concluded he had been killed two days earlier because Harter's white Tacoma pickup truck had been involved in a hit and run on the afternoon of March 11. Witnesses saw the driver abandon the truck shortly after the accident and provided enough details for a police artist to draw a sketch of the perpetrator, but no one was ever arrested. Harter's murder remains unsolved.

Harter's murder reverberated throughout the arts and museum community of New Orleans, and it devastated Stewart, as well as many of the family members. Joullian remembers:

> We met Burt with John Foster during a short time that he and Rich were seeing other people. It was a one of the series of "Faerie Gatherings" as Stewart was fond of calling in Sea Grove, Florida begun by our Montgomery friend Lawrence Jetton. It was here that Alabama friend couples Terry B. and Tim-look-alike Fredrick R. as well as Joey and Shane from Montgomery, now with a home in New Orleans became part of the Alabama Gang at the Playhouse. Burt, although

quiet, due partly to his severe hearing loss, grew to be a beloved member of those gatherings as well as at The Faerie Playhouse. In The Faerie Playhouse Butler Correspondence files are a series of photos from Sea Grove as well as several pages of small colored drawings of much of that group. Along the staircase wall, portraits are displayed of many of these Faerie Playhouse friends. Thus with these and several larger portraits including the iconic Stewart portrait probably constitutes the largest of one if not the largest Harter collection outside of the John Burton Harter Foundation original holdings. In The Faerie Playhouse Stewart Butler Correspondence files is a large collection of photographic as well as painting notecards that Burt was fond of giving to us. This too may be a unique collection at The Faerie Playhouse.[14]

Harter's life was a fascinating glimpse into the internal drama of a talented artist trapped in a self-imposed closet.[15] As such, his life and career are typical of so many gay folk of yesteryear who never lived to witness and enjoy the incredible strides we as a LGBT+ community have made in recent years.

In the 1990s, Harter created what he called the AIDS Wall, a series of portraits of his friends and acquaintances who had died of AIDS or were living with HIV. In addition to drawing inspiration from people and places he knew, Harter was also greatly influenced by Paul Cadmus and Eastern philosophy, particularly Hinduism. In 2005, the New Orleans Contemporary Arts Center honored Harter with an exhibition entitled "The Culture of Queer: A Tribute to J. B. Harter." The exhibit was to run from July through September but was cut short by Hurricane Katrina. The exhibition was reopened at the Leslie-Lohman Gay Art Foundation in New York City in May 2006.

The next several years would witness a gradual decline in Stewart's mental and physical health. Stewart and Alfred, both heavy smokers, gave up cigarettes in 2002. At one time, Alfred was up to eight packs a day, and Stewart was at two packs a day. Also that year, Stewart resolved to eat healthier and made an effort to lose weight, going from 180 pounds to 145 pounds. Stewart suffered a transient ischemic attack in 2003 and, in 2004, underwent a hernia operation. Before the surgery, when a nurse asked him for his occupation, Stewart enthusiastically replied, "gay activist!" But Stewart's enthusiasm would come to a grinding halt later that year. The depression Stewart battled periodically for most of his adult life reared itself again and resulted in an emotional breakdown. At the recommendation of his longtime friend Sandra Pailet, he saw a psychiatrist and subsequently spent ten days in a psychiatric unit. While undergoing observation and receiving treatment,

Stewart bonded with his fellow patients, some of whom were financially impoverished. Stewart had his friends Rich Magill and Julie Thompson bring him cash so he could distribute it among these patients. Pailet and friends Ron Joullian and his partner Tim Angle visited Stewart regularly during his hospitalization. After being released, Stewart returned home to the Faerie Playhouse under the watchful supervision of his sister Suzanne, who had come down to care for Stewart, and Alfred and the rest of the family. Stewart gave up, temporarily, alcohol and marijuana, and he visited a therapist once a week for roughly a year. His mental health improved somewhat, but, on the downside, he developed an addiction to lorazepam, more commonly known as Ativan. He became unmotivated and generally lethargic. He would later describe the period from his release through Hurricane Katrina as a time of "incapacitation."

Depression notwithstanding, Stewart and Alfred settled into a nightly routine in the 2000s. Stewart describes a typical evening at the Faerie Playhouse in 2003:

> Alfred and I spend about an hour reading to each other followed by another hour during which he has a beer and I some Scotch on the rocks as we discuss the day's events, upcoming plans or whatever else might come to mind. We continue to that routine. This year we completed all but one of Gore Vidal's series of six or seven historical novels. Now we are on the final pages of his rather lengthy *Creation*, an historical novel dealing with various philosophies and religions of ancient Persia, Greece, India, and China. Quite interesting as seems to be the case with everything I've read by Vidal.

These nightly reading sessions, which were accompanied by fruit and cheese, continued until Alfred's death in 2008. In 2007, Butler recalled that Alfred usually read a passage from the Bible or a selection of his own writings. Examples of Stewart's reading choices included *Animal Farm*, *1984*, *The Travels of Marco Polo*, *Democracy in America*, *Gay American History*, *The Hobbit* and *Lord of the Rings*, *The Velveteen Rabbit*, and *The Golden Bough*. The routine was interrupted only on Wednesdays and Saturdays, when they met their friends at the Golden Lantern for drinks or on Sundays when they dined at Café Degas.

In 2004, on Alfred's sixty-eighth birthday, Stewart threw Alfred a party at the Faerie Playhouse, which was attended by several members of the family.[16] At the party, Stewart gifted Alfred with a book, *Three Plays*, which consisted of Alfred's writing. The three plays Alfred had written, and which appear in the book published by Two Rooms Press, are *Peter Puck, The Divine Love Play*, and *The Sun*. Two Rooms Press was owned by Steve McKinney (another Birmingham, Alabama native) and Jonathan Aaberg, family members through Hagler, Joullian, and Angle who lived in San Francisco. At the birthday party, Stewart, Alfred, and the other partygoers drank three and a half jugs of wine that had been made the year before by Bill Hagler.[17] Stewart also recalls that three "five generation joints" were smoked.

The publication of *Peter Puck* was the realization of a dream of sorts for Alfred. Educated as a classicist, Alfred considered himself first and foremost a writer. And he wrote a lot, filling dozens of yellow legal pads with notes, ideas, poetry, music, phrases that fancied him, and, most interestingly, visions. Some of the scribblings are incoherent or illegible, but those that are decipherable are laced with religious symbolism and classical allusions. Much of his writing was directed at Stewart—"You are the wildness of night and darkness. You are the sexy wild moon." His affection for Stewart was most evidenced in his poetry. For example, here is a poem he wrote for Stewart on the occasion of his seventy-seventh birthday:

> *Beloved Stewart,*
> *Happy birthday to the*
> *Most loving man in the whole world*
> *The loved man I love*
> *Care for, and believe in*
> *For the love of*
> *Stewart*
> *Who loves me*
> *Who is closest to me*
> *Who I cannot live without*
> *I love you, Stewart*
> *As*
> *Myrrh incense*
> *Rubbed on my breast*
> *Love breathes in as*
> *Sweat*
> *Love for beloved*
> *My love*
> *I love you Stewart*
> *As the wine of love*
> *Drinks deeply*

As Stewart and Alfred
Drink
Golden chateau
Y'bien
Sweet golden
Grace
Poured
Forth

What his poetry lacked in quality was made up for by its authenticity. And if his verse lacked sophistication, his letters to world leaders, real and imagined, were fantastic. Consider this letter addressed vaguely to "Emperor":

Emperor,
  I am nirvana on earth.
  I have conquered Russia and Egypt and have given [unintelligible] legionary peace process.
  I am the center of television and world-wide communications.
  I am also the Holy of Holies Most Holy cherubim angel that sits in the throne of God and stands around the throne.
  What is spiritual sex?
  I believe in the Kama Sutra the nail rubbing of the body to music and a golden circle amidst music and nail rubbing that creates a circle of evermore relaxation and senses of the skin, and hearing evermore the word which no one has.
  And pictures and incense and myrrh and music and poppers and orgy and beautiful [unintelligible] birth faces of angel.
  I believe in God and Buddha's wisdom and the Bible's understanding and knowledge and wisdom.
  I do not believe in death.
  I believe in life eternal the first and great commandment of God to love God with all your heart, body, and mind and you shall live eternally.

  Love,
  Alfred Cherubim

And then there is this letter from Alfred to the prime minister of Iran, no date:

Beloved Prime Minister of Iran,

The Seraphims (angels) are wounded with blood flushing hungry for love, the she-camel of Allah. The she-camel has love and beauty to give like the fires of the sun's splendor which sun's splendor is her's and Allah's.

Allah is overshadowing her words with himself, and his angels, which is a secret! Overshadowing her for her BABY the prophet's baby. Allah, God, Vishnu Nirvana, the Supreme August Heavenly Emperor [unintelligible].

Sunburnt in her glory she burns with love. Her baby is due February 28th.

Love,
The She-Camel, Alfred

And here is one simply addressed to China:

The Dragon King sends rain as incense from the Jade Emperor on the people of China. Incense, myrrh, frankincense, sandal wood, mush, aloes, [unintelligible], streams of incense on China, rivers of incense, streams y gardens y [unintelligible] of living water and incense [unintelligible] you.

Love in torrents, like incense, love from the Jade Emperor, love for the Jade Emperor, love for the Chinese people blood flushed lungs of the breath of love from the dragon king to the rulers and people of China.

Love,
The Dragon King,
Alfred

When not writing, Alfred spent a lot of time on the couch reading the Bible, monthly financial statements, and trust portfolios and watching TV stock market news. He also enjoyed watching sitcoms, especially *Keeping Up Appearances* and *Two and a Half Men*. The dogs were another great source of joy. In the mornings, Putz would eagerly wait for Alfred to wake because Alfred would kiss him after rising. And in the afternoon, Alfred included the dogs in his ritual of taking coffee (in a fancy cup) with tea biscuits by giving them two or three crackers served on fine china. Psychologically he was still given to periodic manic episodes, and knives and other sharp objects had to be hidden from him. Physically he was growing weaker, and by 2005 he had to sit down in order to brush his teeth and required help dressing and with other routine daily tasks, like opening a pill bottle. After Hurricane Katrina, Alfred would have to be hospitalized for not being able to walk. Stewart was of some assistance, but he was still recovering from his mental breakdown in 2004.

Stewart's persistent depression lifted in January 2004 when he traveled to New England to attend his sister's fiftieth wedding anniversary. He spent the night with his niece Alicia in Upper Grandview, New York, at her home on a bluff overlooking the Hudson River before renting a car and driving to Burlington, Vermont, through a snowstorm. He later recalled spending

> three hours in a snow-bank into which I skidded in freezing weather. I vowed then and there to never again drive in snow. But it was all worth it, for after spending two nights at my sister's, we drove to the southern part of the state to a country inn which Sue and Dave had entirely booked. All four children's entire families along with many close friends gathered for two nights of celebration. It was a grand time I'll never forget.[18]

If 2004 was a year of highs and lows, 2005 would bring more of the same. The year started off on a positive note with Stewart's reconciliation with Bill Hagler and Rich Magill and would end with Alfred in the hospital with a ruptured back disc. And there was also Katrina.

In August, as Hurricane Katrina churned in the Gulf, Stewart and Alfred initially decided to remain at home. They had never evacuated before for a hurricane and saw no need to do so for Katrina—that is until Rich Magill called from Prattville, Alabama, where he was visiting his mother and urged them to leave New Orleans and drive to Alabama to stay with him. The same day Mayor Ray Nagin issued a mandatory evacuation order. Stewart and Alfred decided to go to Alabama. Stewart later remembered:

> Most of our close friends had already gone, but Steve Willey hadn't left yet and accepted our invitation to go with us. The next couple of ours we frantically got together what essentials we thought we'd need over the next three or four days and headed out about noon. What with the two dogs, Tara and Putzy, we were so cramped it made for a pretty miserable twelve hours, the time it took us to get to Prattville. Those there—Rich, Pat, and Bill Hagler—did everything they possibly could to make us comfortable.[19]

After a few days in Alabama, it became clear they would not be returning to New Orleans anytime soon. As the devastation unfolded on national
television, Stewart's sister invited them to come to Vermont to her home
in Jericho. Leaving Tara with Rich Magill and his mother Pat, Willey drove
three days and, after dropping Stewart and Alfred off at his sister's, drove
to Delaware to stay with his mother. Then the waiting game began. Stewart
and Alfred stayed in Vermont for about a month, all the while not knowing
if the Faerie Playhouse had flooded or been looted. They eventually made
contact with friends Toni Pizanie and Elwood Richardson, both of whom
had ridden out the storm in New Orleans, who reported to them that the
Faerie Playhouse seemed to be okay. They were not sure because even after
the floodwater receded, they could not get closer than three blocks from the
house because of all the fallen trees and debris. On September 17, Ron Joullian
and Tim Angle returned to the city and the following day called Stewart to
inform him the Faerie Playhouse had not flooded (the water had risen to
within inches of the floorboards), nor had it been looted. The backyard was
a mess and a few sideboards had flown off the home, but for the most part,
the home was undamaged.

Joullian remembers:

Not knowing what to expect on the trip back, we departed 12:00 am
17 September and headed home to allow enough time to queue up at
the Jefferson/Orleans parish checkpoint at daybreak. We had to travel
on the north shore of Lake Pontchartrain as the I-10 bridge across the
lake had been damaged. It was eerie traveling along darkened stretches
of the interstates usually ablaze with lights. We made better time than
we anticipated with such little traffic. We pulled into a truck-stop in
Mandeville and slept for a couple of hours. We then proceeded to the
south shore.

We stopped for breakfast at the welcoming lights of Dots Diner in
Jefferson Parish one of the few such places open. There we readied all
the necessary papers such as identification, the business license for our
approval for entry into Orleans Parish. Excited about getting to return,
I was wearing my NOFD tee-shirt and my NOFD Fire Chief cap that
I had purchased at local fire stations. With all our papers in order, we
waited our turn in the relatively short line of cars. As we approached
the checkpoint, the National Guardsman, seeing my tee-shirt and cap,
saluted and waved us through! Tim and I were becoming two in a then
estimated 500 people now permitted back in the city.

We proceeded through the tree strewn streets to our place on Magazine Street. A *USA Today* reporter was on the street and we offered a few words. As he left we allowed a *New York Times* reporter there as well to accompany us into our place to view any the damage. As we went from room to room downstairs as well as upstairs we could not ascertain any damage. With that the *New York Times* reporter left having nothing sensational to note or photograph. Living on the high ground of the "natural levee," we suffered no flooding. Later upon inspection, we noted roof damage. It was a waiting game until the next rain, approximately five weeks away to discover the leaks throughout the place, despite our having the very first blue tarp the roof on the street. Ironically, on Christmas Eve, the most significant leak brought the plaster crashing to the floor in the front room as we were preparing for the "family" Christmas Potluck! Remarkably, the Home Depot was doing a brisk business that night and we were able to obtain a tarp that we affixed over the gap in the ceiling and the potluck continued as scheduled.

The next day after our return, we were assured by a member of the National Guard that we could visit the French Quarter. We found ourselves in a virtual "ghost town" as we attempted to assess damage to Rich Magill's old place on Royal and his newly rented space on Barracks. Little did we realize that the soon-to-be Faerie Playhouse family member, Carmine would occupy the other half of that double. We drove then to the Faerie Playhouse and discovered that Katrina's flood waterline came within two inches of entering the home. We cautiously opened the door to the darkened house with flashlights in hand. The only thing stirring was the large resident gecko crawling along the ceiling that had somehow taken refuge in the house.[20]

On their journey back to New Orleans, Stewart and Alfred stopped in Pennsylvania where Alfred was able to visit with his sister for a few days. Regarding the drive home, Steve Willey later recalled:

I drove them to Vermont when we evacuated and it was long hours on the road and he wasn't a very good traveler anyway and we made it to Vermont and dropped them off, got them settled, and I went to Delaware and came back and got them in Vermont and brought them back. Well, he had a little fit on the way back down and he says, "I hate you. I never want to see you again, but I know I need you for the next

two days to drive me home. Then I'm never going to see you again!"
Even in his off-reality he bounces back to reality in the next second.

Upon arriving home, Stewart and Alfred were relieved to find the house
in good shape and the backyard cleaned up by longtime friend "Skateboard"
Stephen, who had been staying there with Stewart's permission since his
own house flooded.

The effects of Katrina on the Faerie Playhouse were many: Steve Willey
moved temporarily into the backyard cottage because he had lost electricity
at his home. Tara died while at Rich's in Alabama. An avocado tree Stewart
had had since 1967 was lost. Housekeeper Monica Williams and friends
Todd Bachman and Pete Dickinson all relocated. The nightly and weekly
routines were disrupted. Larry Graham moved into the cottage (and did the
covers of the Christmas cards as well as maintaining the yard and garden).
New siding was installed along the main house. Stewart's niece Alicia, her
husband Stewart Lewis, and their daughter Serena, all of whom had come to
volunteer cleaning up Katrina debris, visited for a week. Alfred's psychiatrist,
Dr. Roniger, relocated and did not return from his Katrina exile.

In addition to reassembling their own lives and restoring some sense of
normalcy to the Faerie Playhouse, Stewart and Alfred also assisted others
who were attempting to pick up the pieces after Katrina. Friend and artist Larry Graham had lost his studio, cameras, and lighting equipment in
the storm. Stewart, Rich Magill, Ron Joullian, and Tim Angle organized an
exhibition and benefit for Graham at Magill's home in the French Quarter.
At the time, Graham had been working for three and half years on a series
of photographs he called "The Face of God: Biblical Tableaux." The series
consisted of biblical scenes with French Quarter residents serving as models.
The fundraiser was a success later in the year: the series was featured at the
Perrin Benham Gallery. Born in Alabama and raised in East Texas, Graham
had been in New Orleans since 1995.

As the city began to recover from the devasting flood, St. Anna's Episcopal
Church, which is directly across the street from the Faerie Playhouse, began a
weekly outreach to musicians affected by the storm, which, in part, included
a jazz mass on Wednesday evenings. Stewart and Alfred began attending
these services and eventually caught the eye of the pastor, Reverend Bill
Terry. Father Terry remembers:

Somewhere in the craziness of late 2007 I spied, in the pews, a very
odd couple. It takes a bit to be an "odd couple" in New Orleans. Stewart
often wore marijuana-themed clothing and jewelry to church, sporting

his signature brightly-hued tube socks with plaid shorts. Alfred was a tall and very slender man, with wild grey hair and bushy eyebrows. He always looked rather intense, and his features shifted from serious and somewhat dark, to smiling and delightfully bright. Alfred's expressive emotional fluidity would manifest during the mass. Yet Alfred showed a devotion to prayer and to the sacraments that was sincere and focused, at least most of the time. He did have the penchant to wander a bit. But for me, the more interesting one of the pair was Stewart Butler. It was obvious for me, a pastor, that Stewart was Alfred's caregiver and protector. He would very gently guide his lover here and there. As he attended these services, Stewart always looked serious and spoke to me very little. He would never come to the altar rail to receive communion, as Alfred did. I mentioned to him that he was welcome to receive, but he politely said that he "wasn't there yet." And so, Alfred would pray, and Stewart would provide his companionship and warmth.[21]

Although Stewart lacked the faith to which Alfred was so devoted, he was incredibly tolerant and longsuffering of it. Years earlier, Alfred had purchased a number of Bibles and distributed them to their friends, most of whom were anything but religious. When these friends glanced at Stewart with puzzled looks upon receiving the Bibles, Stewart's response was to shrug his shoulders and brush it off. Years later, as Alfred faced death, Stewart would have a conversion of sorts, but for their thirty-five years together Stewart did not share Alfred's faith. He did, however, respect it. If something was important to Alfred, it was important to Stewart.

After Katrina, Alfred wanted to rent space in Baton Rouge in case they needed to evacuate again. Gradually, as the city recovered from the devastating flood, Stewart and Alfred resumed their weekly routine, which included bar nights with the family and Sunday dinner at Café Degas. At Café Degas, Alfred invariably ordered pate and cheese plates. Alfred also enjoyed occasional meals at Commander's Palace. Before he had to be fitted for dentures, which he hated wearing, Alfred loved a good steak. His standard diet in his last years consisted of raw eggs stirred into skim milk and heated in the microwave, along with tomatoes, cottage cheese, bananas, raw liverwurst, and strawberry ice cream. He also drank olive oil right out of the bottle.

The year 2007 proved to be significant for Stewart and Alfred in a number of respects. Several family members passed away, Bill Hagler returned to the Faerie Playhouse, Stewart was honored for his activism and resumed his advocacy for criminal justice reform, and both Alfred's and Stewart's health worsened.

Friends Skip Ward, the Reverend Bill Richardson, Louise McFarland (a former Louisiana State epidemiologist and AIDS activist in the 1980s), and Sandra Pailet all passed away in 2007. Parts of all these family member's remains were placed in the memorial garden behind the Faerie Playhouse. Also in 2007, a ceremony was held to lay to rest in the garden some of the remains of Charlene Schneider, who had died the year before. Memorial garden ceremonies were as much about celebrating life as they were about death and saying goodbye. Stewart, always sentimental, sometimes tempered his emotions with his obsession with strictly regimented schedules. Charlotte Aitken remembers attending one ceremony when Stewart, standing by her side, surveyed the table full of food and full bar and remarked to her, "Damn, I will never get rid of these people."[22]

Also in 2007, the Bienville Foundation placed a plaque on the front façade of Stewart and Alfred's home indicating the Faerie Playhouse as a historically important site of LGBT+ organizing as well as noting the memorial garden as the final resting place of many significant figures from local LGBT+ history. And on December 12, the LGBT Community Center of New Orleans gave Stewart its Founder Award, along with Betty Caldwell and Niki Kearby.

Around this time, Stewart began publicly advocating for a cause dear to his heart—the reform of marijuana laws. For years he had often berated the "so-called war on drugs," believing it was ineffectual and a complete waste of time, money, and resources. In 2002, he and Alfred gifted everyone on the Faerie Playhouse mailing list with a membership in the Drug Policy Alliance, stating in the newsletter, "It is our hope that you will carefully consider the information they'll be sending you and that you come to appreciate the work they do in spreading the word on the evils of our so-called 'War on Drugs.'"[23] Stewart had been an avid consumer of marijuana since the early 1960s, and his two arrests for marijuana possession only strengthened his resolve to speak out against what he considered "unjust laws." At the end of 2007, Stewart attended the International Drug Policy Reform Conference in New Orleans. The following year, in his annual Valentine's Day newsletter, he promoted "LIBERATE MARIJUANA," a series of marches held around the world in two hundred cities on May 3, 2008. He did not participate in protests and marches but rather confined his advocacy to letters to newspaper editors. Sometimes in his annual newsletter he would spend no small amount of ink editorializing against the war on drugs, specifically railing against the racism and xenophobia that underlies it. In 2010 he wrote to the *Times-Picayune* arguing:

Re—"Drug exhibit looks at colorful La. History" The article's assertion that the Drug Enforcement Administration's current exhibit at the Old U.S. Mint makes "a forceful claim that the Sept. 11, 2001, terrorists financed their activities by trafficking in drugs" is right on. However, it was not the drugs per se that did the financing but rather the fact that we've made them illegal that has made the trafficking profitable. Stop and think about it for a moment. We're financing BOTH sides of the war with our TAX DOLLARS. Not only are we financing the D.E.A., our judicial system, our jails, but also the murderous cartels as well as the terrorists and monstrous costs of our security. We need to make drugs legal and regulate and tax them and treat addicts and hold them responsible for criminal acts. Not only would we be better off financially, but also we'd be safer.[24]

Stewart began losing his hearing and obtained a hearing aid in 2006, but he refused to wear it. His ability to concentrate had been gradually diminishing since 2004, and that trend continued. Alfred faced more serious medical issues. He had finally started taking his medications on a consistent basis and kept regular appointments with his psychiatrist, Dr. Joseph J. Roniger, whom Alfred referred to as "Jo Jo the Clown." But as his mental health stabilized, Alfred's physical condition continued to deteriorate, and he sometimes had trouble standing. In addition to schizophrenia, Alfred also had a history of sustained ventricular tachycardia (a fast, abnormal heartrate) and lumbar disk hypertension and melanoma.

On January 15, 2008, Alfred complained of chest pain and shortness of breath and was prescribed benzatropine and clorazepate. A week later he had trouble breathing and went to the emergency room at Touro Infirmary but left the hospital before seeing a doctor. Another breathing episode occurred the following day and Stewart called 911, but Alfred refused to go to the hospital. Stewart convinced him to see a doctor the following day, and after an EKG, Alfred was immediately sent to the emergency room where a ventilator was placed in his throat. He remained in the hospital for twelve days. A week after being released, an angiogram was performed, and the following day a feeding tube was administered. On February 12, he went to the emergency room again because of shortness of breath. While he was in the hospital, perhaps sensing the end was near, Alfred asked Ron Joullian for a copy of Emily Dickinson's *Complete Poems*. He asked Stewart to read the following poem:

THE bustle in a house
The morning after death

Is solemnest of industries
Enacted upon earth,—
The sweeping up the heart,
And putting love away
We shall not want to use again
Until eternity.

Stewart and Alfred had always shared a love of literature and this poem was especially poignant given the circumstances. During his hospitalization, Alfred also requested Communion. Father Terry was summoned to his bedside and remembers:

> It was a beautiful, clear day, and the sun was bright in the Spring sky. As Alfred laid propped up in his bed, his beloved Bible next to him, Stewart sat beside him. By now Stewart had accepted the inevitability and imminence of Alfred's passing. He was serious but serene. This seemed to be part of Stewart's organized process of understanding Alfred's death, as well as his own inward, spiritual reflection upon "Life." On that particular day I brought a "home communion kit" with me, including a miniature chalice and all things needed to do a full communion service at Alfred's bedside. So we did. Alfred received the bread with the words, "The body of Christ. The bread of heaven" and then the chalice, "The blood of Christ. The cup of salvation." Alfred's countenance reflected a serenity that accepted with complete awareness his own state of being, within the framework of his faith and those ritual actions. At the same time, Stewart continued watching. Alfred, turning his head slightly, asked once again the same question he had been asking Stewart for years, "Will you take Communion (with me)?" On this occasion, Stewart said simply "Yes." And so Stewart received Communion. At the moment Stewart took that piece of bread into his mouth, a tear crept from Alfred's eye, and a smile of gratitude and hope framed his face. And, like Alfred, a peacefulness and serenity came across Stewart's face. They looked at each other and communicated a thousand thoughts and feelings in an instant— a life-time of hopefulness in Alfred and fulfillment in Stewart at that precise moment in their own sacred history. That was the moment of conversion for Stewart Butler.[25]

Alfred was later discharged and returned to the Faerie Playhouse to convalesce. Surrounded by Stewart, Bill Hagler, and a sitter named Maria, Alfred died at 11:55 p.m. on Sunday, March 2, 2008, at home at the Faerie Playhouse. Alfred died of complications from pneumonia. The death certificate lists atherosclerotic cardiovascular disease as the cause of death.

Alfred's funeral was at St. Anna's Episcopal Church on Saturday, March 8, 2008. Alfred was laid out in his favorite white-striped suit in a white casket with gold crosses on its corners. The casket was covered in white flowers along with a brass crucifix and Alfred's golden statue of an angel blowing a trumpet. Father Bill Terry conducted the High Mass. Alfred's funeral was attended by seven of his family members: brother Jefferson and his daughter Susie, sister Jean and her husband Chuck and their daughter Jeanie, a second cousin, and Patsy Pope. About forty people attended Alfred's interment at the Chapel of Peace Mausoleum at the Garden of Memories Cemetery in Metairie. A lock of his hair was added to the Faerie Playhouse memorial garden. Alfred left everything to Stewart in his will. Alfred's nephew and nieces gave Stewart their share of Alfred's trust.

Testimonials at Alfred's memorial service at the Faerie Playhouse were given by Larry Graham, Steve Willey, Toni Pizanie, Patsy Pope, Jack Sullivan, Jean Henry, and Ron Joullian. Regarding the death of Alfred, Ron Joullian summed up the thoughts of many in a sympathy card:

Dear Stewart,

On this occasion we reflect on the life of Alfred. I was fortunate to be a part of his life, which he shared with us and particularly you. I look back on Alfred's unabashed pursuit of life, art, passion; his intelligence, his humor, his demons and his angels. Who can forget that arched eyebrow when his interest was peaked. We all recall his last journey in this life. I'll never forget those remarkable days when he returned to be with you and us. Who can forget those agonizing days before his transition. I will always remember the great sense of peace and calm when last seeing him. I think this was his peace with you and peace he sought and knew. We all miss him but will never forget him.

Love, Ron

Other family and friends eulogized Alfred at the gathering as well. Toni Pizanie testified to Alfred's generosity, citing the time Alfred paid for her dog, Freddie's, operation. Larry Graham commented:

One time we went to Michelle and Jonathan's for Thanksgiving. I admit it was kind of boring with some old ladies there and it was kind of stuffy in the living room. So everyone went to the balcony, you know, the smokers. So we're out there about ten minutes and Alfred comes out and says, "Oh, there you are," he sits and he says, "It's boring in there. Who's got a cigarette?" So I said I had a really bad back problem. I was kind of bitching about it then and Alfred has his cigarette lit up and he says, "Have you ever tried high heels"?

Steve Willey remembered:

One year, Alfred and Stewart were going to Alaska for a vacation and I had them in the car taking them to the airport and then Alfred decides, "I'm not going to Alaska." So Stewart says, "Well, I'm going, Steven, you have to take care of him for the next 14 days." So we're at the airport and taking things out of one suitcase and putting them in another suitcase. Stewart's making lists for me of what pills he needs to take. And so we get home and spend a nice week. When Stewart got back Alfred said, "He's too dominant a male; he eats too much beef. He stripped me down and ran me up Esplanade in chains." And I'm like "where did this come from?" As soon as I leave, he says, "I don't want him back in the house, I want the locks changed." But that was just one of the many incidents Alfred and I had.

Jack Sullivan read a letter Alfred wrote to him and his late partner Chris:

Beloved Chris and Jack,
    Alfred, a saint of Jesus Christ, the son of God, to the beloved lovers Jack and Chris.
    Grace of the Holy Ghost unto you, Beauty love and truth of Jesus Christ's Word be multiplied unto the two lovers.
    Blessed be the sun face of God Almighty the Absolute Beauty of His Face shining as the sun in its power.
    And blessed be the Greek breasts of Jesus Christ encircled with a golden girdle for love.
    And of the beautiful Greek body of Beauty that shines forth as the Light and Joy of the mind.
    Blessed be the love of God for us in the amounts and sweetness and sensuousness sublime that no man has ever expressed.
    And of the truth of Jesus the Christ's Words which sanctify us his saints and give everlasting Life.

    Love, Alfred

Jean Henry, Alfred's sister, spoke about Alfred's faith:

Alfred grew up in an agnostic family. My father went away in the
Second World War and came back. He had been something of a hero,
and it was a difficult time for all of us. It was difficult particularly
for Alfred, but he found faith and humanity with a Jesuit priest at St.
Ignatius High School in San Francisco. I don't know if he was head-
master or what. So that's the place he found religion at first, then the
Episcopal Church and the Anglo-Catholic Church, and that was his
saving grace. But through all of this he found love and Stewart.

After Alfred's passing, Stewart remained faithful, attending church regularly. St. Anna's commitment to social justice appealed to Stewart. Of all the
mainline Christian denominations, the Episcopal Church was perhaps the
most progressive, embracing the ordination of women and preaching tolerance for LGBT+ people and inclusivity for all. According to Father Terry, who
would visit Stewart at the Faerie Playhouse regularly, Stewart "read a tract
produced by the Episcopal Church, *Forward Day by Day*. That text provided
a scripture passage followed by a mediation. If he did not get his *Day by Day*
on time, a call would soon be made to the church office demanding that he
received his copy." Some may have found Stewart's conversion puzzling, but
as Stewart explained to those who questioned him, he was convinced it was
the only way he would ever see Alfred again. Stewart was officially confirmed
in the Episcopal Church on March 9, 2009. He brought to his newfound
spirituality certain conditions. For example he rejected the notion that Jesus
was a king and that heaven was a kingdom, preferring instead to think of a
heaven as a dominion and Jesus as a brother. As Father Terry notes, even in
his newfound faith, Stewart "demanded a radical equality."[26]

At the time of his passing, Alfred's financial standing was on sound foot-
ing. His investment portfolio (which began in 1997 with ten shares each in
Microsoft, Intel, and WorldCom) was worth $194,890.66. There were also
the four trusts previously set up by his family, his inheritance, and the Faerie
Playhouse. Stewart would be financially secure for the remainder of his life.
A PFLAG scholarship in memory of Alfred was created by his friends in
New Orleans, and Alfred's sister Jean donated $100,000 to the University of
California, Merced to endow a scholarship fund in Alfred's name.

The death of Alfred hit Stewart hard, and he fell, not unexpectedly, into
a deep depression. To help navigate the grieving process, Stewart visited a
psychiatrist, who recommended electroshock therapy, but Stewart felt that
would be too invasive. Instead he sought the help of a social worker, who

not only helped him but also became a friend. A few years later, when this woman became ill, Stewart sent her money to help with medical expenses.[27]

In the fall after Alfred's death, Suzanne and Dave Eaton hosted a family reunion at their home twenty-five miles outside of Burlington, Vermont, on the occasion of nephew Tim's twenty-fifth wedding anniversary. Stewart learned of the reunion a month after Alfred died and was in such an emotional state that he was convinced he wouldn't be able to attend, but his sister wouldn't take no for an answer.

> But Suzanne and everyone else who knew of it kept nagging me to go. Finally, I came to the conclusion that I needed to show myself that I could do it. And I am so gratified that I did because everyone did show up: Suzanne and David, all four of their children along with the spouses of two and girlfriend and a friend of the other two, and all seven grandchildren along with the boyfriend of one. I arrived Friday evening, August 1st. Everyone already there poured out of the house to greet me as though I were the guest of honor. On Saturday, games, meals and conversation dominated the gathering as it built momentum toward the evening climax. Almost everyone had selected a chapeau from the large portion of my collection that I had brought along for that very purpose. The evening began with a boiled lobster dinner. We were entertained by background music emanating from one of the corners of the huge backyard. Older son Kent had gotten the trio, or quartet or whatever it was that he played with on a somewhat regular basis to volunteer their services for the occasion. They were wonderful. After dinner a couple of the guests twisted my arm and drug me away to some secluded place where we were joined by two or three others and they tortured me so horribly that ultimately I had no other choice but to give in and share some absolutely grand grass with them. I don't know what it was but this strange feeling of euphoria gradually enveloped me just as what was in effect a family jam session was getting underway. Some seven or eight family members gradually joined all or various members of the band. Alicia's two daughters, Liana and Sarina, sang both solo and as a duet; Jennifer played the violin; Tim's son Jasper, or "Jazz," was absolutely wicked on the drums; Tim played a totally down and dirty harmonica (the band's bassist switched back and forth between bass and harmonica and had brought along his whole set of harmonicas [could this possibly have been plotted in advance?]); and, of course, Kent was pretty mean, too, on his guitar. And there were two or three

others who I hope will forgive me for not being able to remember more particulars. I wonder why. In summary, I'm so glad I decided to go. Such a family reunion is rare due to its totality. It gave me an opportunity to know my grand nieces and nephews better; I showed myself I could do it and I learned that the next time I fly I need to wear slip-ons, not lace-up tennis shoes. The trip was my Number One fun time for 2008.[28]

In 2012, Stewart began his last great project—preserving local LGBT+ history by cofounding the LGBT+ Archives Project of Louisiana. This organization, and Stewart's role in forming it, is discussed in greater detail in the epilogue. After getting the Archives Project "off the ground," Stewart was tired, exhausted from a lifetime of passion and activity. His health continued to gradually decline, and he began staying at home more and more.

In 2014, the ACLU of Louisiana presented to Stewart its prestigious Ben Smith Award, which honors people who have demonstrated a commitment to the advancement of civil liberties in Louisiana. Ben Smith was a civil rights lawyer who was arrested for his work to end segregation and for participating in mixed-race gatherings. He cofounded the ACLU of Louisiana in 1956. In his acceptance speech, Stewart spoke briefly and credited Alfred with enabling his activism. This award was just one of many Stewart had received; his other awards and honors include the Gittings-Hay Award (1985), Louisiana Council for Equal Rights "We're Here" Award for politics (1991), HRC (1993), Pride parade co–grand marshal (1998), and Equality Louisiana "Community First Award" (2004).

The following year, 2015, Anthony DeJacimo and other friends helped plan a surprise party for Stewart's eighty-fifth birthday. When Stewart and Bill showed up to their regular bar night at Mag's 940 (formerly Charlene's), Stewart was shocked to see a packed house of friends, many of whom he hadn't seen in years. The party featured performances by Savannah Summers (DeJacimo's drag persona) and the legendary drag performer Princess Stephanie (who also bartended at Mag's); remarks by Father Bill Terry, Judge Miriam Waltzer, Courtney Sharp, Julie Thompson, Roberts Batson, Johnny Jackson, and Stewart himself; mayoral and city council proclamations honoring Stewart; donations to PFLAG New Orleans and the LGBT+ Archives Project of Louisiana; a beautiful flower arrangement donated by Wayne Christenberry; and a poignant slideshow prepared by Larry Graham and Tim Angle. Also in attendance were Larry Raybourne—a friend of Alfred's from before Stewart—and his partner, Paul Arrington, both of whom had traveled to New Orleans from Florida for the party.

Over the next few years, Stewart withdrew more and more and often complained of being tired. He even talked of suicide. By 2020 he had made up his mind. He was ready to die.

Charles Paul remembers:

> Looking back, there was a bar night in January when he asked when we would be back. He wanted to make sure we were supplied with brownies for the next time we would be at a bar night. I told him it would be the weekend before Mardi Gras weekend or Mystic Krewe of Barkus weekend. He called me on the 11th of February to make sure we were still coming down (also to see if I would donate again to his Church). He called again on the 15th and asked Pete and me to come over to pick up some brownies. Of course, there was a time window provided—the next 45 minutes to an hour. We went over and he handed us a huge bag of brownies and I gave him the check for St Anna's. We had a conversation that I figured out shortly thereafter was his saying goodbye to us. He told us how much we meant to him, how much he loved us and that he always looked forward to seeing us. It was also in that conversation that he spoke of "being done" and of going into hospice, how miserable he was because he could no longer write, would fall while walking and was having trouble swallowing. When leaving, Bill followed us out and spoke to us on the sidewalk for a few minutes. The pain and sadness were apparent in his eyes.[29]

On Sunday, February 16, 2020, as Stewart and Bill were preparing to walk across the street to attend church, Stewart told Bill, "I'm done" and then expressed his desire to forego his oxygen tank, medications, and food. Stewart was tired and ready to die. Bill suggested he take a nap and they could talk about it later. As Stewart lay in his bed, Bill began to process the import of Stewart's desire to die. He summoned to the Faerie Playhouse family members Ron Joullian and Charlotte Aitken. Later in the afternoon, Hagler called Father Bill Terry to apprise him of the situation. Bill, Ron, and Charlotte respected Stewart's wishes and urged him to get some rest and contact hospice in the morning. Stewart agreed and then went back to bed. Ron left. Charlotte remained with Bill at the Faerie Playhouse.

Charlotte and Bill then discovered that Stewart had harmed himself in an attempt to commit suicide. Joullian returned along with his spouse, Tim, to the Faerie Playhouse immediately. Stewart was rushed to the hospital, where doctors successfully treated him. Joullian, as the executor of Stewart's estate and having medical power of attorney, submitted Stewart's do-not-resuscitate form to the physicians in the event it might be required. They also notified the hospital that Stewart had a living will. Joullian recalls, "The attending physicians acknowledged it and said once Stewart was released from the trauma center, he would be referred for psychiatric evaluation. We asked would this jeopardize Stewart's request for at-home hospice care and it was his opinion that it would not." Later in the day, Father Terry visited Stewart and provided spiritual counseling. Complicating the matter was a urinary tract infection, which in patients of advanced age can cause hallucinations.

A few days later, Stewart was transferred to a mental health facility in Kentwood, Louisiana, for psychiatric evaluation. Suicide is illegal in Louisiana, and legally, Stewart had to be declared "of sound mind" in order to make the decision to stop eating and taking his medication. After a week of observation and evaluation, he was discharged and returned home on Ash Wednesday, February 26, confused and exhausted. That evening, Bill, Ron Joullian, Tim Angle, Charlotte Aitken, and Evan Kirk gathered to discuss the immediate plans for Stewart's care regarding his primary care physician, hospice, Medicare, and so forth.

On Wednesday, March 4, family members were summoned to the Faerie Playhouse to say their goodbyes at an evening potluck farewell dinner. Lying in bed and drifting in and out of various stages of consciousness, Stewart received a steady flow of visitors. Joullian recalls:

Wednesday's forecast for the evening was not promising. It was an unpleasant blustery, rainy, somewhat chilly night for any sort of gathering. Friends coming across the Huey P. Long Bridge reported winds with almost horizontal sheets of rain. It was scheduled to be essentially a gathering of the "extended family" to visit and to offer Stewart their goodbyes. Despite the elements, the gathering numbered twenty-five, with Frank Perez, his biographer and Father Bill Terry, his priest in attendance. Pair~A~Dice Tumblers' band leader John Birdsong along with bandmember Iray Nabatoff as well as attorney Jack Sullivan dropped by prior to the potluck.

Although a "light" potluck was requested, there was a large quantity of food, desserts, along with bottles of champagne with the arrival of the "extended family." Bill had recently secured quite inexpensively, a sizable number of votive candles some of which provided light for the dining room. Many congregated in the kitchen as usual while some ate in the dining room and others drifted out back. There was a quietness amidst it all as many learned of the recent events in the life of the old man, Captain Butler, a couple of the nicknames for our patriarch. Individuals availed themselves of the opportunity to visit Stewart in his room. There were silent times together while others offered comments.[30]

Sometime in the early morning hours of March 5, Stewart Butler died in his sleep.

GETTING OUR HISTORY OUT OF THE CLOSET

I have come to the conclusion . . . that one has arrived in life when one
becomes fully comfortable with the notion that in the final analysis one's
life is but a footprint upon the sands of time.

—STEWART BUTLER

IN 2012, STEWART BUTLER, OTIS FENNELL, AND MARK GONZALES FOUNDED
the Legacy Project with the goal of compiling oral histories to document
local LGBT+ history. Completing one interview, with Stewart as the inter-
viewee, the group realized that the time, logistics, and money involved in
conducting oral histories were overwhelming, and the Legacy Project slowly
dissipated. The need and desire to preserve local gay history was still strong,
however, and from the ashes of the Legacy Project, the LGBT+ Archives
Project of Louisiana rose.

In June 2013, at Stewart's urging, a handful of dedicated and interested
people began meeting once a month at the Faerie Playhouse to discuss the
necessity of preserving local LGBT+ history and how this endeavor might
be undertaken. Attendance at these monthly meetings varied, but the core
group included Stewart, Mark Gonzalez, Clay Lattimer, Lee Miller, Wayne
Phillips, Bill Hagler, Emily and Sebastian Rey, and Larry Bagneris.[1] It was
a diverse group consisting of people from all sexual orientations, ages, and
cultural and educational backgrounds. A few professional archivists and
one museum curator notwithstanding, the group had no formal training in
historiography or library sciences.[2]

Consisting mostly of laypeople, the steering committee decided early on
not to reinvent the wheel; in other words, the group would not start its own
museum or archival repository. Rather, the organization would be an inter-
mediary resource between potential donors, existing institutions, and future

researchers. To that end, one of the organization's first steps was to survey local libraries and collections to determine what LGBT+-related holdings already existed. Questionnaires were sent to archivists at several local institutes, and several on-site visits were made to local repositories. In October of that same year, the Society of American Archivists held its national conference in New Orleans, and a few members of the group's LGBT+ roundtable met with members of the steering committee to offer insight and guidance.

Holding a community meeting in November, the steering committee set out to gather input from the public. After numerous months of information gathering, the LGBT+ Archives Project of Louisiana was officially born in June 2014 at a public meeting at the Marigny Opera House, where bylaws were adopted and officers elected. Since that time, the LGBT+ Archives Project has flourished. In addition to establishing a yearly calendar of events ranging from workshops and panel discussions to social events and gala fundraisers, the project has also established a modest grant program, an internship program with Tulane and Loyola Universities, and an active oral history program. The project has facilitated the donation of major collections to the Louisiana Research Collection at Tulane, the Amistad Research Center, the Newcomb College Institute Archives, the Historic New Orleans Collection, the Louisiana State Museum, the Center for Louisiana Studies, the Special Collections Division at Louisiana State University, the T. Harry Williams Center for Oral History at LSU, and others. These donations include the personal papers and organizational records of the following: Stewart Butler, Alan Robinson, Valda Lewis, Larry Best, Bob Stuart, Frank Perez, Rich Magill, Greg Manogue, Harold Short, BreakOUT!, Southern Decadence, and PFLAG New Orleans. In addition, a wide variety of ephemera and rare copies of long-gone LGBT+ newspapers, magazines, newsletters, and other publications have found permanent homes as a result of the LGBT+ Archives Project of Louisiana.

The LGBT+ Archives Project of Louisiana was Stewart's last great undertaking. From its inception in 2013 to 2019, when Stewart's health took a turn for the worse, the Archives Project board of directors met monthly at the Faerie Playhouse, sitting around Alfred's grandmother's table, the same table that over the decades had been the gathering place of so much queer activism in New Orleans. Stewart was active in the Archives Project until the very end of his life, when he became essentially homebound. Even then, he would still call board members and committee chairs with notepad in hand, checking on various ongoing projects and offering suggestions.

When asked about Stewart's legacy, the people who knew him and worked with him "in the trenches" inevitably say kind things about him. Phrases like "a role model," "a very special person," "incredibly powerful," "charming," "that man could get away with anything," "sage," and "I wanted to sit at his knee and learn" are common. Those that knew him intimately echo these sentiments but also point out his less admirable traits: "stubborn as a mule," "quietly controlling," "cruel streak," and "he could be obsessive."

Recalling the first time he met Stewart at a PFLAG meeting in 2009, Kenny Tucker remembers Stewart as being the oldest person in the room and describes him as having "very long hair, and wearing a colorful, political T-shirt. He was wearing socks with sandals and his glasses were on the tip of his nose. He was 100 percent sincere in his convictions. And when he spoke, he had a slow delivery that commanded attention. He had a special way of making the listener both weary and grateful."

Barbara Dobrosky on Stewart and Alfred: "They tempered each other. Their personalities suited each other."

Roberts Batson on Stewart: "He brought incredible energy to LAGPAC and had such a determination to do the unglamorous work."

Jean Henry Jr. on Stewart: "Alfred would have spent his life in an institution if it weren't for Stewart."

Sincerity and commitment are the two common themes that arise whenever anyone discusses Stewart. To these two admirable characteristics, I would add a third—foresight. Perspective is a gift that comes with time and experience, and Stewart readily accepted that gift. He always had "the big picture" in view.

Stewart Butler once wrote, "I have come to the conclusion . . . that one has arrived in life when one becomes fully comfortable with the notion that in the final analysis one's life is but a footprint upon the sands of time." His was a big footprint.

ACKNOWLEDGMENTS

This book could not have been written without the help and cooperation of Bill Hagler and Ron Joullian. To them I owe a considerable debt of gratitude.

I am also grateful to Stewart's and Alfred's siblings and extended families—Suzanne and Dave Eaton, Alicia Eaton Lewis, Jean Henry, and Jean Henry Jr. The family research, genealogical and otherwise, they shared with me was crucial in reconstructing the early parts of Stewart's and Alfred's lives.

Although recording history is a solitary endeavor, it cannot be done without drawing on the work of others. To that end, I wish to thank those who have previously written books on the subject of New Orleans LGBT+ history: Johnny Townsend, Clay Delery, Howard Smith, and Robert Fieseler. Not only did I rely on their research and published works in compiling this biography, my friendship with each of them has grown and strengthened over the course of the project.

Much of the primary research for the book was conducted at various archival repositories throughout New Orleans, including the Historic New Orleans Collection, Amistad Research Center, and the Special Collections Division of the Howard-Tilton Memorial Library at Tulane University. I owe a special debt of gratitude to Lee Miller and the staff of the Louisiana Research Collection at Tulane, where Stewart's papers reside.

Another valuable source of information was personal interviews. I appreciate all the people who agreed to be interviewed for the book. Those names are listed in the bibliographic essay.

I also wish to thank Charlton Buckley, Anne-christine d'Adesky, Roberts Batson, Courtney Sharp, and Chris Trentacoste.

THE MEMORIAL GARDEN

Cremains located in the memorial garden at the Faerie Playhouse and date added.

PEOPLE

Pierre "Peter" Rene DeLancey, April 18, 1998
John Horn Foster, November 8, 1999
Jack "Ruby" Gentry, May 2000
Gregory Robert Manella, October 14, 2001
John Burton "Burt" Harter, November 2, 2002
"Dugie" E. Rohrbacker, May 15, 2004
Paul "Pogo" Joseph Orfilla, October 24, 2004
Chester Wisniewski, May 28, 2006
Carlos Clifton "Cliff" Howard Jr. (dirt from grave), 2006
John J. Ognibene Jr., October 8, 2006
Charlene Ann Schneider, March 25, 2007
Alfred McLaughlin Doolittle (lock of hair), March 8, 2008
"Pete" Dickinson, August 2008
Blanchard "Skip" Ward, September 26, 2009
Cynthia Louise Joullian, October 1, 2011
Elwood John Richardson (dirt from grave), November 9, 2014
Harvey D. "Buck" Shofner (dirt from grave), November 9, 2014
Richard M. Magill, July 10, 2016
Terry Carter, August 30, 2017
Stewart Butler, August 21, 2020

PETS

Adoni, Cocker Spaniel, April 18, 1998
Tara, Mixed Shephard, October 1, 2011
Putzy, English Springer Spaniel, October 1, 2011
Holly, Labrador Retriever, April 21, 2019

BUTLER AND DOOLITTLE
FAMILY HISTORIES

In addition to the unique environment in which he came of age, Stewart's life of adventure and consequence was also, as they say, "in the genes." Indeed, his family history was one of wanderlust. Stewart Butler's family tree extends from Scotland to Alaska to Burma. Stewart's earliest known ancestor is a man known to history as Hervius, Count de Brion of Normandy, who accompanied his kinsman, William the Conqueror, to England in 1066. After fighting valiantly in the Battle of Hastings, Hervius was given large tracts of land in Norfolk, Suffolk, and Lancaster Counties. Hervius gave birth to a son, Hervius Walter, who in turn had sons—Theobald, Hubert, Walter, Roger, and Hamon. Theobald, the firstborn, was made chief butler of Ireland around 1172 by King Henry II in reward for his military service. His primary duty was to attend the coronation of the kings of England and to present the newly crowned kings with their first cup of wine. It was from this hereditary office that the Butler family took its name. Service is at the heart of the Butler name.

Stewart's paternal great-grandfather was born in Inverness, Scotland, in the mid-1800s and by 1870 had immigrated to America, where he settled in a small unincorporated community in southern Mississippi called Smithdale. In 1916, Stewart's paternal grandmother, Wilena, died giving birth to his uncle, John Butler. The boy was sent to live with Stewart's great-grandmother who lived nearby. Years earlier, Stewart's grandparents had taken in a girl of mixed-race ancestry, Minnie Cloy. Minnie served as a housekeeper in the Butler home when Stewart was a child. Minnie was sent to help raise baby John. Minnie remained a part of the family for the rest of her life. Stewart's parents served in her wedding, a highly unusual thing to do in very segregated times. Baby John's father, Decatur Poindexter Butler, was a medical doctor whose ancestors had emigrated from Ireland. After settling in northern West Virginia near present-day Charlottesville, they eventually traveled along part of the fabled Trail of Tears as they made their way to south central Mississippi.

On his mother's side, Butler's great-grandparents hailed from the Alaska Territory and by the early 1870s had moved to Edgarton, Wisconsin, where his maternal grandfather, Oscar Crandall Perry, was born. In 1902, Oscar married a woman who was born in Rangoon, Burma, Matie Bertha Sloan.

The Sloan branch of the family tree is fascinating and embodies many of the traits that would mark Stewart Butler's life—a penchant for wanderlust and a strong sense of social justice, tempered by a rebellious streak and a love of storytelling. Matie's grandmother Eliza Sinclair (Stewart's great-great-grandmother) recounted her life story to her daughter, Marian Sloan Russell, who included the tale in her memoirs, a book called *The Land of Enchantment*.

Eliza tells us her father and uncles had been among the first to settle the Western Reserve, an area of roughly 3.5 million acres in what is now north-eastern Ohio. By the time her two children, William and Marian, were old enough to understand, Eliza told them their father, William Sloan, had died in the Battle of Monterey (July 7, 1846) during the Mexican-American War. But this was a lie. William Sloan, who worked as a surgeon in the army, actually died decades later. Sometime around 1849, Eliza remarried an Irishman named Jeremiah Mahoney.

For reasons that are not clear, Eliza wanted to make sure her first husband had nothing to do with their children. She felt so strongly about this that she packed up her life and took her kids, aged seven and nine, west in 1852, traversing the rough-and-tumble Santa Fe Trail before settling in Albuquerque in 1854 and then Santa Fe in 1856. She had waited two years for her father-in-law, who had promised to come and collect her and the kids and bring them to California. When she decided they had waited long enough, she lied again and told William and Marian that he had been murdered by Native Americans on a scouting expedition. Records indicate he died in Minnesota in 1899.

In New Mexico, Eliza carved out a new life by running a boardinghouse on what is now the site of the New Mexico Museum of Art in Santa Fe. As fate would have it, she left abruptly in 1856 when her ex-husband was stationed in Santa Fe. She fled with the children to Missouri, where she stayed until 1860 when she learned Dr. Sloan had left Santa Fe. There she returned for a year before relocating to Fort Leavenworth, Kansas, in 1861. Why she returned to the Midwest is uncertain, but the Civil War may have been a motivating factor. Shortly after the war broke out, the Confederacy attempted to extend their territory to the Pacific Ocean. Controlling New Mexico was a strategic priority since it would have facilitated access to Pacific shipping routes as well as mining resources in Colorado and California. New Mexico witnessed two major battles and several skirmishes in which over three hundred Union and Confederate soldiers were killed.

When the war erupted, Eliza's son William joined the Union army. By 1864, Eliza and Marion had once again returned to New Mexico, where they settled in Fort Union. There Eliza took a job as a cook at a boardinghouse for Union soldiers. In 1865, Marian married Lieutenant Richard Russell. By the early 1890s, Eliza was living in Los Angeles. There is also some evidence she lived in Trinidad, Colorado.

Before enlisting as a private in the Seventeenth Kansas Volunteer Infantry, William Sloan worked as a journalist for the *Kansas City Journal*. In the army, his occupation was printer. This experience would serve him well after the war. Devoutly religious, William felt called to the ministry and in 1873 was graduated from the Rochester Theological Seminary in New York. While studying to become a minister, he married Ida Augusta Preston and would eventually have eight children with her. He served as pastor at several Baptist churches throughout the eastern United States and worked as a missionary in Burma (now Myanmar) in Southeast Asia from 1875 to 1877. It was here that Stewart Butler's maternal grandmother, Matie Bertha Sloan, was born. Bertha, as she was called, eventually married Oscar Crandall Perry, who was from Edgerton, Wisconsin. While in Burma, William also served as superintendent of the American Baptist Mission Press. He later did missionary work in Mexico from 1884 to 1888 and from 1893 to 1907. It was in Mexico City that Stewart Butler's mother, Bertha June Perry, was born in 1905. Matie died four days after giving birth. When she was four, Bertha's grandmother moved her to Wisconsin to begin her schooling. The family would later relocate to Maine. It was also in Mexico where William Sloan converted to Roman Catholicism. By 1911, he was living in Las Cruces, New Mexico, where he published a religious magazine, *La Bandera Catolica*. After Bertha's father died when she was eight years old, she went to live with her Yankee grandparents who were living in Citronelle, Alabama (just north of Mobile), after a bankruptcy resulting from a theft of liquid assets by a then-partner in their joint mercantile business forced them to abandon their lives in Edgerton, Wisconsin.

In a letter written to his daughter, William Sloan described a family history he had either compiled or acquired. The Sinclairs (sometimes spelled St. Clair), the history claims, trace their family back a thousand years to the year 890 in northern France. According to the family history, the Sinclairs immigrated to New Hampshire in 1648.

♥ ♥ ♥

Like Stewart's, Alfred's family tree is peppered with colorful characters. Alfred's family, on both sides, can be traced back to fifteenth-century England. Samuel Smith and his wife, Elizabeth, both from Ipswich in Suffolk County, sailed from England in 1634 and arrived in Boston later that year. The couple founded Wethersfield, Connecticut, in 1636 and later Hadley, Massachusetts, in 1659. Samuel and Elizabeth's great-granddaughter, Sarah Morton, married Colonel Ephraim Doolittle, a veteran of both the French and Indian and American Revolutionary Wars. In 1761, Colonel Doolittle and Sarah founded Shoreham, Vermont. The farm they established in Shoreham is one of the oldest in Vermont and is listed on the National Register of Historic Places. Ephraim and his wife, Sarah, had three children—Sarah, Joel, and John.

Alfred's maternal great-great-great-grandfather was David Olcott Shattuck, a native of New London, Connecticut, born on March 21, 1800. After growing up in New England, Shattuck made his way down the Eastern Seaboard before settling in South Carolina at the age of twenty. He then moved to Duplin County, North Carolina, in 1821. For two years he taught and studied for the ministry before he was ordained by the Methodist Episcopal Church. After the death of his first wife, Lydia Watrus, he married Elizabeth Ann Saunders in 1827, with whom he had ten children. In 1829, he moved to Haywood County, Tennessee, where he studied law. By 1833, he was in Carroll County, Mississippi, in the north central area of the state, where he served as a district judge. There he became very involved with politics and ran for governor in the 1841 election as a Whig, but narrowly lost to Democrat Tilghman M. Tucker. Leaving the political arena, Shattuck entered academia in 1843, serving first as a law professor before becoming president of Centenary College, which was then located in Brandon, Mississippi. In 1849, Shattuck and his wife left Mississippi and set sail for San Francisco by way of Panama. He arrived in California in April 1850 and by the fall of that year won election to the superior court. He ran unsuccessfully for Congress in 1861, and after his defeat, he retreated with his wife to Mexico for the duration of the Civil War. Upon returning to California after the war, he settled in Sonoma County in 1867. He died in 1892.

Alfred's great-grandparents, Henry Moffat and Adriana Swett, arrived in California in 1857 and established a wholesale meatpacking business. The business was very successful and enabled Alfred's maternal grandmother, Emma Moffett, to grow up as a socialite in San Francisco. Emma's parents instilled in her a strong sense of social consciousness and commitment to community, values shared by her husband, Dr. Alfred McLaughlin, a physician who catered to the needs of low-income immigrant families. After his death in 1908, she carried on his legacy by serving on the Certified Milk and Baby Hygiene Committee of the American Association of University Women.

Her work with the committee was the first of a long line of philanthropic projects. From 1917 to 1919 she chaired the San Francisco Children's Year Committee—an effort that focused on the health of infants. She became very involved with the Institute of Pacific Relations at its founding in 1927, which, twenty years later under her leadership became the World Affairs Council of Northern California. The council grew out of the 1947 conference in San Francisco that gave birth to the United Nations. She was also involved in the League of Women Voters, serving as its president from 1920 to 1921. She was also involved with several other community and civic organizations, including the San Francisco Foundation, Baby Hygiene Committee, Women's Central Committee, and Women's Board of the Golden Gate International Exhibition. For her lifetime of community service, she was awarded honorary degrees from both the University of California, Berkeley, and Mills College.

In addition to her public works, Emma loved to entertain. The dinner parties and cocktail soirees she hosted were not-to-be-missed affairs. An Episcopal priest who was a friend of the family once remarked to Stewart, "If you get an invitation to one of Granny's dinners, you accept immediately and then check your calendar to see what you have to cancel." The dinner table at the Faerie Playhouse, around which so much LGBT+ activism was planned, was once hers.

While Alfred's mother's family made its fortune in the meatpacking business (as a young man, Alfred worked briefly in the family-owned slaughterhouse), his father, Jefferson J. Doolittle struck it rich in gold. According to the *California Historical Courier*, Jefferson, along with John Hayes Hammond and E. A. Wiltsee, formed the La Grange Gold Dredging Company in 1907 near the Tuolumne River in eastern Stanislaus County. The company was successful and became exponentially profitable in 1938 when the company developed a much larger dredging machine with a loan from the Reconstruction Finance Corporation. It had the longest digging career of any dredge in California. La Grange was reorganized in 1951 and remained a family business for the duration of Alfred's life.

When Jefferson James Doolittle married Jean McLaughlin, two prominent and financially secure families joined forces. James and Jean had three children: Jefferson Doolittle Jr., Alfred Doolittle, and Jean Doolittle. Jeff Jr. would eventually move to Larkspur, California, and have two children—Susan and Carolyn. Jean would become Jean Doolittle Henry, eventually settle in Lebanon, Pennsylvania, and bear four children—Rebecca, Amy, Jean, and Charles.

NOTES

CHAPTER 1: WANDERLUST

1. *Faerie Playhouse Newsletter*, 2014.

2. Butler, *Star*.

3. Sontag, *Illness as Metaphor*.

4. Christiansen, "Story of Leprosy and the National Hansen's Disease Museum."

5. Gaudet, *Carville*.

6. Bertha's parents died when she was four years old, and she was raised by her grandparents.

7. This hospital later became the Public Health Service Hospital and today is Children's Hospital.

8. In addition to saving the letters his friends and family wrote him, Stewart also kept newspaper and magazine articles about his family.

9. Growing up, Stewart was always referred to as Perry. Sometime around 1954, the year he moved to Alaska, he began going by Stewart.

10. Letter from Stewart to his parents, November 22, 1952.

11. Email to the author from Dave Eaton dated July 11, 2019.

12. In a letter written to the author dated November 6, 2019, Suzanne writes, "Thoughts of her [Minnie] role in our lives surely has played a part in my interest to serve on the Committee of Uprooting Racism, sponsored by the Vermont Conference of the United Church of Christ."

13. Letter from Barbara Cooper Duhe to Stewart Butler, August 4, 2003.

14. Email to the author from Dave Eaton dated July 7, 2019.

15. Dave Eaton speculates that the motivation for sending Stewart to GCMA was "to place him under the watchful eye of his uncle Powell, who at the time was on the faculty there. Keeping him under a watchful eye might be equated with keeping him from doing something foolish. Both were probably considered worthy steps at that time." Email to the author from Dave Eaton dated July 11, 2019.

16. Letter from Suzanne Eaton to Stewart, August 17, 2000.

17. *Faerie Playhouse Newsletter*.

18. Interview with the author, date unknown.

19. Letter from Stewart to his parents, June 1948.

20. Letter from Stewart to Wilds Bacot, June 23, 1950.

21. OUTWORDS is a national project that records LGBT+ oral histories.

22. Stewart's transcripts from LSU.

23. Letter from Stewart's parents to him, April 23, 1951.

24. Letter from Stewart to his parents, December 1952.

25. Letter from Stewart to Wilds Bacot, November 24, 1953.

26. Letter from Stewart to Bill Finn, January 11, 1954.

27. Letter from Stewart to his parents, March 30, 1953.

28. Letter from Stewart to his parents, March 30, 1953.

29. Letter from Stewart to his parents, March 30, 1953.

30. Letter from Stewart to Wilds Bacot, September 7, 1952.

31. Letter from Wilds Bacot to Stewart, September 13, 1952.

32. Letter from Wilds Bacot to Stewart, September 13, 1952.

33. Letter from Wilds Bacot to Stewart, September 13, 1952.

CHAPTER 2: TERRITORIAL POLITICS

1. Email to the author from Dave Eaton dated March 20, 2020.

2. Email to the author from Dave Eaton dated March 20, 2020.

3. Email to the author from Dave Eaton dated March 20, 2020.

4. Interview with the author, date unknown.

5. From Stewart's handwritten draft notes, date unknown.

6. This itinerary was reconstructed from a scrapbook of photographs and road maps Stewart compiled during the journey.

7. Letter from Stewart to Bob Pattison dated November 19, 1994. Pattison died a few weeks later on December 4.

8. Letter from Stewart to his parents, August 1954.

9. Letter from Stewart to his parents, September 1954.

10. Letter from Stewart to his parents, September 1954.

11. Letter from Stewart to his parents, September 1954.

12. Letter from Stewart to his parents, September 1954.

13. According to Stewart's brother-in-law, Dave Eaton, Pattison returned to the East Coast, where he worked briefly for Agway, an agricultural concern that sold feed for livestock and poultry, before settling in West Redding, Connecticut, where he developed a successful carpentry business.

14. Much of this history was gleaned from Terrence Cole's *The Cornerstone on College Hill: An Illustrated History of the University of Alaska.*

15. Interview with the author, March 20, 2014.

16. Cole, *Cornerstone on College Hill.*

17. Letter from Stewart to Henrick Wessel, 1992.

18. Letter from William Cashen to Stewart's father, date unknown.

19. Letter from Stewart to his parents, October 28, 1956.

20. Interview with the author, March 20, 2014.

21. Interview with the author, March 20, 2014.

22. Stewart's thoughts on the movies and other information in this paragraph were gleaned from letters Stewart wrote to his parents during this time.

23. Coen, "Not Old Enough to Vote but Able to Support Statehood."

24. Letter from Stewart to his parents, date unknown.

25. Letter from Stewart to his parents, date unknown.

26. This plank in Stewart's platform was somewhat ironic considering he had been an "out of town" summer worker during his years at LSU.

27. Letter from Stewart to his parents, date unknown.

28. Letter from Stewart to his parents, date unknown.

29. *Faerie Playhouse Newsletter.*

30. Ernest Gruening had served as territorial governor of Alaska from 1939 to 1953 and as US Senator from Alaska from 1959 to 1969. Mike Stepovich served as the last territorial governor of Alaska from 1957–1958.

31. The nine candidates included: Eugene Miller, a conservative past president of the Democratic Club, a local attorney, and new on the divisional committee; Ed Orbeck, the Secretary Treasurer of the divisional committee, former city councilman, and president of the Labor Union; Johnny Coonjohn, a division committee member; Ed Merdes, a young conservative attorney; Paul Palmer, a division committee member and bush pilot; and Stewart Butler.

32. Sophie and Stewart kept in touch well into Stewart's life in New Orleans with Alfred.

33. Letter from Stewart to his parents, 1960.

34. Letter from Sophie Butler to Stewart's parents, 1960.

35. Letter from Suzanne Eaton to her parents, 1960. Suzanne and Dave Eaton would eventually have four children: Alicia, Kent, Tim, and Jenn.

36. Sophie Gutierrez in an email to the author, April 26, 2020.

CHAPTER 3: PRYTANIA STREET

1. Boyd, *Wide-Open Town.*

2. Welch, "Homosexuality in America."

3. Interview with the author, March 20, 2014.

4. Letter from Gregory Manella to Stewart, March 1969.

5. Letter from Stewart to Minnie Cooper, December 25, 1989.

6. Letter from Stewart's mother to Stewart, April 1973.

7. Letter from Stewart to his parents, May 9, 1973.

8. Letter from Pat to Stewart, May 1971.

9. Letter from Annie Garza to Stewart, August 31, 1967.

10. The home at 2115 Prytania Street was destroyed by fire in 2011.

11. Notes in Stewart's collection of papers, date unknown.

12. Letter from Greg Manella to Stewart, December 3, 1968.

CHAPTER 4: ENTER ALFRED

1. Fieseler, *Tinderbox*, 51.

2. Fieseler, *Tinderbox*, 5.

3. Fieseler, *Tinderbox*, 55.

4. Stewart's letter to Ann Landers was never published. A copy remains in his collection of personal papers.

5. Email from Jean Henry to Stewart Butler, July 15, 2008.

6. Burton, "Brief History of Schizophrenia."

7. Letter from Morse to Stewart Butler, 2008.

8. Notes in Stewart's collection of papers, date unknown.

9. Letter from Stewart to Freddie Lavre, December 8, 1997.

10. Letter from Jean McLaughlin to Stewart Butler, May 1974.

11. Interview with Steve Willey, April 4, 2020.

12. *Faerie Playhouse Newsletter*, February 2018.

13. Delery-Edwards, *Up Stairs Lounge Arson*, 21.

14. Johnny Townsend, "The Banality of Good," an email to the author, March 20, 2020.

15. Fieseler, *Tinderbox*, 103.

16. Fieseler, *Tinderbox*, 114.

17. Fieseler, *Tinderbox*, 115.

18. Delery-Edwards, *Up Stairs Lounge Arson*, 138.

19. Lind, "Fire Bares the Grisly Face of Death."

20. Fieseler, *Tinderbox*, xxxvi.

21. Interview with the author, date unknown.

22. Letter from June Butler to Stewart Butler, October 1974.

23. Letter from June Butler to Stewart Butler, October 1974.

24. Interview with Barbara Dobrosky, April 9, 2020.

25. Quote is from an interview between Stewart and Clayton Delery. Delery provided me a transcript of the interview in an email dated March 31, 2020.

26. The Jean M. Doolittle Irrevocable Living Trust for the Benefit of Alfred M. Doolittle, the Jefferson Doolittle Trust, the Emma Moffett McLaughlin Trust, and the Alfred McLaughlin Doolittle Trust.

27. Letter from Alfred, October 5, 1989.

28. Email from Jack Sullivan to the author, May 13, 2020.

CHAPTER 5: SETTING THE STAGE

1. Bossu, *Travels in the Interior of North America, 1751–1762.*

2. Minutes of the Superior Council, December 18, 1724. The incident is also discussed in Richebourg Gaillard McWilliam's *Dramatic History of Dauphin Island* (Chamber of Commerce and Dauphin Island Land Sales Corporation, 1954).

3. Baron Ludwig von Reizenstein was an immigrant who fled a number of legal scandals in his native Germany. He arrived in New Orleans around 1850 and began editing and writing

for a number of German-language newspapers. *The Mysteries of New Orleans* was serialized from 1854 to 1855 in *Louisiana Staatz-Zeitung.* The entire work was translated and edited into a single volume by Steven Rowan in 2003.

4. Perez and Palmquist, *In Exile.*

5. Conversation with the author, March 2012.

6. The information in this paragraph is sourced from Roberts Batson's "Claiming Our Past series, which appeared in *Impact* in 1994 to commemorate the twenty-fifth anniversary of Stonewall.

7. Campanella, *Bourbon Street*, 107.

8. "Curb Advocated on Homosexuals."

9. "Dayries Cites No. 1 Vice Problem." *New Orleans Times-Picayune*, June 30, 1955.

10. "Curb Advocated on Homosexuals."

11. Perez and Palmquist, *In Exile*, 48.

12. *Roy Maggio et al. v. City of New Orleans.*

13. For a more in-depth study of the Rios murder, see Clayton Delery's book *Out for Queer Blood.*

14. Sidney Barrios, Carter Church, Scott Hoy, Vincent Indovina, Roeling Mace, and Vic Scalise.

15. Jerry Loner, Scott Morvant, Wendell Stipelcovich, and Don Stratton.

16. Founders include Jerry Radke, Roy Bell, Bob Keesee, Joe D'Antoni, Tom Greenwood, Wallace Sherwood, George Simons, Jim Williams, and Shawn S.

17. Evans Alexander, Thomas J. Franklin III, and Byron Hogans.

18. The definitive book on the history of gay Carnival in New Orleans is Howard P. Smith's *Unveiling the Muse.*

19. For a more in-depth study of gay Carnival, see Smith, *Unveiling the Muse.*

20. Marshall Harris and Carl Mack.

21. Allured, *Remapping Second-Wave Feminism*, 206.

22. Allured, *Remapping Second-Wave Feminism*, 201.

23. "Gay Liberation Group Marches."

24. Vaid, *Virtual Equality*, 44.

25. Liz Simon, Donna Myhre, Mary Capps, Sandy Carp, Sue Laporte, Lynette Jerry, Barbara Trahan, and Judith Cormier.

26. Clay Latimer, Gayle Gagliano, Kim Gandy, Barbara Bullock, Anita Ganachaux, and Janet Riley. For a more in-depth study of the women's movement in Louisiana, see Janet Allured's *Remapping Second-Wave Feminism.*

27. Quote is taken from Sears, *Rebels, Rubyfruit, and Rhinestones*, 273.

28. For a more in-depth study of the Up Stairs Lounge fire, see Johnny Townsend's *Let the Faggots Burn*, Clayton Delery's *The Up Stairs Lounge Arson*, and Robert Fieseler's *Tinderbox.* In addition to these books, see also the following documentary films: Royd Anderson's *The Up Stairs Lounge Fire*, Robert Camina's *Upstairs Inferno*, and ABC News's *Prejudice and Pride.*

29. This core group included Michael Evers, his boyfriend David Randolph, Frederick Wright, Maureen and Charlie Block, Robert Laurent, Tom Tippin, Robert King, Robert Gore, Preston Hemmings, Bruce Harris, Kathleen Kavanaugh, David Red, Ed Seale, Judy Shapiro, and Jerome Williams.

30. For a more in-depth study of Southern Decadence, see Howard Smith and Frank Perez, *Southern Decadence in New Orleans*.

31. Welch, Testimonial on the LGBT+ Archives Project of Louisiana website.

32. Sears, *Rebels, Rubyfruit, and Rhinestones*.

33. Perez, "FAB."

34. Perez, "FAB."

35. Perez, "FAB."

36. Newlin, "Madame John Dodt's Legacy #24."

37. Interview with Rip Naquin, October 2016.

CHAPTER 6: GETTING ORGANIZED

1. Martinez, Editorial.

2. Thompson, "You Make Me Feel."

3. Batson, *Impact*, April 11, 1997.

4. Batson was elected to Orleans Parish Democratic Executive Committee in 1986. Batson observes: "In 1986, LAGPAC leaders initiated a coalition with four other political groups to issue joint endorsement ballots of candidates for the Orleans Parish Democratic Executive Committee, the county-level party organization. Fourteen candidates from each of the five city council districts were elected; I was one of them. The Parish Committee Members, elected by popular vote on the same ballot as city officials, receive no salary and have little authority, but had parole power. In an era when gay people were still harassed by police, this meant we could get people out of jail without posting bail."

5. Essay by Roberts Batson for Out and Elected in the USA, http://outhistory.org/exhibits/show/out-and-elected/early-1980s/roberts-batson.

6. Sullivan interview with Mark Cave as part of a series of oral histories about J. B. Harter for the Historic New Orleans Collection, MSS 628.9, October 25, 2011.

7. Cibellis, "Black, Gay, and Republican."

8. LAGPAC Newsletter, "Great Strides for Gay People in New Orleans."

9. Interview with Glenn Ducote, June 14, 2019.

10. Interview with Glenn Ducote, June 14, 2019.

11. Letter from Roger Nelson to Kyle Scafide, August 24, 1998. Scafide was the owner and publisher of *Impact* at this time. Nelson sent a similar letter dated August 22, 1998, to Rip Naquin, owner and publisher of *Ambush*.

12. Upon returning to New Orleans after securing his degree, Udick served as chair of the mayor's advisory committee on LGBT+ issues. He also chaired the administrative assessment committee on the New Orleans Regional AIDS Planning Council.

13. LAGPAC Newsletter, June 1990.

14. LAGPAC Newsletter, June 1990.

15. Email from Burford to the author, March 26, 2020.

16. Interview with the author, April 1, 2011.

17. Interview with the author, April 1, 2011.

18. Shannon, "Celebration '86 at Tulane," *Impact*, 1986.

19. Butler interview with Mark Cave as part of a series of oral histories about J. B. Harter for the Historic New Orleans Collection, MSS 628.3, June 2, 2011.

20. Interview with Ron Joullian, May 7, 2020.

21. Interview with Ron Joullian, May 7, 2020.

22. Email from Joullian to the author, August 7, 2020.

23. Letter from Pat Denton to LAGPAC co-chairs Jean Carr and Roberts Batson, February 21, 1981, Stewart Butler Papers, Louisiana Research Collection, Tulane University, Box 1.

24. Instant Message from Simon to the author, March 20, 2020.

25. Letter from Ed Frost to Stewart Butler, August 2, 1982. Stewart Butler Papers, Louisiana Research Collection, Tulane University, Box 1, Folder 17.

26. Letter in the Stewart Butler Collection, Louisiana Research Collection, Tulane University, Box 1, Folder 17.

27. Interview with the author, November 16, 2018.

28. Bert de la Houssaye, Effie Silas, Paul Viator, Darrell Johnson, Judy Cadoret, Elizabeth Pizzati Vicki Grant, and Roy Racca, who also served on the state board.

29. Central Louisiana is parochially referred to as CEN-LA.

30. Letter in the Blanchard "Skip" Ward Papers at the Louisiana Research Collection, Tulane University.

31. Letter in the Blanchard "Skip" Ward Papers at the Louisiana Research Collection, Tulane University.

32. Letter in the Blanchard "Skip" Ward Papers at the Louisiana Research Collection, Tulane University.

33. Letter in the Blanchard "Skip" Ward Papers at the Louisiana Research Collection, Tulane University.

34. Interview with Glenn Ducote, June 14, 2019.

35. Email from Domingue to the author, July 8, 2020.

36. Email from Domingue to the author, July 8, 2020.

37. Letter in the LAGPAC files in Stewart Butler's papers at the Louisiana Research Collection, Tulane University.

38. Interview with Wayne Phillips, November 29, 2016.

39. In 1993, the New Orleans City Council passed an ordinance that recognized domestic partnerships between unmarried but cohabitating gay and lesbian couples. The ordinance was largely symbolic and had few immediate effects as the ordinance did not change the state law banning same-sex marriage. Forum for Equality leader Judy Montz noted at the time the ordinance would extend benefits to domestic partners and hoped that private industry would follow suit.

40. Notes in the Stewart Butler Collection, Louisiana Research Collection, Tulane University.

41. Email from Domingue to the author, July 8, 2020.

CHAPTER 7: WORKING WITH OTHERS

1. Jim Wiggins, Richard Weeks, Lloyd Bowers, and Dr. Brobson Lutz.

2. Interview with Randy Evans, March 26, 2020.

3. Interview with the author, April 3, 2011.

4. Email from Domingue to the author, July 8, 2020.

5. Email from Best to the author, March 24, 2020.

6. Interview with Randy Evans, March 26, 2020.

7. Interview with Courtney Sharp, July 19, 2019.

8. Interview with Courtney Sharp, July 19, 2019.

9. Interview with Dr. Jody Gates, April 8, 2020.

10. In 2001, James Donovan, a member of the Tulane law school faculty and former chair of the New Orleans mayor's advisory committee on LGBT+ issues had argued against Frank and Pelosi's approach in an article called "Baby Steps or One Fell Swoop? The Incremental Extension of Rights is Not a Defensible Strategy," which was published in the *California Western Law Review* (Fall 2001).

11. Feinberg, "Grassroots Revolt Against Trans Exclusion from Federal Jobs Bill."

12. Letter dated May 17, 1997, in the author's personal papers, courtesy of Courtney Sharp.

13. Letter dated January 15, 1999, in the author's personal papers, courtesy of Courtney Sharp.

14. Interview with Louis Volz, January 28, 2020.

15. *Faerie Playhouse Newsletter*, January 2013.

16. Quote taken from Clayton Delery's notes of his interview with Stewart Butler on July 2, 2009, for his book *The Up Stairs Lounge Arson*, shared with the author in an email dated March 31, 2020.

17. Other members of the committee included Clay Latimer, JoAnne Hingle, Jeanne Leblanc, Mindy Milam, Jeann Boothe, Michael Thompson, and Robin Kemp. Committee coordinators included Rembert Donelson, Terry Mayer, Lee Goldsby, Mary Stuart, George Young, and David Moynan. Jeremy Clulow, Brenda Laura, and Charlene Schneider volunteered to make flags and banners for the march. Sponsoring and contributing money were Celebration, GayFest, LAGPAC, NO/AIDS Task Force, the Knights d' Orleans, the Lords of Leather, the Krewe of Polyphemus, the Langston/Jones Society, Lambda He, Pontchartrain NOW, PFLAG New Orleans, Glen Munroe, Eve's Market, Kathy Nance, the Other Side, Vera Cruz, Cheshire Cat Tearoom, Mama Rosa's Slice of Italy, Jeanne Booth, Scotty's Toulouse Grocery, Quarter Scene Restaurant, Fins and Feathers, the Elizabeth-Alexander Gallery, Paw Paw's, and American Plant Interiors.

18. Interview with the author, August 6, 2019.

19. Interview with the author, August 6, 2019.

20. *Ambush*, October 1987.

21. *Ambush*, October 1987.

22. Interview with the author, April 1, 2011.

23. LAGPAC records in the Stewart Butler Collection, Louisiana Research Collection, Tulane University.

24. Interview with the author, April 8, 2020.

25. Perez and Palmquist, *In Exile*.

26. Bond, "Charity and the Treatment of AIDS Patients."

27. Email from Kaiser to the author, April 4, 2020.

28. Interview with Dr. Catherine Roland, April 4, 2020.

29. An excellent bibliography of local newspaper coverage of the AIDS crisis in New Orleans was compiled by Philip Ross when he interned with the LGBT+ Archives Project of Louisiana and is available at https://www.lgbtarchiveslouisiana.org.

30. Smith and Perez, *Southern Decadence in New Orleans*.

31. *Flaming Crescent Design*, May 22, 1992.

32. Letter dated May 15, 1989 in the Stewart Butler Collection, Louisiana Research Collection, Tulane University.

33. Email from Rich Sacher to the author, April 1, 2020.

34. Email from Rich Sacher to the author, April 1, 2020.

35. Some of these people included Rue Morrison, Thomas Norman, Robert Kremitzki, Louise McFarland, Harlee Kutezen, Leonard Doty, Richard Devlin, Craig Henry, Henry Schmidt, Carole Pindaro, Jim Kellogg, Dr. Brobson Lutz, Jonathan Clemmer, and Father Bob Pawell.

36. Pope, "Ex-Director of AIDS Agency Jeff Campbell Is Dead at 48."

37. *NO/AIDS Task Force News*, September 1983.

38. *NO/AIDS Task Force Newsletter*, May 1986.

39. *Times-Picayune*, June 5, 1992.

40. Barthelemy was generally sympathetic to LGBT+ causes, but he did run afoul of the community in 1993 when he vetoed a city council ordinance that would have extended city health-care benefits to the partners of LGBT+ city employees. In defense of his veto, Barthelemy argued the city could not afford the additional costs.

41. "Judy Montz Issues Statement on Ryan White AIDS Funding." *Forum Focus*, April 1995.

42. Frank Perez, "How the Greed of an Insurance Company Almost Killed John East." *Ambush*, December 2, 2014.

43. Perez, "How the Greed of an Insurance Company Almost Killed John East."

44. Perez, "How the Greed of an Insurance Company Almost Killed John East."

45. The support team included Dr. Ted Wisniewsky, nurses Carol Pindaro, Jeanne Dumestre, Mike Callais, Paul Holthaus, and Maurice Geisel, who kept books for the facility.

46. Supporters and volunteers in those early years included Armeinius Captain Jon Lee Poche, Arthur Roger, Robert Gordy, Madeleine Kohl, Al McMahon, Robbie Haywood, Don Ezel, and Ginger Snap.

47. "Quilt Returns to Washington Oct. 8," *Ambush*, July 1988.

48. Email from Arthur Roger to the author, April 3, 2020.

49. Robinson, "Artists to Benefit AIDS."

50. Blackstone, *Ambush*, July 1988.

51. The New Orleans Regional AIDS Planning Council was revamped by the Ryan White HIV/AIDS Treatment Modernization Act of 2009. Today the council consists of approximately twenty-five volunteer members from the local community. On average, roughly half of council members are people living with HIV.

52. Oral history interview with Valda Lewis conducted by Mordecai Chapman for the LGBT+ Archives Project of Louisiana, May 13, 2019.

53. Rawls and the other petitioners were seeking to have the crimes against nature law—La. R.S. 14:89—declared unconstitutional as well as several statutes extending its effects: 12.1041, 15:535, 15:536, 15:538, 15:540, 15:542, 15:542.1, 15:543, 15:544, 15:545, and 15:549.

54. *Impact*, March 18, 1994.

55. *Electorate* 1, no. 4 (1994). The *Electorate* was the newsletter of the Louisiana Electorate of Gays and Lesbians (LEGAL). Located in the Larry Best Collection, Louisiana Research Collection, Tulane University. Plaintiff Rhonda Leco eventually withdrew as a petitioner and plaintiff John Foster died before the case reached the Louisiana Supreme Court (Louisiana Supreme Course Case Number 2001-CA-2106.) LEGAL had been founded in 1993 by John Rawls and Brian Hartig.

56. In 1998, Connick established a task force to study the constitutionality of Louisiana's sodomy statute. Representatives from the Forum for Equality and Louisiana Log Cabin Republicans were chosen to head the task force, which also included representatives of NOPD, the mayor's office, and other LGBT+ organizations.

57. The Jefferson Parish district attorney was excluded from the class action because he had filed an application for writs with the Fourth Circuit Court of Appeals, which was denied, but was then granted by the state supreme court on appeal.

58. Finch, "Sodomy Trial Opens with Biology Lesson."

59. These witnesses were neurobiologist Cheryl Weill; plaintiffs Jeanne LeBlanc, Johnny Baxley, Larry Best, Rick Cosgriff, Kevin Besse, and John Rawls; activist Randall Beach; genetics researcher Michael Bailey; psychologist David Schnarch (via deposition); and Egan.

60. This information was gleaned from a series of newspaper articles written by Susan Finch.

61. This information was gleaned from a series of newspaper articles written by Susan Finch.

62. Finch, "Sodomy Law Seen Through Eyes of Gay Man."

63. Finch, "Sodomy Law Likened to Marriage Ban."

64. Pizanie, "The Sodomy Trial." Bailey did not appear at trial but offered his testimony via a deposition.

65. Peristein, "Statute Forbidding Sodomy Violates Privacy, Judge Says."

66. Email from Larry Best to the author, March 24, 2020.

CHAPTER 8: THE ORDINANCE

1. All episodes of *Just for the Record* are currently housed at the Amistad Research Center and are free and available to the public via the Amistad Research Center's Vimeo channel.

2. Email from Larry Best to the author, March 26, 2020.

3. Perez, "Remembering Charlene Schneider."

4. Perez, "Remembering Charlene Schneider."

5. Perez, "Phoenix Rises from the Ashes of Smoky Mary."

6. Perez, "Remembering Charlene Schneider."

7. Perez, "Remembering Charlene Schneider."

8. Perez, "Remembering Charlene Schneider."

9. Email from Joan Ladnier, May 19, 2020.

10. Interview with the author, March 11, 2020.

11. Interview with the author, *Ambush*, October 2, 2015.

12. Interview with the author, *Ambush*, October 2, 2015.

13. Perez, and Palmquist, *In Exile*, 90.

14. Perez, and Palmquist, *In Exile*, 90.

15. Magill interview with Mark Cave as part of a series of oral histories about J. B. Harter for the Historic New Orleans Collection, MSS 628.8, July 1, 2011.

16. Interview with the author, April 3, 2011.

17. *Impact*, 1984.

18. *Impact*, 1984.

19. *New York Times*, April 15, 1984.

20. Email from Rich Sacher to the author, April 1, 2020.

21. Interview with Roberts Batson, April 27, 2020.

22. Interview with Mike Early, May 5, 2020.

23. *Impact*, December 26, 1986.

24. *Impact*, December 26, 1986

25. Interview with Rich Sacher, March 31, 2020. The excerpt printed here is taken from a document Sacher penned in January 2020.

26. The committee consisted of eight members: Rich Magill and Judy Montz represented the mayor's advisory committee, Stewart Butler and Sandra Pailet represented PFLAG, Jim Wiltberger and Joan Ladnier represented LAGPAC, and Susan Clade and Randy Evans represented the Forum for Equality. The mayor's advisory committee (MAC) on lesbian and gay issues had been created Mayor Sidney Barthelemy in July 1988 and consisted of sixteen members: Rich Magill (co-chair), Marilyn McConnell (co-chair), Danielle Duncan, Karen Gibson, Reverend Shelley Hamilton, Yul Knighten, Joan Ladnier, Clay Latimer, Ourelia Manchester, Kipp Mullen, Brad Mullineaux, Sammy Oubre III, Liz Simon, Leif Eric Spivey, Lorenzo Williams, and Jim Wiltberger.

27. Helping distribute the survey were: the television show *Just for the Record*; publications such as the *Rooster*, *Impact*, and *Ambush*; political organizations like LAGPAC and the Langston/Jones Society; women's groups (Sappho's Circle, Women in Harmony); lesbian bars (Charlene's, Lace, Pinstripes); AIDS organizations (NO/AIDS Task Force, ACT UP, NOWAA); PFLAG; businesses (FM Books, Mystic Moon Books, Van Gogh's Ear card shop, Petunia's, Quarter Scene, the Dinner Table, the Launderette Royale); religious groups (MCC, Dignity, Grace Fellowship, First Unitarian); several gay Carnival krewes; the Vietnam Veterans of America; and a host of individuals.

28. Magill, *Exposing Hatred*.

29. Rich Magill, John Ognibene, Charlene Schneider, James Kellog, Reverend Shelley Hamilton, John Rawls, Leonard Green, Rich Sacher, and Johnny Jackson.

30. *Report of the Louisiana Advisory Committee to the United States Commission on Civil Rights*, 1988.

31. New Orleans City Council hearing, December 12, 1991.

32. Interview with Randy Evans, March 26, 2020.

33. Quote is taken from a video of the proceeding, which aired on *Just for the Record*, episode 110, January 1992. All of the *Just for the Record* episodes are available on the Amistad Research Center's Vimeo channel.

34. The ordinance hearing took place not in the regular council chamber but rather in the basement of city hall, which, years earlier, had been a cafeteria.

35. Magill interview with Mark Cave as part of a series of oral histories about J. B. Harter for the Historic New Orleans Collection, MSS 628.8, July 1, 2011.

36. Email from Domingue to the author, July 8, 2020.

CHAPTER 9: PUTTING TRANS RIGHTS ON THE RADAR

1. Interview with Kyle Scafide, May 11, 2020.

2. Perez, "Jeanne Manford & New Orleans PFLAG."

3. Interview with the author, March 4, 2020.

4. Email from Rich Sacher to the author, April 1, 2020.

5. Founders included Ana Simo, Sarah Schulman, Maxine Wolfe, Anne-christine d'Adesky, Marie Honan, and Anne Maguire.

6. Interview with Margaret Coble, April 19, 2020.

7. Yanez, "Womyn on the Move."

8. Pizanie, "Dyke March."

9. Email from Julie Thompson to the author, October 12, 2018.

10. Interview with Stewart Butler, August 6, 2019.

11. Interview with Stewart Butler, August 6, 2019.

12. Interview with Courtney Sharp, July 19, 2019.

13. Interview with Courtney Sharp, July 19, 2019.

14. Stover, "Tulane Preserves Digital Histories of LGBTQ Activism in the South."

15. Interview with Courtney Sharp, July 19, 2019.

16. Interview with Courtney Sharp, July 19, 2019.

17. Interview with Courtney Sharp, July 19, 2019.

18. "Shame on Winne-Dixie: 3rd Anniversary of Peter Oiler's Firing."

19. Southwest Virginia LGBTQ+ History Project, "Oral History Interview with Mary Boenke," Virginia Room Digital Collection, accessed May 1, 2020, http://www.virginiaroom .org/digital/document/BoenkeMary.

20. Interview with Randy Trahan, March 4, 2020.

21. Stewart Butler Papers, Louisiana Research Collection, Tulane University. Currently, the word *transgendered* is considered insensitive and not politically correct. Such was not the case when Stewart deployed the term.

22. Personal Papers of Larry Best. Currently, the word *transgendered* is considered insensitive and not politically correct. Such was not the case when Best deployed the term.

23. Butler, Letter to the Editor, *Impact*, May 22, 1998.

24. Currently, the word *transgendered* is considered insensitive and not politically correct. Such was not the case when Stewart deployed the term.

25. "Sandra Pailet: Honored Citizen."

26. Butler interview with Mark Cave as part of a series of oral histories about J. B. Harter for the Historic New Orleans Collection, MSS 628.3, June 2, 2011.

27. Magill, "Peter."

28. Magill, "Peter."

29. Note from Michael Kaiser to Stewart and Alfred, 1998.

30. Email from Anthony "Robby" DeJacimo to the author, May 19, 2020.

31. Email from Anthony "Robby" DeJacimo to the author, May 19, 2020.

32. Email from Anthony "Robby" DeJacimo to the author, May 19, 2020.

33. Email from Anthony "Robby" DeJacimo to the author, May 19, 2020.

34. Email from Anthony "Robby" DeJacimo to the author, May 19, 2020.

35. Interview with Bill Hagler, August 7, 2020.

36. Interview with Ron Joullian, August 7, 2020.

37. Stewart's co–grand marshal, Toni Pizanie, had led, like Stewart, a fascinating life. Originally from Metairie and of Scottish/Italian heritage, Pizanie attended LSU before moving to New Jersey in 1968 to work as a lesbian activist. She was a race car driver in the 1970s and became active in the Methodist church before joining the Vieux Carre Metropolitan Community Church. She also worked as head of bookkeeping for a national accounting firm and as controller for an architectural firm. She began working in New Orleans politics by joining Dutch Morial's mayoral campaign. Pizanie was also involved with NO/AIDS Task Force, NO/AIDS Walk, AIDS Candlelight Memorial, Lesbian and Gay Community Center of New Orleans, SOLOC, LAGPAC, Celebration, and HRC. She and her husband lived in Gulfport, Mississippi, for a while and were active in a number of civic organizations there before returning to New Orleans in 1992. She wrote a column for *Ambush* entitled "Sappho's Psalm," as well as a number of works with her husband, including, two mysteries, four plays, dozens of short stories and poems. They also created more than one hundred pieces of art, composed a score of songs, gave free art lessons to pre-puberty and elderly students, and entertained constantly.

38. Interview with Jason Ezell, April 19, 2020.

39. Interview with Mark Gonzalez, April 20, 2020.

40. Interview with Mark Gonzalez, March 27, 2020.

41. Interview with Robert Brunet, April 19, 2020.

42. Email from Rich Sacher to the author, March 31, 2020.

43. Interview with Leo Watermeier, April 8, 2020.

44. Founding members included Stewart Butler, Betty Caldwell, Alfred Doolittle, Mark Harper, Niki Kearby, Rip and Marsha Naquin-Delain, Toni Pizanie, Dianne Ranna, Alan Robinson, J. Michael Tetty, Leo Watermeier, and others.

45. Email from Larry Best to the author, March 26, 2020.

46. Letter from Ray Ruiz, realtor, and Rip Naquin, co-chair of the center, to Sam Poche, February 6, 1996. This letter is housed in the Larry Best Collection at the Louisiana Research Collection at Tulane University.

47. Letter from Larry Best to Ray Ruiz, February 1, 1996.

48. *Ambush* 17, no. 4, 1999.

49. The *Center Line*, the community center's newsletter, March 2001.

50. Interview with the author, 2014.

CHAPTER 10: LION IN WINTER

1. *Faerie Playhouse Newsletter*, December 23, 1996.

2. Note from Sophie Gutierrez to Stewart, dated March 2, 2009.

3. Of all Stewart's friends in Alaska, the most colorful was Niilo Koponen. The two probably met at the University of Alaska, Fairbanks, when they both worked on behalf of gaining statehood for Alaska. Their paths also crossed in political circles; both were active in labor unions. Koponen eventually served five terms in the Alaska legislature, where he earned a reputation as the most liberal politician in the state. Koponen was also a progressive educator. He and Stewart corresponded regularly until Koponen's death in 2013.

4. Stewart and Hagler participated in a peace demonstration during the visit.

5. *Faerie Playhouse Newsletter*, February 2015.

6. *Faerie Playhouse Newsletter*, December 1999.

7. *Faerie Playhouse Newsletter*, Fall 1997.

8. *Faerie Playhouse Newsletter*, December 2001.

9. *Faerie Playhouse Newsletter*, December 2004.

10. Email from Charles Paul, May 10, 2020.

11. Email from Charlotte Aitken, May 22, 2020.

12. Facebook post in the Faerie Playhouse group, October 7, 2020.

13. Facebook post in the Faerie Playhouse group, October 7, 2020.

14. Email from Ron Joullian to the author, August 8, 2020.

15. Born in Jackson, Mississippi, in 1940, Harter studied art history at the University of Louisville and studio arts at Louisiana State University. He then did graduate work at the University of Pennsylvania, Hebrew University (Jerusalem), the University of Vienna, and Arizona State University. In 1967, Harter joined the staff of the Historic New Orleans Collection before becoming a registrar at the Louisiana State Museum in New Orleans. He was promoted to curator and eventually, in 1986, director of collections, a position he held until he retired in 1991. In addition to being recognized as an extremely effective leader and administrator (especially after the 1988 Cabildo fire and the 1989 theft of sixty John James Audubon prints), Harter was also an accomplished artist. He was skilled in photography, still lifes, abstract art, and landscapes. In 1999, the Louisiana State Museum of Art featured an exhibit of his landscapes. Harter was also a master of homoerotic art, but he kept this aspect of his work a secret for thirty years. Harter chose not to come out until after his mother died in 1996. Of his choice to remain closeted, Harter once observed it was "partly . . . in deference to family, partly in deference to employment." In 1997, Harter published a collection of his art called *Encounters with the Nude Male*. Another book, *The Drawings of J. B. Harter*, was published posthumously in 2003.

16. Bill Hagler, Ron Joullian, Tim Angle, Cindy Joullian, Tom Lonegin (Cirello), Steve Willey, Rich Magill, Stephen Samuel, Hammer, Gary Griffin, Don Dupre, Paulette Pickett, Elliott and Elizabeth Hammer, Anthony DeJacimo, Sandra Pailet, Steve Freeman, and Monica Williams.

17. The wine was a big hit. Hagler's efforts yielded twelve bottles, upon which were affixed labels that read:

"Nouveau / Vieux Carre / Orleans Rougeur / A Unique blend of red and green grapes / Locally grown in strict accordance / With the Vin Franchise Gastronomic / U.S.A." And on the back of the bottles:

"Nestled between Congo Square and the Faubourg Marigny in Orleans Parish, Louisiana runs the Esplanade Ridge. The picturesque region has long been noted for its unique mixture of local and faerie cultures. Quaint creole Cottages and ever changing discards dot the landscape of stately Oaks and Night Blooming Jasmine. Here deep in the heart of Creole Country rests a small Plantation known for its exotic Fruits and Residents. The Faerie Playhouse Plantation has long been a noted draw for the undiscriminating bon-vivant."

18. *Faerie Playhouse Newsletter*, December 2005.

19. *Faerie Playhouse Newsletter*, December 2005.

20. Facebook post in the Faerie Playhouse group, September 17, 2020.

21. Email from Father Bill Terry, May 5, 2020.

22. Email from Charlotte Aitken, May 22, 2020.

23. *Faerie Playhouse Newsletter*, December 2002.

24. Unpublished letter to the *Times-Picayune* written by Stewart in March 2010.

25. Email from Father Bill Terry, May 5, 2020.

26. Ibid.

27. Interview with Anne Freedman, July 8, 2019.

28. *Faerie Playhouse Newsletter*, February 2009.

29. Email from Charles Paul, May 10, 2020.

30. Email from Ron Joullian to the author, date unknown.

EPILOGUE: GETTING OUR HISTORY OUT OF THE CLOSET

1. Other members of the steering committee included Susan Tucker, Rich Sacher, Liz Simon, Roberts Batson, Sam Stover, Josh Goodman, Gene Cizek, Daniel Morvant, and others.

2. Adapted from Perez, "LGBT+ Archives Project of Louisiana."

BIBLIOGRAPHIC ESSAY

I learned it's impossible to completely pin down history. There is always conflicting information. It leaves you feeling you haven't learned enough, done enough. But the truth is no one else can ever pin everything down perfectly, either.

—JOHNNY TOWNSEND

A NOTE ON THE RESEARCH

Any attempt to document a person's life, especially one who has lived a long time, and in many different places, can be an overwhelming undertaking. This was certainly true of Stewart Butler. Not only was he eighty-nine years old when he died, he lived in six different states. Fortunately, Stewart was a prolific letter writer. He wrote constantly, especially to his family, who, even more fortunately, saved all of his letters and returned them to him before he died. Stewart also saved almost every letter ever written to him. It is almost as if he sensed his life would be consequential and therefore preserved this correspondence for future researchers. I derived the most valuable information about his life from these letters. Another valuable source of information were his military records and the papers associated with his various jobs and careers, including those having to do with his activism in New Orleans. Many of these records are now housed in the Special Collections Division archival repository of the Howard-Tilton Memorial Library (formerly the Louisiana Research Collection) at Tulane University.

Organizational newsletters also proved to be an invaluable source of information. These include newsletters from NO/AIDS Task Force, PFLAG New Orleans, LAGPAC, Forum for Equality, Gertrude Stein Society, Langston/ Jones Society, LEGAL, and others.

The excerpts in this book from Alfred's letters and writings are from the original yellow legal notepads Alfred used when composing. Alfred wrote a lot of letters to world leaders and gave them to Stewart to mail. Stewart saved those too. Because much of Stewart's career was in the public arena, newspaper articles proved to be a priceless source of information not found in other places. This was also true of organizational newsletters and minutes from board meetings of the various organizations to which Stewart belonged. Much of the Butler and Doolittle genealogies were compiled by Stewart's and Alfred's siblings. Personal interviews also yielded much information and insight into not only Stewart's life but also his work in the political arena. I have listed all the people I interviewed for this project in a section below, but a few bear mentioning now. I have formally interviewed Stewart numerous times since 2008, and for the last several years of his life we spoke on the phone weekly. In addition, we saw each other at least once a month when the LGBT+ Archives Project of Louisiana board of directors met at the Faerie Playhouse. I must also mention Bill Hagler, who has lived at the Faerie Playhouse on and off since 2001 and who, in 2008, assumed the role of Stewart's caretaker. As Stewart's health declined and his capacity to concentrate diminished, Bill was an incredible help and a wealth of knowledge. The same can be said for Ron Joullian, Stewart's longtime friend and the executor of his estate. And although Rich Magill passed away before I began working on this biography, I did formally interview him in 2013 for another project and many more times informally at Café Lafitte in Exile, where we would occasionally meet for Scotch and hours of casual conversation.

PERSONS INTERVIEWED

When possible, I interviewed people in person. When circumstances did not permit that luxury, interviews were conducted over the phone or via email. Sometimes, casual conversations at social events or in bars or otherwise outside the context of a formal interview setting yielded useful information. I have included conversations with a few of those people in the following list.

Tomy Acosta, Charlotte Aitken, Tim Angle, Larry Bagneris, Roberts Batson, Larry Best, Saundra Boudreaux, Robert Brunet, Josh Burford, Stewart Butler, Jennifer Callan, Wayne Christenberry, Gene Cizek, Margaret Coble, Michael-Chase Creasy, Anne-christine d'Adesky, Deyette Danford, Anthony DeJacimo, Clayton Delery, Barbara Dobrosky, Edward Domingue, Glenn Ducote, Steve Duplantis, Mike Early, John East, Alicia Eaton, Dave Eaton, Suzanne Eaton, Randy Evans, Jason Ezell, Otis Fennell, Robert Fieseler, Anne

Freedman, Misti Gaither, Dr. Jody Gates, Mary Gehman, Mark Gonzalez, Larry Graham, Mary Griggs, Bill Hagler, Billy Henry, Jean Henry, Jean Henry Jr., Michael Hickerson, Ron Joullian, Dr. Michael Kaiser, Dr. Niki Kearby, Evan Kirk, Joan Ladnier, Brenda Laura, Celeste Autin LeBoeuf, Valda Lewis, Crystal Little, Rich Magill, Connie Manella, Gary Martin, Marilyn McConnell, Ken Mitchell, Rip and Marsha Naquin-Delain, Charles Paul, Wayne Phillips, Pete Pietens, Chloe Raub, Larry Raybourne, Sebastian Rey, Arthur Roger, Dr. Catherine Roland, Rich Sacher, Kyle Scafide, Elizabeth Schexnyder, Liz Simon, Jack Sullivan, Julie Thompson, Johnny Townsend, Randy Trahan, Kenny Tucker, Linda Tucker, Noel Twilbeck, Louis J. Volz III, Wes Ware, Leo Watermeier, Steve Willey, and Sheri Wright.

DOCUMENTING QUEER NEW ORLEANS HISTORY

The biggest challenge for LGBT+ historians is that much of queer history remains in the closet. Until very recently, being queer was not something people wanted to document; being publicly identified as LGBT+ could result in being arrested and jailed, being committed to a mental asylum, the loss of a job, eviction from an apartment, social ostracization, and, in some cases, death by suicide. Consequently, primary sources are scarce. The names and addresses of people arrested at raids of gay bars were routinely published in the newspapers, and the raids were usually reported in sensational style. There are also arrest records. Property records and chains of title in New Orleans date back to 1718 and sometimes yield information on the sites of gay bars, but the information in these records relates to property ownership and often excludes information about lease holders. Newspapers in New Orleans covered virtually nothing gay related, other than bar raids, arrest records, and criminal trials, until the 1970s.

The advent of gay periodicals helped remedy this dearth of primary source material. The earliest of these publications were organizational newsletters, the first of which in New Orleans was *Sunflower*, published by the Gay Liberation Front, which was founded in 1971 and lasted less than two years. A few years later, the Gertrude Stein Society, founded in 1975, published *Gertrude's Notes*. LAGPAC (1980) sent out a regular newsletter as well, as did PFLAG (1982), the *Banner*. The Forum for Equality (1989) had *Forum Focus*, and the Louisiana Electorate of Gays and Lesbians had the *Electorate*. These newsletters, and others, provide an in-depth history of not only the organizations that produced them but also of the larger social and political context in which they were written.

The organizations that produced these newsletters also produced other records—internal memos, letters, membership rosters, media coverage, agendas, and minutes of board meetings. Some of these organizational records have found permanent homes in area archival repositories. Of these institutions, the Louisiana Research Collection at Tulane University has the largest collection of gay organizational records as well as the personal papers of several prominent activists. Other archival institutions in New Orleans actively preserving LGBT+ material include the Louisiana State Museum, the Historic New Orleans Collection, the Newcomb College Institute Archives, and the Amistad Research Center. Thanks to the efforts of the LGBT+ Archives Project of Louisiana, a statewide collective, other archival repositories, museums, and libraries throughout Louisiana are also preserving queer material. Many of these institutions also preserve LGBT+ ephemera.

The 1970s also witnessed the first of the entertainment guides, which provide valuable information about the bar scene. *The Cajun Queen: A Complete Guide to New Orleans Gaydom* was published in the early 1970s and consisted of paragraph descriptions of gay and lesbian bars, popular restaurants, and other gay owned or themed businesses. In later years there were *Headlines: New Orleans' Foremost Entertainment and Information Guide*, the *Pink Pages of Greater New Orleans*, *New Orleans Gay and Lesbian Yellow Pages*, *This Week Guide: New Orleans Entertainment in the Gay and Lesbian Community*, and the *Whiz*.

The *Zipper*, a statewide publication produced in Baton Rouge, appeared in 1977 and was the first sustained effort at LGBT+ journalism in Louisiana, featuring news stories as well as entertainment coverage. In 1977, Roy Letson began publishing *Impact*, which ran for twenty-three years. In 1981, *Zipper* editor Rip Naquin started the *Alternative*, which in 1982 became *Ambush Magazine*. Still in publication, *Ambush* is one of the longest-running LGBT+ themed publications in the nation. Other, shorter-lived publications included the *Big Easy Times*, the *Rooster*, and the *Times of Louisiana Communities*. These periodicals are valuable to researchers for a variety of reasons. The advertisements alone are a wealth of information.

The first person to do any sustained work on New Orleans LGBT+ history was Roberts Batson. Batson had been involved in the Gertrude Stein Society in the 1970s and cofounded LAGPAC in 1980. In 1993, when PFLAG had its national conference in New Orleans, the conference co-chairs (Stewart Butler, Sandra Pailet, and Billy Henry) asked Batson, who was working in the tourism industry at the time, to organize tours for the conference attendees. At that time, Batson developed the Gay Heritage Tour, which explored the city's colorful queer history. The following year, on the twenty-fifth anniversary of

Stonewall, Batson wrote a series of columns in *Impact* called "Claiming Our Past." Since then he has written over four hundred articles on New Orleans LGBT+ history. Batson has participated in numerous panel discussions and other public programming, including the first LGBT+ themed panel discussion at the Louisiana State Museum in 1995. At that time, Batson said, "If we don't tell these stories, no one will know. All they'll know is what's there in the public record and newspaper files—who got arrested in bar raids. I feel an impulse I can't quite articulate—an emotional obligation, a responsibility to document these lives and experiences." Academically trained in theater and communication, Batson was nominated for an Emmy in 2007 for his one-man show, *Amazing Place, This New Orleans.*

Batson's Gay Heritage Tour was the first of its kind. Since then, similar tours have emerged. I founded the Rainbow Fleur de Lis Tour in 2012, the late Glenn DeVillier began the Twirl a year or so later, Quinn Bishop began the NOLA Drag Tour in 2019, and Tylyn Anson started the LGBT Queer History Tour in 2019.

A number of books documenting New Orleans queer history have been published in the last decade or so. The first significant research on the Up Stairs Lounge fire began in 1989 when Johnny Townsend began compiling biographical profiles of that arson's victims. Townsend's research was ultimately published as a book, *Let the Faggots Burn*, in 2011. The following year, *In Exile: The History and Lore Surrounding New Orleans Gay Culture and Its Oldest Gay Bar* was written by Jeffrey Palmquist and me. This book, while not an exhaustive history, does provide a cursory survey of local queer history. *The Up Stairs Lounge Arson: Thirty-Two Dead in a New Orleans Gay Bar, June 24, 1973*, was published in 2014 and offers a detailed account of the tragic fire. Two years later, Perez and Palmquist followed up *In Exile* with an anthology—*My Gay New Orleans: 28 Personal Reminiscences on LGBT+ Life in New Orleans* (Bedford, TX: LL Publications, 2016). The year 2017 saw the publication of two important books: Howard P. Smith's *Unveiling the Muse: The Lost History of Gay Carnival in New Orleans*, the definitive treatment of gay Carnival, and Clayton Delery's *Out for Queer Blood: The Murder of Fernando Rios and the Failure of New Orleans Justice*. Two more books appeared in 2018. Robert Fieseler's *Tinderbox: The Untold Story of the Up Stairs Lounge Fire and the Rise of Gay Liberation* added to the growing body of scholarship on the Up Stairs Lounge fire. Drawing on the work of Townsend and Delery, *Tinderbox* positions the fire within a national context. That year also saw the publication of Howard P. Smith and Frank Perez's *Southern Decadence in New Orleans*. Resurrecting the jovial spirit of Trey Bienville's *The Gay Gourmet* (Bloomington, IN: Writers Club Press, 2003), Poppy Tooker's *Drag Queen*

Brunch (New Orleans: Pelican Publishing) came out in 2019. In addition to these works, local queer history has been discussed in part in a number of other books as chapters or sections, as well as in a number of journal and magazine articles.

Local LGBT+ history has been the subject of four documentary films. Tim Wolff's *The Sons of Tennessee Williams* (2010) explores the history of gay Carnival. The Up Stairs Lounge fire has inspired three documentaries: Royd Anderson's *The Upstairs Lounge Fire* (2013), Robert Camina's *Upstairs Inferno* (2015), and ABC's *Prejudice and Pride* (2018). The Up Stairs Lounge fire has also inspired two theatrical musical productions: Wayne Self's *Upstairs* (2013) and Max Vernon's *The View UpStairs* (2017).

Also available to researchers are episodes of *Just for the Record*, an LGBT+ themed open access television program that aired from 1987 to 1993. Producer Valda Lewis donated footage of the show to the Amistad Research Center. Digitized with a grant from the LGBT+ Archives Project, the episodes are available on Amistad's Vimeo channel and the LGBT+ Archives Project of Louisiana website. Additional film footage of a wide variety of events from the 1980s and 1990s pertinent to the LGBT+ community in New Orleans, including Pride festivals, HIV/AIDS conferences, protests, Carnival balls, and other events, are also available at the Amistad Research Center in the Valda Lewis collection.

Last Call: The Dyke Bar History Project has also done an excellent job of documenting the lost lesbian bar scene in New Orleans and features interviews with key players in not only bar culture but also the activist scene. In addition to two seasons' worth of podcasts, *Last Call* has also produced live performances and sponsored panel discussions.

In addition to the aforementioned sources, there have been at least eight doctoral dissertations and six theses written about queer Louisiana history. These include: Thomasine Marion Bartlett, "Vintage Drag Female Impersonators Performing Resistance in Cold War New Orleans" (PhD dissertation, Tulane University, 2004); Robert D. Byrd Jr., "When the Pretending Stopped? AIDS Coverage in New Orleans' Mainstream, Gay, and Alternative Presses from 1981–1991" (MA thesis, University of South Alabama, 2011); Richard Clark, "City of Desire: A History of Same-Sex Desire in New Orleans, 1917–1977" (PhD dissertation, Tulane University, 2009); Thomas B. David Jr., "Perceptions and Experiences of Growing Up Gay in Rural Louisiana: A Reflexive Ethnography of Six Gay Men" (PhD dissertation, University of Louisiana at Monroe, 2003); B. M. David, "The Only Safe Closet Is the Voting Booth: The Gay Rights Movement in Louisiana" (Unpublished doctoral dissertation, University of Louisiana at Lafayette, 2016); Gareth F. Griffin,

"Flames of Hate: The New Orleans Upstairs Lounge Fire, 24 June 1973" (MA thesis, University of Louisiana at Lafayette, 2008); Lawrence M. Knopp, "Gentrification and Gay Community Development in a New Orleans Neighborhood" (PhD dissertation, University of Iowa, 1989); Heidi S. Kulkin, "A Qualitative Retrospective Study of Lesbian Youth: The Journey toward the Resilient Self" (PhD dissertation, Tulane University, 2001); Caroline Olsson, "Not All That Easy: Survival Strategies in Lesbian Bar Life in New Orleans, 1950–1970" (MA thesis, University of New Orleans, 1999); Rachel O'Pry, "Louisiana Social Workers: A Study on Attitudes toward LGBT Youth" (MSW thesis, Louisiana State University, 2012); Ryan B. Prechter, "Gay New Orleans: A History" (PhD dissertation, Georgia State University, 2017); D. C. Manuel, "We Are Able to Find Pride and Dignity in Being Gay: Culture, Resistance, and the Development of a Visible Gay Community in Lafayette, Louisiana, 1968–1989" (Unpublished doctoral dissertation, University of Louisiana at Lafayette, 2014); Mary Elaine Stuart, "An Examination of Tolerance in New Orleans: Voter Attitudes toward Lesbians and Gays" (MA thesis, University of New Orleans, 1992); Jelisa Thompson, "You Make Me Feel: A Study of the Gay Rights Movement in New Orleans" (BA thesis, University of Southern Mississippi, 2011).

ARCHIVAL RESOURCES

The official repository of the Stewart Butler Papers is the Louisiana Research Collection at Tulane University. These papers, which consist of seventeen linear feet, include letters, notes, minutes, ephemera, and other materials from his career as a political activist. The collection has been divided into eight series: LAGPAC, Celebration-Louisiana State Conference, SECLGM, PFLAG, National March on Washington for Lesbian and Gay Rights, organizations/events/fundraisers, personal correspondence, and photographs. The vast majority of Butler's personal correspondence remained in his personal possession until after his death but will eventually be housed at Tulane University as well.

The Louisiana Research Collection is also home to the LAGPAC records, as well as several other organizations and persons relevant to Butler's activism in New Orleans. These include: the LGBT Community Center of New Orleans records, the Rich Magill Papers, the Skip Ward Papers, a variety of LGBT+ themed periodicals, and an enormous collection of ephemera.

Due in large part to the efforts of the LGBT+ Archives Project of Louisiana, of which Butler was a founding member, several other archival repositories, libraries, and museums, in addition to the Louisiana Research Collection, have begun collecting materials that chronicle Louisiana's LGBT+ history. These include: the Historic New Orleans Collection, the Newcomb College Institute Archives, the Louisiana State Museum, the Amistad Research Center, the Center for Louisiana Studies, the East Baton Rouge Public Library, the New Orleans Public Library, the Special Collections Library at LSU, the T. Harry Williams Center for Oral History, the Earl K. Long Library at UNO, and the Monroe Library at Loyola University. A wealth of information is also available on the LGBT+ Archives Project of Louisiana website, including an extensive bibliography.

WORKS REFERENCED AND CONSULTED

ACT UP, New Orleans Chapter. Letter to ACT UP, National Headquarters. May 15, 1989. Stewart Butler Collection, Tulane University.

Aitken, Charlotte. Email to Frank Perez. May 22, 2020.

Allured, Janet. *Remapping Second-Wave Feminism: The Long Women's Right's Movement in Louisiana, 1950–1997.* Athens: University of Georgia Press, 2016.

Anderson, Royd. *The Up Stairs Lounge Fire.* Documentary film. 2013.

Babovich, Wayne. Quoted in *Impact.* 1984.

"Basil Speaks Out." *Ambush.* August 1987.

Batson, Roberts. "Claiming Our Past." *Impact.* 1994.

Batson, Roberts. "Essay." *Out and Elected in the USA.* http://outhistory.org/exhibits/show/out-and-elected/early-1980s/roberts-batson.

Batson, Roberts. *Impact.* April 11, 1997.

Batson, Roberts. Personal interview. April 27, 2020.

Bell, Kevin. "Partners' Health Care Is Vetoed—Council May Vote to Override." *New Orleans Times-Picayune* November 11, 1993.

Best, Larry. Letter to Ray Ruiz. February 1, 1996. Personal collection of Larry Best.

Best, Larry. Email to Frank Perez. March 24, 2020.

Best, Larry. Email to Frank Perez. March 26, 2020.

Blackstone, John. *Ambush.* July 1988.

Blumer, Markie Louise Christianson. "Gay Men's Experiences of Alaskan Society in Their Coupled Relationships." Dissertation. Iowa State University, 2008.

"Board Member Profile." *Banner,* July 2002.

Boenke, Mary. Interview. Conducted by Mariana Araujo. October 6, 2019.

Boenke, Mary, et al. *Our Trans Children.* Washington, DC: PFLAG Transgender Network, 1997.

Bond, Gay Lynn. "Charity and the Treatment of AIDS Patients." *New Orleans Times-Picayune/States-Item.* July 9, 1985.

Bossu, Jean Bernard. *Travels in the Interior of North America, 1751–1762.* Translated by Seymour Feiler. Norman: University of Oklahoma Press, 1962.

Boyd, Nan Alamilla. *Wide-Open Town: A History of Queer San Francisco to 1965.* Berkeley: University of California Press, 2003.

"BRAGPAC Faces Crisis with Downtown B.R. Crackdown on Gays." *Impact*. May 18, 1984.

Brunet, Robert. Personal interview. April 19, 2020.

Burford, Joshua. Email to Frank Perez. March 26, 2020.

Burton, Neel. "A Brief History of Schizophrenia." *Psychology Today*. September 8, 2012.

Butler, Bertha. Letter to Stewart Butler. April 1973. Personal collection of Stewart Butler.

Butler, Bertha. Letter to Stewart Butler. October 1974. Personal collection of Stewart Butler.

Butler, Bertha, and Stewart Butler. Letter to Stewart Butler. April 23, 1951. Personal collection of Stewart Butler.

Butler, Sophie. Letter to Dave and Suzanne Eaton. 1960. Personal collection of Stewart Butler.

Butler, Stewart. Letter to Bertha and Stewart Butler. June 1948. Personal collection of Stewart Butler.

Butler, Stewart. Letter to Wilds Bacot. June 23, 1950. Personal collection of Stewart Butler.

Butler, Stewart. Letter to Wilds Bacot. September 7, 1952. Personal collection of Stewart Butler.

Butler, Stewart. Letter to Wilds Bacot. September 13, 1952. Personal collection of Stewart Butler.

Butler, Stewart. Letter to Bertha and Stewart Butler. November 22, 1952. Personal collection of Stewart Butler.

Butler, Stewart. Letter to Bertha and Stewart Butler. December 1952. Personal collection of Stewart Butler.

Butler, Stewart. Letter to Bertha and Stewart Butler. March 30, 1953. Personal collection of Stewart Butler.

Butler, Stewart. Letter to Wilds Bacot. November 24, 1953. Personal collection of Stewart Butler.

Butler, Stewart. Letter to Bill Finn. January 11, 1954. Personal collection of Stewart Butler.

Butler, Stewart. Letter to Bertha and Stewart Butler. August 1954. Personal collection of Stewart Butler.

Butler, Stewart. Letter to Bertha and Stewart Butler. September 1954. Personal collection of Stewart Butler.

Butler, Stewart. Letter to Minnie Cooper. December 25, 1989. Personal collection of Stewart Butler.

Butler, Stewart. Letter to Bob Pattison. November 19, 1994. Personal collection of Stewart Butler.

Butler, Stewart. *Faerie Playhouse Newsletter*. 1996. Personal collection of Stewart Butler.

Butler, Stewart. *Faerie Playhouse Newsletter*. 1997. Personal collection of Stewart Butler.

Butler, Stewart. Letter to Freddie Lavre. December 8, 1997. Personal collection of Stewart Butler.

Butler, Stewart. "Letter to the Editor." *Banner*. May 1998.

Butler, Stewart. "Letter to the Editor." *Impact*. May 22, 1998.

Butler, Stewart. *Faerie Playhouse Newsletter*. 1999. Personal collection of Stewart Butler.

Butler, Stewart. *Faerie Playhouse Newsletter*. 2001. Personal collection of Stewart Butler.

Butler, Stewart. *Faerie Playhouse Newsletter*. 2002. Personal collection of Stewart Butler.

Butler, Stewart. *Faerie Playhouse Newsletter*. 2004. Personal collection of Stewart Butler.

Butler, Stewart. *Faerie Playhouse Newsletter*. 2005. Personal collection of Stewart Butler.

Butler, Stewart. Interview. Conducted by Clayton Delery, July 2, 2009.

Butler, Stewart. Letter to the Editor (unpublished). *New Orleans Times-Picayune*. March 2010.

Butler, Stewart. Personal interview. April 1, 2011.

Butler, Stewart. Personal interview. April 3, 2011.

Butler, Stewart. Interview. Conducted by Mark Cave, June 2, 2011.

Butler, Stewart. *Faerie Playhouse Newsletter*. 2013. Personal collection of Stewart Butler.

Butler, Stewart. *Faerie Playhouse Newsletter*. 2014. Personal collection of Stewart Butler.

Butler, Stewart. Personal interview. March 20, 2014.

Butler, Stewart. Personal interview. August 6, 2019.

Butler, Stewart. Title unknown. *Star* (Carville Newsletter), n.d.

Butler, Stewart. Letter to Ann Landers (unpublished). Date unknown. Personal collection of Stewart Butler.

Butler, Stewart. Interview. Conducted by Hattie (last name unknown). Date unknown.

Butler, Stewart, et al., Letter to Elizabeth Birch. May 17, 1997. Personal collection of Frank Perez.

Byrd, Robert D., Jr. "'When the Pretending' Stopped? AIDS Coverage in New Orleans' Mainstream, Gay, and Alternative Presses from 1981–1991." MA thesis, University of South Alabama, 2011.

Caldwell, Betty. "A Brief History of New Orleans PFLAG, 1982–1992." *Banner*. May 2002.

California Historical Courier. January 1975.

Camina, Robert. *Upstairs Inferno*. 2015. Documentary film.

Campanella, Richard. *Bourbon Street: A History*. Baton Rouge: Louisiana State University Press, 2014.

Carlton, Lee H. "A Thank You to New Orleans." *Headlines*. June 26, 1987.

"Celebration '84 Snags Troy Perry." *Ambush*. March 1984.

"Celebration '87 Set." *Ambush*. May 1987.

Center Line. March 2001.

Chapman, Nathan. "Community Must Join Together." *Ambush*. August 1988.

Christenberry, Wayne. Personal interview. March 11, 2020.

Christiansen, Kristy. "The Story of Leprosy and the National Hansen's Disease Museum." https://www.louisianatravel.com/articles/story-leprosy-and-national-hansens-disease-museum.

Cibellis, Matthew. "Black, Gay, and Republican." *Washington Blade*, April 24, 1992.

Clark, Richard. "City of Desire: A History of Same-sex Desire in New Orleans, 1917–1977." PhD dissertation, Tulane University, 2009.

Claverie, Laura. "View from a Different Window." *New Orleans Magazine*. 1986.

Coble, Margaret. Personal interview. April 19, 2020.

Coen, Ross. "Not Old Enough to Vote but Able to Support Statehood: University of Alaska Students and the Statehood Movement." *Alaska History Journal* 24, no. 2 (Fall 2009).

Cole, Terrence. *The Cornerstone on College Hill: An Illustrated History of the University of Alaska Fairbanks*. Anchorage: University of Alaska Press, 1994.

Coyle, Pamela. "Connick Sets Up Study of State's Sodomy Laws." *New Orleans Times-Picayune*. January 21, 1998.

"Curb Advocated on Homosexuals." *New Orleans Times-Picayune*. April 28, 1951.

David, Thomas B., Jr. "Perceptions and Experiences of Growing Up Gay in Rural Louisiana: A Reflexive Ethnography of Six Gay Men." PhD dissertation, University of Louisiana at Monroe, 2003.

DeJacimo, Anthony. Email to Frank Perez. May 19, 2020.

Delery, Clayton. *Out for Queer Blood: The Murder of Fernando Rios and the Failure of New Orleans Justice*. Jefferson, NC: Exposit, 2017.

Delery-Edwards, Clayton. *The Up Stairs Lounge Arson: Thirty-two Dead in a New Orleans Gay Bar, June 24, 1973.* Jefferson, NC: McFarland, 2014.

Denton, Pat. Letter to Jean Carr and Roberts Batson. February 21, 1981. Stewart Butler Collection, Tulane University.

Dobrosky, Barbara. Personal interview. April 9, 2020.

Dodds, Richard. "Rallying the Arts World Against AIDS." *New Orleans Times-Picayune/States-Item.* November 6, 1987.

Domingue, Edward. Email to Frank Perez. July 8, 2020.

Donovan, James M. "Baby Steps or One Fell Swoop? The Incremental Extension of Rights Is Not a Defensible Strategy." *California Western Law Review* (Fall 2001).

Doolittle, Alfred M. *The Divine Love Play and Other Plays.* San Francisco: Two Rooms Press, 2004.

Doolittle, Alfred M. Letter to Freddie Lavre. October 5, 1989. Personal collection of Stewart Butler.

Ducote, Glen. Personal interview. June 14, 2019.

Durant, Will, and Ariel Durant. *The Age of Louis XIV.* New York: Simon and Schuster, 1963.

Early, Mike. Personal interview. May 5, 2020.

Eaton, Dave. Email to Frank Perez. July 11, 2019.

Eaton, Dave. Email to Frank Perez. March 20, 2020.

Eaton, Suzanne. Letter to Bertha and Stewart Butler. 1960. Personal collection of Stewart Butler.

Eaton, Suzanne. Letter to Stewart Butler. August 17, 2000. Personal collection of Stewart Butler.

Eaton, Suzanne. Letter to Frank Perez. November 6, 2019. Personal collection of Frank Perez.

Electorate: The Newsletter of the Louisiana Electorate of Gays and Lesbians 1, no. 4 (1994).

Ellis, Scott S. *Madame Vieux Carre: The French Quarter in the Twentieth Century.* Jackson: University Press of Mississippi, 2010.

Evans, Randy. Personal interview. March 26, 2020.

Ezell, Jason. "Returning Forest Darlings: Gay Liberationist Sanctuary in the Southeastern Network, 1973–80." *Radical History Review* no. 135 (2019): 71–94.

Ezell, Jason. Personal interview. April 19, 2020.

Feinberg, Leslie. "Grassroots Revolt against Trans Exclusion from Federal Jobs Bill." Workers World. October 13, 2017. www.workers.org.

Fieseler, Robert W. *Tinderbox: The Untold Story of the Up Stairs Lounge Fire and the Rise of Gay Liberation.* New York: Liveright, 2018.

Finch, Susan. "Local Marchers United in Fight." *New Orleans Times-Picayune.* April 26, 1993.

Finch, Susan. "Sodomy Trial Opens with Biology Lesson." *New Orleans Times-Picayune.* October 27, 1998.

Finch, Susan. "Sodomy Law Seen through Eyes of Gay Man." *New Orleans Times-Picayune.* October 28, 1998.

Finch, Susan. "Sodomy Law Likened to Marriage Ban." *New Orleans Times-Picayune.* October 30, 1998.

Fitzgerald, Thomas. "Gay Rights March a Mix of Protest and Celebration." *New Orleans Times-Picayune/States-Item.* October 12, 1987.

Flaming Crescent Design. May 22, 1992.

Freedman, Anne. Personal interview. July 8, 2018.

Frost, Ed. Letter to Stewart Butler. August 2, 1982. Stewart Butler Collection, Tulane University.

Galatus, Marie. *Just for the Record*. Episode 110. January 1992.

Garza, Annie. Letter to Stewart Butler. August 31, 1967.

Gates, Jody. Personal interview. April 8, 2020.

Gaudet, Marcia. *Carville: Remembering Leprosy in America*. Jackson: University Press of Mississippi, 2004.

Gay and Lesbian Review. March–April 2019.

"Gay Liberation Group Marches." *New Orleans Times-Picayune*, January 24, 1971.

"Gays Raise $2,100 for N.O. Police Vests." *Ambush*, June 1983.

Gonzalez, Mark. Personal interview. March 27, 2020.

Gonzalez, Mark. Personal interview. April 20, 2020.

Green, Leonard. *Ambush*, October 1987.

Gruening, Ernest. *Many Battles: The Autobiography of Ernest Gruening*. New York: Liveright, 1973.

Gutierrez, Sophie. Letter to Stewart Butler. March 2, 2009. Personal collection of Stewart Butler.

Gutierrez, Sophie. Email to Frank Perez. April 26, 2020.

Hagler, Bill. Personal interview. August 7, 2020.

Horner, Tom. "Gay Festin.'" *Impact*, June 29, 1984.

Joullian, Ron. Personal interview. May 7, 2020.

Joullian, Ron. Email to Frank Perez. August 7, 2020.

Joullian, Ron. Email to Frank Perez. August 8, 2020.

Joullian, Ron. Facebook post. October 7, 2020.

Joullian, Ron. Facebook post. September 17, 2020.

"Judy Montz Issues Statement on Ryan White AIDS Funding." *Forum Focus*, April 1995.

Kaiser, Michael. Letter to Stewart Butler and Alfred Doolittle. 1998. Personal collection of Stewart Butler.

Kaiser, Michael. Email to Frank Perez. April 4, 2020.

Ladnier, Joan. Email to Frank Perez. May 19, 2020.

"LAGPAC Demonstrates at Mike Early Fundraiser." *Ambush*, February 1988.

LAGPAC Newsletter. "Great Strides for Gay People in New Orleans." Stewart Butler Collection, Louisiana Research Collection, Tulane University. Box 1.

Lawrence, Jill. "Thousands March for Gay Rights." *New Orleans Times-Picayune*, April 26, 1993.

Lewis, Valda. Interview. Conducted by Mordecai Chapman. May 13, 2019.

Lind, Angus. "Fire Bares the Grisly Face of Death." *New Orleans States-Item*. June 25, 1973.

Log Cabin Federation Newsletter, August/September 1993.

Magill, Rich, ed. *Exposing Hatred: A Report on the Victimization of Lesbian and Gay People in New Orleans, Louisiana*. New Orleans: Louisiana Lesbian and Gay Political Action Caucus, 1991.

Magill, Rich. "Peter." *Ambush*, February 20, 1998.

Magill, Rich. Personal interview. April 3, 2011.

Magill, Rich. Interview. Conducted by Mark Cave. July 1, 2011.

Maginnis, John. *The Last Hayride*. N.p.: Gris Gris Press, 1984.

Manella, Gregory. Letter to Stewart Butler. December 3, 1968. Personal collection of Stewart Butler.

Manella, Gregory. Letter to Stewart Butler. March 1969. Personal collection of Stewart Butler.

"The March on Washington—An Update." *Ambush*, November 1987.

Martinez, Ed. "Editorial." *Vieux Carre Star*, 1977.

McLaughlin, Jean. Letter to Stewart Butler. May 1974. Personal collection of Stewart Butler.

McWilliams, Richebourg G. Dramatic History of Dauphin Island. Chamber of Commerce and Dauphin Island Land Sales Corporation, 1954.

"Membership Response Increases." *Banner*, December 1997.

Mitchell, Kenneth. Personal interview. November 16, 2018.

Morse, Robert. Letter to Stewart Butler. 2008. Personal collection of Stewart Butler.

Naquin-Delain, Rip. "Louisiana Celebrations Highly Successful." *Ambush*, July 1983.

Naquin-Delain, Rip. Editorial. *Ambush*, 1999.

Naquin-Delain, Rip. Personal interview. October 2016.

Naquin-Delain, Rip, and Ray Ruiz. Letter to Sam Poche. February 6, 1996. Personal collection of Larry Best.

Naske, Claus-M. *A History of Alaska Statehood*. Lanham, MD: University Press of America, 1985.

"National March on Washington for Lesbian and Gay Rights." *Ambush*, September 1987.

"National Sexual Privacy Challenge." *Impact*, October 17, 1986.

Negley, Jennifer. "Walkers from All Walks of Life–6000 Step Out to Join AIDS Fight." *New Orleans Times-Picayune*, October 10, 1991.

Nelson, Roger. Letter to Kyle Scafide. August 24, 1998. Personal Collection of Stewart Butler.

Newlin, Jon. "Madame John Dodt's Legacy #24." *Ambush*, June 26, 1998.

New Orleans Police Report. Item number C-11013–89. April 14, 1989.

"New Orleans Rejects Homosexual Rights Bill." *New York Times*, April 15, 1984.

"N.O. Inmates Must Wear Pink Uniforms." *Ambush*, October 1988.

NO/AIDS Task Force News. September 1983.

NO/AIDS Task Force Newsletter. May 1986.

NO/AIDS Task Force. Press Release. *Impact*. December 26, 1986.

"NORCO/LAGPAC Endorses Papal Visit Coalition." *Ambush*, September 1987.

"Off the Presses." *Ambush*, October 1983.

Oliva, Bonita, and Leo Oliva. "A Few Things Marian Sloan Russell Never Told or Knew About Her Mother and Father." *Wagon Tracks: Santa Fe Trail Association Quarterly* 7 no. 2 (1993): 1–6.

Olsson, Caroline. "Not All That Easy: Survival Strategies in Lesbian Bar Life in New Orleans, 1950–1970." MA thesis, University of New Orleans, 1999.

"Our Loss Is Nation's Gain." *Banner*, February 1997.

OUTWORDS Interview with Stewart Butler conducted by Mason Funk, recorded July 12, 2017.

Pailet, Sandra. Letter to Barney Frank. January 15, 1999. Personal collection of Frank Perez.

Pat (last name unknown). Letter to Stewart Butler. May 1971. Personal collection of Stewart Butler.

Paul, Charles. Email to Frank Perez. May 10, 2020.

Perez, Frank. "Climate of Hostility" *Ambush*, November 20, 2012.

Perez, Frank. "Jeanne Manford & New Orleans PFLAG." *Ambush*, January 22, 2013.

Perez, Frank. "The Persecution of Tony Bacino's Bar." *Ambush*, April 16, 2013.

Perez, Frank. "Project Lazarus." *Ambush*, May 28, 2013.

Perez, Frank. "Rich Magill Exposes Hatred." *Ambush*, June 11, 2013.

Perez, Frank. "The Gay Liberation Front Marches on City Hall." *Ambush*, July 9, 2013.

Perez, Frank. "FAB: Faubourg Marigny Arts and Books." *Ambush*, August 6, 2013.

Perez, Frank. "Anita Bryant Comes to New Orleans." *Ambush*, November 19, 2013.

Perez, Frank. "Stewart Butler: Lion in Winter." *Ambush*, December 3, 2013.

Perez, Frank. "Gay Interest Walking Tour." In *Treasures of the Vieux Carre: Ten Self-Guided Walking Tours of the French Quarter*. Bedford, TX: LL Publications, 2014.

Perez, Frank. "Activism & Ink." *Ambush*, January 14, 2014.

Perez, Frank. "LGBT Community Center of New Orleans." *Ambush*, March 25, 2014.

Perez, Frank. "Pioneering Lesbian Barbara Scott Was Ahead of Her Time." *Ambush*, April 22, 2014.

Perez, Frank. "Crimes Against Nature." *Ambush*, May 6, 2014.

Perez, Frank. "NO/AIDS Task Force." *Ambush*, May 20, 2014.

Perez, Frank. "Alice Brady." *Ambush*, June 3, 2014.

Perez, Frank. "Queer Pioneer Skip Ward." *Ambush*, November 18, 2014.

Perez, Frank. "Remembering Burt Harter." *Ambush*, January 13, 2015.

Perez, Frank. "The Southeastern Conference of Lesbians and Gay Men." *Ambush*, March 10, 2015.

Perez, Frank. "The Louisiana Lesbian and Gay Political Action Caucus (LAGPAC)." *Ambush*, May 5, 2015.

Perez, Frank. "Johnny Jackson: An Early Ally and Straight Leader for LGBT Rights." *Ambush*, July 28, 2015.

Perez, Frank. "Belle Reve." *Ambush*, August 11, 2015.

Perez, Frank. "Remembering Charlene Schneider." *Ambush*, October 13, 2015.

Perez, Frank. "Rich Magill and His Times." *Ambush*, May 23, 2016.

Perez, Frank. "The Phoenix Rises from the Ashes of Smoky Mary." *Ambush*, November 8, 2016.

Perez, Frank. "The LGBT+ Archives Project of Louisiana as a Community Organizing Success Story." In *Queering Education in the Deep South*, edited by Kamden K. Strunk. Charlotte, NC: Information Age Publishing, 2018.

Perez, Frank, and Jeffrey Palmquist. *In Exile: The History and Lore Surrounding New Orleans Gay Culture and its Oldest Gay Bar*. Bedford, TX: LL Publications, 2012.

Peristein, Michael. "Statute Forbidding Sodomy Violates Privacy, Judge Says." *New Orleans Times-Picayune*, March 10, 2001.

"PFLAG At Celebration '97." *Banner*, July 1997.

Phillips, Wayne. Personal interview. November 29, 2016.

Pizanie, Toni. "The Sodomy Trial." *Ambush*, November 13, 1998.

Pizanie, Toni. "Dyke March." *Ambush*, September 20, 1999.

Pope, John. *Getting Off at Elysian Fields: Obituaries from the New Orleans "Times-Picayune."* Jackson: University Press of Mississippi, 2015.

Pope, John. "AIDS: Plague of the '80s—Killer's Trail has Left Few Clue to Cure." *New Orleans Times-Picayune/States-Item*. August 11, 1985.

Pope, John. "AIDS: Plague of the '80s—Safe Sex Leader: Little Done Locally to Defuse Time Bomb." *New Orleans Times-Picayune/States-Item*, August 12, 1985.

Pope, John. "AIDS: Plague of the '80s—$139,000 a Patient Spent, Study Says." *New Orleans Times-Picayune/States-Item*, August 12, 1985.

Pope, John. "AIDS: Plague of the '80s—Charity Cradles the Dying." *New Orleans Times-Picayune/States-Item*, August 13, 1985.

Pope, John. "AIDS Memorial Quilt to be Displayed in N.O." *New Orleans Times-Picayune/States-Item*, March 28, 1988.

Pope, John. "Ex-Director of AIDS Agency Jeff Campbell Is Dead at 48." *New Orleans Times-Picayune*, April 9, 1994.

Prechter, Ryan B. "Gay New Orleans: A History." PhD dissertation, Georgia State University, 2017.

"Quilt Returns to Washington October 8." *Ambush*, July 1988.

Rawls, John. "Advertisement." *Impact*, March 18, 1994.

Report of the Louisiana Advisory Committee to the United States Commission on Civil Rights. 1988.

Rey, Sebastian. Personal interview. 2014.

Ripley, Robert S., and Sandra Pailet. "PFLAG's HRC Ad—An Omission." *Banner*, September 1998.

Robinson, Alan. Quoted in *New York Times*, April 15, 1984.

Robinson, Alan G. "Letter to the Editor." *Impact*, July 25, 1986.

Robinson, Alan. "Artists to Benefit AIDS." *Ambush*, October 1987.

Roger. Arthur. Email to Frank Perez. April 3, 2020.

Roland, Catherine. "Farewell to the American Aquatic Gardens: Celebrating the History and Courage of Two Pioneers." *Ambush*, November 5, 2019.

Roland Catherine. Personal interview. April 4, 2020.

Roy Maggio et al. v. City of New Orleans. Civil District Court of the Parish of Orleans, Division F. 1958.

Russell, Marion Sloan. *The Land of Enchantment: Memoirs of Marian Russell Sloan Along the Santa Fe Trail.* Albuquerque: University of New Mexico Press, 1985.

Sacher, Rich. Unpublished note. January 2020. Personal collection of Rich Sacher.

Sacher, Rich. Personal Interview. March 31, 2020.

Sacher, Rich. Email to Frank Perez. April 1, 2020.

Salvaggio, John. *New Orleans Charity Hospital: A Story of Physicians, Politics, and Poverty.* Baton Rouge: Louisiana State University Press, 1992.

"Sandra Pailet: Honored Citizen." *Banner*, December 1997.

Scafide, Kyle. Personal interview. May 11, 2020.

Sears, James T. *Rebels, Rubyfruit, and Rhinestones: Queering Space in the Stonewall South.* New Brunswick, NJ: Rutgers University Press, 2001.

"Shame on Winne-Dixie: 3rd Anniversary of Peter Oiler's Firing." GayToday.com. January 7, 2003. http://gaytoday.com/world/010703wo.asp.

Shannon, Patrick. "Celebration '86 at Tulane: Politics, Pride, Protest." *Impact*, June 13, 1986.

Shannon, Patrick. "Early Recall Rally: Too Early?" *Impact*, December 26, 1986.

Sharp, Courtney. "The Beef People." *Banner*, January 2001.

Sharp, Courtney. Personal interview. July 19, 2019.

Smith, Howard P. *Unveiling the Muse: The Lost History of Gay Carnival in New Orleans.* Jackson: University Press of Mississippi, 2017.

Smith, Howard P., and Frank Perez. *Southern Decadence in New Orleans.* Baton Rouge: Louisiana State University Press, 2018.

Sontag, Susan. *Illness as Metaphor and AIDS and Its Metaphors.* New York: Farrar, Straus, and Giroux, 1978.

Stover, Sam. "Tulane Preserves Digital Histories of LGBTQ Activism in the South." Tulane News. November 17, 2017. https://news.tulane.edu/news/tulane-preserves-digital-histories -lgbtq-activism-south.

Stuart, Mary. Quoted in *Impact*, December 26, 1986.

Stuart, Mary Elaine. "An Examination of Tolerance in New Orleans: Voter Attitudes toward Lesbians and Gays." MA thesis, University of New Orleans, 1992.

Sullivan, Jack. Interview. Conducted by Mark Cave, October 25, 2011.

Sullivan, Jack. Email to Frank Perez. May 13, 2020.

Terry, Bill. Email to Frank Perez. May 5, 2020.

Thompson, Jelisa. "You Make Me Feel: A Study of the Gay Rights Movement in New Orleans." BA thesis, University of Southern Mississippi, 2011.

Thompson, Julie. Email to Frank Perez. October 12, 2018.

"Today's Chuckle." *New Orleans States-Item.* 1959.

Townsend, Johnny. *Let the Faggots Burn: The UpStairs Lounge Fire.* Bangor, ME: Booklocker, 2011.

Townsend, Johnny. Email to Frank Perez. March 20, 2020.

"Tracks." *Rooster*, February 14, 1990.

Trahan, Randy. Personal interview. March 4, 2020.

Treadway, Joan. "Gay Community Surfaces in Tragedy of New Orleans Fire." *New Orleans Times-Picayune*, September 11, 1973.

Treadway, Joan. "Independent Route Taken for Personal Objectives." *New Orleans Times-Picayune*, September 12, 1973.

Treadway, Joan. "Homosexuals Disagree on Behavior's 'Sickness.'" *New Orleans Times-Picayune*, September 13, 1973.

Treadway, Joan. "Psychiatric and Clerical Views—a Wide Spectrum." *New Orleans Times-Picayune*, September 14, 1973.

Treadway, Joan. "It's Not Illegal to BE Gay—Certain Acts are Criminal." *New Orleans Times-Picayune*, September 15, 1973.

Tucker, Linda. Personal interview. October 2, 2015.

United States Commission on Civil Rights, Louisiana Advisory Committee. *The Administration of Justice for Homosexual Persons in New Orleans.* Washington, DC: The Commission, 1989.

"Unwed Couples Affirmed." *New Orleans Times-Picayune*, September 2, 1993.

Vaid, Urvashi. *Virtual Equality: The Mainstreaming of Gay and Lesbian Liberation.* New York: Doubleday, 1995.

Vella, Christina. Personal interview. March 2012.

Volz, Louis. Personal interview. January 28, 2020.

Von Reizenstein, Ludwig. *The Mysteries of New Orleans.* Translated by Steven Rowan. Baltimore: Johns Hopkins University Press, 2003.

Watermeier, Leo. Personal interview. April 8, 2020.

Welch, James. Testimonial on the LGBT+ Archives Project of Louisiana website.

Welch, Paul. "Homosexuality in America." *Life*, June 26, 1964.

Wightman, Steve. "About the Cover." *Ambush*, June 1987.

Willie, Steve. Personal Interview. April 4, 2020.

Yanez, Lindsay. "Womyn on the Move." *Ambush*, February 23, 1994.

INDEX

ABOUT THE AUTHOR

Frank Perez serves as president of the LGBT+ Archives Project of Louisiana. He is a columnist for *Ambush Magazine* and *French Quarter Journal* and has authored several books on New Orleans history, including *In Exile: The History and Lore Surrounding New Orleans Gay Culture and Its Oldest Gay Bar* (with Jeffrey Palmquist), *Treasures of the Vieux Carre: Ten Self-Guided Walking Tours of the French Quarter*, and *Southern Decadence in New Orleans* (with Howard P. Smith). He is also the coeditor of the anthology *My Gay New Orleans: 28 Personal Reminiscences on LGBT+ Life in New Orleans*.

As a licensed tour guide, Perez developed the Rainbow Fleur de Lis, an interactive walking tour of the French Quarter focusing on New Orleans's rich LGBT+ history, which has earned national and local critical praise in *The Advocate*, ABC News, *USA Today*, queerty.com, *Out Traveler*, NPR, WGNO, WHIV, and other media outlets. Perez teaches part-time at Loyola University. He and his partner and their dog live in the French Quarter. Learn more at frenchquarterfrank.com.